THE PEOPLE OF THE SEA

THE PEOPLE

*Published with the support
of the School of Hawaiian,
Asian, and Pacific Studies,
University of Hawaiʻi*

PAUL D'ARCY

OF THE SEA

Environment, Identity, and History in Oceania

 UNIVERSITY OF HAWAI'I PRESS • HONOLULU

Library of Congress Cataloging-in-Publication Data

D'Arcy, Paul.
    The people of the sea : environment, identity
and history in Oceania / Paul D'Arcy.
        p. cm.
    Includes bibliographical references and index.
    ISBN-13: 978-0-8248-2959-9 (hardcover :
alk. paper)
    ISBN-10: 0-8248-2959-X (hardcover :
alk. paper)
    1. Oceania—Social life and customs. 2. Pacific
Islanders—Social life and customs. 3. National
characteristics—Oceania. 4. Seafaring life—
Oceania. 5. Navigation—Oceania—History.
6. Maritime anthropology—Oceania. 7. Oceania—
Environmental conditions. 8. Oceania—History.
9. Ocean and civilization. I. Title.
    DU28.D37 2006
    995—dc22

                          2005029353

Designed by Leslie Fitch
Printed by The Maple-Vail Book
Manufacturing Group

For Xiaoqin and Christopher Jiayi

CONTENTS

ILLUSTRATIONS

ABBREVIATIONS

AJCP   Australian Joint Copying Project

AJHR   Appendices to the Journals of the New Zealand House of
Representatives

ANU   Australian National University

BPBM   Bernice Pauahi Bishop Museum

CNMI   Commonwealth of the Northern Marianas

EEZ   Exclusive Economic Zone

FAO   Food and Agriculture Organization of the United Nations

HRAF   Human Relations Area Files, microfilm copies held in Hamilton
Library, University of Hawai'i at Mānoa and MARC Library,
University of Guam

LMS   London Missionary Society

MARC   Micronesian Area Research Center, University of Guam

MFM   microfilm

MS   manuscript

N.D.   no date indicated

RSPAS   Research School of Pacific and Asian Studies, ANU

SSJ   South Seas Journals of the London Missionary Society

UNCLOS   United Nations Convention on the Law of the Sea

UNESCO   United Nations Educational, Scientific and Cultural Organization

ACKNOWLEDGMENTS

SCHOLARSHIP IS a collective enterprise. While I have devoted many years of hard work into producing this book, I am also mindful of the huge debt that I owe to many people who gave freely of their time, expertise, and friendship. I feel privileged and blessed to live on the shores of the Pacific and to study and be with the peoples who have made their homes here. My enthusiasm for the idea of writing a history of the Pacific as a history of sea peoples arose in the early 1990s, when Television New Zealand's Natural History Unit was seeking researchers for a series on the world's oceans. Although the project did not go ahead, I became so interested in the concept that I continued my own independent research. In 1995 I received a scholarship to the Australian National University to complete a doctorate on this topic. The offer of a lectureship in Pacific history at Victoria University (ANU) in Wellington in 1997 cut short my ANU scholarship. Heavy teaching loads delayed completion of my doctorate and its subsequent conversion into a book. In all this time, I can honestly say that I have experienced nothing but warmth, enthusiasm, and kindness from every person I have come in contact with in regard to this project.

My time at the Division of Pacific and Asian History in the Research School of Pacific and Asian Studies at the ANU was the happiest and most intellectually stimulating time of my life. The ANU gave me a generous scholarship and ample travel funds for my fieldwork. They funded two trips to Micronesia and one to Hawai'i, and would have funded another to Fiji if I had not cut short my scholarship to accept the position at Victoria University. All staff and students came to be friends, and still are. I was particularly fortunate with my advisory panel: Donald Denoon, Niel Gunson, Deryck Scarr, Athol Anderson, and Anthony Reid. All were helpful and friendly, but offered trenchant criticisms when needed. Donald and Niel have been particularly helpful. This work has been immeasurably improved by their careful editorial comments. Niel also gave me a number of valuable primary sources and helped my research many times with his unrivaled knowledge of Pacific primary sources. Donald was a wonderful supervisor, combining acute attention to detail with a breadth of vision. He also has a great deal of patience and a wonderful sense of humor, which certainly helped him through my initial drafts. My thanks also go out to the division's administrative staff: Dorothy McIntosh, Marion Weeks, Jude Shanahan, Julie Gordon, and Oanh Collins. They have always been a delight to deal with; nothing is ever a problem for them.

Other scholars who assisted and inspired me were Bob Langdon and Dorothy Shineberg at ANU, Gordon Parsonson at Otago University, and Ron Crocombe. Bob lent me his notes on Anaa and the Tuamotus, Dorothy her manuscript of the *Acis* journal of Andrew Cheyne, and Gordon his voluminous transcriptions of numerous missionary journals on Polynesia. Gordon was also the person who first suggested I apply the concept of sea power to Polynesia. The intellectual audacity and breadth of vision of his Pacific history courses had first fired my enthusiasm for the Pacific. The recent deaths of Dorothy and Bob have made my Pacific a sadder place. Professor Terry Hughes of James Cook University advised me on aspects of marine biology and gave me copies of his articles on tropical reef ecosystems. The enthusiastic and warm reception my ideas always received from my colleagues at Victoria University—Teresia Teaiwa, Sean Mallon, Peter Brunt, Steve Behrendt, Richard Hills, and Doug Munro—encouraged and inspired me to publish this work more than they perhaps realize. A meeting with Susan Jones of Oxford TV and subsequent correspondence about a series on the Pacific also encouraged me to press on with the publication of this book.

My work has been particularly influenced by the environmental histories of John McNeill, Mark Elvin, and my former supervisor and *wantok* Judy Bennett, and the Pacific visions of Kerry Howe and Ian Campbell. Kerry was an examiner for my doctorate. The other examiners were Gerry Ward and Geoff Irwin. My initial postgraduate worries about using top scholars from history, geography, and archaeology as examiners proved groundless, as their insightful criticisms were offered as helpful suggestions to improve the manuscript for publication rather than statements of condemnation. The same is true for the reports on my manuscript commissioned by the University of Hawai'i Press. This generous mentoring role is typical of every scholar mentioned here.

I hope I can emulate their example. The daily joys of lecturing and supervising students serve as constant reminders of why I became an academic. Sharing their enthusiasm for the Pacific and for knowledge keeps me young and optimistic. To the thousands of students I have been fortunate enough to share knowledge of the Pacific with—thank you. You probably do not realize that I learn much more from you than you ever learn from me.

Permission to use illustrations or other material produced by others was given by everyone I approached. Ratu Sela Rayawa granted permission to use an illustration from a Fiji Museum publication for Figure 8. Professor Jon Jonassen allowed me to reproduce part of his translation of a Cook Island chant to conclude my study. James Siers granted permission to use his wonderfully evocative photo of a spear fisherman in Kadavu Lagoon for the cover illustration. Kay Dancey and her team at the RSPAS Cartography Unit produced Maps 3 to 9 and Figures 3 and 5 and granted permission for their use. Taylor and Francis, the publisher of the *Journal of Pacific History*, granted permission for Maps 7 and 9 from my article in that journal to be used here. Joel Bradshaw and Agnes Hiramoto of the University of Hawai'i Press granted permission to reproduce Map 1 and Figure 6 from their publications. Dennis Kawaharada gave permission for the use of the photo in Figure 2 and provided an electronic version. Ward H. Goodenough and the editor of *Expedition*, James R. Mathieu, granted permission to use an illustration from an article by Professor Goodenough in *Expedition* for Figure 4. Professors Christopher Lobban and Mark Lander of the University of Guam allowed me to reproduce Map 2, Table 1, and Figure 1, and provided electronic versions of Map 2 and Figure 1. Peter Bellwood gave permission to reproduce Figure 7. Karen Nero and Dave Chappell granted permission to use unpublished material and provided advice on Palau and indigenous beachcombing, respectively.

Although we eventually opted to use alternative versions of their maps or diagrams, the following also agreed to my requests to use their material: Judith Huntsman as editor of the Journal of the Polynesian Society gave permission for the reproduction of the some of the originals that Maps 3, 7, and 8 are based upon. Ken-ichi Sudo of Kobe University granted permission for me to reproduce one of his maps as Map 6. Junko Edo helped me contact Professor Sudo. Patty Persich of Cambridge University Press granted permission to reproduce Map 4. Scarlett R. Huffman of Harvard University Press was also helpful and courteous in responding to my inquiries about using one of their maps for Map 8.

My fieldwork was greatly assisted by the generosity of local scholars: Tina Rehurer on Palau, Paul Palemar and Margie Falanruw on Yap, Fran

Hezel on Pohnpei, and Scott Russell on Saipan. Bruce Campbell has been my host, guide, mentor, and friend throughout my time in Micronesia. This study also benefited from his editorial comments and profound knowledge of Micronesia. The Micronesian sections of this book could not have been written without his assistance. Bruce's hands-on, practical approach to community development and environmental education in the Pacific has also helped me to keep a healthy perspective on the potential benefits and limits of academic endeavours as a means of improving the lives of Pacific peoples.

Magrit Davies and Torsten Juelich of the Australian National University and Edward Dickinson of Victoria University helped to check or supplement Human Relations Area Files German translations, while Mista Sos Middleton (Misomi) of Chuuk translated local lore contained in the *Uruon Chuk*.

The Pacific librarians I have dealt with over the years are, without exception, a talented and dedicated group. They are also warm and patient people, who are a pleasure to work with. I was assisted at the Hamilton Library's Pacific Collection of the University of Hawai'i by Karen Peacock (Pacific Curator), Lynette Furuhashi (Pacific Librarian), Joan Hori (Hawaiian Curator), Chieko Tachihata (Emeritus Hawaiian Curator—now retired), James Cartwright (University Archivist), Nancy Morris (Emeritus Curator of The Charlot Collection), and support staff; Andrea Nakamura, Sherman Seki, Wesley Poka, Mary Gushiken. My research time at the University of Guam's Micronesian Area Research Center was facilitated by Monique Carriveau Storie, John P. Sablan, Lourdes T. Nededog, Omaira Brunal-Perry, and Marjorie G. Driver. Judy Caldwell of the Micronesian Seminar Library in Kolonia, Pohnpei, Dianne Wood and Robert Petre of the Alexander Turnbull Library, Maureen Kattau of the Australian National University's Menzies Library, Nancy Kwalea of the Forum Fisheries Agency Library in Honiara, and the late David McDonald of the Hocken Library in Dunedin also gave freely of their time. In addition, Karen, Monique and Omaira promptly answered my frantic e-mail requests to recheck footnotes.

A number of friends and family have also been dragged into the vortex of this book's production. Dave French rechecked incomplete references for me at the Hamilton Library, while Ewan Tempero of Victoria University's Computer Science Department and my wife, Xiaoqin, helped convert the electronic maps into a useable format. Xiaoqin, Pennie Gapes, and David Tulloch assisted with other formatting problems. Greg Reeves of James Cook University helped to reformat all illustrations and maps into TIFF format to meet University of Hawai'i Press requirements. My mother and father have always supported my academic career and been there for me when I needed them. They have long given up waiting for me to get a real job, but hopefully the birth of their first grandchild and a book in 2005 will more than compensate.

I am glad I chose to publish with the University of Hawai'i Press. All the staff I have been fortunate to come into contact with bring a wonderful combination of professional flair and *aloha* to their work. My initial approaches to the Press were warmly received by Linley Chapman and Pamela Kelley. Both made extremely helpful comments and encouraged me to submit my manuscripts. My commissioning editor Masako Ikeda and copy editor Maria denBoer have been delightful to work with. Their editing and suggestions have significantly improved this work. I look forward to a long, enjoyable, and fruitful relationship with the Press in the years to come.

I owe a special debt of gratitude to you, Xiaoqin. You have always been an inspiration to me ever since I fell in love with you while working on my Ph.D. in Canberra. I have always valued your sound judgment and common sense, and your warmth, love, and support throughout the long birth of this book. *Wo ai ni.*

Introduction:
The All-encompassing Sea

THIS STUDY examines the influence of the sea on the actions and out-
looks of the inhabitants of those Pacific islands that lie within a truly
oceanic domain. This area, sometimes referred to as Remote Oceania,[1] is
characterized by large sea gaps between islands and archipelagos and by
a relatively limited area of land within a vast expanse of ocean. It broadly
coincides with the older conceptual divisions of Polynesia and Micronesia.

This book covers the maritime dimension of Remote Oceania's history
for the period from 1770 until 1870. The study emphasizes Pacific Islanders'[2] varied relationships with the sea as evolving processes during a crucial transitional era. Particular attention is paid to the flux in the natural
marine environment, how such a state instilled an expectation and openness toward outside influences, and, accordingly, the rapidity with which
cultural change could occur in relations between various groups in this
era. This runs counter to the dominant paradigms of recent Pacific Islands'
historiography.

Although this is one of the few truly oceanic habitats occupied permanently by humankind, surprisingly little research has been conducted on
the maritime dimension of the region's history. Most studies of island
communities with a maritime theme are oriented toward the initial exploration and colonization of the region. They speculate on the nautical
technology and navigational ability of these early explorers by examining
the vessels and sea knowledge of Oceania's cultures at the time of first
encounters with Western/European[3] outsiders. They also examine this
issue by studying communities in the twentieth century whose maritime
practices were partially preserved by relative isolation from Western
influences during the colonial period. A host of ethnographies consider the
use of the sea as a food source, often as part of a wider analysis of the total

subsistence base. These studies emphasize longer-term continuities rather than short-term change, so there is little historically specific detail in them.

Pacific historians have been more focused on instances of rapid change in the period of sustained Western contact from the 1770s onward. However, they usually emphasize Western influences as the main reasons behind the transformation of Islander communities in this period. Indigenous relations with Europeans receive the lion's share of attention, while ongoing and new interactions between local communities tend to be neglected. Such studies rarely examine the degree to which the realities of living in an oceanic environment promulgated openness to external influences among Islanders. As a result, the impact of Westerners is perhaps exaggerated.

This work attempts to fill these gaps by combining hitherto uncoordinated studies of various maritime topics, and by using neglected historical material from the period under review. The book uses a combination of detailed case studies and region-wide surveys, depending on the availability of sources and the intention of each section. The focus is fairly evenly divided between high island and low-lying coral island communities. The case study in chapter 7 concentrates on the Caroline Islands in Micronesia, while the remainder of the book has a slightly more Polynesian than Micronesian focus. Primary material is used, although financial and time constraints meant that this was not always possible. The Human Relations Area Files' (HRAF) English translations of French, German, Russian, and Spanish sources provided an invaluable first point of reference for continental European sources. All have been subsequently checked against the original sources with the assistance of the translators noted in the acknowledgments. Footnotes cite both HRAF translations and original sources. Information that is not specific to the 1770–1870 period is identified as such. It is usually included only to fill lacunae in the historical evidence, or because it is particularly germane to the topic.

Both imperial and metric measurements are used in keeping with the sources from which they were obtained to avoid messy, poorly rounded conversion measurements. For readers unfamiliar with one of the two systems, one mile equals 1.609 kilometers, one nautical mile equals 1.852 kilometers, one fathom equals 1.828 meters, one acre equals 0.0404 of a hectare, one pound equates to 0.453 kilograms, and one ton is equivalent to 1.016 metric tons.

Chapter 1 examines the ways in which modern studies have characterized the region. It first looks at approaches to the sea among the disciplines involved in Pacific Studies. The Western scientific vision of Oceania is then traced. Modern scientific data on the maritime environments of the region are reviewed to set the stage for an examination of the people who made their homes there and to suggest ways in which these environments may have influenced them.

The major part of this study consists of a comprehensive survey of the ways in which living in this great expanse of ocean shaped societies between 1770 and 1870. It is organized into five chapters around the theme of cultural spaces within the sea. Beginning with what was near and familiar in the sea world of Remote Oceania, the chapters move outward to the increasingly distant and unfamiliar realms of the sea. No single narrative encompasses all aspects of Islanders' relations with the sea. General patterns of sea use are examined from a variety of perspectives to flesh out ways of exploring the maritime dimension of Pacific history. Previous neglect of the topic means that much of this study is dedicated to constructing an extended and detailed conceptual framework. This conceptual framework is outlined in chapters 1 to 6. Chapter 7 then applies these concepts by exploring the influence of the sea on the history of the western Caroline Islands.

Islander actions and narratives reveal the importance of the sea. Chapter 2 examines the sea in the day-to-day life of Islanders. This chapter's environmental focus is the near-shore environment around settlements where most Islanders had the majority of their interactions with the sea. Chapter 3 explores peaceful interactions between communities involving sea travel. Chapter 4 outlines the infrastructure necessary for sea travel. Sea travel was also influenced by the ways in which Islanders resolved conflicting interests over access to the sea. Chapter 5 examines how maritime boundaries were decided. Principles and forms of tenure are reviewed, and the degree to which communities could protect or contest tenure is discussed. Chapter 6 examines Islanders' attitudes to unheralded arrivals from beyond the horizon. The chapter also outlines Islanders' conception of the world beyond their usual voyaging spheres, and their willingness to travel to such areas when opportunities arose.

The study concludes by examining the influence of the sea on historical processes in Oceania from 1770 until the present. Chapter 7 is a regional case study whose history is reevaluated in light of the conceptual framework already outlined. This chapter examines inter-island exchanges in the western Caroline Islands, particularly the *sawei* system. This is followed by the conclusion, which begins by tracing how Islanders' relationships with the sea were profoundly altered during colonial rule. Only recently have many inhabitants of the region begun to rediscover and reestablish the ties that bound their ancestors to this great expanse of ocean. It then discusses the implications of its findings for Pacific Studies. By focusing on the sea and its place in the lives of Islanders, the way is opened for new explorations of the region and its inhabitants. Oceania was, and still is, one of the few places on earth where the sea figures so prominently in human activities and thoughts. Dissatisfaction with neglect of the maritime dimension of Pacific history has risen in recent years. The time has come to reevaluate the influence of the sea on Oceanic history.

The Oceanic Environment

THE PAST few decades have been exciting and unsettling times for Pacific scholarship. Calls for reorientation have become increasingly frequent. Some of the changes proposed require greater attention to human interactions with the sea. In particular, there have been consistent calls for more regional perspectives instead of isolated island or single community studies, and for more focus on human-environment relations rather than on cultural norms and sociopolitical relations.[1] To answer these calls effectively, Pacific scholars need to become familiar with the diverse but fragmented literature on Islander interactions with the sea, and to investigate neglected dimensions such as scientific studies of ocean ecosystems.

Islands and Oceans in Recent Pacific Scholarship

Until quite recently those studying Islanders tended to treat individual island communities in relative isolation. Arbitrary colonial boundaries assisted by cutting the Pacific into administrative units of study that bore no resemblance to voyaging spheres.[2] Modern academic writings of even the most geographically wide-ranging field of study, the pre-European period of Oceanic history, portray external contacts as being of limited significance in the development of individual islands after their initial colonization by humans. Pre-European cultural development is usually depicted as driven by the interaction of internal processes. These include adaptation of the founding culture to a new environment; population growth on a limited land area; environmental change, both natural and human-induced; and cultural emphasis on competition for status channeled into warfare, or the intensification of production for redistribution to forge social and political obligations. The possibility of new arrivals introducing cultural innovations is not dismissed, but it is almost always considered of secondary importance.[3] Douglas Oliver's view of Tahitian indigenous history is typical:

> The picture I perceive . . . is of numerous landings on the Society Islands throughout a millennium or more, from other archipelagoes near and far, and ranging in size from a lone and near-dead survivor in a drifting canoe to a modest-sized fleet. Most newcomers would have added some new ideas and objects to the local cultural inventory, and during the earlier centuries some of the larger-scale immigrations were probably near revolutionary in their influence. But as time passed and the local population made settlements on all the islands of the archipelago, subsequent new arrivals, (say after about AD 1200), even large-scale ones, could not have been large enough or culturally "superior" enough, to have effected radical changes in the technological and social patterns that had by then become fairly well consolidated.[4]

Concern at this tendency to treat islands as closed cultural systems was expressed in the late 1970s when a series of well-argued articles called for an end to the pervasiveness of narrowly focused studies. Historian Kerry Howe called this approach "monograph myopia," which he and others characterize as "finding out more and more about less and less."[5] These critics noted that there seemed to be no guiding direction or overall purpose beyond accumulating information and filling gaps. Oskar Spate observed that such historians "may on occasion not see the Ocean for the Islands, may be content to be marooned on the tight but so soft confines of their little atolls of knowledge, regardless of the sweep of the currents which bring life to the isles."[6] Howe offered a comprehensive strategy to correct the shortcomings. He proposed a variety of approaches ranging in scale from precise studies to inter-group regional history, and more general studies still, that focused on Pacific islands as part of wider regions, or even the global economy.[7] This work is intended as a contribution to Howe's second and third approaches.

Calls for academics to view the sea more as a means of communication than as an isolator have mounted. Now island communities are increasingly portrayed as connected "in a wider social world of moving items and ideas."[8] Local traditions, the distribution of cultural traits, and observations by literate outsiders all attest to inter-island voyaging within most archipelagos. Voyaging between archipelagos was also apparent in the eighteenth and nineteenth centuries in at least three regions of Remote Oceania.[9] Such external contacts probably waxed and waned, as did their impact. For example, historian Ian Campbell notes that archaeological, linguistic, and traditional evidence all suggest that the period from c. AD 1100 to 1500 was an era of significant upheaval and inter-island movement through much of Oceania.[10]

Such a world created a wider sense of community and belonging. Perhaps the most articulate voice for this new vision has been Tongan scholar Epeli Hau'ofa. In his 1994 article "Our Sea of Islands," Hau'ofa asserts that

> the world of our ancestors was a large sea full of places to explore, to make their homes in, to breed generations of seafarers like themselves. People raised in this environment were at home with the sea. They played in it as soon as they could walk steadily, they worked in it, they fought on it. They developed great skills for navigating their waters, and the spirit to traverse even the few large gaps that separated their island groups.
>
> Theirs was a large world in which peoples and cultures moved and mingled, unhindered by boundaries of the kind erected much later by imperial powers.[11]

This vision was a response to the "basket case" MIRAB stereotype used to describe many of the smaller nations of contemporary Oceania. MIRAB refers to the main funding sources of these economies: migration, remittances, aid, and bureaucracy. The MIRAB image is one of tiny, nonviable economies forever condemned to dependency on aid from former colonial powers. Hau'ofa argues that these basket cases were the result of barriers created by colonial boundaries and policies that imposed an artificial sense of isolation and separation on Islanders. They must now decolonize their minds, and recast their sense of identity by rediscovering the vision of their ancestors for whom the Pacific was a boundless sea of possibilities and opportunities. Hau'ofa's vision has generated much praise in academia,[12] but is virtually lacking in evidence. Thus far, it has inspired few scholars to produce detailed studies in support of its claims about the world of the ancestors. This study is intended as a contribution to that process.

Others have begun to argue for the need to incorporate the sea into our vision in ways that go beyond merely tracing the highways of sea travel between islands. Geoff Irwin notes that "most prehistorians have concentrated on the evidence for intervals of *time* between islands but it could help our explanations to give more consideration to the intervening *space*—which is ocean—and the changing social and environmental circumstances of the islands and people in it."[13] While Irwin suggests a way forward, he does not discuss the ocean environment in detail. His work also remains rooted in Western scientific discourse. The only discussion of Islanders' conceptions of the ocean relates to their navigational techniques.

The sea must also be seen as a cultural space in the worldview of the inhabitants of the islands. Hau'ofa makes this point in a sequel to "Our Sea of Islands." He notes "for us in Oceania, the sea defines us, what we are and have always been. As the great Caribbean poet Derek Wolcott put it, the sea is history."[14] Once again Hau'ofa provides little evidence for his contention that the sea is part of Islanders' identity. This book moves to fill this lacuna by exploring the Pacific as both a physical and cultural space.

Few studies examine the sea from this perspective. Three works on Pacific seascapes are noteworthy in this regard: Bob Johannes's *Words of the Lagoon,* Michael D. Lieber's *More Than a Living,* and Edvard Hviding's *Guardians of Marovo Lagoon.*[15] Johannes's book is essentially a study of fishing knowledge and practice, reflecting his background in marine biology. An anthropologist by training, Lieber traces the role of fishing activities in the social, political, and ritual life of the inhabitants of Kapingamarangi Atoll. Hviding's work is the most comprehensive. Also trained in anthropology, he attempts to knit together the physical and cultural worlds that make up the territory of the people of the Marovo Lagoon in the Solomon Islands. To Hviding, "the sea plays a crucial role in Marovo as a focus of cultural and social relations; it is the context for practice, interaction, and encounters, and is a cornerstone of Marovo identity, history, and material sustenance."[16]

An exploration of the way in which maritime environments shape the cultures of Oceania has the additional merit of providing an alternative to the increasingly contentious tripartite cultural division of Oceania. into Melanesia, Micronesia, and Polynesia. These are geographically discrete regions, but they are often also portrayed as culturally and linguistically distinct. This tripartite division is generally attributed to the nineteenth-century explorer Dumont d'Urville. His classification reflected European thinking by associating the three cultural regions with different racial types.[17] There was little questioning of this classification until the late 1970s. In 1979, however, Bronwen Douglas challenged a long-standing claim by fellow anthropologist Marshall Sahlins that Melanesia and Polynesia were distinct cultural entities on the basis of their divergent political organization. Douglas produced evidence of the great diversity of organization within both areas.[18] Others have noted that Micronesia's cultural diversity makes it even less amenable to generalizations than either Polynesia or Melanesia.[19] Despite mounting dissatisfaction with this tripartite cultural classification and the association of culture with race, scholars persist in ascribing usefulness to them as broadly similar groupings. Most academics continue to specialize in one or other region.

Part of the reason for this unsatisfactory state of affairs is the perceived lack of any other viable classification. Alternatives do exist, however. For many years archaeologist Roger Green has advocated the use of Oceania's biogeographical divisions as units for studying human colonization.[20] These divisions map the progressive diminution of terrestrial and marine species' diversity eastward into the Pacific as the gaps between islands increase. Green emphasizes the distinction between Near Oceania and Remote Oceania when describing the settlement of the region. Near Oceania is located in the western Pacific and encompasses most of the islands designated as Melanesia under the existing classification. This area demonstrates a great deal of environmental continuity with island Southeast Asia in terms of its large continental islands and small gaps between islands. In contrast, Remote Oceania, broadly coinciding with Micronesia and Polynesia, is characterized by large gaps between islands and archipelagos. It is also notable for its very limited land area relative to ocean area.

Remote Oceania is a truly oceanic environment, one of the few extensively settled by humans. This study examines the extent to which this oceanic environment links the cultures of Polynesia and Micronesia. Vanuatu and New Caledonia are excluded from this study, as both are well within Melanesia, whereas Fiji is included because of its extensive links with Polynesian communities farther east. Occasional reference is also made to maritime aspects of the coastal New Zealand Māori way of life as a Polynesian people inhabiting an abnormally large landmass by Remote Oceanic standards. The literature pertaining to maritime aspects of Remote Oceania's cultures is diverse and fragmented. There is no comprehensive overview of Islanders' many relationships with the sea. There is not even a work that does this for a single archipelago or island. This work seeks to build upon this substantial but fragmented legacy to integrate the multiple ways in which the inhabitants of this truly oceanic environment interacted with the sea. Given the current discontent with the conventional cultural divisions, the application of this biogeographical unit Green found applicable to the initial settlement of the Pacific to later phases of Oceania's history is worthy of consideration.

The boundary between Near and Remote Oceania lies east and south of the present-day Solomon Islands.[21] It then passes east and north of the

Bismarck archipelago, extending westward off the north coast of New Guinea before turning north to pass east of the Philippines. To the west of this line humans can usually travel between islands without losing sight of land because of the high mountains on these islands and the relatively narrow sea gaps between them. In contrast, Remote Oceania is made up of islands clustered into archipelagos that are now separated by at least 350 kilometers of ocean. Islands in this region tend to be smaller than those in Near Oceania, and their flora and fauna more attenuated. This is because it was populated by an extremely limited Indo-Malayan biota that dispersed from the larger islands in Near Oceania. New Caledonia and Aotearoa/New Zealand are exceptions. Both are continental in terms of size and diverse resource base, although New Caledonia is nevertheless relatively impoverished compared to islands of a similar size in Near Oceania. Both lie west of the Andesite Line, which is the main geographical division within Remote Oceania. East of this line no andesite lava or continental rocks occur. The only island landforms in this eastern sector are high volcanic islands, coral atolls, and other kinds of coralline islands.

Within Remote Oceania there is great variation between localities in terms of relative isolation and immediately accessible resources. For example, while there are only ten inhabitable islands within an 800 kilometer radius of Rarotonga in the Cook Islands, the same radius centered on the Ha'apai group in the Tongan archipelago encompasses hundreds of islands with 2400 square kilometers of land.[22] Anthropologist William Alkire divides the coral islands of the Pacific into four groups on the basis of relative isolation and accessible resource base. He makes a convincing argument that these variables play a significant role in determining cultural patterns.[23] Essentially Alkire's argument is that the larger the environmental system, the greater the cultural development, until the population reaches the limits of its environment's carrying capacity.

Alkire's four categories in ascending order of resource availability are: isolates, clusters, complexes, and fringing reef islands. He demonstrates that environmental constraints *and cultural patterns* differ significantly between the categories. Isolates are atolls and raised coral islands such as Niue and Kapingamarangi, which are separated from their neighbors by large enough bodies of water to make travel infrequent or impossible. Clusters are small groups of coral islands in close proximity whose inhabitants can use the resources of the group as a whole. The Tokelau chain is an example. Complexes are coral islands that are part of an extensive chain of islands that either contains high islands or are near to high islands. Complexes contain a range of island types and sizes, as well as climatic diversity. The Caroline Islands and the Tuamotu-Society Islands group are examples. The final category is fringing reef islands, like Kayangel and Peleliu in Palau. These are coral islands so close to high islands that they can be considered part of the latter's cultural and environmental systems.

Alkire's thesis was not the first to propose that the environment played a significant role in shaping human affairs in the Pacific. However, most modern ecologically oriented studies focus on single communities and terrestrial environments. This is in keeping with modern anthropology's emphasis on in-depth analysis of cultures as complex and distinct entities. As Hviding wryly points out, it is also easier and less dangerous to observe a community's economic and social activity on land, than to share the perils and uncertainties of their activities at sea.[24]

Cultural ecology in the Pacific has tended to view cultural perceptions of landscapes, and occasionally seascapes, as cultural orders imposed upon neutral topography. The physical environment is set apart from the cultural order, and culture rather than nature determines the perception and use of the environment. Rarely is modern scientific data consulted to evaluate whether cultural perceptions of the environment correlate with Western scientific explanations, or at least to ascertain whether there are

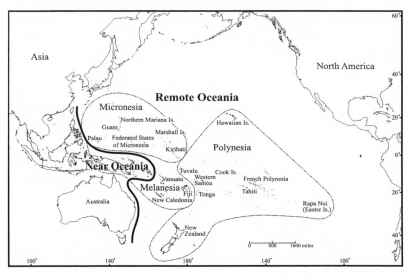

MAP 1 Near and Remote Oceania in relation to Melanesia, Micronesia, and Polynesia. The boundary between Near and Remote Oceania is between Vanuatu and the Solomon Islands. (Merlin, 277)

phenomena in nature that might account for these perceptions. Thus the Māori legend of Paikea riding to Aotearoa on the back of the whale is usually viewed as merely a cultural analogy.[25] The fact that it might allude to early explorers following the annual migratory routes of certain species of whales from the tropical Pacific is not even contemplated.

Hviding offers an exciting alternative to this cultural determinism. In *Guardians of Marovo Lagoon* he suggests that the inhabitants of the lagoon construct their perception of nature through their day-to-day use of that environment. It is not a cultural system that is merely transferred from the minds of the elders to the memories of the young. Such a system would be imposed upon the environment, but not influenced by it. There is no nature-culture dichotomy here. The Marovo people's view of nature emerges from engagements with the environment in multiple forms of knowledge and practice.[26] Hviding's work is also significant in demonstrating that some maritime environments can be endowed with as much cultural value and detail as terrestrial environments. To truly understand the history of Oceania, we need to map its cultural seascapes as well as those on land.

Pacific historians have not been inclined to consider the environment as a significant influence on cultural and historical patterns. In most books and articles the environment is relegated to the general introduction that outlines environmental and cultural structures to set the stage for the human drama that then unfolds. A few relatively unheralded works by archaeologists explore the potential of a more thorough integration of environmental considerations into historical narratives. In Tom Dye's study of Marquesan fishing, and Patrick Kirch and Marshall Sahlins's collaborative study of Anahulu Valley on Oʻahu, changes in resource use are related to historically specific cultural events.[27] This study will also seek to demonstrate that while more regular, seasonal events shaped the rhythm of human activity, shorter-term, less predictable elements of the environment also intruded into the actions and attitudes of Islanders. On occasion, such intrusions had dramatic and far-reaching implications for the communities that they affected.

The Pacific Ocean as a Dynamic Environment

Oceanographers now generally accept that all marine ecosystems are in constant flux, and that they are open systems affected by marine and climatic influences generated elsewhere. Such ecosystems are characterized by short-term perturbations and disruptions as well as by more regular, seasonal patterns. People who live in such environments must view the world differently from those who inhabit more closed, stable environments. Short-term environmental perturbations and unpredictable changes from external elements foster expectations of unheralded elements intruding from beyond the horizon, curiosity about where these elements came from, and flexible, opportunistic strategies to cope with this, at times, uncertain world.

Remote Oceania's dominant spatial characteristics influencing human occupation are its vast area of sea relative to land and significant sea gaps between archipelagos. The Pacific Ocean is a vast body of water, covering an area greater than all land in the world: 9200 miles separate Bering Strait in the north from Antarctica in the south. The Pacific is 10,400 miles wide at the equator. The rest of the world's oceans would fit comfortably within the Pacific.[28] About 80 percent of the world's islands lie within the area bounded by Tokyo, Jakarta, and Rapanui, which incorporates Remote Oceania.[29] These islands are the result of volcanic extrusions that eventually rise above the ocean's surface from the seabed where the earth's surface is fractured as tectonic plates collide. The islands of Remote Oceania consist of high volcanic islands and more low-lying coral islands. Most are grouped in clusters or arcs, with few individual islands in total isolation.[30] High islands generally have steep mountainous interiors that force moisture-laden oceanic winds upward, resulting in high rainfall on the windward side. With most of the moisture released, the air descends on the leeward slopes as hot, dry winds that draw moisture from the land. The windward slopes of the Koʻolau Mountains on Oʻahu receive 6250 millimeters annual rainfall, while less than 500 millimeters fall on the leeward coast at Ewa.[31] This rainfall pattern also gives rise to permanent and semipermanent watercourses. In contrast, coral islands are smaller and narrower, most are only a few meters above sea level, and none have permanent watercourses, so their flora depends on subterranean freshwater lens replenished by seasonal rainfall.

The geological forces giving rise to islands over the centuries also intruded into people's lives as volcanic eruptions, earthquakes, and tsunami. Scientific records in the southwest Pacific for the past 70 years reveal a weak tendency toward gaps of 13 and 29 years between phases of volcanic activity. If this pattern is consistent, then members of each generation of Islanders experienced some form of volcanic activity.[32] Where seismic activity occurred on land, the main threats to humans came from lava, gasses, and debris from volcanic activities. Earthquakes were frightening, but do not seem to have caused great loss of life during the century being examined.[33]

Seismic activity at sea was more of a problem. Tsunami are sea waves generated by seismic disturbances on the sea floor. They radiate across the ocean surface as barely detectable shock waves less than a meter high. These travel at speeds in excess of 700 kilometers per hour, until they encounter shallow coastal waters, where they are slowed by the drag of the sea floor. The result is that water coming from behind at speed begins to pile up to form crests up to 30 meters in height. Such waves hit the shore with incredible destructive force just minutes after the telltale recession of inshore waters as they are sucked into the oncoming wave.[34]

Despite the magnitude of the geological forces underlying these episodes, climatic conditions had more impact on the lives of Islanders. Short-term changes in temperature, rainfall, and the atmospheric circulation patterns were the most important environmental influences. Weather varies across both time and space. Knowledge of this variation was vital to people dependent upon agriculture and fisheries for subsistence, as flora and fauna are very responsive to these variations. Such knowledge was also important for any society committed to traveling by sea. Traditional lore is rich with information on the more regular aspects of these cyclical changes: the transition from wet to dry season; the transition from winter to summer; seasonal changes in wind direction; the seasonal cycles of crops from planting to harvesting; and the behavior of birds and fish.[35] There is little sense of uncertainty or irregularity in these accounts, but the importance of prophecy and appeals to the gods for bountiful harvests suggest that this was not the case. Recent climate research increasingly supports this proposition; major short-term irregularities do and did punctuate the broad climatic patterns that characterize the region.

Regular voyaging between islands requires intimate knowledge of wind patterns. The climate of Oceania is influenced by both atmospheric and oceanic circulation systems. A number of wind systems operate in the Pacific. In the more open eastern two-thirds there are zones crossing the ocean from east to west, each with a distinct pattern of surface winds. In the higher latitudes of both hemispheres, strong westerly winds blow for most of the year. Between these two belts are two zones of trade winds. In the Northern Hemisphere these blow from the northeast, while south of the equator they blow from the southeast. Their strength diminishes in the western third of the Pacific. The trade winds are not continuous, but generally blow for at least part of every month. They are most consistent between May and September. For the remainder of the year winds blow from both east and west. The equatorial area between these belts of trade winds is known as the doldrums, which generally experiences light, variable winds, and total calm. However, it is also subject to occasional squalls, heavy showers, and thunderstorms.[36]

The western Pacific is dominated by monsoon and typhoon weather patterns arising from the periodic heating and cooling of the Asian landmass. The monsoon winds blow from the northwest away from Asia in the Northern Hemisphere winter, and from the southeast toward Asia in the Northern Hemisphere summer. Typhoons or hurricanes occur in much of the western tropical Pacific.[37] These spiral storms begin as areas of slowly circulating cloud that gather energy from the warm ocean waters that they pass over. They develop into giant mobile whirlwinds that can last for weeks. Their high winds and torrential rains carve a path of destruction, while the accompanying storm waves devastate coastal areas and low-lying coral islands.

Typhoons vary in intensity. Although an island may encounter up to five or six per generation, most Pacific locations suffer only one severe typhoon per century. Typhoons can intensify or weaken quickly for reasons that are still not fully understood. In the Southern Hemisphere they generally coincide with the summer monsoon period from November to March, typically forming at about 8 degrees south and tracking west then south. In the Northern Hemisphere they originate between 7 and 20 degrees north in the vicinity of the eastern Carolines, and move west toward the Philippines before swinging north toward Japan. Almost half of the world's tropical storms occur in this area. The typhoon season in this part of the Pacific is from July to November.[38]

There is great variability within these seasonal patterns. Typhoons can occur during any month of the year. Similarly, storms with gale force winds may occur during any month over much of the region. Winds in excess of 43 kilometers per hour make up 5 percent or more of modern wind measurements for any month.[39] Rainfall also varies widely. Generally areas near the equator experience high rainfall with limited seasonal variation. Farther from the equator annual rainfall diminishes substantially, and is subject to marked seasonal variation.[40]

The movement of seawater influences life at sea, just as terrestrial flora is influenced by atmospheric circulation. Much of the daily and seasonal behavior of near-shore marine biota is oriented around tidal patterns.[41] Seawater also circulates in ocean currents. Two vast loops, or gyres, dominate the Pacific. The one north of the equator flows clockwise, while the other flows anticlockwise. The currents on the western side of these gyres increase in intensity as they flow away from the equator. Islands deflect these currents, particularly the southern, westward-moving flow. Between these two gyres is the equatorial countercurrent, which flows from the Carolines across to Panama. These tropical currents vary seasonally in strength, and even location. Seasonal wind shifts account for much of this variation. As well as these larger, general flows there are smaller, irregular currents that result from local eddies, islands, and other barriers to flows on the ocean floor. Such currents may also exhibit seasonal variation because of changing winds and weather conditions.[42]

These currents have important consequences for life in the ocean. Surface currents affect human travel and subsistence. They either facilitate or hinder boat travel. Either way, their variability required that mariners acquire an intimate knowledge of local conditions. In February 1817, for example, a Russian expedition negotiating a passage through the atoll chain of the Marshall Islands found that a current carried them just over 12 miles in 24 hours.[43] Currents also affect subsistence economies by influencing the distribution of ocean-borne flora and fauna. These terrestrial and marine species spread by drifting with the currents. Plankton, the basis of all ocean food chains, is one such organism.[44] Deep ocean currents also affect the food chain by transporting decomposing organic matter that falls from surface waters enriched by the sun's penetration. Such currents transport this matter away from tropical seas toward the polar seas, where it rises to the surface and moves back toward the equator along surface currents. The result is that most tropical seas have much poorer offshore habitats than their temperate and polar equivalents. Tropical seas tend to consist of intense concentrations of marine biota surrounded by large tracts of relatively impoverished seas.

Most zones of concentration are in coastal waters just offshore. The exceptions are zones where localized upwellings bring sunken nutrients back to the surface. This infusion of nutrients creates rich ecosystems that support many species. One such area is off the coast of Peru. A phenomenon known as the El Niño involves the periodic disruption of the upwelling of nutrient-rich cool waters into the relatively shallow warmer surface layer off the coast of Peru. When deprived of this infusion, the catches of coastal fisheries have been estimated to diminish by as much as 90 percent.

This phenomenon is explained in terms of variations in the strength of the southeast trade winds. At one time it was thought that when strong, these winds allowed upwelling by displacing surface water westward away from the coast. Thus, El Niño conditions resulted from a weakening of these winds. Contemporary explanations increasingly emphasize atmospheric pressure differences across the Pacific, for which the Southern Oscillation is a measure. Much of the world's climate is determined by the exchange of heat and moisture between ocean and atmosphere. As the largest body of water, the Pacific has a crucial role. Modern explanations now link the two together as the El Niño Southern Oscillation (ENSO) phenomenon. When pressure gradients lead to weaker than usual easterly winds in the eastern Pacific, this leads to a deeper level of warm surface waters off Peru that is far less productive than the upwelling mix that occurs otherwise.[45]

Rather than being abnormal, El Niño is merely the extreme warm surface phase of an 18- to 24-month cycle that also exhibits an extreme, cool surface water phase known as La Niña. The occurrence of these cycles is irregular, although they seem to happen on average every 3 to 7 years. Historical records also suggest that these cycles vary in intensity. In a La Niña phase the opposite conditions apply. These conditions may cause strong trade winds that push water westward, so that the sea level in the western Pacific is up to 2 feet higher than in the east.[46]

What does this mean for Remote Oceania? Above all, it means that annual variation may have been as important as seasonal variation in the lives of Islanders. Climatic conditions and weather patterns can vary dramatically from year to year. Onotoa Atoll in Kiribati recorded 85 inches of rain in 1946, but only 6.6 inches in 1950.[47] This is not an isolated example. Geographer R. F. McLean notes that "rainfall data in the dry belt suggest a biennial oscillation and throughout the central Pacific a 5.3-year cycle is indicated. Drought is thus a frequent and persistent feature of the region's climate."[48] In such variable conditions, the worst-case scenario rather than the overall average determines the viability of a community. Some droughts last for years. Kapingamarangi had a 2-year drought in 1916–17, which is reputed to have killed eighty to ninety people.[49] During El Niño conditions zones of convergence that cause heavy rainfall in this part of the Pacific move toward the equator. The usual areas of convergence such as the Carolines and Fiji then experience a decline in rainfall. Variation even occurs within the Caroline Islands. Islands that normally have high rainfall like Palau and Pohnpei may experience drought, while drier areas farther east such as the Marshalls may experience high rainfall.[50]

Wind patterns also alter during El Niño occurrences. The trade winds weaken in the eastern Pacific and may even be reversed west of the International Dateline. The area where typhoons form moves eastward, so that areas like Hawai'i and Tahiti may experience major typhoons. Such changes may also influence the strength and position of ocean currents by altering the winds that drive them.[51] Annual variation is not merely the result of El Niño. McLean suggests that tropical storms and hurricanes in the southwest Pacific may operate on a 3- to 5-year cycle, as well as more long-term cycles of up to a decade. His investigation of recent weather patterns in the central Pacific revealed that over a 30-year period the number of tropical storms and hurricanes in one season ranged from one to twelve.[52]

Some flora and fauna have adjusted to these conditions. Short-term fluctuations in rainfall, wind, and temperature mean that species must be opportunistic and flexible. Some delay their procreation until wet periods, rather than mating at regular times of the year. A number of species that cannot tolerate a great range of conditions become nomadic to seek out desired conditions.[53] Not all adjust. During El Niño wind conditions the sea level of the western part of the tropical Pacific drops, exposing upper layers of certain inshore reefs and killing many organisms that

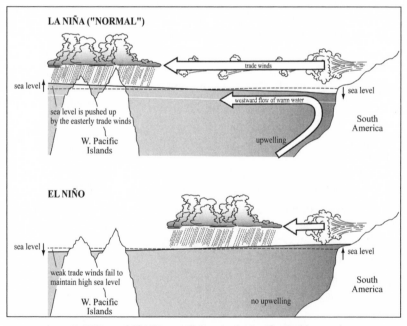

FIGURE 1 La Niña and El Niño conditions in the Pacific. (Lobban and Schefter, 105, after Wallace and Vogel)

depend on near-surface ecological niches.[54] This natural history perspective raises interesting issues for the study of Islander communities. Did an oceanic environment make Islanders more adaptable or nomadic than other premodern peoples? To what extent did the ability of humans to modify their environment ameliorate problems elsewhere in the food chain?

The inhabitants of Remote Oceania had to live with a biota that was uneven across time and space and less well endowed than those of Near Oceania. Most terrestrial flora and fauna came originally from the Pacific's western margins. There is a marked diminution of terrestrial and marine species as one moves east. Tahitian waters contain only half the marine species that the waters surrounding New Caledonia have. This west-east gradient is by no means steady or consistent as it is not only a function of distance from Asia, but also of vectors of diffusion and the suitability of landfalls. The land crab *Cardisoma longipes* is found in New Caledonia, Niue, and Makatea, but nowhere else in Oceania. Terrestrial flora and fauna colonize new islands by flotsam drifting on ocean currents, or they are blown by the winds or attach themselves to birds.[55] Few marine species move across the oceans independently. Like many of their terrestrial counterparts, near-shore maritime colonizers often depend on the whim of the currents to found new colonies.[56]

A host of factors promote the rich fisheries so valued by sea peoples. Most marine species inhabit the benthic (ocean floor) or neritic (near-shore) zones rather than the pelagic (open ocean) zone. Sunlight is a key factor. Most of the marine biomass is made up of phytoplankton, tiny plant plankton that combine sunlight, carbon dioxide, and nutrients to

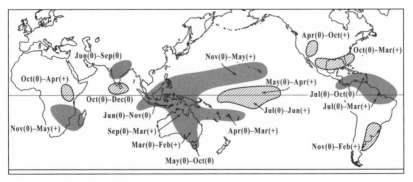

MAP 2 Effects of El Niño on global rainfall. Stippled areas inside solid lines experience drier than usual conditions, whereas areas inside dashed lines are wetter than usual. (Lobban and Schefter, 107, after Lander)

produce organic matter in a manner similar to terrestrial plants. To enable photosynthesis they concentrate in the upper level of the sea where sunlight penetrates, which is down to 100 or 150 meters in clear conditions. Phytoplankton form the basis of the marine food chain.[57] Shallow seas concentrate marine life and organic fallout near the surface. Areas with a lot of turbidity or upwelling recirculate decomposing organic matter back into the living ecosystem. Landmasses with high runoff periodically flush land nutrients into offshore waters. Infusions of fresh water are also important, as even marine organisms can suffer excessive water loss in conditions of high salinity. Not all areas of high productivity are geographically fixed. Examples of mobile productive areas include tidally driven sea fronts on continental shelves, fronts along subtropical climatic transition zones, areas of counter currents, gyres, and eddies.[58]

There is growing recognition of the variability of marine ecosystems across time as well as between localities. This has major implications for Islander fishing patterns and marine tenure. Empirical data and historical records show that the biomass of individual species varies from year to year, and also over longer periods. While the impact of year-to-year fluctuations is modified by the total species population being made up of many yearly cohorts, longer-term fluctuations can considerably alter a species' total biomass. Such long-term changes result from alterations to the environment and changes to species relations with predatory and competing species. Research suggests that change in the ratio of predators to juvenile fish is a significant factor in demographic fluctuations.[59]

All marine species have limited tolerance to changes in water temperature, salinity, physical-chemical conditions, and viscosity, as well as the availability of preferred food sources. Even small changes can have large consequences. For example, phytoplankton require eighteen minerals for healthy growth. The reduction of even one of these can therefore alter the whole food web, built as it is upon phytoplankton.[60] Most marine species are particularly sensitive to temperature changes. The climatic variations outlined above can result in great annual variation in particular species' numbers in local ecosystems. Such changes are particularly devastating for juvenile stock during their first year of life. It appears that these declines are offset by increases in other species' numbers so that the total biomass of any ecosystem demonstrates little fluctuation.[61] But species-specific instability has implications for fisher-folk, who may not eat all species, or who may restrict access to the full range of marine resources through cultural considerations and rules of tenure.

Marine scientist G. D. Sharp proposes a dynamic model for neritic ecosystems that recognizes the complex interactions between fish, habitat, and climate that has major implications for fisher-folk. In such a changeable environment, species must either be flexible enough to adjust to new conditions, or mobile enough to find conditions they prefer. Sharp is particularly challenging when he suggests that species do not adapt or fail as a whole, but exhibit variable success between individuals. The successful adaptors may form the core of a new genetically adapted group as others fade out through a narrowing of their options. The new successful strategy of adaptation has ramifications for the whole ecosystem, as feeding patterns change and the species' predators must adjust their behavior to match the adaptation of their prey.[62] Humans are among these predators.

Sharp goes on to note that

> under the present forced recognition of inherent ecological variations and the clear absence of "equilibria," man will have to accept that he will need to become more versatile as most predators must, and more economic and less disruptive, if he is to live in harmony with the seas and their varying resources.[63]

The fact that instability in individual species' numbers can occur alongside stability in the overall size of the ecosystem biomass suggests that there can be continuity in marine harvests for fisher-folk not rigidly tied to harvesting a few species only.

Inter-relationships between Pacific Maritime Ecosystems

Islanders used a variety of marine environments. The links between these environments drew them out to sea and forever reminded them of a world beyond their home shores. The main ecosystems in the coastal waters of Remote Oceania are coral reefs, lagoons, and mangrove swamps. Some locations lack these buffers, allowing waves to break directly against the shoreline. The reef-lagoon complexes are among the most productive ecosystems on the planet. Only tropical rain forests rival reef-lagoon complexes in terms of productivity and diversity. The 150-kilometer-long barrier reef surrounding Palau has nine species of sea grass, more than three hundred species of corals, and approximately two thousand species of fish.[64]

Coastal waters are zones of transition where forces shaping land and sea interact. They are uneasy spaces for those seeking precise boundaries. While the boundary between land and sea might be defined by the high or low tide mark, the boundary between the neritic and oceanic provinces is more problematic. Without a clear physical border such as the outer margin of fringing reefs, one must fall back on some arbitrary definition based on depth of water or distance from the coast.[65]

Open ocean ecosystems tend to be much less productive than reef-lagoon complexes. The only exceptions are areas of shallow water shoals, or areas where upwelling enriches the upper layers with nutrients. Terrestrial runoff and shallower waters mean that the neritic zone is more turbid than the open ocean, and subject to greater seasonal variation in temperature, salinity, and light penetration. Current and wave forces are also very strong in the neritic zone. Oceanic fish are less capable of withstanding wide differences in temperature and salinity. The open ocean's relative stability of temperature, salinity, and other physical conditions means that there are few barriers to fish movement in search of preferred regimes.[66]

There is significant overlap between these provinces. Life came to the islands and their coastal waters from the surrounding sea. New elements were continuously introduced by the forces of nature, as the following quote from the journal of nineteenth-century trader Peter Dillon demonstrates:

> About seven o'clock yesterday morning, we entered the channel between Mannicolo [sic Vanikoro] and the barrier reef which surrounds the island. Perceiving something lying on one of the dry sandbanks on the reef, we pulled out, and found it to be drift wood, thrown up there by the sea. There was a solitary young cocoanut tree in a flourishing condition growing there, which will no doubt come to perfection if not molested by the natives.[67]

Elements from across the ocean also influence local marine ecosystems. Near-shore species colonize other coastal locations by drifting as larvae on ocean currents. Such colonization can succeed providing the currents actually encounter islands, and the sea passage is not too extensive or devoid of nutrients so that a sufficient number of larvae survive to form a viable population.

The wealth of these inshore ecosystems can attract concentrations of predators from just outside the reef and beyond. The temporary entry of these predators can have a significant effect on fisheries. A foray by a school of migratory tuna, for example, can consume a huge amount of fish. Some schools of tuna captured by modern seine fishing have weighed over 200 tons. At times in their lives tuna may need to consume 20 percent of their body weight per day. Multiple species' aggregations of juvenile tuna may contain over 100,000 tons of fish. Such a grouping can consume 600,000 tons of fish per month.[68] Coastal sea birds are also significant predators, but they also make a major contribution to the ecosystem by introducing nutrients in the form of guano. Similarly, lagoon shores inhabited by humans receive more human waste and other organic matter than waters off uninhabited shores.[69]

External influences not only affect inshore fish populations, but also the structure of the reef. Most classic studies of reef and lagoon fishing were based on assumptions about the physical environment that have been challenged by marine biologists unknown to most of those who study the human populations of Oceania. Johannes, for example, argues that coral reefs are highly sensitive to man-induced changes because they evolved in relatively stable environments that were characterized by a narrow range of physical and chemical variation. A new school of thought portrays reefs as "temporal mosaics." Coral reefs are seen to be in a state of dynamic flux, formed of a patchwork of reef communities in different stages of recovery from various natural disturbances. Change is seen as more typical than constancy.[70]

Climatic conditions generated beyond the reef produce many of these disturbances. High waves associated with tropical storms and typhoons can cause massive mortality to many reef species. In some cases storms return an entire reef community to an early stage of development with low species diversity. There are documented cases of a single typhoon destroying tens of kilometers of reef. Typhoons damage reefs through unusually strong waves and currents. Major increases in sedimentation brought about by terrestrial runoff from unusually high rainfall can also smother the reef community.[71] Typhoons may also create new features on the lagoon floor that may change the relative value of existing marine tenure units. For example, a sandbank appeared in the middle of Woleai Atoll's lagoon in the wake of a powerful typhoon in 1907. The German ethnographer Augustin Krämer noted that

> according to the natives, there exists an old story which claims that there was an island in the same spot in the past and that it was destroyed by a typhoon in a similar manner to that in which Raur was washed away in 1907. The same typhoon deposited the sand formation which is known as the sand cay in the old place.[72]

Changes in sea temperatures also affect the growth of coral reefs. Corals have a narrow band of tolerance to sea temperatures. When their threshold is exceeded they "bleach," the visible result of the loss of zooxanthellae, coral's symbiotic algae. This algae helps the coral to photosynthesize and to fix carbon. As a result, coral growth is inhibited. In the eastern Pacific, a one-degree rise in sea surface temperature off Moorea resulted in 20 percent of bleached corals dying. The 3 to 4 degree rise in sea surface temperature experienced in the eastern Pacific during the 1982–83 ENSO produced mass bleaching, and led to coral mortality rates in excess of 90 percent in certain localities. Recovery may also be affected by the reduction of the surviving coral's ability to reproduce. In keeping with this flux, recent research indicates an "ongoing evolution of temperature tolerance" among corals, resulting in a broad spectrum of sensitivity to temperatures.[73]

The impact of these disturbances can vary considerably depending on the characteristics of the reef community. The range of species in the reef, the age of the reef, and the alignment of the reef to prevailing weather patterns all influence the impact of storm waves and other disturbances. Reef communities that experience frequent disturbances are mainly younger, with high species diversity. More stable reef communities tend to be monopolized by the larger, older growth of a few species. Such sheltered communities often take 20 to 50 years to recover from major disturbances, while systems that never advance beyond the early stages of development due to frequent interruptions recover to their former immature stage more quickly.[74]

Reefs act as filters rather than barriers to exchanges between lagoon waters and the ocean. Waves break on the seaward margins, and water flows over the reef into the lagoon and back with tidal patterns. Water also flows through gaps in the reef. This influx may bring nutrients into the reef-lagoon system if they come from areas of upwelling or currents offshore.[75] The open sea also receives influences from the terrestrial and neritic provinces. The influence of the land and inshore waters can be detected well out to sea. In an oceanic environment, islands represent a concentrated source of nutrients and natural fertilizers rich in nitrogen and other materials that phytoplankton feed on. Much of this material is eroded by wind, rain, and flowing water, carried to the sea along water courses, and then washed out to sea by waves and tides. Some then settles on the seabed near to the shore, but a significant amount is carried out to sea through reef channels. The heavier detritus is eventually carried down to the deep sea floor offshore via submarine canyons. Lighter material floats on the surface. Driven by surface currents, these plumes of nutrients may extend for 100 miles or more downstream from their island of origin.[76] These plumes enrich offshore ecosystems, and indicate the presence of rich inshore waters to those traveling the open sea, be they migratory tuna or human seafarers.

Islands enrich offshore waters in other ways. Wind action over leeward shores may produce minor upwelling offshore by generating currents that disturb the surface layer. This allows colder and nutrient-laden subsurface waters to rise. Other upwelling occurs as a result of eddies that arise from the deflection of moving water masses by islands or shallow water formations such as offshore reefs.[77] Land-based sea birds may be drawn to these enriched fisheries. While they deplete the fishery, their guano also enriches its nutrient base.[78]

A number of species that make their homes on the reef acquire food elsewhere, through daily foraging or longer absences. Island fishermen have long been aware of the tendency of lagoon and reef fish to migrate seaward to spawn. These migrations occur along predictable routes. They proceed to spawning sites along the outer reef, or in channels leading out to sea. Spawning generally lasts for only a few days before the fish return to their normal habitats. The location and timing of spawning is designed to ensure that the eggs are swept out to sea by the tide or currents. Spawning tends to occur around new and full moons when tidal ranges and tidal currents are greatest. Such a strategy ensures that fry emerge from the eggs in the open ocean. They emerge as planktonic larvae, and only later develop into free-swimming fish. They return to their parents' reef or lagoon habitat any time from a few days to a few months later.[79]

Little is known about their activities at sea. It seems likely that they spend their early lives in this impoverished environment to escape the host of predators that inhabit the rich reef and lagoon ecosystems. Studies of reef and lagoon zooplankton indicate that these relatively helpless drifters lose from 50 to 90 percent of their populations to the host of predators in these areas.[80] Spawning behavior seems designed to ensure that larvae not only escape inshore predators, but can also return inshore once they are ready. It makes sense for eggs to be dispersed out to sea, but not too far out. Johannes notes that peak spawning times in tropical seas seem to be when prevailing winds and currents are at their weakest. Similarly, the most favored spawning areas for a wide variety of reef and lagoon species are submarine promontories on the seaward side of reefs. Gyres tend to form there. Whereas currents may take fry away from land, these gyres circulate larvae and fry back toward the shore.[81] Evidence from the Hawaiian archipelago suggests eddies on the leeward side of the islands may fulfill a similar role. These eddies may be as large as 50 miles in diameter, but they are not a regular or permanent year-round phenomenon.[82]

The return of the fry is a bountiful time for fishermen. Large numbers suddenly appear from the ocean, attracting equally large concentrations of predator fish and birds. Because the open ocean is much more uniform than inshore waters, many oceanic fish can migrate to exploit such concentrations. This also enables them to avoid seasonal shortages in any locality or seasonal changes in sea temperature. Perhaps the fish best adapted to migratory life in the ocean are the fifty-eight species of tuna and related fish such as wahoo and marlin. Skipjack tuna tagged in the Pacific have been found 10,000 kilometers away, while albacore tuna are known to travel from Japan to California in less than a year.[83]

Modern ocean mapping shows that the open sea also contains neritic-like environments. Relatively shallow areas of ocean well away from land are found across Remote Oceania. Fijian fishermen refer to one as Thakau Lala, the "Empty Reef." It has no land, just a circular reef enclosing a shallow, sheltered body of water.[84] Bukatatanoa is the name given to a reef 11 miles east of the island of Lakeba that encloses a lagoon nearly 200 square miles in extent.[85] Similarly, the Marshallese were familiar with a huge, current-free area of ocean south of the atoll of Ailingalaplap. They call it Eon Woerr, literally "over coral" in reference to its presumed shallow depth.[86]

Eon Woerr, Thakau Lala, and Bukatatanoa were all cultural representations of the marine environment, in the same way that designations such as neritic and oceanic are products of Western oceanography. Modern oceanography's depiction of marine ecosystems as dynamic, variable, and open to external influence has major implications for fisheries management and sea travel. The rhythms and currents of this oceanic environment link Polynesia and Micronesia. The sea dominates the lives and consciousness of the inhabitants of both areas as nowhere else on earth. In this ocean setting, the sea cannot be ignored.

2

Local Worlds:
The Sea in Everyday Life

HUMANS HAVE an ancient biological relationship with the sea. Most evolutionary scientists now believe that all life on earth originated in the water.[1] Vestiges of our aquatic past remain. British writer James Hamilton-Paterson points out that

> the salt which is in seawater is in our blood and tears and sweat. The lungs of an infant *in utero* can be seen rhythmically breathing as it inhales and expels amniotic fluid, even as its oxygen supply comes from the mother's bloodstream via the umbilicus. Each of us has breathed warm saline for days and survived. The lungs themselves derive from fused pharyngeal pouches, and branchial clefts ("gill slits") still form temporarily in all chordate embryos, including humans, reminding us that something which became *Homo* did crawl up a beach many millions of years ago.[2]

We are unique among land animals in having a dive reflex. When our faces touch water there is an automatic reduction in our heart rate and oxygen consumption. We are also three-quarters liquid. Our bodies are insulated with subcutaneous fat like marine mammals, so that we are buoyant and streamlined.[3] Attitudes matter as well as physique. The more relaxed you are in the water the less chance you have of drowning. Something like 15 percent of all drownings in developed, urbanized societies are "dry drownings," as people panic when they first inhale water, sending their larynx into violent spasms that result in suffocation.[4]

At Home with the Sea

People of the sea need to feel truly at home with the sea. Most of the inhabitants of Oceania lived along the coastal margins of their island homes. The sights, sounds, and smells of the sea pervaded their lives, while the tastes of the sea were often on their lips. Dwellings on atolls were almost always along the lagoon shore of the larger islets. The lagoon shore was generally the most protected from stormy and seasonal rough seas. Most family dwellings were located beside the major lateral paths that ran parallel to the lagoon shore, among coconut trees and, if soils permitted, other food-producing trees such as breadfruit and banana. Taro swamps were often excavated in the interior of the larger islets, where the freshwater lens was most developed. Canoe houses lined the shore of the lagoon. They served as the focal point for men's activities, as well as repositories for the canoes that were so valued by atoll dwellers. Men spent much of their days there, and often slept there, attracted by the cool breezes of the lagoon and the camaraderie of men from the same lineage.[5] There were isolated cases of settlements on seaward shores, particularly when the lagoon shore faced into prevailing winds.[6]

Settlements on larger, high islands were still predominantly sited along the coast. In Palau, most villages were situated within a few hundred meters of the shore. Preferred sites were usually low ridges near freshwater streams. The ridges provided security, while the freshwater was used for cooking, bathing, and irrigation of taro fields. The marine wealth of the reef and lagoon near the coast was a major consideration in village location. Mangrove swamps curtailed shoreline locations over much of Palau. Villages' portals to the sea were usually canoe landings at the head of natural or man-made channels through the mangrove. Land was less intensely cultivated away from the villages, with a buffer of uncultivated land often demarcating the border between antagonistic villages.[7] On neighboring Yap most villages had rocky or beach frontages rather than mangrove. Jetties made from coral stone, with canoe houses on them, thrust out from the shore. Inland villages populated by people of lower rank lacked access to localities suitable for both cultivating taro and harvesting marine resources.[8] Most settlements on the high islands of eastern Micronesia were also concentrated along the shoreline.[9]

European observers of eastern Polynesia noted that while dwellings were generally on the coast, they were scattered throughout the coastal plain and the lower and middle reaches of valleys. Settlements might form an almost continuous ribbon of individual dwellings set alongside the coast or be scattered among fields and groves of fruit trees. Large clusters of dwellings were found only in areas of particular agricultural wealth, or perhaps around the residence of eminent individuals.[10] The explorer La Pérouse described such a pattern when he wrote of Hawaiian dwellings on a fertile section of the southeast coast of Maui:

[they] are so numerous, that a space of three or four leagues may be taken
for a single village, but all the houses are upon the sea shore, and the
mountains seem to occupy so much of the island, that the habitable part
of it appears to be scarcely half a league broad.[11]

The ideal location was fertile and well watered with good offshore fishing. Hawaiian sociopolitical units tended to be centered upon such areas,
while boundaries between political units were often less well endowed.[12]

Most settlements recorded by literate observers in western Polynesia
were beside lagoons, inlets, or bays, yet variations in geography resulted
in diverse patterns. In the Tongan archipelago, for example, four patterns
are discernible. The low-lying Haʻapai group replicated the atoll lagoon
shore pattern found throughout Oceania. The more rugged interior of
ʻEua restricted settlement to the coastal plain and the lower reaches of
some valleys, while the rolling hill country of Vavaʻu produced both
coastal and interior villages. On the largest island, Tongatapu, a gently
sloping topography resembling a continuous coastal plain extended across
its entire width. Dwellings were dispersed among cultivation until civil
unrest led to a concentration into fortified villages at the beginning of the
nineteenth century.[13]

This pattern of fortified villages was apparently learned from Fijians,
with whom Tongans had frequent contact. Most of the population of eastern Fiji lived in fortified villages on coastal plains, but the larger islands
also contained groups who were recognized as distinct from the coastal
population. On Vanua Levu the coastal peoples referred to them as ʻai le
kutuʻ (bush people).[14] These peoples traded with the coastal peoples on
occasion, but rarely came to the sea. On December 26, 1840, the missionary Jaggar met one such group in the densely populated Rewa Delta of
eastern Viti Levu:

This afternoon some strangers from inland came to see Rewa for the 1st
time—the Rewa people do not understand their Dialect. They had not
before seen the sea and had some necklaces of shells to take back to their
town as great riches.[15]

Lovoni people from the interior often raided the coastal population of
Levuka on Ovalau.[16] Western travelers to Chuuk in the nineteenth century also noted antagonism between coastal and inland peoples. They
described the people of the interior as being of dark complexion with
woolly hair, while those on the coast were lighter-skinned.[17]

Other islands contained populations who had moved from the interior to the coast. Only a small proportion of the interior of Samoa was permanently occupied by the mid-nineteenth century. This may have been a relatively recent state of affairs, as the missionary Dyson noted that there had been movement from the interior to the coast in the first half of the century in response to the attractions of European trade goods.[18] Similarly, Rotuma's interior seems to have been abandoned within a generation of sustained European contact in the nineteenth century. Visitors in the 1870s found only a half dozen dwellings in an interior valley, but were told that not long before the whole island had been heavily populated.[19]

For most of the region's inhabitants the sea was integral to daily life. They felt at ease in the sea, and excelled at swimming and diving. The missionary William Ellis went so far as to describe Hawaiians as "almost a race of amphibious beings." He detailed how

> familiar with the sea at birth, they lose all dread of it, and seem nearly as much at home in the water as on dry land. There are few children who are not taken into the sea by their mothers the second or third day after birth, and many who can swim as soon as they can walk.[20]

Ellis's description is not isolated. Numerous observers were struck by how comfortable Islanders were in the water, and often described them in terms usually reserved for marine creatures. Captain David Porter related how Marquesans "would swim off to the ships, about meal time, in large shoals, and wait there for the sailors to throw them pieces of bread, although the harbor was much infested with large and ravenous sharks, and one of the natives was devoured by them soon after our arrival."[21] The English captain Frederick Beechey described a group of Rapanui women crowded together like seals onto a small rock, and how among "these Nereids three or four would shoot off at a time into the water, and swim with the expertness of fish to the boats to try their influence on their visitors."[22]

There are a number of accounts of Islanders surviving for long periods in the water, or swimming long distances in rough seas. After the schooner *Marianne* capsized between Kaua'i and O'ahu in August 1852, many of the Hawaiian passengers swam to Kaua'i, 6 miles distant. A number of the mothers swam with children on their backs.[23] When the Tahitian Tamaha took offense at the treatment meted out to him by the boatswain's mate on a U.S. vessel sailing from the Marquesas Islands, he jumped overboard and swam off. This despite the fact that their last port of call was 20 miles distant, and "it was blowing fresh with a considerable sea."[24] Yet accord-

ing to a marine left behind to garrison the American base in the Marquesas, Tamaha made it back safely, claiming to have been in the water for
one day and two nights.[25]

There is little information on the swimming techniques of Islanders at
the time. The most detailed account is ethnologist Basil Thomson's
description of Fijian swimming:

> In long-distance swimming the natives adopt a sort of side-stroke, in
> which nothing but the head is above water. They move smoothly and rap-
> idly through the water, the legs and the right arm giving the propulsion,
> and the left hand striking downwards under the body. When a quick spurt
> is required, they use the overhand action with both arms alternately, with
> the cheek resting flat on the water as the arm on that side is driven aft.
> With this action they can swim at greater speed than all but the best Euro-
> pean swimmers.[26]

Interestingly, Thomson notes that even the hill tribesmen of the interior
were good swimmers and divers, being as good as, if not better than
coastal Fijians.[27] The only precolonial reference located that contradicts
this picture of a people universally at ease in water comes from the trader
Peter Dillon, who noted that a Rotuman woman on a canoe that capsized
had to be assisted by her companions as she could not swim, but only
after they had righted the canoe.[28]

Islanders were also at ease under water. The French artist Jacques
Arago observed how Carolinians were "supple and active, swim like fish,
and keep their head almost always under water, which is much less fatigu-
ing to them than it would be to us."[29] Islanders were also accomplished
divers, who often amazed Western sailors with their ability to dive and
retrieve coins and nails thrown overboard. European captains and traders
specifically recruited Islanders for their diving ability, either to collect
pearl shell or for work such as untangling cables and repairing ships' hulls
below the water line.[30] Ability varied. Yapese, Raivavaens, and Rotumans
seem to have been preferred for commercial diving.[31] Thomson observed
that Fijians preferred to jump into the water feet first, and once on the
bottom could propel themselves at incredible speed along the sea floor by
lying flat with their noses in the sand and their hands behind their backs,
then digging their toes into the sand and pushing off.[32]

There were limits to the depth one could dive to, and the amount of
time one could stay underwater without breathing apparatus. A European
witness to Islander pearl diving in the Tuamotu Archipelago noted that
none of the divers on his vessel ever stayed down longer than 50 seconds.

He did, however, admit that they could perhaps remain underwater longer if circumstances required. If divers went below 14 meters the water pressure could rupture the membrane in their ears and cause nosebleeds. A number of divers suffered these complaints, although they claimed that most of the side effects, such as inflamed nostrils and swollen eyes, disappeared within a few days.[33]

Islanders derived great joy from being in the sea. Children spent much of their time on the beach or in the lagoon. They were regaled with tales of endurance and strength involving paddling and canoe surfing. Water sports and activities were popular with adults—body, board, and canoe surfing; diving; canoe races; and swimming races.[34] Hawaiians in particular delighted in surfing. Their inventory included hardwood boards ranging from 2 to 20 feet in length. When conditions were right, whole villages, men, women, and children, would abandon the day's activities to take to the surf. Hawaiian records list a host of surfing spots throughout the archipelago, each with distinct features. Ruling chiefs were expected to be expert surfers. Certain types of board were reserved for their use, as were particular surf beaches on occasion. Surfing contests attracted great interest, and there were even temples dedicated to the sport. The greater the danger, the greater the prestige of surfing a particular spot, such as Puaa in North Kona on the island of Hawai'i, where a famous surf called *Kooka* surged over a coral head just beyond a point of lava rocks.[35]

Islanders appear to have adapted physically to their oceanic environment. A study by anatomy professor Philip Houghton notes that body mass among Islanders increases the farther east one moves across the Pacific. Hawaiians are the most bulky. Polynesians and Micronesians (the inhabitants of Remote Oceania) have large body size and strong musculature that set them apart. Most other inhabitants of tropical seas have slim bodies that maximize their surface area in relation to mass, which enhances their bodies' ability to lose heat, but Polynesians and Micronesians have a low surface area to mass ratio, which facilitates the retention of body heat. Houghton accounts for this apparent anomaly by suggesting that the key feature is low temperatures at sea rather than high air temperatures in this part of the world.[36]

Surface temperatures on tropical seas can become chilly, particularly at night, or during rainy and windy conditions. Oceanic canoes offered limited protection. Once a person begins to lose heat, she or he slips into hypothermia, and may ultimately die. Houghton calculated the survival rates for people of varying body masses on ocean voyages in Pacific conditions. He found that bulky people clearly had better rates of survival under all conditions likely to be encountered, so that larger people had the best chance of surviving the longer inter-island voyages in Remote Oceania. This physique evolved in Remote Oceania as predominantly bulky colonists passed these features on to their descendants. Cold maritime conditions also gave rise to other physical adjustments. People did not necessarily become fat (fat is a poor insulator), but developed larger, denser bones, and greater musculature.[37]

There are problems with Houghton's theory. The first humans to colonize the Pacific Islands may already have been large-bodied maritime peoples, perhaps originating from colder latitudes. Also, much is made of the necessity of surviving long voyages of exploration and colonization. Island traditions suggest that intentional, two-way voyaging was the norm, with initial discovery being followed by deliberate voyages of colonization toward a known target. As Houghton himself points out, a bulky frame requires more food to sustain it, which is a disadvantage for voyages of indeterminate length into areas of unknown food resources.[38] Did the majority of the gene pool continue to make open sea voyages often enough to require such thermal insulation after the initial settlement of islands? By the era of this study's focus, many no longer sailed regularly out of sight of native shores, and other factors had come into play to create significant differences in physique. Although Hawaiians are the bulkiest population in the region on average, Lieutenant James King noted significant differences in physique when he visited Hawai'i with Cook in the 1770s. While ali'i (chiefs) and toa (warriors) towered above British sailors and marines, the common folk were a "very tawny, thin and small, mean looking people."[39]

Overall, Houghton's observations hold. The inhabitants of Remote Oceania are bulky compared to other maritime peoples, but such adaptations have their limits. Houghton's modeling shows that survival rates decline as average temperatures drop in proportion to distance from the equator. Historical examples of Islanders sailing on Western vessels still suggest that their physique enhanced their chance of survival in colder seas. They certainly had an advantage over Europeans. When a ship's boat was swamped in cold seas off Oregon's Columbia River in 1811, two Hawaiians onboard were able to save a Western crewman. However, one died of cold soon afterward.[40] Yet in 1820 a Marquesan on a sealing vessel off the South Shetland Islands in the far south Atlantic survived a fall overboard. He cut off his boots with a knife and remained afloat until the vessel could turn around and rescue him. Although requiring hospitalization when the ship docked in Boston, he survived an ordeal that would have finished off most others.[41]

Western observers noted other adaptations. The trader Kobelt told the ethnographer Damm that the Puluwatese had far better long-distance vision than Europeans. This was a great advantage at sea. Kobelt noted that Puluwatese observed things like sea birds and variations in water color and shade that indicated the presence of reefs long before he could.[42] The German missionary Salesius also noted that

> the vision of the Yapese is excellent. He recognizes people at very great distances and without difficulty distinguishes fish, crabs, and mollusks in the water, even though their shape and coloring are marvelously adapted to the surroundings; with sure aim he impales on his spear even small fish in motion; he early distinguishes ships and flags, even when they are far out to sea.[43]

This may have been as much the result of learning what to look for as of superior eyesight, as Europeans with field glasses still had difficulty detecting objects Islanders could see.[44]

Islanders enhanced their vision into water by means of oils placed on the surface. Lutké noted that the inhabitants of Murilo and Fananu improved their underwater vision "by chewing coconut, which they spit into the sea, in order to make the water calmer and more transparent by means of the oil which is separated from it, and after that they quickly succeed in their hunt."[45] Hawaiians were also able to see clearly down to 20 fathoms after they had chewed roasted *kukui* nuts and spat them out onto the surface.[46]

Sustenance from the Sea

The ability to see underwater was important because marine species made up a significant part of the diet. The chroniclers of Cook's expeditions recorded 150 types of fish known by Tahitians in the 1770s, at least forty-eight of which were identified as edible.[47] It is difficult to quantify the role of marine products in the diet between 1770 and 1870 solely on the basis of the historical record. Root crops such as taro, yam, and sweet potato, or tree crops such as breadfruit and pandanus seem to have made up the greater part of the diet, with fish and shellfish forming the main protein component.[48] The sea also provided salt for preserving fish.[49] Salt from evaporated seawater was a valued addition to the diet in Hawai'i and Fiji, while in Tonga, a small amount of saltwater might be drunk at mealtimes. A drink of seawater was the universal remedy employed by Hawaiians to overcome the nausea, stomachaches, and dizziness that sometimes accompanied a change in the usual diet from taro to 'uala (sweet potato) or from 'uala back to taro.[50]

Modern studies suggest that marine foods make up between 10 and 20 percent of energy supplied to the body. In a study of the Fijian community of Batiki, Bayliss-Smith concluded that root crops and vegetables made up 71 percent of the diet, coconuts 20 percent, and marine products 9 percent. These figures were derived by multiplying the hectares cultivated or fished by the average yield per hectare for each category. In a study using a similar methodology, Bayliss-Smith concluded that the diet of inhabitants of the atoll of Ontong Java was made up of 29 percent taro, 21 percent coconut, 3 percent other crops, 19 percent marine products, and 25 percent imported food.[51] While the maritime contribution appears limited, ethnologists regard a society to be fisher-folk if marine species make up 10 percent of the diet.[52]

The contribution of seafood varied. Typhoons and storms, drought, heavy rains, or infestations of ants or rats could devastate crops. In such circumstances, fishing took on more prominence, as a supplement to the remaining crops and foods drawn from the forests that were used in times of hardship. Kotzebue was informed that typhoons could destroy all the crops on Carolinian Islands, "so that the inhabitants are compelled to subsist for a long time only by the fishery."[53] In the wake of a devastating hurricane that hit eastern Fiji in 1886, a steamer carrying food relief found that although many crops were destroyed, all localities still had enough fish and pumpkins for everyday use, so their relief supplies were devoured in one large feast.[54]

The accessibility of marine resources varied across time and space. As well as periodic fluctuations of individual species, fishers also had to contend with storms that prevented offshore fishing and disrupted the inshore fishery by increasing turbidity.[55] Reef fisheries are periodically tainted by ciguatera, a food poisoning caused by toxins from microscopic algae on the sea floor called dinoflagellates. Their toxins pass through the food chain via herbivorous fish, which are consumed by carnivorous fish. Humans contract ciguatera by eating reef fish. Although rarely fatal, ciguatera causes highly unpleasant and long-lasting digestive and neurological symptoms. Ciguatera is so common on some atolls that it is considered an occupational hazard.[56]

Many fishing activities were highly seasonal. Most Islanders divided their calendar into two distinct seasons: a calm season of rich fishing, and a windy season in which little fishing was conducted.[57] Seasonality and the life cycle of marine species influenced fishing. The Tahitian year was divided into a rainy season and its immediate aftermath when fishing and breadfruit were abundant, and a dry season when taro and other food crops prevailed. The whole summer from November to March was a time of alternating storms and calm periods. Stormy weather brought increased rainfall, which disrupted near-shore ecosystems with silt. The swollen streams also enriched the inshore fishery by washing nutrients into the lagoon, and attracted shoals of sea fish, lured by small fry washed into the lagoon from the streams. When calm spells returned, Tahitians could take to their canoes to harvest the enriched fishery.

Most lagoon and reef fish spawned when currents swept their eggs out to sea. Here they hatched, banded into schools, and moved back inshore, pursued by bonito and albacore. This process occurred from mid-October to early June, when inshore fishing prospered. However, the offshore fishery was less accessible during April and May due to stormy conditions. From June to September the storms subsided, but winter swells prevented canoes from venturing far from shore. Smaller, species-specific perturbations occurred within this pattern. The ina'a (whitebait) ran when the to'erau, a northerly and northwesterly wind, blew. Fishermen were aware that other species of fish reacted to particular phases of the moon or shifts of the current.[58]

Alkire has noted that the differences in dietary resources between high islands and low coral islands are more a matter of scale than kind. Although high islands generally have more reliable and abundant terrestrial resources than coral islands, their dietary patterns are broadly similar.[59] Marine topography does influence diet, however. Marine resources vary considerably. The coral reef of Ulithi Atoll encloses a 460-square-kilometer lagoon, while the lagoon of Ifalik Atoll is only 2.42 square kilometers in extent.[60] Palau is particularly blessed with 2130 square kilometers of reef, lagoon, and mangrove, as well as a significant land area, so Palauans rarely venture into the open sea beyond their protective reef.[61] But in a number of areas reef development was limited, or even nonexistent, necessitating greater reliance on terrestrial resources or open sea fisheries. The small raised coral island of Fais has only a limited reef fishery, prompting its inhabitants to become one of the few groups in the region to hunt and eat sharks.[62] The inhabitants of the coral islands of Lamotrek, Ifalik, Satawal, and Tobi all derive much of their fish from offshore fisheries such as shoals, as a result of the limited lagoons or reefs surrounding their home islands.[63]

In the 1820s Dillon noted that fish were not plentiful on Tikopia "owing to the deep water round the island."[64] Steep slopes offshore and a lack of sheltered reefs and lagoon complexes also restricted the wealth and safety of much of the Hawaiian shoreline. Similar conditions prevailed in the Marquesas. Cultural factors also contributed to dietary deficiencies in both the Hawaiian and Marquesan populations. Fishing equipment and canoes were reserved for chiefs in the Marquesas by the early 1800s.[65] King attributed the poor physique of the Hawaiian maka'ainana (commoners) to their diet and hard work.[66] Modern studies support this theory. The apparently widespread nature of commoners' physical deficiencies suggests a diet that was largely made up of carbohydrates and deficient in body-building protein. The main vegetable staples were taro and 'uala. To be truly nutritional, these foods need supplementing with foods rich in proteins, fats, minerals, and vitamins, such as fish and coconut. Ali'i had access to such supplements through their fishponds. Maka-'ainana did not, and relied on fisheries off their immediate coastlines.[67]

Islanders evolved several strategies to overcome disruptions in their access to marine resources. Joseph Banks noted that Tahitians would eat almost everything that came out of the sea. A wide variety of marine species was eaten, and most parts of these species were considered edible, including entrails and gills. Tough seafood such as jellyfish was simply allowed to decompose until it was considered palatable. While Europeans found the smell repugnant, it does not seem to have harmed those consuming it.[68] Most Islanders seem to have preferred their fish raw or lightly boiled. An English sailor stranded on Palau in the 1780s had to concede that fish gutted and preserved by smoking was "not so well flavored as when eaten raw."[69] In addition to smoke-cured flesh, drying and salting were also used to preserve fish. Fish cured in this way were obtained by Cook at Ni'ihau in 1778, and were found to keep well and to be very good to eat.[70]

When fish were scarce, the whole community might be mobilized to search the inshore fishery. Tahitian women would "flock to the reef in droves, and in any scarcity of fish remain up to the middle in water the greater part of the day,"[71] while at night thousands of fishermen might scour the reef. In the atolls of the Hall Islands fishing with fishhooks was reserved for the three months of the year when fish were hard to come by, as sea conditions made nets and traps ineffective. Fortunately, this time of scarcity coincided with the egg-laying season of *Sterna stolida,* a sea bird found in large numbers on these islands.[72] Hawaiians built fishponds to overcome the vagaries of the marine environment. These were generally stone constructions along shallow coastlines. The main fish kept in these ponds were *awa* (milkfish) and *'ama'ama* (mullet). A study suggested that these fishponds yielded an average of 166 kilograms of fish per acre.[73] As such, they were a highly concentrated and reliable resource for the chiefs to whom they belonged. Tahitians also constructed enclosures to contain fish. In this case they placed "deep-sea fishes"[74] within walls of coral in lagoons and bays, so that they could harvest them with nets.

Fishing bans were imposed on some species while they were spawning, while others like turtle were reserved solely for consumption by the chiefly class or only for special religious occasions. These restrictions promoted the preservation of such species and enhanced their cultural status.[75] Certain marine products were regarded as items of prestige. Whales' teeth were highly valued in most societies, and were largely reserved for persons of rank and consequence.[76] In Palau, bracelets of dugong bone and tortoise shell ornaments were symbols of chiefly status.[77] Rare shells were often sought after beyond their area of origin. Regional alliances might be forged, or threatened, by the control of such resources.[78] Even such common items as fishhooks, fishing gear, and shells used for fish hooks were listed as valued items by the Hawaiian historian David Malo.[79]

During the period under review similar methods were used across the region to exploit comparable environments.[80] Fishing was generally concentrated between the shoreline and the outer edge of the reef. Here, small fish and shellfish were gathered by hand, while other fish were speared or harpooned, netted, trapped, or caught by angling with a variety of hooks.[81] The different techniques reflected the diversity of species. Herbivores such as the scarid family clearly will not take a baited hook like a carnivorous fish will. Scarids such as the ubiquitous parrotfish are small and plentiful, and tend to be found in shallow water, so that nets were the best method to catch them. Many reef and lagoon fish, such as squirrel-fish *(Holocentridae)* and goatfish *(Mullidae),* spend much of their time ranging from the lagoon to the reef flats and even to the seaward edge of the outer reef in search of food. Knowledge of their daily pattern is therefore essential to ensure they can be intercepted when they funnel through channels and can be caught with nets or traps. Bottom-dwelling fish such as grouper *(Serrandae),* snapper *(Lutjanidae),* and bigeye scad *(Carringae)* are concentrated in certain parts of the lagoon, and on the outside of reef passes at depths of 150 meters or more. The outer reef slope was a rich fishery, but wave action restricted the use of nets and traps, so that most fishing had to be done by hand line or by diving. Knowledge of a species' location, depth, and preferred bait was vital to the success of the angler or spear fisherman.[82]

Deeper offshore waters were exploited less regularly by trolling, angling, netting near the surface, and long lining, or more rarely by the use of traps. Traps might be set down to depths of 75 fathoms, while some Hawaiian long lines used for benthic species could reach down 1200 feet.[83] Offshore fisheries were less reliable, but could still provide rich catches. Pelagic predator fish such as *mahimahi* (dolphinfish, *Coryphaenidae*) and *aku* (skipjack tuna, *Scombridae*) were particularly sought after.[84] Nineteenth-century Hawaiian sources imply that a catch of 100 *aku* a day was not an unreasonable expectation. Small *aku* average 5 to 12 pounds, while some weigh up to 22 pounds. Even allowing for weight reduction due to gutting and drying, a moderate catch of *aku* represented a significant source. In 1810 a European resident of Honolulu noted that one expedition landed 10 to 12 canoe loads of fish caught in nets.[85]

Pelagic trolling was not only potentially lucrative, but also thrilling. The Hawaiian master fisherman Kahaulelio left a detailed account worth quoting at length. He recorded how fishermen were alerted to a school of the carnivorous *aku* pursuing their prey by the presence of *noio* (Hawaiian noddy tern), *'uwa'u* (petrel), and *koa'e* birds (white-tailed tropic bird)[86] circling overhead. The canoes were then paddled at full speed toward a school of *makiawa* (round herring)[87] that the *aku* were pursuing:

> We followed them [the school of *makiawa*] and in less than half an hour they would surge up to the surface and the *aku* would rush among them. This lasted a few minutes then the sharks that looked white in the water, the *ahi*,[88] the voracious *mahimahi* and many others appeared. We *aku* fishermen never failed to keep ourselves supplied with small scoop nets to dip up the remaining *'iao*[89] fish that cling close to the canoe, after the fishing. With the scoop net the *makiawa* was scooped to be used as bait. The fishing had to be quickly and expertly done in order to catch a hundred *aku* fish in less than an hour's time. The *makiawa* fish was soon devoured by the sharks and other big fish. Like the roaring of the sea in a storm, so it sounded with the fish. The canoe remained amidst the school of *makiawa* fish with the sharks all about with open jaws and the *aku* fish has to be drawn in with skill. The *aku* fishermen enjoyed this kind of

fishing. If there were from five to ten canoes, they were filled with *aku* fish.[90]

It was little wonder that this type of fishing was a favorite pastime of the chiefs.

Although Islanders used a variety of fishing techniques, favored methods varied between locations. According to Lewis, spearing and trapping were preferred from Southeast Asia to western Polynesia. In contrast, open sea techniques were rarely used, except for trolling in Tonga and Samoa. No fishing was done with baited hooks. In Micronesia and eastern Polynesia a wide range of techniques was developed so that these regions' inhabitants could exploit the full range of their marine environments. In his classic study of oceanic fishing Reinman noted that the main features differentiating these regions from the Southwest Pacific was the formers' development of a variety of fish hooks to exploit a range of marine environments, particularly deep sea angling gear. Reinman attributed this to cultural and historical factors as well as environment. He noted that Micronesia and eastern Polynesia are more oceanic than Melanesia and western Polynesia, but did not dismiss the possibility that these differences may have also been due to different cultural origins.[91]

The Sea in Thoughts and Beliefs

Marine creatures were considered much more than a source of food. The categories that modern scientists use to classify the ocean and the life forms that inhabit it bear little resemblance to those used by Islanders. In their world all things were connected; fish might be relatives as well as food, and gods and ancestors could take multiple forms. Instead of being relegated to the world of the supernatural as they tend to be today, these beings figured in the daily lives of Islanders.

Gods could convey their wishes through human mediums, omens, and other signs. A Tahitian chant records how:

> *E tari'a to te mau mea atoa o te*
>   *fenua e te moana;*
> *to te mata'i to te vero, to te fafatutiri,*
>   *to te puahiohio, e to te ureure*
>   *ti'a moana, e fa'aro'o;*
> *e tari'a to te feti'a, to te ava'e,*
>   *to te rā, to te uira, to te tau ma*

> Every thing in the land and in
>   the sea had ears;
> the winds, the storm, the thunder,
>   the whirlwind, and the water-
>   spout, all had ears to hear;
> the stars, the moon, the sun,
>   the lightning, the seasons,

te tiaʻo, to te moana haʻuriuri,   the sea of rank odor, things
to te mau mautai, i faʻaroʻo   innumerable obeyed the
anaʻe ia i te reo o te nuʻu atua.   bidding of the host of gods.[92]

Signs from the gods might consist of natural phenomena such as thunder, or the actions of species associated with a particular god or ancestral spirit. The Tongan god Taufa might manifest himself in his priest Kautae, in a shark, or in a gecko. Such species were *vaka* (vessels) of the god.[93] Only those whose family or clan god was associated with a particular sacred species revered them.[94] This could cause problems. A Rarotongan visiting Tonga with some early missionaries got into trouble when he inadvertently offended fishermen by grabbing a sea snake without realizing that it was their god.[95] Some Islanders were even more specific, revering individual creatures as incarnations of their god, rather than the species as a whole.

There were many marine incarnations of gods and ancestral spirits. The most notable and widespread seem to have been sharks, eels, squids, limpet shells, and cowry shells.[96] These are most thoroughly reviewed by Polynesian scholars Teuira Henry and Samuel Kamakau. Henry records how in Tahiti the *putu* or *ruru* (the common albatross, genus *Diomedea*) was considered the "shadow" of the great sea god Taʻaroa that would aid distressed canoes manned by his worshippers. The *mauroa-hope-uo* (a tropic bird with white tail feathers) and the *mauroa-hopeʻura* (a tropic bird with red tail feathers) were also considered shadows of Taʻaroa. On Raivavae and Maupiti they were worshipped as gods and never harmed or interfered with. Tahitians were not so deferential, using their tail feathers in helmets. Aquatic shadows of Taʻaroa included the *tohura* (whale), the *papahi* (sunfish), and the *pa-taʻaroa* (a small parrot fish), held sacred at Pari in the Taiʻarapu district of Tahiti Nui. Worshippers of Taʻaroa believed that they would die if they ate the shadows of their god.[97]

Ancestral spirits were also associated with creatures of the land, sea, and sky. In Kiribati each ancestral spirit was associated with one or two creatures. If they were associated with just one, it was usually a sea creature, while those with dual associations paired a sea creature with one from the land or sky. Thus, Tabakea was associated with the turtle and the tern, Auriaria with the giant clam and the rat, Riki with the eel, Nei Ati with the bonito, Bue and Rirongo with the porpoise, and Tabuariki with the shark.[98] Hawaiians believed that their *ʻaumakua* (ancestral spirits) could change back and forth between the forms associated with them.

The spirit associated with the *opelu* (mackerel) could transform itself back and forth between this fish and a lobelia plant also known as *opelu,* on account of its leaves resembling the shape of a mackerel.[99]

The fact that more sea creatures are listed as sacred than land creatures in Kiribati may be due to a number of factors. There are many more marine than terrestrial species in coral island environments. This is even the case on larger, high islands. Most domesticated animals are clearly unsuitable as vessels for revered or feared gods and ancestor spirits. The sea is also more dangerous than the land. In the 1860s visiting German naturalist Karl Semper was told by Palauans that

> we call everything kalid [sacred] that lives in the ocean or in fresh water, as well as all animals which we fear. We believe our ancestors live in them. For that reason, each of us has a different kalid. But everything on shore, the birds and lizards, pigs and chickens, we call karam. We especially refer to animals always living among us in the village near our houses by that name. These will never be our kalid.[100]

Some ancestral spirits eventually became gods. The most famous god of Niuatoputapu was Seketoa, originally a chief who lost a battle for the leadership with his brother. He manifested himself as a large fish with the unusual ability to change color, and would appear to assist his worshippers in times of danger at sea. Catholic priests on Niuatoputapu not only recorded these beliefs, but also witnessed interventions by Seketoa in the early twentieth century. Father J. B. Mace was on a boat that was accompanied for a few hours by a large fish, that he estimated to be 5 meters long. The Nuiatoputapuans on the boat called it Seketoa, offered *kava* to it, and continuously addressed it with compliments, wishes, and prayers. When another priest and some local people were in danger of drowning as their raft began to sink, a similar fish appeared and buoyed it up until they reached the shore.[101]

Another god who took the form of a large fish was the Fijian shark god Dakuwaqa. In December 1909 an usually skeptical European captain reported how a 40-foot shark rolled on its back and clasped his 32-foot cutter. His Fijian crew addressed the creature as Dakuwaqa, and promised it *kava* if it did not harm them. Dakuwaqa had a history of fierce retribution against seafarers who did not respect him, but had rescued his worshippers from trouble at sea on a number of occasions. He was particularly associated with the leading lineage of Cakaudrove, a polity centered on the southeastern shores of Vanua Levu and the island of Taveuni.[102] The behavior of Seketoa and Dakuwaqa cannot adequately be explained by modern marine science. It might simply be a manifestation of the tendency for fish to be attracted to flotsam noted by Wood, or a way of rubbing off unwanted attachments and parasites. But scientific investigation is now impossible, as this type of fish behavior is no longer reported. Denied the power that worship gave them, the gods no longer make their presence felt.

Much more immediate and personal links connected marine creatures and humans. Fish might be manifestations of people who had died at sea, particularly those who had drowned. Tahitians associated the *mahimahi* with the spirits of those who had died at sea. Its change in color as it dies was believed to be a sign of the spirit leaving its body. *Hihi* (freshwater periwinkles) were mediums for the spirits of premature infants who died at birth.[103]

Hawaiians believed that they could transform dead relatives into a particular *'aumakua* form through offering the deceased person's bones to the *'aumakua* in the *kākūʻai* ceremony. Families related to sharks performed the *kākūʻai* ceremony and placed the bones of the deceased in the sea. The *'aumakua* shark was then supposed to take the bundle of bones, cover it with a belly fin, and care for it until the transformation was complete. Not all who died at sea shared this fate. Hawaiians believed that souls without a link to marine *'aumakua* could not transform, and were doomed to drift helplessly, formless on the currents.[104]

Many sharks were believed to be manifestations of the spirits of the deceased who protected their human relatives at sea. Shark *'aumakua* were the most popular family guardians among fisher-folk in Hawaiʻi. Individual sharks were recognized as *'aumakua* by markings on their body, which conformed to the marks on the *tapa* (bark-cloth) in which the deceased had been wrapped or to their birthmarks. An intense bond formed between the family and their shark *'aumakua*. The shark was fed daily by them, and was believed to assist them by driving fish into their net and rescuing family members in times of danger, such as when their canoes capsized.[105]

Sharks were particularly associated with chiefly lineages. Besides Dakuwaqa, another such relationship existed between the Tahitian high chief Moe of Mataʻoae in Taiarapu and the shark god Vivi-te-Fua-ehu (Spray-of-light-cavern). The latter lived in a great hole in the offshore reef, with an immense eel god of the same name as its attendant and messenger. This shark god attacked all humans who ventured into the sea in the area, except Moe and his family. The same shark god seemed to be aware of the movements at sea of Moe and his family, and was always at hand to pro-

tect them. When a new ruler was installed as the paramount chief of
Ra'iatea at the coastal *marae* (sacred enclosure) of Opoa, part of the ceremony was said to involve validation from two deified sharks. The paramount chief stood in the water facing the sacred passage through the reef,
awaiting the two sharks, Tuu-mao (Let-go-shark) and Ta-hui (By-the-
clan). If the new ruler was legitimate they swam in through the passage
and rubbed against him gently, before returning to sea. They would not
appear for a usurper.[106]

Shark *'aumakua* and gods could transform themselves into human
form. Dakuwaqa occasionally appeared in human form in the Rewa Delta
of Viti Levu searching for his favored turtle meat.[107] Hawaiians were
wary of shark men, who took human form when on land but would turn
into man-eating sharks in the sea. Their only distinguishing feature was
a shark's mouth on their back, which they usually tried to cover with
mats.[108] However, other sharks were believed not merely to resemble
humans, but to have a human parent. A girl from Ka'u on Hawai'i gave
birth to a shark after dreaming of visits from a lover from the ocean. Her
parents realized that the dream alluded to the shark god Ke-'lii-kaua-o-
Kau. The baby was wrapped in green *pakaiea* (a coarse seaweed) and cast
into the sea. It grew into a green shark that protected locals along the
coast. From that day onward the family worshipped the shark as a family
'aumakua and never ate shark or *pakaiea*.[109]

A number of traditions mention human ancestors who lived in the
sea, or who mated with sea creatures to produce hybrid descendants. A
Palauan legend relating to the ancient era of Chuab speaks of a time when
people were like fish.[110] Even today, Palauans believe that the influence of
the moon and the tides affects not only fish, but also humans. Both fish
and women are believed to give birth on outgoing tides.[111] Legends also
recount that when Palau was being formed from the sea the children of
Latmikaik could live on land and in the sea.[112] Similarly, Malo records
how Wakea, the first chief of Hawai'i, was vanquished and driven out to
sea with his people. Here they swam around until they could regroup and
swim ashore to defeat their enemies. Part of their success was attributed
to offerings they made to their god while they were at sea. Stories of such
aquatic people persisted into the nineteenth century. One variation of the
legend of Wakea claimed that some of his followers were still swimming
out at sea. Malo records other legends from Hawai'i where fishermen
learn of underwater villages on reefs offshore inhabited by aquatic
humans, after fellow fishermen reveal themselves to be from these settlements. When a human attempts to marry a female from one such village,

her parents come looking for her. They cause the sea to rise and inundate the coast, killing many before the waters subside.[113] The Hilo coast where this occurs is notorious for tsunami.

Other stories of aquatic people suggest that they were growing distant from humans. A story recorded in Kosrae by the German ethnographer Sarfert relates how two human beings were caught in a net full of fish. According to Sarfert:

> The heavy net was gradually pulled ashore, and the two men were brought into a house. They were people who were able to live only in symbiosis with fish. During their stay in the house, water constantly poured forth from their ears, eyes, noses, and mouths. They were unable to breathe like human beings breathe; they breathed like fishes do. Their hair consisted of fine coral, but their bodies were like those of human beings. When they were addressed they could not talk.[114]

However, when an old man was summoned to speak to them in the old Kosraean language, he was able to have a brief conversation. The conversation was cut short by their deteriorating condition. The Kosraeans put them back in the sea, and they swam off.

Stories of humans mating with dolphins and porpoises are common throughout Micronesia. Associated clans refrained from killing or eating them, and often had porpoise tattoo designs on their bodies.[115] The following tale from Yap is typical. On certain nights two dolphins used to swim ashore, bury their fins in the sand, and turn into beautiful women. They ran inland and secretly watched the women's dances until just before dawn, when they hurried back to shore, dug up their fins, turned back into dolphins, and swam out to sea. One night a man spotted them and hid one's fins, so that she could not return to the sea. After her companion had swum off the man came out of hiding and led the girl to his house and made her his wife. They lived together until she discovered where he had hidden her fins. She put them on, returned to her original form, and swam out to sea. Some time afterward the man was out fishing with his son when a large fish came up and circled his canoe. He speared it and hauled it aboard whereupon it turned into his former wife. Stricken with grief, he took her ashore and buried her. Some Yapese still traced their descent from this union as late as the early twentieth century. It is significant that the story was said to have taken place in Rumung in northern Yap, whose inhabitants are believed to have come from Sepin, an island that disappeared under the sea some generations before, according to Yapese traditions.[116]

Islanders' perceptions of the sea reflected both their practical knowledge as fishers and sailors, and their beliefs in a world where gods, spirits, humans, and other creatures coexisted. The most complete picture of Islanders' perception of the ocean in the nineteenth century comes from Hawai'i. Descriptions of the zones and moods of the sea recognized by Hawaiians are almost as detailed as their terrestrial equivalents. The zones were named according to their color, motion, wave action, tides, and the type of fishing conducted there.[117] The inter-tidal area where the waves washed over the land was *pahola* or *pahala*. The rising tide was known by such names as *kai-pii* (rising sea), *kai-nui* (big sea), and *kai-piha* (full sea), while the ebbing tide was *kai-hoi* (retiring sea) or *kai-make* (defeated sea). *Kohala* was the general name for waters within the reefs that protected certain parts of the coast. It was divided into such areas as *po'ina kai* (where breakers scoop out sand near the shore) and *kai 'elemihi* (inshore waters where the *'elemihi* crab is found). Coral reefs were divided into fishing grounds such as *papa he'e* (octopus grounds) and *kai 'ohua* (feeding grounds of young fish). Waters farther from the shore were largely distinguished as fishing grounds. Thus, *Kai paepae* were sea areas for pole fishing, and *kai luhe'e,* squid fishing areas. These seas were known generally as *kai uli* (blue seas).

Shallow inshore waters are generally more transparent than deeper seas. Aaron Buzacott recorded that any observer on the surface could clearly discern objects 10 fathoms down in the sheltered waters of lagoons.[118] Hawaiian categories reflect this in their wealth of information on near-shore zones. Indeed, ethnographers across the region found local knowledge of lagoon and reef topography and fauna both accurate and detailed. What is fascinating about the Hawaiian material is its breadth of coverage of deeper waters farther from shore. The writings of Kahaulelio and others reflect a detailed knowledge of fish and sea floor characteristics as deep as 200 fathoms. Kahaulelio knew a hundred fishing grounds that were 10 or more fathoms deep. Each was described in terms of its location relative to the shore, its depth, and seabed conditions.[119] The following description of part of the seabed between the islands of Maui, Lana'i, and Kahoolawe gives some indication of this rich lore:

> The kinds of fishing grounds both deep and shallow are as follows: From Point Hawea at Kaanapali to Lae-hima-lani point, the fishing grounds are very shallow, from twenty to thirty fathoms in depth. It is also true with these that at close to the writers dwelling place in front of Kamaiki point, the depth is the same. In between these places the sea floor is flat with no

cliffs and mountains that are overgrown with trees that grow in the sea. From Launiupoko to Papawai Point the sea outside of them hold most of the fishing grounds and contain some deep depressions good for *kaka* fishing. Allowing six feet to a fathom, they are 1,200 feet deep and that is about the height of a mountain in the ocean all grown over by *okaha* trees. With these mountains in the sea, the lines and hook often get entangled among the trees. They have many branches and leaves and find a sale among sea captains because they think it strange that trees grow in the ocean. The fishing ground called Laepaki (Kealeikahiki) is five miles distant, from fifteen to twenty fathoms deep, that is the shallowest one. Three miles straight out, on the seaward side of Laepaki we used to fish. It is only fifteen fathoms deep. The sea floor and the fish swimming to and fro are plainly visible and that is one of the most productive of the three fishing grounds of Kahoolawe.[120]

The sea surrounding the Hawaiian islands was also divided into regions on the basis of which aquatic *'aumakua* and gods held sway. The waters off Oʻahu were protected from man-eating sharks by order of the shark gods Kanehunamoku and Kamohoaliʻi. Hawaiians claimed that in 1834 a rogue shark was killed by guardian shark *'aumakua* off Waikiki when it came seeking food.[121] A number of fishing grounds were marked out by ʻAiʻai, the son of the fishing god Kūʻula-kai. Various sites mark places of significance on ʻAiʻai's voyages of discovery. Thus, a long thin outcrop of *pahoehoe* lava on the Hana coastline at Lehoʻula is the backbone of the giant *pūhi* (eel) slain by ʻAiʻai for raiding his father's fishponds. The *pūhi* was called Koona, and had made its home in a nearby sea cave called Ka-puka-ulua (the hole of the crevalle). Prior to this it had lived in the sea at Wailau on the windward coast of the neighboring island of Molokaʻi. However, it had moved to Hana after a battle with a large *mano* (shark) at Wailau. A large sea cave, 5 fathoms deep, marked the spot where Koona had killed the *mano* by causing part of a sea cliff to collapse upon it.[122]

Feared creatures such as Koona were as much part of the familiar seas of daily activities as they were features of more distant, less frequently visited seas. The missionary Williams might comment on how Fijians passed over certain parts of the open ocean in silence, with uncovered heads, through fear of the spirits of the deep,[123] but other Islanders believed danger was closer to home. The inhabitants of Fananu avoided a particular passage through the fringing reef known as Lauis because misfortune plagued all who entered it. Lauis was the home of an evil spirit called Sou-Fana.[124] The inhabitants of Kapingamarangi believed that the souls

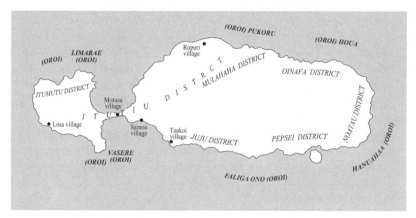

MAP 3 The *Oroi,* or underwater spirit abodes, of Rotuma. (RSPAS Cartography after Russell, "Rotuma," 231)

FIGURE 2 The backbone of the giant eel hooked and killed by 'Ai'ai, son of Ku'ula-kai—a pahoehoe rock formation at Leho'ula Beach, Hana. Maui. (Courtesy of Dennis Kawaharada)

of the dead lived at Tikaunga, in a section of the lagoon only 15 feet deep. Every night a procession of these spirits came across the lagoon as sharks, and then changed form and moved among the dwellings on land, before returning to the lagoon. Their entry and exit from the islets was marked by a swirl of water when there was no fish present to cause it.[125] On the Carolinian atoll of Ifalik religious markers were hung from branches around the shore to deter malicious spirits from coming ashore from the lagoon.[126] On Rotuma a series of underwater spirit abodes were believed to exist offshore. They were known collectively as *Oroi*. These locations were generally conceived as underwater variations of human villages.[127] Similar beliefs were expressed about the homes of fish.[128]

Local spirits also protected their living kin from outsiders. Two reef rocks known as Nengoria and Nunguria would warn the inhabitants of Pulap Atoll of the approach of strangers by moaning.[129] The Tuamotuan sea god Te-a'u-roa moved inshore during the cold weather to Takume Atoll, where he guarded the reef passage from hostile outsiders.[130] Features such as the reef passage of Takume served as cultural markers that demarcated local seas from the seas of outsiders.

Reef passages and other cultural boundary markers were also pathways of opportunity through which local worlds could be enriched and expanded by contacts with other communities. Most scholars now acknowledge that Islanders were not isolated on their small islands in this vast sea. However, the full extent to which the people of the sea went beyond their local worlds is still not widely recognized. In the following chapter we examine Islanders' mobility between 1770 and 1870, and the extent to which the sea served as a highway rather than a barrier.

Communication and
Relative Isolation in
the Sea of Islands

RECENT SCHOLARSHIP on the collapse of Rapanui (Easter Island) society as a result of self-inflicted environmental degradation has inadvertently raised the international profile of Pacific islands as small, bounded, and vulnerable ecosystems.[1] Rapanui is the most isolated inhabited island in Oceania, 2250 kilometers southeast of its nearest inhabited neighbor, Pitcairn Island. By the eighteenth century the people of Rapanui had isolated themselves by cutting down all timber suitable for ocean-going canoes. When Captain Cook's expedition made contact with the inhabitants in March 1774 they had no knowledge of other lands.[2] The deforestation of the island promoted leaching and soil erosion, and reduced the soil's ability to retain water. Faced with environmental degradation and no means of escaping the island, violence and destruction reigned as groups competed for increasingly scarce resources on the denuded island and its immediate near-shore waters. The history of Rapanui is not typical, however. Most of the inhabitants of Remote Oceania were not bound by the sea, but rather embraced it as both habitat and pathway to resources and opportunities beyond their home islands. A web of social, economic, and political ties linked them with other communities and localities.

Mobility and Exchange

A number of studies investigate why Islanders traveled and the extent of their sailing range or geographical knowledge.[3] Most were conducted to throw light on initial colonization, so they focus on long-distance voyaging. Few ask how pervasive travel was. This section seeks to ascertain how many people usually traveled, and how often they traveled. The region is surveyed by locality, and in terms of high island communities versus coral island communities, to determine the degree to which cultural and ecological factors shaped mobility.

Long voyages between archipelagos were still undertaken in several areas after 1770. Regular voyaging occurred between the Societies and Tuamotus in central eastern Polynesia; between Tonga, Samoa, and Fiji in western Polynesia; and between the coral islands of the western Carolines and their high island neighbors in Micronesia.[4] In a study of voyaging distances and linguistic relationships between islands in Micronesia, Jeffrey Marck concluded that a 100-mile sea gap was a crucial boundary. Islands closer than this were found to have mutually intelligible dialects. Sea gaps of this size mark the distance that can be covered by traditional vessels overnight with suitable winds. These voyages were considered safe enough to be conducted by junior navigators, and could be instigated with little preparation. As such, they were far more frequent than longer voy-

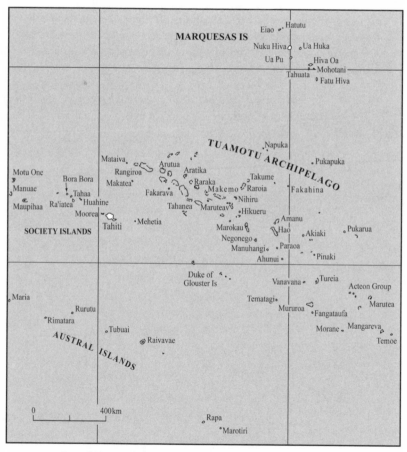

MAP 4 Central Eastern Polynesia. (RSPAS Cartography)

ages that required great planning and the services of the limited number of skilled navigators. The frequency of these shorter voyages led to greater interaction and linguistic intelligibility.[5]

The people of the sea traveled beyond their immediate landscapes and seascapes for a variety of reasons. The desire for certain material goods figured prominently in accounts between 1770 and 1870. Smaller, resource-poor islands had perhaps the greatest need. European visitors to the drought-prone Tuamotus noticed that many of the occupants had to live migratory lifestyles because of food shortages. They depended on *fara* (pandanus) and fish as their staples, and regularly visited neighboring uninhabited islands in search of birds' eggs. Thousands of eggs might be taken in a single visit. One observer noted how

> they live in small hordes, emigrating from one part of the Island to another as food became scarce. The scarcity of food obliging them to live in small parties, and at some distance from each other make them an easy prey to the marauding parties of Ana or chain islanders, who are constantly making descents on the different Islands within their reach.[6]

Most communities could gain access to valuables through exchanges with other communities. Goods were exchanged on a regular basis. Where food was exchanged between coral island communities, it reinforced social ties as well as providing sustenance. The social ties forged by such

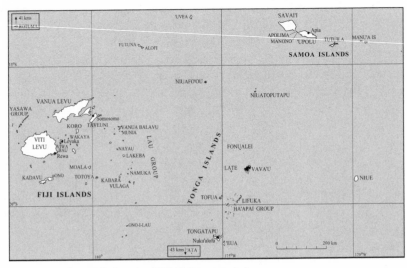

MAP 5 Western Polynesia. (RSPAS Cartography)

relationships could be called upon in times of need, such as drought or the aftermath of storms.[7] Rare items were traded far and wide, particularly decorative manufactures, to which great symbolic meaning was attached. *Faibōbo* were red pieces of spondylus shell incorporating materials gathered from Eauripik to Woleai that were highly prized throughout the central Carolines. Bracelets of tridacna shell collected at Eauripik, Ulithi, and Yap were also traded widely throughout the archipelago.[8] Rotumans sailed to Tonga for white shells to decorate chiefs' houses and canoes. They also sailed to Vythuboo (Vaitapu) for prized white shells.[9] The best source of the canoe wood *kanava (Cordia subcordata)* in the Tokelau atoll chain was Atafu. Although Atafu was the smallest of the chain's three atolls, it could elevate its status by occasionally providing *kanava* to the others.[10]

Differences in natural resources led to regular interactions between high island communities and nearby coral island communities. Tahitian communities had regular access to pearls, pearl shell, turtles, dog fur, and mats from the Tuamotus, in exchange for high island products.[11] Carolinians made an annual voyage to the high island of Yap, during which products were exchanged. The coral islanders gave shells highly prized by the Yapese and manufactures such as sennit twine and woven cloth in return for turmeric, pots, and woods unavailable at home.[12] Mopelia and other uninhabited atolls to the west of the high islands of the Society group were used as reserves for coconuts, birds, fish, and turtles. The offshore islands of Hatutu, Motu Iti, and Fatuhuku fulfilled a similar function for the Marquesas Islands.[13]

Food items were also exchanged between high islands despite their relatively greater resource base. The chiefs of Tahiti procured parakeet feathers and well-built *pahi* (canoes) from Leeward Islands such as Ra'iatea and yams from neighboring Moorea, Tupuai Manu, and Huahine. Regular exchanges were also made with Tahaa and Borabora, with Tahitian *tapa* exchanged for those islands' prized manufacture, bamboos filled with coconut oil.[14] Tumeric and arrowroot were made exclusively by certain districts in Samoa, and exchanged for other local specialities such as nets, paddles, and bowls.[15] In Fiji local scarcity created regional exchanges. Salt could only be obtained from saltpans on mangrove tidal flats and cooking pots from clay pits found only on certain islands.[16] Areas with advantages in natural resources tended to develop craftsmen skilled in manufacturing items from them. Islands such as Kabara, rich in the hardwood *vesi (Intsia bijuga),* were renowned for their wooden *kava* bowls and ocean-going canoes. Low, dry islands produced the best war clubs from the heavy *nokonoko* wood *(Casuarina equisetifolia)* that grew well in their poor soils.[17]

By the late eighteenth century Tongans were increasingly drawn to eastern Fiji for items that were rare in Tonga. *Vesi* wood canoes, parrot feathers, and sandalwood for scenting coconut oil were highly prized by Tongans, and could be traded for bark-cloth, sennit, stings from stingray tails for spear points, whales' teeth, pearl shells, and finely woven Samoan mats. By the nineteenth century they were also offering their services to Fijian chiefs in their wars in return for their hospitality and valuables.[18]

These exchanges were as much about forging and reinforcing social and political relations as they were about supply and demand. The process mattered as much as the goods exchanged. The inhabitants of coral islands probably had the greatest need. Although their agricultural land and offshore fisheries could provide their subsistence needs most of the time, these low-lying islands were highly susceptible to drought and to storm damage. Competition for land between clans on the same island could be intense. These circumstances led to interactions with other islands as competing clans sought allies, additional sources of food, and refuge from natural disasters and their enemies.

Individual atolls in the Marshall Islands might contain as many as fifteen clans. Clans were also dispersed over many islands. Clans were little more than aggregates of lineages loosely bonded by the belief that they had descended from a common ancestor. The lineages that made up these clans expanded and contracted according to the fecundity of their females and their success in war and obtaining sustenance. Some lineages expanded until they splintered into new, independent lineages. By this means some clans extended across almost all the atolls of the archipelago. The Jerikrik clan, for example, was settled throughout the Ratak chain and extended into the Marshalls' other chain, the Ralik, where it went by the name of Ijjirik.[19]

These links and a limited resource base resulted in high mobility. The number of apparently abandoned habitations puzzled Chamisso until he saw Marshallese moving from one island to another "with all their goods and families."[20] Beachcombers from the American whaler *Globe* confirmed Chamisso's suspicions after their lengthy stay on Mili (Mille), noting that "when [the Marshallese] are not fishing, or otherwise employed, they are generally travelling about, and visiting each other."[21] These movements could involve a large part of the population. Reverend L. H. Gulick noted that Ebon was reduced to a population of only five hundred during the winter that he visited on account of all the high chiefs and eight hundred inhabitants sailing north in forty *proa* (canoes). They remained in the northern atolls from September 1857 until March 1860.[22]

The close proximity of islands in the western Carolines promoted inter-island ties. Many clans had members on a number of islands that kin could call on in times of need. Anthropologist William Lessa records that the Mongolfach clan had members on ten atolls from Ulithi to Puluwat, and beyond to the high islands of Chuuk lagoon.[23] Ethnographers Burrows and Spiro note that clans on Ifalik had links with Yap, Woleai, Puluwat, and Pulap.[24] Inter-island exchanges were usually conducted between members of the same kin group.[25] In the 1820s the Russian explorer Lutké noted that the population of Woleai was "greatly mixed due to the migrations of the natives of the surrounding islands."[26]

Clans on each coral island in the Carolines were ranked. Each clan's status varied between islands and was largely related to length of residence. Members of a chiefly clan could only marry individuals from another chiefly clan. This restricted the range of potential spouses. Only three of Lamotrek's eight clans were of chiefly rank. A member of these clans could marry into a chiefly clan from another island, even though that clan might not hold chiefly status on its own island. Inter-island chiefly marriages were popular ways of extending the pool of candidates, as well as increasing clan links.[27]

Travel between coral island communities was often conducted for the pure enjoyment of voyaging and socializing. The beachcomber Floyd told Lutké that trips by inhabitants of his island home of Murilo

> were not always made in the interest of commerce or some other business. They sometimes take them for fun, and then the men take their families with them. The natives of Mourileu [Murilo] and of the other eastern islands do not like to sail with their wives: but their western neighbours often come visiting with their families. In 1829 they were expecting a large gathering at Fananou [Fananu].[28]

Lutké enlarged on Floyd's testimony. He noted the passion for song and dance, and how communities derived great pleasure from new performances:

> In this respect a continual exchange of ideas takes place by means of navigation. If, for example, the young people of one island are seized by the desire to make their musical talent shine in some other island, more or less distant, they do not hesitate to set off, certain in advance of being received with the most sincere demonstration of the satisfaction and pleasure

which this sort of visit never fails to produce. There are cases in which these meetings are arranged for dates very far ahead.[29]

Visits could involve as many as seventy canoes, and seem to have taken place at least once a year. Competition prevailed as each community witnessed the dances of other islands, and sought to imitate and improve on them.[30]

Communities on the high islands of the western Carolines were also characterized by residential mobility and regular interactions. Visiting ethnographers noted the fluidity of village sites in Palau. Krämer recorded 253 village sites in 1910, only eighty-four of which were occupied. Kubary recorded only seventy occupied villages in 1872. This was not solely due to the ravages of Western diseases, as evidence dating from the 1780s also reveals a pattern of more sites than actual villages. Palauan traditions are full of tales of migration by individuals, families, and whole villages.[31] A village contained a number of clans. Each had associations with fellow clan members in other villages. Men's clubs and women's clubs bound men and women of similar ages together in organizations that cut across clan and territorial divisions.[32]

Some Palauan communities were also linked to communities from Yap, 400 kilometers to the northeast. Stone discs made from Palauan aragonite were highly prized by the Yapese, as were certain types of pearl shell and dugong teeth unavailable on Yap. Yapese would travel to Palau for these items, and quarry the aragonite *in situ,* before transporting it home. This required a significant commitment in terms of men and time. When Kubary visited Palau in 1882, he traveled with sixty-two Yapese bound for the quarries. Upon arrival, he found four hundred Yapese already collecting aragonite. Their presence was only possible through the cooperation of local rulers. The Yapese had to act respectfully to their hosts, and perform menial tasks such as gathering firewood and building fish weirs in return for the right to quarry. Marriage links and other exchange relations between villages on Yap and the host communities on Palau, Koror, and Ngkeklau reinforced this arrangement.[33]

More people participated in community exchanges in western Polynesia than in the high islands of the western Carolines. Peaceful interaction between Samoan villages was promoted through institutional arrangements. Inter-village marriages created widespread kin networks. While marriages might disperse individuals from one village to a host of others, the *malaga* was a tour by large numbers of people from a village. They would visit a number of communities and be hospitably received by people who expected the same treatment in return. *Malaga* parties often contained hundreds of people.[34] The missionary Aaron Buzacott also implied that they were a frequent and pervasive feature of Samoan life:

> The Samoans are rightly named navigators as they are frequently visiting their neighbours on the neighbouring islands. When they are about to go on a *"malaga"* (or journey) the chief with nearly the whole of his people get into their canoes & start so that it is not an unfrequent case on going to a Samoan village to find it almost deserted.[35]

Formal exchanges were also conducted between Fijians in the form of *solevu*. These involved the presentation of gifts by one community to another. They might be conducted as tribute or as a reward for services. At other times they involved exchanges between equal parties. These latter *solevu* involved prior arrangement to allow time to gather the goods to be exchanged and to prepare to host the party. Months or even years might pass between the initial approach and the *solevu,* which involved the ceremonial exchange of gifts, accompanied by feasting and dancing. There was an expectation of reciprocity, although it might be years before a community gathered enough goods for another *solevu.*[36]

Tongans were perhaps the most wide-ranging travelers in western Polynesia. In addition to frequent voyages within the archipelago and visits to Fiji, strong links were maintained between Tongan and Samoan communities. Ties were especially strong between Manono, Savai'i, and A'ana in Samoa, and Vava'u in Tonga. A number of Tongan and Samoan chiefly lines had strong ties, involving ongoing marriage links, frequent visits, and occasional large-scale movements between the two island groups to assist in power struggles or to settle. Tongan fleets that sailed to Samoa between 1770 and 1870 generally consisted of three hundred to five hundred people in seven to ten double canoes.[37] Others came to Tonga. Some Tongan chiefly retinues contained *muli,* or foreigners, who were valued for being outside of the Tongan *tabu* restrictions, and therefore able to attend to their chiefs without infringing on their sacred status.[38]

A number of young Tongan chiefs organized expeditions for adventure, fueled by frustration at domination by more senior chiefs at home. Beachcomber William Diapea noted that these expeditions were not only common, but also extensive,

> being not infrequently absent a year or two from home, wandering and gadding from island to island, going all through Samoa, Fiji, and the Friendly Islands, not omitting even the more distant ones of Wallis' Island,

Futuna, Nieuafou [Niuafoʻou], Nieuatobutabu [Niuatoputapu], as well
as the three nearer groups of Tongatabu [Tongatapu], Vavao [Vavaʻu]
and Hapai [Haʻapai].[39]

The English beachcomber William Mariner witnessed the return of the
Tongan chief Kau Moala, after an excursion of fourteen years.[40]

Tongan chiefs like Kau Moala became feared and respected for their
martial prowess at home and abroad. They particularly favored Fiji as a
destination. By the 1790s, contingents of Tongan warriors led by chiefs
such as Finau ʻUlukalala I, Finau Fisi, and Tuihalafatai were a force to be
reckoned with in Fiji. Mariner noted that Tooi Hala Fatai (Tuihalafatai)
made a number of visits to Fiji in the latter eighteenth century, returning
there when he became tired of his relatively idle life in Tonga. On his last
visit of the century he took 250 young men of "some unquiet disposition"
in three large canoes. He remained in Fiji for two and a half years, giving
support to one side or the other in local disputes, plundering and collecting valuables in payment for these services. This lifestyle was considered
"active, noble, and glorious."[41] He returned to Tonga in the 1790s, and
became embroiled in a bitter war that erupted after the murder of the
chief Tukuʻaho.

Farther east, funerals and marriages drew Tahitians from afar, particularly from chiefly ranks that had kin relationships and political alliances.
Other visits or tours were conducted simply for social interaction. These
touring parties could be quite large. Banks refers to one containing over
thirty canoes. The trader John Turnbull mentions that one tour around
Tahiti by an important chief and a large retinue lasted for three months.
Such events often required much advance planning. It might take over a
year to prepare a tour of the Leeward Islands from Tahiti, for example.
Although commoners visited kin, they generally preferred to travel in the
retinues of their chief, as such retinues of highly ranked chiefs received
better treatment than less powerful visitors. Their parties were lavishly
hosted. A generous host enhanced his own prestige, cultivated allies, and
ensured similar treatment when it came time for him to tour. Nevertheless, there must have been limits to hospitality.[42]

Sizable touring parties were also formed by members of the *Arioi* society, a group associated with the worship of the ascendant god ʻOro. The
Arioi were drawn from all ranks of society and from all localities. Large-
scale tours seem to have been their principal activity, during which they
entertained their hosts with dances, songs, plays, and social satire. The

size of *Arioi* touring parties varied. The largest recorded was a fleet of sixty to seventy canoes carrying around seven hundred people between Huahine and Ra'iatea in 1774. There is no evidence of how frequently *Arioi* toured. The fact that the *Arioi* was probably the largest social group in Tahiti suggests that their tours were infrequent. Local communities could not cope with the logistical demands created by the absence of so much manpower and the resources to feed them. The *Arioi* probably merged into their local communities when not on tour.[43]

Much of the population of the other high islands of the eastern Pacific seemed to have led more confined lives. Only the chiefly elite and their retainers traveled as much as Tahitian people. Most of the population of the Marquesas Islands, for example, spent their lives within the valleys of their kin group territory. Only members of the chiefly class and *tuhuna* (religious specialists) maintained social networks transcending tribal boundaries. Rival chiefly families intermarried to cement alliances, while famed *tuhuna* were in demand throughout the islands. Only chiefs could own canoes. This gave them control over fishing as well as sea travel.[44]

A similar pattern occurred in Hawai'i. The vast majority of the population were *maka'ainana,* who spent most of their lives within local territorial units called *ahupua'a.* Most *ahupua'a* extended from the mountains to the sea, but were only a few kilometers wide at the coast. *Ahupua'a* communities were generally self-sufficient, and had few social interactions with their neighbors.[45] They were not totally discrete, however. Drought-affected communities received supplies from elsewhere, or were temporarily evacuated to other *ahupua'a* or even to other districts within the realm of their ruling chief.[46] Cook's visit to Kealakekua Bay seems to have attracted *maka'ainana* from surrounding areas for the duration of the visit.[47] Similarly, in the 1790s Menzies noted that Vancouver's presence at Kealakekua Bay drew *maka'ainana* from "several leagues" north and south.[48]

Ali'i and their retainers were altogether more mobile. The Hawaiian Islands were divided into polities known as *moku. Moku* comprised a number of *ahupua'a,* and occasionally incorporated more than one island. Although the ruling chief and his court favored the fertile heartlands of the *moku,* they did move around to spread the burden of feeding them. These tours also allowed the paramount chief to assess the state of his lands, and to reaffirm his rule over subordinate *ali'i* on whom he depended for local administration.[49]

The importance of high-status marriage partners meant that ties among the upper echelons of the *ali'i* extended between districts and islands.[50] Visits to relatives and the search for marriage partners took *ali'i* out of their own polities. Inter-district and inter-island travel by *ali'i* seems to have been frequent, as the following passage implies:

> Following the custom of the times, Lonokahaupu set out from Kaua'i with a suitable retinue of men and canoes, as became so high a chief, to visit the islands of the group, partly for exercise and practice in navigation, an indispensable part of a chief's education, and partly for the pleasures and amusements that might be anticipated at the courts of the different chieftains where the voyagers might sojourn.[51]

Resettlement by Exiles and Colonists

All these activities involved temporary, if sometimes lengthy, absences from home. A significant minority intended to settle elsewhere. By 1770 most of these migrants only left when forced by natural disaster or human animosity. Most settled in areas already known to them, but an idea persisted that there were still new lands to be found. Unoccupied islands continued to be found at this late stage. For many, the Pacific was still a sea of opportunity.

Tongan chiefs exercised increasing influence over Fijian affairs in the early nineteenth century. More and more Tongans were attracted to Fiji by the lure of adventure and enrichment. A number of colonies were established to use local wood for canoe building. Initially, they had paid Fijian chiefs to get local carpenters to construct canoes. But now, Tongan chiefs sent their own canoe builders to Fiji, and paid local chiefs for materials and provisions. These craftsmen might take seven years to complete a large canoe *in situ*. During this time some married local women and their progeny became the next generation of canoe builders in these specialist settlements.[52] Tongans came to dominate the canoe-building industry of eastern Fiji, as Tongan chiefs supporting these carpenters began to relocate to Fiji. Chiefs such as the Vava'uan brothers Tupoutotai and Lajike, and Ma'afu, became powerful players, exercising great influence over the affairs of Lau, Cakaudrove, and Bau.[53]

There was significant migration back to Tonga from about 1840. In April 1842 over one thousand Tongans left Lakeba to return to Tonga,[54] but large groups of Tongans also took up permanent residence in eastern Fiji. The Tongan colony at Sawana on Vanua Balavu has been extensively analyzed. Sawana was established by force as a strategic colony to enhance Tongan control of the northern Lau group. It was situated at the southern end of Vanua Balavu, a large island on the western side of a large lagoon. Sawana had a climate similar to that of Tonga, but better soils and a more dependable water supply.[55] The colony was culturally conservative, having few interactions with Fijian communities, and retaining most of the features of Tongan social organization.[56] Most of Sawana's Tongans came from small islands in the northern part of the Tongan archipelago. Even in the postwar period they traced their origins to their lineages' particular Tongan homeland; the Tao lineage traced its origins back to the Lulunga cluster of islands, for example.[57] Its population grew slowly as the settlers' offspring were occasionally boosted by the recruitment of spouses, relatives, and craft specialists from home. These connections were weakened as the community became socially self-sufficient. While the male founders either brought their wives with them, or returned to Tonga to seek wives, their sons and daughters generally married within the Sawana community.[58]

A number of those who journeyed to Fiji did so to escape constraints. Others had no choice. Exile was a widespread punishment. Many were set adrift in small canoes for crimes such as murder, adultery, breaching social norms, or causing offense to their ruler.[59] The beachcomber Floyd was threatened with transportation to a deserted island "if he continued to show himself lacking in the respect due to women, by using expressions forbidden in their presence."[60] Occasionally, whole families or communities were expelled. In the late eighteenth century the Butoni people of Bau were banished for trying to avoid the customary offering of part of their fish catch to the ruler of Bau.[61]

Many societies made provisions for incorporating new groups. Even before the rise of the Tongans, Fijian society was characterized by kin group fission and fusion, which meant a great deal of relocation. Indeed, d'Urville claimed that the Fijian and Samoan islands were often awash with refugees. A function of the *veikau* (forest lands) that surrounded the agricultural core of each Fijian polity was to provide land for groups seeking refuge or separation from their former associates.[62] Marshallese tenure also allowed for the incorporation of groups expelled from the lands of other chiefs. These new groups increased the military and agricultural strength of their new ruler.[63]

Coral island dwellers had particular reason to welcome outsiders. With populations rarely exceeding five hundred people, division into clans and lineages meant that smaller units might number as few as thirty, who could be virtually wiped out by a single catastrophe. The removal of just one social unit created imbalance, as all groups were intermeshed by reciprocity. Surviving clan members might marry into other kin groups, or the balance could be restored by repopulating the clan's land through immigration. A flexible system of land tenure was developed to allow new kin and territorial units. When off-island kin could not be attracted, it might well be passed on by other means such as gifting or simply by right of residence.[64]

Only 25 to 30 people survived a typhoon that hit the eastern Micronesian atoll of Mwaekil in the 1770s.[65] The surviving kin groups were rebuilt by bringing in women from other islands. When information was collected on clan affiliations in the 1940s, there were 319 people on the atoll. Only 5 of the 14 clans had resided on Mwaekil prior to the typhoon. The rest had come in from the neighboring atoll of Pingelap, or from atolls in Kiribati and the Marshall Islands.[66] Mwaekil's population was still only 87 in the 1850s.[67] This was above the population of 30 to 50 people that Alkire assessed as necessary to allow a coral island community to weather losses from natural disasters.[68]

Alkire believed Eauripik was the smallest size atoll that could sustain a population. Eauripik's land area is about 20 hectares, while its lagoon area measures only 4.6 by 1.6 kilometers.[69] Eauripik was recorded as having a population of over 100 people when visited by the trader Andrew Cheyne in 1844.[70] Cheyne returned in 1864 to find only 16 Yapese drift voyagers. While 10 of this party sought a ride back to Yap, 6 chose to stay. The Yapese told Cheyne that they found only one man, 10 women, and 4 children on the atoll when they arrived.[71] Traditions record that this was because the island had been abandoned after a devastating typhoon in the 1850s. The atoll could only be recolonized after the vegetation began to regenerate.[72] The first to resettle Eauripik had been the family of Tarmai, from Gilman in Yap, who had married a woman from Woleai, Eauripik's nearest neighbor.[73] By 1907 there were 87 people on Eauripik.[74] The willingness of such a small group to resettle the atoll may have been because it was one of only three sources of spondylus shell in the western Carolines, a shell much sought for Yapese *gau* (shell money).[75]

People continued to seek new lands to colonize. Drought and war prompted many Marquesans to search for new lands. Droughts might last for years, withering breadfruit trees and exhausting stores of *ma* (preserved breadfruit paste). The beachcomber Edward Robarts was in the Marquesas during one such drought, and recorded that hundreds died of starvation in his valley.[76] Such events prompted the departure of canoe loads of refugees. When Cook's expedition first arrived, the Marquesans believed they had come from a land experiencing famine.[77] They had very limited knowledge of other archipelagos in their vicinity, but their traditions told of "islands abounding in bread-fruit, cocoa-nuts, tarra [taro], kava, and such other productions as are to them in higher estimation than any other."[78] Although colonizing expeditions were never heard from again, well-equipped and provisioned Marquesan fleets continued to sail away. Porter was told that eight hundred men, women, and children had departed on such expeditions in only a few years.

Priests sought to allay fears about the unknown. Porter noted that

> three or four days after the departure of the canoes, on these voyages of discovery, the priests come lurking to the houses of the inhabitants of the valley, whence they sailed, and in a squeaking affected voice inform them that they have found a land abounding in bread-fruit, hogs, cocoa-nuts, every thing that can be desired, and invite others to follow them, pointing out the direction to sail, in order to fall in with this desirable spot. New canoes are constructed, and new adventurers commit themselves to the ocean never to return.[79]

In a similar manner, parties of Rotumans and Futunans would set out to look for new land when the population looked like it was outstripping the island's ability to feed them. Priests would consult the oracles, and it was largely at their behest that these expeditions were launched.[80]

More than desperation and blind faith drove colonization expeditions. Islands continued to be fished from the ocean. Steep, volcanic 'Ata was one such island. 'Ata is only 90 miles south of Tongatapu, yet Tongan traditions suggest it was only settled in the eighteenth century. The Dutch explorer Abel Tasman saw no signs of human settlement in 1643. Tongan traditions attribute the first settlement to Motuapuaka, a chief who stumbled upon the island while fishing for bonito. He chose to settle on 'Ata to escape the wrath of Tui Tonga Fakanaanaa after he eloped with his daughter Tapuosi. A second group of settlers arrived after their canoes were blown off course on a trip between Tongatapu and Tungua in the Ha'apai group. A third group settled on the island in the early 1800s, fleeing from their enemies.[81] Other islands on the fringes of the collective memory were rediscovered. Hundreds of Carolinians were able to draw upon ancient navigational chants to sail to the Marianas when the opportunity arose to trade and settle there in the 1800s. It was the renewal of an ancient link that had been severed for over a hundred years after the Spanish subjugation of the Chamorro people.[82]

The Sea as a Highway

The seas of Oceania were bridges as well as barriers. The sheer volume of movement attests to Islanders' willingness and ability to travel. They traveled mainly by sea, even to destinations on the same island. Some islands had fairly well-established pathways, but most did not, and they were generally poorly developed. Travel was easiest where reefs and currents caused the buildup of long beaches. Frequently used paths along flat littoral zones were usually well maintained and compacted, although prone to becoming quagmires after heavy rains. The most developed were in Tonga and Hawai'i. A map of Tongatapu from the 1790s shows its flat terrain crossed by roads 6 to 12 feet wide. The most impressive was a road that ran from the east end of the island through the center to the western tip.[83] The northern Tongan groups of Ha'apai and Vava'u were crisscrossed by sunken roads of varying widths and depths.[84] Maui was completely ringed by a well-formed trail known as the *Alaloa* (great road), dating from the reign of Kihapi'ilani in the sixteenth century.[85]

Paths through the interior were particularly difficult and usually poorly maintained. Most became almost impossible to traverse during the rainy season because they followed the beds of streams in the upper valleys and crossed into neighboring valleys by way of steep slopes at the head of the valleys. The density of vegetation away from regular cultivation meant that rapid movement was only possible on trails maintained through the woods.[86]

Coastal trails were also difficult to negotiate at times. In 1861 the missionary Martin Dyson noted that the paths around Samoa's coast

> are neither macadamised nor surveyed. Here & there a little order is observed but in general they are narrow, irregular paths overgrown with brushwood & overshadowed with tall trees, swimming through mud & water as the case may be. Poles lying loosely across a river sometimes form an apology for a bridge, but the beach in many places proves as useful & more pleasant to pedestrians than our metropolitan commercial Road.[87]

On some windward coasts sea wind and wave sculpted cliffs. Here, coastal paths might be reduced to narrow ledges that cut across the cliff face above the pounding surf.[88]

Windward coasts were also difficult to negotiate by canoe. Tahitians preferred to haul their canoes across the 2-mile-wide Taravao isthmus to avoid the passage around the southern tip of the Taravao peninsula where southern swells crashed directly against steep cliffs and rocky shores. The canoes were hauled across the low-lying, muddy isthmus with ropes and rollers.[89] Other isthmus portages simply saved time rather than avoiding danger. The Tamaki isthmus allowed Māori to move their canoes between the upper North Island's east and west coasts in a few hours. The alternative was a voyage of many days around the northern tip of Muriwhenua.[90] Another well-known portage was Na are Bale on the Fijian island of Kadavu. Na are Bale was relatively narrow and low-lying, in the middle of this long, narrow island, and overcame the need to sail around either end.[91]

Islanders were willing to go to all this effort because canoes were the most efficient transporters of bulk cargoes. Islanders' lack of the wheel and beasts of burden meant that any heavy load moved over land had to be transported by human muscle. Heavy weights might be carried in slings suspended from shoulder poles or on sleds dragged by teams of men. While the size of these teams is unknown, estimations by American scholar Edwin Ferdon suggest that Tongan sleds might have been capable of carrying loads in excess of 2 tons. Such propulsion was slow and cumbersome.[92] One or two canoes could carry out the same task far more efficiently. When a five thousand-man Tongan army from Haʻapai ran short of supplies while attacking Vavaʻu, sending just two double canoes back to Haʻapai for provisions quickly rectified the problem.[93]

Many coastal communities could transport most of their population by canoe. European explorers were often confronted by a host of canoes. The following account of Otto von Kotzebue's reception at Manono is typical. Arriving off Manono in 1824, he noted:

> Some idea may be formed of the dense population of the Flat Island from the fact that, small as it is in extent, above sixty canoes, each containing seven or eight men, came to us from it in less than an hour, and had we stayed longer, the canoes must have amounted to some hundreds, as the whole sea between us and the island was rapidly covering with increasing numbers.[94]

The Manono people seem to have preferred to travel farther in a few larger double canoes, but not all followed this practice. In 1847 a delegation of two hundred from Savaiʻi made the open sea passage to Manono in a fleet of forty-eight canoes.[95]

The most thorough surveys of canoe numbers relative to population took place in the postwar period and only dealt with atoll communities that relied on seafaring. Alkire's survey in 1962–63 on Lamotrek, Elato, and Satawal is probably the most detailed. He found that Lamotrek, with a population of 201, had 13 sailing canoes and 23 paddling canoes. At any time, 9 sailing canoes and 19 or more paddling canoes were seaworthy. Its smaller neighbor Elato had only 2 sailing canoes for its 49 people, and one was not seaworthy (he did not count their paddling canoes). Fourteen sailing and 30 paddling canoes served the needs of Satawal's 326 people. Several sailing canoes were also under construction.[96] A decade earlier a study of Ifalik had shown that its 245 inhabitants could call on 23 sailing canoes and 68 paddling canoes.[97]

Coastal travel within the reef sheltered canoes from the full force of bad weather. Lagoons are not always benign environments, however; other hazards needed to be guarded against. Most travelers preferred to travel within the reef during high tide to avoid becoming grounded on reefs or sandbanks.[98] While the barrier reef protects the lagoon from ocean swells, winds over the confined waters can generate sharp and choppy waves. These can be more difficult to deal with than the larger but more gradual, even swells generated on the open ocean.[99] Canoes can also be overturned by sudden squalls in the lagoon. In September 1783, canoes carrying English sailors were hit by a sudden squall in Palau's lagoon. One was overturned when it could not get its sail down in time. The others were driven some distance away, and reached the shore with difficulty.[100]

Man-made hazards also caused problems. Stone and reed fish weirs were particularly troublesome in Yap and Fiji. Kubary noted that fish weirs were built so solidly and so frequently in Yap that it was all but impossible for a stranger to travel by canoe in coastal waters without running into one, even at high tide.[101] Fish fences littered the sandy and muddy inlets of Fiji. They were 100 to 200 yards long, and built of reed work supported by stout stakes driven deep into the mud. While capable of snaring a canoe, they were not robust enough to survive storm waves. These waves would breach the fences, rendering them useless. New fences were generally built in different locations so that they soon covered the near-shore seascape.[102]

Negotiating reef passages out to sea could also be a problem. These narrow passages funneled water in quite strong currents at times. A Russian naval vessel lying off a reef passage in the Marshalls noted a current a full 50 fathoms from the reef opening. The current doubled in intensity through the narrowest part of the passage.[103] Putting out to sea through narrow openings was especially difficult in high seas, when winds created heavy surf at the seaward edge of the reef.[104]

The Pacific is not particularly treacherous to travel on. Commentators compare it favorably with the Atlantic.[105] Experience and skill are still needed to read its signs and anticipate its moods. The sea has always been a harsh mistress to mariners, and the Pacific has its share of surprises and variations, but overall its wind and current patterns are reliable. Sporadic and seasonal wind shifts allow annual voyaging in most directions for those incapable of sailing into the wind. The sun and stars are seldom obscured for more than three days, so that those skilled in celestial navigation can maintain their bearings. Clouds tend to disperse at night over the open ocean, and periods of cloud cover tend to be highly seasonal and therefore predictable.

Islanders usually waited for favorable winds rather than sail in dangerous conditions. Western Polynesians rarely ventured beyond the reef to fish or travel during times of westerly winds. These winds were only used to travel from Fiji to Tonga, and even then, the weather was carefully observed for weeks beforehand. The English scientist William Harvey encountered a Tongan fleet at Lakeba in 1855 waiting for such a wind, and was told that they would never embark on a long voyage without a leading wind.[106] Sarfert was told that the Puluwatese also lessened the dangers by sailing when winds, weather, and stellar conditions were most favorable. They broke up long voyages by sailing via intermediary islands rather than taking shorter routes over stretches of ocean devoid of havens. They also ensured they had several alternate routes in case of trouble along the way.[107]

Perhaps the greatest danger to seafarers was being caught in a storm. Records garnered since 1770 suggest that Islanders were remarkably skilled at avoiding these dangers. While studying the traditional navigational ability of Puluwatese in the 1960s, Thomas Gladwin noted that 73 voyages ranging from 15 to 150 miles in length were conducted in 16 months without mishap. The last fatality at sea had occurred in 1945, when a canoe was lost during a typhoon. If this voyaging frequency is typical, then Puluwatese would have conducted 1150 trips between 1945 and 1968 with only one fatality. This figure may have been higher in pre-European times when Puluwat's population was larger and more dependent on canoes. The record for the period prior to the twentieth century is less complete, but suggests a similar pattern. Hommon's analysis of traditions collected by Kamakau and Hawaiian resident Abraham Fornander reveals that only 2 of the 108 inter-island voyages recorded in the Hawaiian archipelago prior to 1795 encountered storms at sea. In both cases the fleets made land safely. Elsewhere, the people of Tubuai remembered only four people lost at sea while fishing.[108]

Accounts of fleets hit by storms suggest that most vessels could survive. There are only five accounts of fleets being overwhelmed by storms between 1770 and 1870. Recently restored Carolinian trade contacts with the Spanish outpost of Guam were curtailed in 1789 when a returning fleet was lost at sea. The relatives of the mariners assumed the Spanish were responsible and suspended voyages to Guam.[109] After links were restored in 1805 an even greater disaster struck. In 1816 a Carolinian fleet of 120 canoes, carrying around nine hundred settlers to Saipan, was hit by a storm at sea and most of the fleet was lost.[110] In 1830 a Marshallese fleet of a hundred canoes was overwhelmed and only one canoe escaped. In 1860 the Marshallese lost two more fleets.[111]

Those that did survive often had to endure long periods before making land. Lewis notes that many drift voyages were carried out in paddling canoes designed only for near-shore use. While these vessels had less ability to withstand the rigors of open sea voyages, a number of their occupants survived to become castaways.[112] These fishing expeditions, and voyages hastily mounted by those fleeing enemies, were also less well provisioned than planned voyages. Although canoes did occasionally break up,[113] the main concern of voyagers caught in storms seems to have been being blown off-course and losing their bearings, rather than sinking.[114] The record is full of drift voyages where Islanders survived for months before making landfall or being rescued.[115] The longest recorded drift voyage lasted nine months. It occurred during the Pacific War, when seven men escaped Japanese rule on Banaba (Ocean Island) in three canoes. Only one survived to make landfall at Ninigo in November 1944, by catching sharks and collecting rainwater in the canoe's sails.[116]

It is difficult to say how many failed to survive these ordeals. Some drowned during the storms that caused their troubles. Others died of hunger or thirst before land was reached.[117] Even those lucky enough to make land still faced difficulties. Infertile islands lacking timber to repair or rebuild canoes were as much prisons as havens. Their infertility might mean that others never visited. Edward Lucatt describes such a plight befalling a family blown out to sea during a gale. They ended up on the unoccupied and infertile islet of Hereheretue in the Tuamotus, and remained there for many years until discovered by another group of voyagers.[118] Some storm-tossed drifters reached inhabited islands and were considered valuable enough to marry into the community. This was the fate of the warrior Sualo of Samoa when he drifted ashore at Tongoa in Vanuatu around 1825.[119] But castaways were often less warmly received. If they were not immediately dispatched, they might remain marginalized on the fringes of their new society.[120]

Islanders exhibited deep ambivalence toward sailing beyond the reef. Their chants and actions reveal a sense of excitement at the prospect of voyaging, but also acute awareness of the dangers. A song from Tikopia clearly expresses ambivalence toward voyaging and divergent attitudes within the community. The song outlines the feelings of a man torn between accepting an invitation to join a voyage and concern for the family he will leave behind, particularly his father. Despite his desire to travel, he stifles his wanderlust.

Ko pa e tangi mai i te tai	My father mourns me on the beach
Ka u ifo ake	I will go down to him alone!
Ka māvae mo te faoa	I'll leave the crowd all by myself
Ko pa koru oro ki te fenua	Father, will you go up inland?

Ko pa e tangi i te tai	My father weeps for me on the beach
Ka u ifo ake	I will go down to him myself
Ku au kuou	Here I am! I have left my brothers
Ku māvae moku taina	Now father! Won't you go back inland?
Ko pa koru oro ki te fenua	

E au tangata muna mai	A man comes up and calls me
Taua ka oro	Let the two of us now go off!
Tau forou e ranga tuā moi	But this voyage makes me anxious

Toku roto kua te e!	So my mind is made up (to stay at home)
Toku roto momori ka riro	And my thoughts of abroad shall be hidden[121]

Another Tikopian song expresses the more adventurous attitude probably held by many young men when it exclaims, "If we stay on land we shall die; if we go to sea we shall die; let us go then."[122] There was some justification in this outlook. Despite the dangers and anxieties, the benefits of sea travel clearly outweighed the costs. Most island societies were geared to sea travel, and institutions associated with maritime activities held pride of place. It is to these institutions, and their activities, that we now turn our attention.

Seafaring in Oceania

THE SEA is unforgiving to the ill prepared. Voyaging required a major commitment of time and resources. Communities needed to build vessels to withstand the rigors of sea travel, and to train navigators and sailors to guide these vessels to their destinations. These skills had to be disseminated widely enough to ensure that they did not die out when disasters struck. Seafarers needed to be able to live with the stresses of voyaging, while the rest of the community had to cope with their absence. The community also needed to equip and feed voyagers.[1] Modern scholars pay great attention to canoe technology and navigational techniques but have generally neglected all other aspects of seafaring. This chapter examines the navigational techniques and ocean-going canoes used between 1770 and 1870 as well as the infrastructure behind seafaring.

After studying Puluwat in the 1960s, Thomas Gladwin concluded that the entire culture was geared toward assuring successful voyages. There were always enough vessels to sail in and crews to man them. Canoes could be provisioned with little notice, and navigators sailed with enough knowledge to adjust course should conditions demand.[2] This chapter examines variation in seafaring infrastructure between 1770 and 1870. The western Carolinian cultures that formed the basis for modern studies of Islander seafaring were by no means typical of the level and spread of skills. Other seafaring cultures had fewer seafarers to call upon, so they were much more susceptible to the erosion of that base. If just one of the elements diminished, the seafaring ability of a culture could decline dramatically. Sea conditions also varied. Seafaring varied across both time and space between 1770 and 1870.

Navigating the Sea

Most voyages between 1770 and 1870 were conducted across seas that communities had been familiar with for generations. Seafarers called on an existing body of knowledge to navigate between known locations. This information was contained in chants and songs that drew together celestial, climatic, and oceanic direction markers. Islanders literally sang their way across the sea. Few stretches of ocean were featureless to those trained in the song-lines.[3]

Songs were designed to keep the crew alert, confident, and aware of dangers and markers. They consisted of a few key words relating to navigational information contained in phrases whose meaning was not always transparent. The phrases often contained archaic words, or were incomplete and disjointed. Marshallese sailing songs in the 1940s intoned each syllable for minutes on end. The way the syllables were intoned was believed to impart protective magic upon the crew.[4] The recital was often accompanied by the continual beating of drums. Leonard Mason recorded the following song in 1947 during a voyage between Likiep and Wotje:

Where are we?
Windward of Wotho.
Fill the water breakers.
The canoe is [now] exposed.[5]
We are way beyond, [way into] the rough windward sea,
    we are afraid.
What sign[6] did you see?
We saw the *kalo*.[7]
Where [did] he land?[8]
[We saw] white places [surf] to the windward of Emejwa
    and Matirik.
[We] anchored and drifted out.
[We see] the signs of the *kone* trees.[9]
Stand up, look, [see] where we are.
Tokeen and Anelen and Malien[10]
Likiep causes death[11]
Aekne and Lolem and Lotto.[12]
To the leeward from Boked and Mole.

Chorus: Emo-o-le-e-e.[13]

Where are we?
We drifted out, way away from the island.
What are we going to do?
I take the *karon* distance.[14]
[I take the distance] beyond the horizon.[15]
Beyond the horizon.[16]
Intensely we search for Mille's wave patterns.

We are racing toward Mille atoll.
Here are the Mille signs.

Chorus.

I will listen—
To that long noise [?] which rolls slowly landward; however,
I take the waves between Lepokna and—
The *le*[17] appears; what happens when he lands?[18]
The calm suddenly strikes the fleet.
We drift outward and back to the north; we saw the *soot*[19]
    on the *konant* tree.[20]
At the Kemla peninsula.
Calm, so calm.[21]
Pillow, the pillow.[22]
I follow the long, long pattern of the calm sea.[23]
The big pillow, bigger than—
The *aol*[24] which goes down and back to the open sea.

Chorus.

Navigators had three main tasks. First, they needed to know the direction of their destination. They then had to maintain that direction and plot their progress. Finally, they needed to ensure that they could make contact, particularly if seeking a small island.[25] Initial bearings might be taken by lining up canoes with landmarks such as mountains, trees, or capes. Kiribati and Cook Island seafarers also laid out stone pointers near their departure points to indicate the direction of their more common destinations.[26]

The sea contained many signposts for trained observers.[27] The song quoted above makes particular reference to sea birds and to wave and current patterns. Currents cause steep waves that rise up sharply, even in the absence of wind.[28] As well as the reefs and shoals mentioned in chapter 1, the open sea has other features such as intersecting currents, convergence zones marked by surface flotsam, concentrations of seaweed, fishing areas favored by birds, and variation in surface temperature and salinity.[29] Patches of smooth water (usually associated with leeward offshore zones) also occurred in the open sea.[30]

Some open ocean navigational markers also serve as food sources. Aggregations of tuna in the open sea are often found around localities where oceanic fronts meet.[31] These are zones between different currents and water masses. Here seasonal or periodic convergence or divergence at the surface occurs as a result of wind stress, eddy motions from cyclonic weather fronts, or the meeting of wind-driven surface currents with ocean currents. The resulting upwelling concentrates nutrients, creating a rich fishery.[32]

These boundary zones are often recognizable by lines of flotsam that straddle their surface. Logs, mats of vegetation, and other flotsam frequently attract large numbers of oceanic fish. This is especially true of large logs that have been in the water for a long time.[33] One of the best descriptions of such a front is found in the memoirs of C. F. Wood, where he describes the crossing of the equator by his vessel on its way north from New Guinea to Pohnpei in September 1872.

> On the 19th and 20th we passed through immense quantities of driftwood. Huge trees and logs of wood were seen floating on all sides, looking as if they might have floated off some suddenly submerged island. Whilst we were among this driftwood, we saw immense flocks of terns and boatswain birds. The water was alive with fish of all sizes. Large albacore splashed and jumped on all sides, evidently in pursuit of the smaller fish that hung round the large floating trees.
>
> They were no doubt, in their turn, preying on the smaller creatures that lived on the timber. Above them all fluttered vast flocks of terns, incessantly darting down in pursuit of small fry. It struck me that in this marine settlement the albacore had certainly the best of it.[34]

Subtle differences in the salinity and temperature of seawater are also apparent. On a passage from the Marshall Islands to Guam in 1817, a Russian naval expedition commanded by Otto von Kotzebue distinguished different seas within their ocean passage. It was noted that

> the sea to the west of Radak and in the stretch where the Carolines were sought (between the 9th and 10th, and in the last three days up to the 11th degree north latitude) had a paler blue color, had a greater salt content, and deep under the surface had a noticeably lower temperature than elsewhere at the same latitude in the Great Ocean.[35]

The Russians concluded that these differences indicated that the sea was less deep there. As soon as they steered farther north for Guam, the sea again took on its usual dark blue color, and its salt content and subsurface temperature returned to normal. Modern scientific measurements confirm these differences, and show that there are seasonal variations in surface sea temperatures. These occur because of seasonal variations in solar intensity and wind strength and direction. The former heats the surface water, while the latter mixes it.[36]

The direction of seasonal winds and swells, and the position of the sun, could be used to check direction. From April to October, for example, the main wind south of the equator was the southeast trade wind, while winds were more variable between November and March. Distinct, local topographical and storm winds also occurred. The direction and strength of the wind was measured by observing the sail and the feel of the wind on the navigator's face. Predominant swells underlay waves generated by short-term local winds. Navigators could identify distinct swell and wave patterns. Canoes pitch if the swell is coming from the front or rear, and roll if the swell is hitting from the side. If the canoe sails at an angle to the swell the vessel will both pitch and roll. The canoe's direction was maintained by ensuring that the pitch or roll remained constant.[37]

While winds and swells are detectable at night, star alignments were the main nocturnal navigational device. Stars trace an east to west arc across the sky. Those rising in the navigator's latitude keep a constant bearing. Stars positioned over the poles remain visible to anyone in the same hemisphere throughout the night, cloud cover permitting. Most other stars appear to rise from the horizon during the night. They can be used as direction markers when close to the horizon. As they rise, the navigator can switch to other stars closer to the horizon. Star paths to destinations consist of a series of rising or setting stars. These stars were lined up against certain parts of the canoe. They need not have the same bearing. The difference in bearing was simply noted by the navigator, and lined up against a different part of the canoe. Navigators always had backup courses in case their preferred star path was obscured by clouds.[38]

A Spanish description of a Carolinian navigational school on Saipan in the 1860s is one of the few extant detailed accounts of celestial navigation from this period. The school was presided over by the navigator Arrumiat. According to Don Eugenio Sánchez y Zayas, Arrumiat

was the most celebrated of the Carolinian pilots, and was really deserving of his reputation. He knew the stars, and could describe their groups. He knew that the pole star was always in the same place, while the others were continually moving round the sky; that the belt of Orion always rose and set in the same part of the horizon, that the planets were wandering stars, different from the rest, which remained the same in their relative positions. By the rising and setting of Orion he knew the East and West points of the horizon, and the North by the pole star; in fact, he had a knowledge of astronomy that was extraordinary for a mere Indian. He knew the positions of all the Caroline Islands and parts of the Marianas, from Guam to Saypan [Saipan]; and would place them on the table by beans, representing them in their true relative positions excepting in actual relative distance.[39]

Figure 3 reproduces the star compass used at this school. It is divided into eastern and western sections. Ueleuel is the pole star, and Mailab the belt of Orion.[40]

Navigators sailed by dead reckoning, which meant that the canoe's location was determined solely by keeping track of the distance and direction traveled since leaving the last known location. Points of reference along the route, the estimated speed of the canoe, and the time since departure were used to estimate how much of the journey remained. The

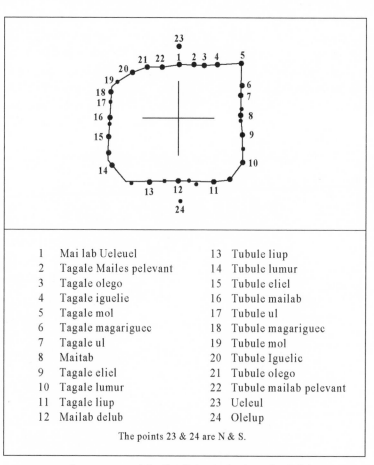

1	Mai lab Ueleuel	13	Tubule liup
2	Tagale Mailes pelevant	14	Tubule lumur
3	Tagale olego	15	Tubule eliel
4	Tagale iguelie	16	Tubule mailab
5	Tagale mol	17	Tubule ul
6	Tagale magariguec	18	Tubule magariguec
7	Tagale ul	19	Tubule mol
8	Maitab	20	Tubule Iguelic
9	Tagale eliel	21	Tubule olego
10	Tagale lumur	22	Tubule mailab pelevant
11	Tagale liup	23	Ueleul
12	Mailab delub	24	Olelup

The points 23 & 24 are N & S.

FIGURE 3 Star compass of the Carolinian navigation school, Saipan, 1866. (RSPAS Cartography after Sánchez y Zayas, 264)

speed of the canoe was judged in relation to the force of wind and currents, while the time lapsed was estimated against the passage of celestial bodies. Sailing chants also served as time markers.[41]

In the Carolines, voyages were divided into unequal sections known as *etak,* which served as section markers on the voyage. *Etak* were determined by the progress of certain stars over a third reference point to the left or right of the voyaging path.[42] The voyage from Woleai to Fais was divided into three stages that were further divided into *gatag (etak).* The canoe sailed northwest for the first four *gatag,* which were measured against the star Ugelik (Polaris?) to the north. The second course consisted of one *gatag* as the navigator sailed west, aligning the canoe to the constellation Magoroger (Pleiades). The final course consisted of two *gatag* measured against the star Mal (Sirius).[43] The *etak* concept was also used to realign a canoe with its destination by providing numerous reference stars from various angles. It was particularly useful when canoes deviated from the usual route because of storms, or had to tack into the wind.

While atolls and other low islands are only visible from 10 miles in good conditions, high islands can be seen 75 miles away.[44] Signs of land occur long before the islands are sighted. Most islands are marked by dis-

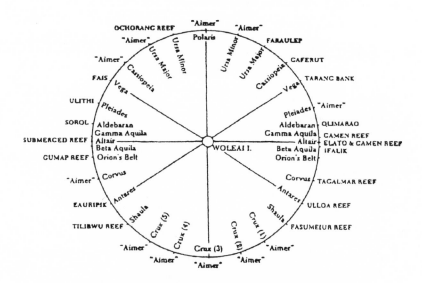

FIGURE 4 Contemporary star compass of Woleai, aligning stars with islands and seamarks. (Goodenough and Thomas, "Traditional Navigation," 5)

tinct formations of high clouds, which are particularly noticeable over high islands. They appear to be stationary from a distance, in contrast to lower clouds that drift over the ocean. Thermal radiation of the land causes a daily buildup of clouds after midday as moist air is lifted by convection. These clouds then disperse at night.

Other signs of land are apparent in the sky and ocean. Clouds often reflect the nature of the earth's surface. Wooded islands reflect as a dark, greenish tinge on clouds, while the brightness of sunlit lagoons or white beach sand can turn clouds a shimmering white or light green.[45] Indicators of land radiate outward as well as upward. Land-based sea birds such as boobies, terns, noddies, and frigate birds fly out to fishing grounds up to 50 miles offshore each day.[46] A form of bioluminescence emanating just offshore causes flashes of light a fathom below the surface that dart up to 100 miles into the ocean. These flashes are most clearly seen 80 to 100 miles from land.[47]

Islands also alter wave and swell patterns. Waves hitting an island's windward shore are reflected back, or refracted around it. All have distinctive patterns. Unique patterns of intersecting refracted and reflected

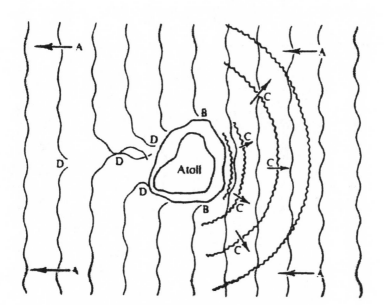

FIGURE 5 Effect of an island on ocean swells. A. Direction of swell.
B. Refracted swell. C. Reflected swell. D. Shadow of turbulence.
(Lewis, *Navigators,* 181, after Davenport, "Cartography")

waves occur in archipelagos. Swell patterns were particularly relied on as navigational aids in the Marshalls. Here, two parallel atoll chains oriented northwest to southeast block the predominant easterly swells. The Marshallese constructed *meddo* charts to represent swell patterns and *rebbelib* charts to represent these local patterns in larger areas.[48]

Islands are best approached from the leeward direction where the wind blows odors and flotsam into the path of approaching vessels.[49] Navigators initially aimed for the screen of signs around their island target. Once this was achieved, they could sail to their specific destination. Even the smallest target, an isolated coral island, creates a circle of signs at least 20 miles in diameter. Large high island archipelagos present overlapping signposts that extend for hundreds of miles.[50]

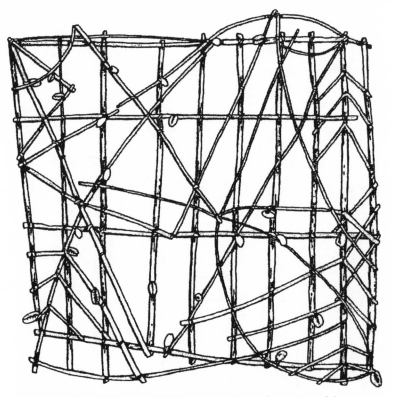

FIGURE 6 Marshall Islands *rebbelib* navigation chart of a portion of the archipelago. Islands are indicated by cowrie shells, while the lines represent swell patterns. (Oliver, *Oceania,* vol. 1, 410, after Haddon and Hornell, 1936–38).

Sailing in Oceania

European explorers were generally impressed with oceanic canoes and the skill with which they were handled. Polynesian and Micronesian sailing canoes differed markedly. Single-hulled outrigger canoes were favored in Micronesia. Known as *proa*, they counteracted the sideways pressure of the wind on the sail by using deep, asymmetric V-shaped hulls. The narrowness of the hull reduced its drag, while the windward side of the hull bowed out to allow the vessel to keep closer to the wind. They were powered by a triangular lateen sail and directed by a steering oar. They could be sailed with either end leading, simply by swinging the sail around from one end to the other—a process known as shunting. The outrigger was always positioned on the windward side of the canoe as the pressure of the wind against the sail tilted the canoe leeward, raising the outrigger to minimize drag. Leeward and central platforms provided space for passengers and cargo without unduly adding to the load. The passengers were generally positioned on the leeward platform to balance the outrigger and to keep it riding high in the water. The speed and maneuverability of *proa* was unequalled in Oceania. They were particularly well designed for sailing into the wind.[51]

Most eastern Polynesian sailing canoes had two equally sized hulls, with symmetrical cross sections. Those with round-bottomed hulls could be paddled in the absence of wind, while their shallow draft suited coastal voyages.[52] The double-hulled canoes of eastern Polynesia were distinguished from those of western Polynesia by their use of both paddles and sails, and their high sterns. The latter assisted in heavy seas and landings through surf.[53] Cook and his officers commented on the ability of Tahitians and Hawaiians to paddle large double canoes in complex maneuvers. Some Tahitian double canoes carried over a hundred paddlers, as well as up to six steersmen and a number of specialist bailers.[54]

Polynesian double-hulled canoes such as the *pahi* of Tahiti were much larger than Micronesian *proa*, and could carry many more passengers on the decks connecting their hulls. Unlike *proa*, Polynesian canoes had bows and sterns, and carried a fixed sail on a vertical mast, so that they had to be steered by arduous tacking.[55] The *drua* of Fiji combined aspects of the outrigger sailing canoes of Micronesia and the larger, double-hulled canoes of Polynesia. *Drua* were double-hulled canoes whose windward hull was shorter than the leeward. They resembled *proa* in their use of lateen sails and hulls that could sail in either direction.[56]

Little has been written on the experience of voyaging before the

1960s.[57] Sailing conditions varied between craft. Voyages on *proa* could be both exhilarating and exhausting. A Chamorro described to Arago how *proa* flew across the waves like birds, and were "the wind itself."[58] While crew members often had little to do for much of the voyage,[59] endurance was required. This was particularly true for *pelu* (navigators), who had to remain alert throughout the voyage to keep track of the canoe's progress. *Pelu* commanded through respect. On Carolinian *proa* they were as much managers of men as navigators.[60] Steering *proa* also required constant attention. Sánchez y Zayas noted "all day and all night during the entire voyage the person steering must hold it [the sheet] regardless of how long the boat is out sailing."[61] The steersman had assistants for long voyages because the *proa* would capsize if the sheet was released. The rest of the crew saw to other duties such as bailing. The distribution of their body weight was crucial for stability, particularly during times of increased wind stress and tacking. At these times, the crew had to move rapidly and precisely into position.[62] Conditions were cramped. Lutké noted that no one slept on *proa* during short trips, and that even on longer voyages, there was only room for one or two people to sleep in the shelter on the platform.[63]

Recalling his experiences on a *proa* in the 1960s, Gladwin noted that

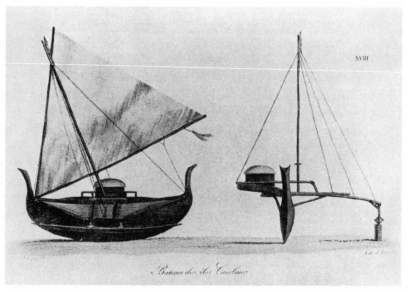

FIGURE 7 *Proa* from the Caroline Islands with asymmetrically cross-sectioned hull, drawn by Louis Choris in 1815. (Bellwood, 296)

if the crew is lucky and the wind holds steady, this pitching and twisting will go on without rest day and night for the day or two or three it takes to reach their destination. But the wind may drop and leave the crew drifting or dawdling along under an equatorial sun. Or it may rise to a storm with gusts wracking the canoe and driving chilling rain into the skin and eyes of the crew. Throughout all of this the navigator, in sole command, keeps track of course and drift and position, guided only by the stars and waves and other signs of the sea . . . Even at night he stays awake and vigilant, trusting only himself. They say you can tell the experienced navigators by their bloodshot eyes.[64]

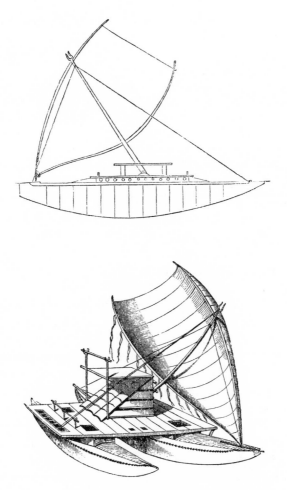

FIGURE 8 A Fijian double-hulled *drua*. (Williams, *The Islands,* 86)

Gladwin's comments highlight the main concerns of mariners in Oceania: relief from the equatorial sun and storms at sea. These are also emphasized in a Tikopian canoe song that celebrates thunder and lightning at sea for clearing stormy skies and bringing rain to parched mariners:

Te rapa mai te kakamo	The lightning flash has come at last
Ku ou o tofu i te moana	Has come to calm the raging sea
Ke kau inukia	And I may drink and so not die[65]

Dehydration was a major concern. Beechey interviewed drift voyagers in the Tuamotus who described

> their canoe, alone and becalmed on the ocean; the crew, perishing with thirst beneath the fierce glare of a tropical sun, hanging exhausted over their paddles; children looking to their parents for support, and mothers deploring their inability to afford them assistance. Every means of quenching their thirst were resorted to; some drank the sea water, and others bathed in it, or poured it over their heads; but the absence of fresh water in the torrid zone cannot be compensated by such substitutes.[66]

Seventeen people perished before the gods heeded their prayers and sent rain. Not all drifters were this unfortunate. Kotzebue records that the Woleai navigator Kadu survived a drift voyage to the Marshalls by gaining liquid and sustenance from raw fish, and collecting any rain that fell. He also dived deep into the sea and used a coconut shell with a small opening to collect water that was cooler and less salty than surface water.[67]

Canoes offered little protection from the elements. *Proa* had only small shelters that might house one or two people. Most Islanders traveled on open platforms barely a meter above the sea, even on the largest Polynesian double-hulled canoes.[68] Some wore woven cloaks or mats,[69] but most relied solely on their unique body mass for protection from wind, sea spray, and rain. Prolonged exposure to the sun, and its reflection off the water, also caused discomfort. Ellis noted that in the Society and Tuamotu islands many sailed at night to avoid sunburn.[70]

The experience of sailing on larger canoes, such as Fijian *drua*, differed markedly from that on smaller vessels like *proa*. Although *drua* carried hundreds of passengers, most tasks onboard were left to specialist seamen. Many hands were needed to hoist the huge sails and to pole the vessel beyond the reef. The oars to steer the vessel could be up to 20 feet long and required many men to control them. Oars were also used to propel the vessel by sculling, as their hulls were too high to allow the use of pad-dles when winds failed. Bailing water that came over the sides or through joints was another constant for all types of canoes, regardless of sea con-ditions. But for much of the time, sailing with suitable winds was enjoy-able. Diapea described the experience as one of "eating, drinking, steer-ing, sailing, and bailing, with the enlivening songs which we were all cheered by, as well as by the beating of the large wooden drum."[71]

Drua were not so comfortable in heavy seas. The missionary Thomas Williams noted that

> in a sea and heavy wind, the deck inclines at a most uncomfortable angle to the water. When running with the small end foremost, a beautiful jet of water, ever changing its form, is thrown up in front to the height of a yard; or, sometimes, the body of the canoe is driven along beneath the sur-face, and only seen occasionally—a dark outline in a bed of foam. When this is the case, a landsman is safest sitting still, but the native sailors move about with surprising security.[72]

Being driven under waves places great strain on twin-hulled vessels. The beachcomber John Jackson was onboard a *drua* when the force of a wave broke away the whole fore-end of the smaller windward hull known as the *thama*. The crew reacted quickly and effectively. All moved to the larger, leeward hull and positioned themselves so as to push the front of the *thama* out of the water, allowing temporary repairs to be made with matting. By this means they completed their 20-mile voyage to Beqa.[73] Others were not so lucky. Diapea describes the sinking of a vessel he was on during a cyclone, in which two-thirds of the crew either drowned or were devoured by hordes of sharks. The boat had been swamped in high seas as waves broke over the deck, sweeping the cargo and crew into the sea.[74]

Diapea's experience does not appear to have been typical. Sailors usu-ally reduced the amount of sail as winds increased, to maintain control. The mast and sail were often dismantled and lashed to the hull during strong winds to reduce the chance of the wind catching an upright and tipping the canoe over.[75] Islanders could not always adjust the sails in time. The fact that they spent much time practicing uprighting overturned canoes suggests that this was a common experience. Arago observed the uprighting of a *proa* that took two hours to complete. The crew of the accompanying *proa* assured him that this was neither unusual nor a cause for concern.[76] Wood and sennit were carried onboard for emergency repairs.

The easiest way to cope with storms at sea is to avoid them. Most records suggest that navigators were skilled at short-term weather prediction. Some signs were obvious to all. The appearance of sea birds near to shore signaled bad weather. Other signs required local knowledge to interpret. The Spaniard Don Joseph de Andia y Varela was astounded that two Tahitians who sailed with him never failed to predict the weather for the following day.[77] Centuries of accumulated knowledge taught Puluwatese that the weather usually changed around noon, and afternoon conditions usually continued through the night.[78] Beyond 24 hours, predictions were restricted to general seasonal conditions that navigators were taught to associate with various star alignments.[79]

Canoes usually traveled in convoys for security. Vessels in convoys could help each other, although maintaining contact at night and during storms was often a problem.[80] Marshallese fleets traveled in an arrow formation, headed by the canoe of the *rimedo* (master navigator). The other vessels followed behind and to the side at intervals of up to 2 nautical miles. This extended formation enhanced their chances of seeing signs of land. At night and during storms, the canoes would draw nearer to the canoe of the *rimedo,* and keep in contact through blasts on shell trumpets.[81] Tahitian fleets maintained contact by means of drums and horns. Deep-toned drums carried onboard were called *ta'i-moana* (sounding at sea), while the conch shell trumpets were called *pp-ta'i-i-te aeha* (trumpet sounding over the sea from horizon to horizon).[82] Carolinian canoes also seem to have traveled in convoys, with five being a common minimum.[83] One of the dangers of traveling in large fleets of small vessels was that there might not be enough navigators. A disaster that befell the Abemana fleet on the 70-mile return journey from Tarawa in Kiribati in the 1780s occurred when the main navigator was thrown overboard during an altercation. The whole fleet was lost at sea while tacking into the prevailing east wind except for one canoe that had stopped to rescue her and was guided back to Abemana.[84]

Superstition and ritual dominated life at sea. Supernatural beings and their maritime familiars made their presence felt. A shark lying in the path of a canoe might be seen as a warning from the god associated with it.[85] While gods were particularly invoked in times of danger, Ellis noted the sense of awe that ocean travel across a calm sea at night could engender:

> Nothing can exceed the solemn stillness of a night at sea within the tropics, when the wind is light, and the water comparatively smooth. Few periods and situations, amid the diversified circumstances of human life,

are equally adapted to excite contemplation, or to impart more elevated conceptions of the Divine Being, and more just impressions of the insignificancy and dependence of man.[86]

Voyages involved ritual and prayer. Oracles were consulted daily before long voyages in the Carolines, until a favorable result was obtained. Special magic or offerings were then used to gain the support of the maritime deities.[87] Most other seafarers also made offerings to their sea gods before departure. Tahitian crews and their relatives deposited a piece of sennit about one foot long in their home *marae* after placing it under the outrigger of the canoe. The priest then put it under a sacred slab, and called on the god Tane to give the voyagers good weather and all sea gods to guide them safely to their destination. The crew again invoked their gods with prayers and cast rolls of *'aute* (paper mulberry) into the sea as the canoe set sail.[88]

Seafarers carried ritual objects and magical chants for protection. Carolinians carried the tail of a special ray believed to remove the danger of being cast adrift. They also carried carved pieces of wood with strips of leaves and ray stings attached known as *osonifél*. When adverse winds or bad weather approached they were thrown into the air, accompanied by magical invocations.[89] Arago noted that Carolinian mariners uttered prayers calling on their patron spirits to repel threatening weather.[90] *Osonifél* were also used to counter the magic of strangers believed to lie behind a failure to make landfall.[91] Magic was needed to protect against hostile conjurers able to call up winds to overturn canoes.[92] Certain foods, such as bananas, were not allowed onboard, as they brought bad luck.[93]

A variety of other sustenance was carried onboard. Fresh breadfruit or taro could be collected just before departure for trips of a few days. Preserved breadfruit and ripe coconuts were also carried as a backup because of their durability. Young green coconuts or fresh water carried in coconut shells were taken to drink.[94] Commenting on a voyage of 80 miles from Rua to Chuuk, Floyd noted that for this day-long voyage "they take with them a dozen fruits of the breadfruit tree, which are broiled; they also prepare a dish of fruit of the Jaquier [pandanus?], which is served in shells. Fish is not forgotten, when it can be obtained, any more than are coconuts."[95] Because the return voyage required at least five days of tacking into the wind, canoes were loaded with a dish called *kois,* prepared from the nuts of inferior breadfruit trees. It was very nourishing, and served as a staple during famine.[96] Preserved breadfruit was a common food on voyages throughout Oceania, as it was compact and lasted well at sea. Pandanus was preserved in the sun, then wrapped into a tight roll and covered with a waterproof cover of dry leaves and coconut sennit.[97] Coconuts were stored in the hull. All other food was stored between pandanus mats secured to the deck or platform.[98] Fish might be obtained along the way, and eaten raw or cooked over fires lit in baskets of sand in *proa* or in boxes containing sand and cooking stones in larger vessels.[99]

The Infrastructure behind Sea Travel

A wide variety of skills was needed for voyaging. Ability at sailing, navigating, canoe building, and ritual expertise were particularly important. There was usually a wide pool of skilled sailors. Training began when young boys learned the mechanics of wind propulsion by playing with miniature sailing canoes in the lagoon. The American missionary Luther Gulick observed Marshallese miniature canoes with 18-inch hulls and large sails that could reach speeds of 15 or 20 miles per hour.[100] As the boys grew, they began to accompany their fathers and other adults on coastal outings. Arago was informed that all young Carolinian men had to pass a sailing test before they were allowed to marry.

> For this examination a time is chosen when the sea is rather high, the candidate is placed at the sheet (for the Carolinians steer their vessels entirely by the sails) and there, surrounded by reefs, and in the midst of foaming waves, he must make his proa sail a certain distance without allowing its balancer to touch the waves.[101]

Seafaring skills varied between and within island groups. The ability to sail was essential on atolls. All adult males were organized into canoe houses whose members sailed together. The bond between members of canoe houses was reinforced through blood ties.[102] On some larger high islands, however, the percentage of the adult males considered capable sailors diminished significantly. The Hawaiians distinguished certain *ma* (lineages) as seafarers. The Kaneakahoʻowaha, Kaiahua, Kuakapuaʻa, and Luia *ma* were the seafaring lineages. All were protected and guided at sea by a shark deity known as Kalahiki.[103] Within Tonga, the inhabitants of the northern isles were more famed as seafarers than those of Tongatapu. While only one god of the sea is recorded for Tongatapu, Mariner recorded five gods of the sea and voyaging in the northern islands. The emphasis on individual gods also varied. Tangaloa was the god of the sky throughout Tonga, but also the god of shipbuilding in Haʻapai.[104] Fijians distinguished between *ai vanua* (landsmen) and *kai wai* (mariners). Groups such as the Levuka, Butoni, and Malaki were the "inhabitants of the water." There were also specialist fishermen like the Lasakau and Soso in Bau, and the Kai Naselai and Kai Vutia in Rewa.[105]

More effort was required to master the art of navigation. Gladwin found that only half of those who undertook navigation training on Puluwat completed their instruction.[106] It took years of formal training and practical sailing experience to become an accomplished navigator. Most initial training was oral, and usually involved skilled navigators teaching small groups of younger relatives. Training began on land with the memorizing of a mass of information in the form of star paths across the sky. Trainees then went on to memorize the star alignments for each voyage between every pair of islands they might sail to. This could involve over a hundred star paths if return voyages are included. These star paths were often accompanied by other knowledge such as sea markers, the behavior of land-based sea birds, and weather prediction. Instruction might be divided between navigators—one teaching about the stars, another about seamarks, and so on.[107]

This material was memorized, as star compasses centered on the navigator's island that incorporated star and sea markers in each direction. The rising and setting points of stars used for direction markers were marked on the compass horizon. The process was repeated for other islands in the vicinity, so that navigators knew each island's relationship to other islands, and the directional markers for all. The form of the information facilitated oral learning. The material was systematic and schematic, and taught in standardized drills and exercises. Memorizing this information was aided by incorporating it into chants.[108]

Details varied between islands according to sea and celestial conditions, but the broad principles were similar. Village elders conducted training in Kiribati, chiefs in the Marshalls, and hereditary navigators in Tonga, while the Carolinians trained in navigation schools.[109] A number of schools might exist on the same island: Puluwat had the Warieng and Fanur schools, both named after revered founders. There was some variation between the teachings of each school, particularly for esoteric information such as navigation ritual and magic.[110]

A variety of ritual knowledge was important, as voyaging involved a great deal of magic and divination to ward off and counter adversity. Carolinian navigators were taught to interpret a series of knots tied into two pairs of coconut leaf strips. The knots were counted in groups of four, so that there were 256 possible combinations, each of which carried a particular omen. The navigator's pool of knowledge also included chants and prayers to calm seas, call up islands they were having difficulty locating, and ward off storms.[111] Graduation from navigation school on Puluwat concluded with a ceremony in which a lucky charm specific to that school was tied around the right wrist of the graduate. These charms were known as *melǎn*, and consisted of a coral wrapped in a woven mat and tied with hibiscus fibers. These charms would keep bad weather away from those wearing them.[112]

Ritual knowledge set navigators apart from other seafarers. They not only needed to observe their personal food and sexual taboos meticulously, but also had to ensure that all rituals were carried out properly during the voyage. Failure to do so would endanger the entire crew. Navigators had to invoke the patron spirits of navigation correctly, ensure all taboos were observed, and know how and when to employ protective bracelets and magic to ward off storms, sharks, and other dangers. They also needed to be familiar with the spells and language necessary to ensure a friendly welcome, particularly when kin would not be on hand to provide hospitality.[113]

The qualities that most distinguished great navigators were memory, strength, wisdom, and courage.[114] Such men inspired confidence and respect. Noting that most Carolinian men were tall, Sánchez y Zayas observed that the navigator Arrumiat was

> a man of low statue, although like the rest of them strong and muscular. He wore no ornament whatever excepting the stones in his ears; and there were no kind of figures on his skin [i.e., tattoos]. His long hair, most carefully cleaned, fell luxuriantly over his shoulders; and, notwithstanding the almost entire nudity of his person, his movements were even graceful and remarkable for decorum, and he conducted himself with an air of gravity and dignity the result of self-confidence and habit of command.[115]

Navigational knowledge was added to and altered as new information came to light during voyages. New sailing directions were incorporated into existing chants as reference points were discovered.[116] Most of these additional pointers were in the sea, as celestial markers remained fixed over the lifetime of humans. Sea features and conditions also altered because of storm damage and climatic variation. This information was shared with a few familiar navigators in the discoverer's family or school, where it would then be taught to future initiates. The knowledge was not widely disseminated beyond this circle. Chants and sailing directions were encoded in archaic and poetic language, so that meanings were not apparent to the untrained listener.[117]

Marshallese sailing chants were deliberately vague and ambiguous to prevent outsiders from understanding the information they contained— for example, a sea marker called the *konant* tree or a patch of sea referred to as the "big pillow." Full information on stars, weather, and sea conditions and the capacity to make and interpret navigational stick charts were reserved for a select few. Members of this group were known as *rimedo*. They were generally drawn from privileged classes in this hierarchical society, although they included women as well as men. *Rimedo* would only impart their knowledge to their favorite children or others identified as worthy of training. There was a high degree of professional rivalry and secrecy between *rimedo,* so that each *rimedo*'s trainees formed a distinct school of navigation. This distinctiveness was reinforced by rivalry between the titled chiefs the *rimedo* worked for.[118]

Navigational knowledge in Tonga was restricted to a few navigator families. All were *eiki* (chiefs) or *matapule* (ceremonial attendants) and carried hereditary titles. These families were known collectively as *toutai.* The anthropologist Edward Gifford describes them as *ha'a toutai,* the navigator lineage. He lists the main families in this lineage as Tuita, Fakatulolo, and Akau'ola.[119] A number of prominent chiefs were listed as navigators. The adventurer Kau Moala was the son of Akau'ola, while Taufa'ahau Tupou, the eventual unifier of Tonga, was also renowned for his navigational ability.[120]

Commoners also served as navigators, using lore taught to them by their fathers. They were *'eikivaka,* or canoe captains. They used star paths and wave patterns to navigate by, but their knowledge was not as detailed as that of the *ha'a toutai. Fanakenga* was a common term for warm and cold seas, but to the Tuita it also referred to stars that indicated island locations. Thus Sirius at its zenith was the *fanakenga* star for Vava'u. Most *'eikivaka* only used horizon stars to trace their *kaveinga,* or star paths.[121] A similar distinction occurred in Tahiti. While expert navigators such as Tupaia were drawn from the ranks of the privileged classes, J. R. Forster gained the impression that the fundamentals of canoe building and navigation were "understood by every person from the last toutou to the first chief of the land."[122] The navigator Mahine told George Forster that very few knew all the secrets of navigation.[123]

Navigational knowledge was restricted in other ways. Navigation seems to have been largely a male occupation. Women were generally believed to endanger maritime activities, and were avoided by those conducting any activity related to the sea, such as planning a voyage, building canoes, or undertaking navigational training.[124] However, women did travel by sea, and they were also trained as navigators, particularly in the Marshalls and Kiribati. Baintabu, the chief navigator on Abemana in Kiribati in the 1780s, was a woman.[125]

Canoe building was another important profession. Canoes were highly valued in most communities. The finest hardwoods, such as *koa (Acacia koa)* in Hawai'i, *'ati (Calophyllum inophyllum)* and *mara (Nauclea forsteriana)* in Tahiti, *vesi (Intsia bijuja)* in Fiji, and *ifilele (Intsia bijuga)* in Samoa, were preferred for the hulls of sailing canoes.[126] The breadfruit tree *(Artocarpus altilis)* was also used for hulls, particularly on coral islands because of their lack of hardwoods. Breadfruit wood is easy to work, and swells in water, so that joins became more watertight. It is also not susceptible to the wood-boring teredo "sea worm."[127] The use of breadfruit as timber was restrained by its prolific fruit-bearing capacity. Indeed, a general lack of suitable wood on coral islands meant that many canoe hulls were a patchwork of smaller pieces.[128]

Canoe building was labor intensive. First, the trees had to be selected, felled, and prepared. The wood for hulls on Murilo was dragged to the shore and exposed to the sun for several months, so that it was completely dry before construction began.[129] Stone and hardwood wedges were driven into the timber along the grain to split it. This was followed by the laborious task of shaping and smoothing the wood. Fire was sometimes used to speed up the process of hollowing out a log. Bone, shell, and shark's teeth tools were used to shape the wood by chiseling, gouging, or drilling. The surface was then polished smooth with sand or coral. When the hull was complete, the outrigger attachment and superstructure were built from smaller pieces of wood, and sails of plaited matting attached. Canoe parts were generally bound together with strips of coconut husk. Breadfruit resin cement provided additional binding, although on Murilo lime putty manufactured from coral was used.[130]

While many were capable of building the smaller paddling canoes, a great deal of ritual and technical skill was required to construct sailing canoes.[131] Much emphasis was placed on ritual. In Tahiti, canoe building was always begun on the last night of the moon with a ceremony to invoke the gods Tane, Ta'ere, Te-fatu, and Ta'aroa to bless the canoe builder's axe. The axe was "put to sleep" in the *marae*, while the canoe builders prepared a sacred, canoe builders' feast on the *marae* grounds and dedicated part of the pig killed to Tane. Offerings were also made to the other gods of the *marae*. They then feasted and retired for the night. They arose before dawn to "awaken the axe" in the sea. This ritual was accompanied by another appeal to the gods. Construction then began. Dressed in working *maro* (loin girdles), the builders went to cut and trim the wood. It was taken to their shed and construction began. They worked diligently throughout the construction phase, taking care to look out for any signs or omens from the gods.[132]

Great importance was attached to the proper launching of the canoe. An incantation was sung as the builders laid rollers from the shed to the water. The canoe was taken out of its shed the day before the launch, placed on rollers, and decorated with garlands and pennants. The builders then gave a lavish feast for others in their profession. That evening the axes were again put to sleep, and a piece of sennit was passed under the foremost end of the canoe's outrigger and then laid to sleep beneath a flat stone in the *marae*. On the morning of the launch the axes were again awakened, and the *marae* stone was lifted to examine the sennit. Straight sennit bode well for the canoe, but a twisted or turned over piece was ominous. Placing a piece of the hull of an old *marae* canoe in the *marae* for the duration of the new canoe's life would nullify the omen. The actual launching was a solemn occasion presided over by the priests and chiefs and watched by the whole community.[133]

When Sánchez y Zayas visited the Carolinian settlement of Garapan on Saipan in the 1860s it boasted a building yard where two vessels were under construction and several others were being careened. The yard also served as a school for canoe building and navigation. Nearby, thick sennit ropes up to 100 fathoms in length were constructed by hanging the fiber from a tall tree and twisting it.[134] On islands like Puluwat, canoe building was a hereditary profession.[135] *Tufunga fou vaka* (canoe builders) were the highest-ranked hereditary professionals in Tonga. They were always drawn from the prestigious *mu'a* or *matapule* classes, and never from the *tu'a* (commoners).[136] Fiji's canoe builders were all drawn from the *mataisau*, a "tribe" of specialist boat builders. Legend described how they were scattered throughout Fiji after incurring the wrath of the god Dengei. They now formed a caste of canoe builders attached to the households of chiefs.[137] Tahitian canoe builders had their own guild and separate places of worship. They were either part of the retinues of powerful chiefs, or hired for specific projects by chiefs unable to include them within their retinues.[138] Ra'iatea appears to have been the major *pahi* building center by the late eighteenth century, although Cook referred to the Tahitian chief Tu's "dock yards," where a number of large canoes were under construction.[139]

Canoes were a major investment. A moderately sized canoe might take a year to complete, while the large canoes of western Polynesia took much longer. Great care was taken of them. Islanders avoided leaving their canoes in the water or sun for too long when not in use. Canoes moored in water are vulnerable to attack from sea worms, while saltwater, sun, and rain are hard on lashings, sealed joints, and the canoe hull. Coconut fiber rots after prolonged exposure to saltwater, so all bindings and fittings had to be regularly checked and periodically replaced. To reduce these problems, canoes were lodged in canoe houses with open sides, placed under the shelter of trees, or covered with coconut fronds if out of the water for more than a few hours. Hulls were often dragged over palm fronds to save wear on the bottom. Housing the sail in canoe houses also helped to stave off rot and mildew.[140] Wooden Carolinian canoes from the modern era seem to have a life-span of around twenty years, particularly if returned to the canoe house straight after use.[141] In other words, canoe builders were needed by each generation.

The construction and maintenance of canoes was a community effort. Only chiefs could muster the manpower and resources needed to construct large voyaging canoes in Polynesia.[142] At least three years of sustained community effort was required to build a *drua*. The chief and his retinue supervised the project, allocated tasks, and ensured there was food to feed workers and supply ritual feasts. They had to keep up the supply of sennit, gum, and wood, as well as coordinate the groups involved. The canoe builders had to be free from other tasks for the duration of the project. Riggers were required to make fittings, women to construct matting sails, and priests to be on hand for ceremonies. The main task for the majority was growing and cooking food for the workers and feasts.[143] A similar community effort was required for the construction of large canoes in Tahiti.[144] Even the smaller *proa* required a group effort. On Puluwat, canoe builders were paid to construct canoes. The purchaser was usually male, although his sisters and brothers and their children all contributed. In return, they were entitled to a share of the benefits derived from the canoe.[145]

Canoes were not just physical assets; they were also symbols of community *mana*. The completion of a large canoe was a source of immense pride. When Tui Nayau sailed his new *drua, Rusa i vanua,* from Vulaga to Lakeba in November 1942, his followers were thrilled to note that its great hulls were longer than those of *Ra Marama,* the canoe being built at Somosomo for their rival Bau.[146] To Hawaiian chiefs, sailing canoes were a means of ostentatious display, as well as tools with which to extend their dominion. The power of a chief was often measured by the expanse of shoreline covered by the beached canoes of his army.[147]

Voyaging also required community support, in varying degrees. Voyages between neighboring atolls in the Carolines required only a few vessels and could be undertaken within a few days of the decision. The *pelu* in charge of each canoe could easily gather the four- to six-man crew needed from within his canoe house or among the co-owners of the canoe. These were often relatives, or men who sailed together regularly. Their provisions required no special preparation. The only reason to delay would be a bad omen or the prospect of poor weather.[148] Undertakings such as the colonizing expeditions of the Marquesans represented the other end of the spectrum, and might involve hundreds of participants. As they were not regular seafarers, it might take months or even years to build the vessels, and set aside enough preserved food to feed the colonizers until they discovered a new home and harvested their first crop.[149]

Seafaring cultures also needed to make provisions for those left onshore. It might be some time before mariners returned. While most voyages were relatively short, mariners might have to wait for a wind change to return home. Some voyages might take people away from friends and relatives for months, or even years. Atoll canoe houses not only provided a pool of familiar seafarers to crew vessels, but also ensured that the families of absent seafarers had support. They could also call on other kinfolk.[150] The concerns of relatives left behind were also catered for by ritual. Tahitians deposited *'aha moa* (sleeping sennit) on *marae* at the beginning of voyages to link voyagers to those left behind. When it was time for the voyagers to arrive at their destination, family and friends went to the *marae* and asked the priest to uncover the sennit and see how they had fared. If the sennit was still lying straight, the canoe had arrived safely before a suitable wind. If it was slightly crooked, the canoe had met with contrary winds, but had still arrived safely. Sennit that was twisted over indicated misfortune. This news obviously caused great anxiety. If the mariners then returned, the priests would claim that evil spirits had deceived them.[151]

The Fragility of Seafaring Institutions

Although most voyages between 1770 and 1870 were successful, the period still witnessed the demise of a number of vibrant seafaring cultures. Most commentators suggest that these declines were symptomatic of a gradual atrophying of seafaring ability. However, this diminished capacity may have been the result of sudden catastrophic events that led to the collapse of seafaring in the space of only one or two generations. This decline was by no means universal, and much of it occurred on islands relatively untouched by Western influence.

There was a marked difference in seafaring ability between peoples living on coral islands and those living on high islands in Micronesia. The retention of seafaring skills was an economic and environmental necessity on the small, low-lying, and storm-prone coral islands, while high islands were self-sufficient. With no reason to leave their islands, the seafaring skills of high islanders gradually diminished. Brower asserts that

> men came to high volcanic islands much as corals do. The coral larvae row in on hair-like oars, attach themselves to the volcanic substrate, and become polyps, building castles of calcium carbonate and shedding these hair-like oars. Men sail in, erect their house stones of calcium carbonate, their cities of basalt, and they reef their sails.[152]

Goodenough noted this tendency in the eastern Carolines. The inhabitants of the high islands had lost the ability to navigate and sail the open seas by the nineteenth century. Few people on Kosrae and Pohnpei even knew how to build sailing canoes. Farther west, Palauans were capable seafarers, but rarely ventured beyond their large and bountiful lagoon. While these high islands were linguistic isolates, the languages of the coral islands of the Carolines were all mutually intelligible, as were those of the Marshalls and most of Kiribati.[153] Knowledge of seafaring existed on Yap and Chuuk, but they still relied heavily on specialists from surrounding atolls. Most Chuukese ocean-going canoes were constructed on atolls, while the Yapese preferred to use canoes built on Woleai for their trips to Palau.[154]

Resource endowment alone does not explain the distribution of seafaring communities. Chuukese and Yapese still sought canoes. Island economies went beyond subsistence needs. Prestige items also mattered for chiefly status and for exchanges to forge alliances. Both required high Islanders to have access to other islands. The expansive low Islander versus atrophic high Islander dichotomy did not apply in Polynesia either, where many high Islanders were capable seafarers.

Catastrophe rather than atrophy lay behind much of the decline. The restricted dissemination of knowledge meant that a community's seafaring expertise could be wiped out in a short time by natural disasters or Western epidemics. Although there was a large pool of sailors to call on, far fewer were trained in navigation and canoe building. Studies from the late 1960s and early 1970s recorded 18 to 26 trained navigators out of Puluwat's total population of just over 400. This represented about half of the total male population over the age of 30.[155] Satawal also contained approximately the same ratio of navigators to adult males at the time.[156] Puluwat had 26 navigators in the early 1970s and 30 in 1910, implying that this was the minimum number needed to maintain a viable seafaring base.[157] The situation was not as robust elsewhere in the Carolines, however. When Lutké visited the Hall Islands where few Europeans had visited in the 1820s, he found only three canoe builders on Murilo Atoll, while navigational knowledge on Rua was restricted to an aging chief and the son of his sister, although the inhabitants of these islands relied on annual trading voyages to Chuuk to secure their main form of sustenance through the lean winter.[158]

The inhabitants of the western Carolinian island of Fais seem to have lost much of their seafaring ability during the nineteenth century. In the early 1900s they told Krämer that they traveled on canoes from neighboring Ulithi, but did not sail themselves. Yet Krämer recorded the names of sailing and navigation deities, and was told of voyages by two locals within living memory. Although Krämer found endogamous marriage patterns on Fais, twenty of its women then resided on Ulithi, and others on Woleai—testimony to the recent practice of marrying out.[159] Lutké commented on Fais Islanders' poor ability at handling canoes in the 1820s,[160] although Chamisso noted that a Western vessel trading at Fais in 1808 found some of its inhabitants waiting to resume trade when they arrived at Palau soon afterward.[161]

When Wood stopped at Rotuma in the early 1870s he was confronted by another seafaring culture in apparent decline. He noted how

> one sees at several places large double canoes, similar to those of Fiji and Tonga, lying in their sheds on the beach. The people assure me that no one now alive, or their fathers before them, have ever seen these canoes in the water. Were they to launch them, they would not know how to manage

them, nor could they make the mat sails suitable for them, so completely have they lost all their former knowledge of navigation.[162]

The loss of men at sea lay behind much of the decline. Wood was told that many ocean-going double canoes never returned home.[163] Dillon had visited Rotuma in 1827 and learned that Rotumans were still voyaging westward to Vaitapu and to Nui in Tuvalu.[164] However, the English resident Emory informed a visitor in 1832 that many canoes had been lost at sea since his arrival in 1827.[165] Another reason for the decline of Rotuman seafaring in the nineteenth century was the expansion of opportunities to crew on Western vessels. By the 1830s Rotumans were already in high demand as crew members for commercial vessels.[166]

European visitors to Mangareva early in the nineteenth century noted that the inhabitants sailed on rafts known as *paepae*. Canoes were the usual form of maritime transport in the rest of eastern Polynesia. Māori academic Te Rangi Hiroa suggested that this unusual feature was a response to the shallow waters of Mangareva's lagoon, but other Islanders in similar environments did not adopt the same strategy. The dominance of *paepae* seems to have occurred late in Mangarevan history. Resident missionaries reported seeing wrecked double canoes on the beaches in the nineteenth century. One reported that the canoes had been destroyed because the continual wars carried out in them had almost obliterated the social and economic fabric of the island.[167] One of the casualties may have been the knowledge necessary to build and sail these vessels.

The loss of seafaring infrastructure was not limited to small island populations. There was a noticeable decline in Fijian canoe building during the nineteenth century. Canoe building was a prestigious, hereditary occupation. The position of Fijian canoe builders was threatened in the middle of the nineteenth century by an influx of Tongan craftsmen. By the end of the century Tongans were preferred as canoe builders by most chiefs, while specialist communities of Fijians remained in only a few places like Bau, Rewa, and Naitasiri. The rest of the Fijian canoe-building clan no longer worked under their own leaders, but were scattered around the retinues of individual chiefs, performing a variety of woodworking tasks. They did not control their own garden lands, nor did they have a political voice in the councils.[168]

There was also a dramatic and rapid reduction in aspects of Tahitian seafaring during the last two decades of the eighteenth century. Cook reported Tahitian war fleets of over a hundred war canoes in the 1770s, yet by the early 1790s these fleets had declined to a few dozen vessels.[169] James Morrison, an English beachcomber on Tahiti in the early 1790s, noted:

> Their Chief Strength consisted formerly in their Naval force, which at present is but triffling, their Navy being put on a very indifferent footing, Otoo [Pomare II] thinking it better to keep peace than make war. At present his naval force does not exceed 20 sail of War Canoes & for the most part of these he is beholden to his Sister Areepaeoa Wahene [Ari'i- paea? Wahine] who brought them from Ryeataya [Ra'iatea].[170]

By the end of the 1790s the missionary Wilson reported only five war canoes in Tahiti.[171] The cause of this decline remains a mystery. Perhaps it was due to the depopulation that occurred because of the introduction of Western diseases. Tahitians simply may not have been able to man this many vessels. The decline may also have been due to the difficulty of maintaining the seafaring infrastructure. Disease may have wiped out many of the small group privileged with navigational and canoe-building expertise. Wilson also reported that

> Pomare and his retinue particularly regretted their want of ships, and knowledge to conduct them to foreign countries; and, addressing himself to me, said in a tone of concern that they were able to go no further than Ulietea [Ra'iatea] or Huaheine; and that at the risk of being driven they knew not whither, to perish: whereas we could sail for many moons, and in the darkest nights and strongest gales, and after all could come exactly to Tahiti.[172]

The loss of maritime skills and technical ability was only one factor determining Islanders' voyaging spheres. Other factors inhibited travel and harvesting of the sea's resources. The Pacific was not only crossed by well-traveled sea lanes, but also by lines that signaled claims of owner- ship and rights of access. The maintenance of these claims required recog- nition from rivals or the ability to enforce compliance. In this tumultuous century, the traveled sea was often a contested sea.

5

Fluid Frontiers:
The Sea as a Contested Space

TENSIONS AND rivalries on land extended out to sea. Islander activities at sea were constrained by an awareness of boundaries not apparent to Europeans. These boundaries were fluid, and divided the ocean into safe and familiar seas of regular use, and seas made hazardous by predatory enemies. Communities were defined by land and sea boundaries. Those on land often followed natural features like ridges or watercourses. In the absence of these features, borders between political units and boundaries between social and economic plots were sign-posted by man-made markers such as stone cairns, bundles of dry leaves hung on trees, or cords tied between trees.[1]

While detailed accounts of land borders between 1770 and 1870 have survived for much of the region, the record of sea boundaries is less substantial. Yet there is enough evidence on sea tenure to suggest that postwar ethnography does not represent the precolonial state of affairs. Modern studies of sea tenure portray it as a relatively static set of rules, rather than an evolving process. The sea is depicted as partitioned, but rarely as contested. Despite the importance of the sea, little has been written about how Islanders attempted to secure and defend their maritime interests. Nowhere has anyone linked sea tenure to sea power.

Marine Tenure in Oceania

Modern studies of marine tenure focus largely on social and political aspects of fishing rights. They distinguish between frequently used near-shore waters and other seas. Most fishing was concentrated close to shore because of the productivity and shelter of lagoons and other inshore waters. These studies generally conclude that fishermen recognized distinct and specific tenure zones near to shore, while the open sea was much less tightly controlled. Information from the nineteenth century suggests a more complex reality, however.

Resource tenure on atolls was based on corporate control by kin groups, which held sections of the land, lagoon, and reef. These sections were then allocated to households. Ulithi in the western Carolines has probably the most thoroughly studied system of atoll sea tenure. Postwar studies by Lessa, Ushijima, and Sudo found land holdings divided into small sections of valuable taro land and larger straight-edged blocks of other land held by individual lineages. Its large lagoon was divided into big district blocks, with the most powerful lineage in the district controlling access to all resources within it. The lagoon was divided into fourteen lagoon sections and eighteen reef sections. Maps of marine tenure on Ulithi and most other atolls show marine divisions as straight-edged blocks of territory incorporating the whole lagoon.[2] On Marshallese atolls, however, lineage tenure only extended out to waist-deep water, which was where people stood to fish with a pole.[3] An unofficial part of sea tenure was individual knowledge of fishing spots and patterns of fish movement. Such knowledge was often closely guarded.[4]

The sacred status of the paramount chief of Ulithi was acknowledged by gifts of specific fish from the atoll's kin groups. Refusal to provide tribute entitled the chief to dispossess the offending group of its maritime territory, although there is no record of any such confrontation. The presentation of part of the catch to the chief was also common on other atolls.[5] Chiefs on most atolls had rights to material that drifted ashore.[6] They also had the right to declare particular zones of the lagoon or reef as theirs to regulate and control. This might be done for a short time to conserve marine resources, or permanently to control a rich fishery. The latter reason figured prominently in the Marshalls, where chiefly power was particularly strong. Chiefs favored reef sections alongside sea passages where fish were plentiful. Marine resources within the lagoon were also the property of the chief, although his subjects did not need his permission to exploit them unless a specific *tapu* was in place. Chiefs also directed the distribution of the day's catch among the population.[7]

Chiefs on high islands held similar rights. They had exclusive use of certain fisheries and the right to expropriate part of any catch. These expropriations were often conducted for religious reasons, and came with an expectation that chiefs would be generous in redistributing their share, particularly in times of want.[8] High island tenure was largely organized around kin-based affiliations. The usual pattern was for a kin group to

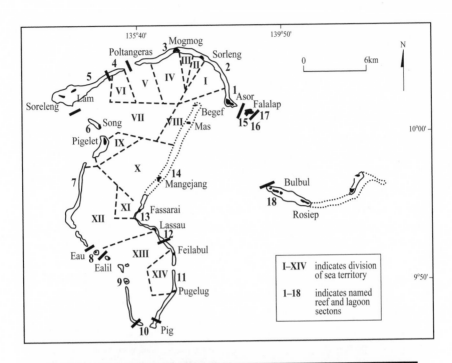

Clan	Location	Reef Section	Lagoon Section
Rigipa	Falalap	15	–
Falchugoi	Falalap	16	–
Falkel	Falalap	17	–
Bogatlaplap	Rosiep	18	–
Efan	Asor	1	VIII
Lugalap	Sorleng	2,5	–
Maifan	Sorleng	–	I
Maiyor	Sorleng	–	II
Fashilith & Numurui	Mogmog	3	IV,V
Falmsy	Mogmog	–	III
Fashilith[1]	Mogmog	4,6	VI,VII,IX
Muroch	Mangejang	7,9,11,14	X
Lebogat	Fassarai	8,13	XII
Tauefan	Fassarai	–	XI
Fachal	Lossau	10,12	XIII
Ligafaly	Lossau	–	XIV

Note: [1] Paramount Chief's clan

MAP 6 Reef and lagoon tenure on Ulithi Atoll. (RSAPS Cartography after Sudo, 218–19, after Ushijima, 1982)

control a section of the island extending from mountain peaks to the outer edge of the fringing reef.[9] These divisions were defined by reference to natural features of the terrestrial and marine environment. The Tahitian clan district of Hitia'a, for example, was defined as follows:

E moti i Vai-o-va'u e horo roa i 'Ea'ea, o Hitia'a te fenua.	From Vai-o-va'u (Water-in-weeds) to 'Ea'ea (Deliberation), Hitia'a (Rising or East) is the land.
Te mou'a i ni'a o Te-vai-tohi, o Mauru, e o Ta-hou-tira.	The mountains above are Te-vai-tohi (Riven water), Mauru (barrenness), and Ta-hou-tira (renewed mast).
Te Tahua i raro, o Te-'iri'iri.	The assembly ground is Te-'iri-'iri (The pebbles).
Te 'outu i tai, o Pape-he'i	The point seaward is Pape-he'e (Gliding waters).
Te vai, o Manini-haorea e o Maha-te-ao.	The rivers are Manini-haorea (Manini [fish] encircled) and Maha-te-ao (World-in-four, or quarters).
Te marae, o Hitia'a e o Taputapu-atea.	The temples were Hitia'a and Taputapu-atea (Sacrifices from abroad).
Te ava i tai: o Pu-tai-maru, (i Pape-ivi e Vai-to-are),	The harbors outside (within the reefs) are: Pu-tai-maru (easy-ocean-pool) at Pape-ivi (water-of-ghosts), and Vai-to-are (Water-of-waves), Te-aau-raa (The-sacred-reef), at Faaone (sand-extension), Te-matoe-o-Hitia'a (The-eastern-crack), and Tapo-ra (Now-strike), at Tai-pa'i'a (Ocean-slipping).
Te-aau-raa, i Faaone, o Te-matoe-o Hitiaa, e o Tapo-ra i Tai-pa'i'a.	
Te motu i tai, o Opu-totara, o Vari-a-raru (oia o	The islets are Opu-totara (porcupine-fish-stomach), Vari-a-raru (Mud-of-insects) called also Ari-o-raro (Waves-below) and Pu-uru (Forest-clump).
Ari-o-raro), e o Pu-uru.	
Teri'i-tua te ari'i.	Teri'i-tua (Sovereign-of-the-ocean) was the chief.[10]

Reefs were prominent features of sea boundaries. In Palau the traditional boundary between Koror and Aimeliik was a stretch of lagoon separating two shallow reefs between the villages.[11] After describing how the boundaries of the district of Ngeremlengui ran from mountain peaks to two river mouths, Parmentier details how they ran out toward two points on the reef. One was a reef opening named Toachelmlengui, while the other was a point on the western reef known as Klairamesech.[12] Thomson relates how the fisher-folk of rival Fijian chiefdoms of Bau and Rewa divided up the reefs off the Rewa coast, and agreed not to interfere with reefs other than their own.[13] The Kingdom of Hawai'i confirmed traditional tenure practices in a written legal code implemented in 1846. The code included a definition of the seaward boundaries of *ahupua'a* land units. These were set where the breakers struck the edge of the reef, or about 1 1/2 miles from shore where there were no breakers.[14]

Fishermen rarely strayed beyond their own area within the near-shore zone. When fish were caught outside of one's own kin group area, it was usual practice to present part of the catch to local residents. These presentations were usually made to the head of the kin group, although each coral bank, fish weir, and other fishing spot within their marine territory was associated with specific families.[15] Inshore fisheries were not always clearly demarcated. A New Zealand government investigation in the 1860s reported that while some coastal mudflats were only accessible to particular *hapu* (subtribes), others were divided between different kin groups. The right to fish on the mudflats of the Thames area was vested exclusively in the Ngati Rautao *hapu* of Ngati Maru, for example, while fishing rights to mudflats in Katikati Harbor were divided between two tribes at the line of the tidal rip. The report asserted that fishing rights on mudflats also varied between species; *pipi* (clam, *Paphies australis*) could be gathered on any mudflat, while the harvest of other species required the permission of local "owners."[16]

Few claims of tenure are recorded in areas out of sight of land or the range of shore-based sea birds. The open ocean is usually described as a fishery open to all,[17] but there were exceptions. Fornander records fishing grounds off Hawai'i 3 miles offshore and 1200 feet deep, yet deemed to belong to the chief and people of the nearest *ahupua'a*.[18] Information on Hawaiian *ko'a* (offshore fishing grounds) was kept secret by individuals to prevent others from exploiting them. Fishermen would only approach these grounds under cover of early morning darkness, and wait until they were well away from the site before hauling in their catch.[19] Kahaulelio recorded ninety-eight *ko'a*.[20]

A number of high islands claimed control over uninhabited offshore islands, and made annual visits to gather coconuts and bird eggs, and to fish. The Tikopians had such a relationship with the island of Fataka. Dillon reports that they went as far as keeping the island cleared of coconuts to deter others from settling. They were particularly wary of mariners who were occasionally blown there from the west. If a settlement was established, they would lose their privileged access. Dillon does not reveal why they did not settle the island themselves, as it certainly had enough land and water to support a colony.[21] It is unclear whether the Tikopians believed their rights over Fataka also implied rights to the intervening seas.

The most thorough study of high island offshore tenure is Hommon's on Hawai'i. He noted that Hawaiian chiefs occasionally extended their control beyond one island, but found no explicit statement about control of the seas between islands. Hommon asserts that political control was expressed through the limitations and prohibitions that Hawaiian chiefs were able to impose on activities at sea. He notes that chiefs were able to ban canoe travel at certain times of the year, and control trading with Western vessels. There were also seasonal bans on fishing for certain species. While trade with Western vessels was largely restricted to within a few kilometers of the coast, fishing for periodically banned species occurred up to 15 miles from the coast, and canoe travel included passages across sea channels up to 117 kilometers wide.[22] In Hawai'i, as on many other islands, chiefs were entitled to flotsam washed ashore and goods arriving by sea.[23] This right was based on chiefs' sacred association with gods and ancestral figures who dwelt in the sea or sky. Objects and people from beyond the horizon carried supernatural associations, as the sea and the sky appeared to merge at the horizon.[24]

Coral islanders also maintained offshore tenure claims. The most detailed studies deal with the western Carolines, where the sea was crowded with fishing banks, reefs, and smaller, uninhabited atolls between inhabited atolls.[25] Coral islanders regularly exploited nearby reefs and fishing banks. Gladwin, for example, mentions that the inhabitants of Puluwat used to place huge fish traps on Uranie Bank, a broad reef that extends 20 miles to the east of the atoll. Each canoe house placed its own fish traps in the area of the reef reserved for it.[26] Damm revealed that weir fishing was also practiced in sight of Puluwat between three reefs east of the atoll. He also noted other fishing grounds. Puluwatese fished on Oraurau-feis (Manila Bank) southwest of Puluwat, Suat Reef (Enderby Bank) to the northwest, Asebar Reef in the east, and Maianjor to the southeast. All these fisheries were less than a day's travel from Puluwat. Canoes would leave about midnight to arrive at the fishing grounds early the next day. After fishing for the remainder of the day, they departed in the evening, and arrived back at Puluwat the following day.[27] Lamotrek Atoll exercised tenure over uninhabited atolls in its vicinity, although these atolls were open to exploitation by others in the area. Lamotrek's right was based on its high status in the wider Carolinian community. Other communities acknowledged this by giving Lamotrek part of the resources gathered on the uninhabited atolls. Lamotrek maintained no presence on these atolls and lacked the coercive capacity to enforce recognition of its rights.[28]

Ken-Ichi Sudo's survey of sea tenure principles in Micronesia reveals a remarkably consistent pattern. Tenure was centered on inshore waters with only vague claims farther offshore. Tenure patterns bore no correlation to environmental features or to fishing methods, and were largely influenced by social and political organization. Groups held access rights by virtue of their membership of social groups, although ownership was vested in groups ranging from families up to the community as a whole.[29] The smaller the basic tenure group, the more subdivided the inshore fisheries.[30]

Sudo's study focuses on principles of tenure rather than their enactment. Groups are portrayed as holding different rights to resources on the basis of relative status, with little sense that the system was flexible or open to challenge. Another factor to consider is the dynamic nature of fisheries. Fixed tenure was surely unsuited to such a fluid environment. European writings on sea tenure adopt a different approach. They emphasize competing claims between nation-states and fluctuating balances of power. In European historiography the sea is a contested space.[31] There is enough evidence to suggest that this approach could also apply to Oceania.

The Sea as a Zone of Conflict

Not all maritime borders were clearly defined. On Satawan Atoll in the Mortlock Islands the political boundary between Satawan and Moch islands was a long reef without islands called Lamoylap. Both communities shared fishing rights along the boundary reef.[32] Size and power influenced marine tenure. The inhabitants of some smaller *ahupua'a* in Hawai'i could only fish out to the depth of a man. Beyond that, the borders of larger neighboring *ahupua'a* swept around to incorporate rich fisheries farther from shore.[33] Maritime rights needed to be constantly protected and asserted. Kubary noted that in Palau it was "considered perfectly natural to rob the traps of the weaker neighbouring villages, although the same offence practiced against kin or fellow villagers would not be accepted."[34] This may explain why the fish traps of high-ranking individuals were not only in the best locations, but also near to the village, while the traps of more marginal families were relegated to poorer fisheries close to sea boundaries.

Confrontations occurred along borders and within maritime territories. The mudflats of the Firth of Thames were considered the best *patiki* (flatfish) fishery in Aotearoa and were fought over by *hapu*.[35] The district of Koʻolau on the Hawaiian island of Molokaʻi went to war with its rival Kona over valuable fishing grounds off Kekaha on the Kona coast. The two clashed at their land border on the Kalaupapa peninsula. The Kona forces emerged victorious and held onto the fishery.[36] When Andrew Cheyne visited Yap in 1864 he found that the people of Tomil and Weeloey were at war after the Tomil people had killed two Weeloey men "on account of having ordered the Tomeel people off their fishing grounds when I was here last voyage."[37] In the late 1820s Tongans claimed that a dispute with Samoans occurred because the latter had encroached upon their fishing grounds.[38] The distance between the archipelagos makes this unlikely, however, unless the Tongans were referring to local fisheries given to them in return for their military assistance in Samoan disputes.

Reefs and fisheries did change hands in this way. The Chuukese enticed allies to join them in their disputes by offering fishing rights to sections of Chuuk's outer reef.[39] The Palauan village of Ngerang in the district of Melekeok controlled a reef off the neighboring district of Ngchesar, gifted by the Ngchesar village of Ngaruingel for services rendered.[40] On other occasions groups forcibly seized fisheries. The Fijian polity of Verata lost control over many reefs during the mid-eighteenth century after being defeated by Bau at Naivonini. Bauan fishermen eagerly moved in.[41] Damm was told that by the end of the nineteenth century Puluwat had taken control of uninhabited Pikelot from Lamotrek and that Puluwatese no longer allowed other Islanders to fish there.[42]

Islanders also went fishing for humans. The dedication of Hawaiian temples reserved for human sacrifices involved a ceremony known as *kapapa-ulua*. The officiating *kahuna* (priest) and several others went fishing for *ulua* to dedicate at the temple. If they failed to catch *ulua*, they went from house to house seeking humans to sacrifice. Anyone unfortunate enough to be caught was dispatched, and a hook was thrust in his mouth. The victim was then carried back to the temple for the ceremony. Malo mentions that households with many people were able to resist the fishing party.[43] The implication is that victims were loners or outcasts. When Marquesan warriors went out seeking victims to sacrifice at the death of a chief or prophet, they also called it fishing—*e ika*. Fishing for victims took place both on land and at sea. Sacrifices were mainly enemy of low status. As Dening notes, the victims' "work or social marginality put them on the dangerous edges of their communities."[44]

Fishermen were vulnerable to attack and needed to be constantly alert, as much fishing was conducted by relatively small groups. Shores lined with mangrove were particularly dangerous, as the dense thickets were ideal lairs.[45] High status did not convey immunity. In the early 1800s the Tongan high chief Tuihalafatai was surprised and killed by men from Nuku'alofa while out fishing on the lagoon of Tongatapu.[46] A similar fate befell Langenmwen, a prominent chief on Mwaekil Atoll. A party of at least ten men attacked him while he was out reef fishing with only two or three relatives. His companions tried to defend him, but were over-whelmed.[47]

Villages were forever wary of incursions from the sea, as the dangers of traveling through coastal waters did little to deter raiders. In 1864, for example, ten men from Gagil launched a night raid in two canoes on rivals gathering *bêche-de-mer* near the barrier reef that marked the edge of their territory.[48] Men's houses were often sited on the shore as a defense against night raids. The approach of canoes from another locality usually required precautions. Warriors might gather at the village meeting house or the waterfront to await their arrival, or a battle-line of canoes might be formed. By the nineteenth century many Palauan villages protected their seaward approaches by thick stonewalls with only one narrow entrance. These walls were either along the shore or across bays.[49] Defenses were rare on the inland side of Palauan villages.

One important way of protecting villages was to ensure that rivals were unfamiliar with seaward approaches. Palauans informed English castaways that they no longer took prisoners as slaves because some had managed to escape and inform their kin about channels and creeks through the protective buffer of mangrove. Their enemies had then been able to negotiate these channels and launch surprise raids at night that caused great harm.[50] Travel in unfamiliar enemy territory was particu-larly risky at low tide, when canoes were vulnerable to stranding or were restricted to narrow channels. A Palauan fleet was crushed at Ngesebokel in 1780 when they became trapped on mud flats at low tide in the terri-tory of their intended victims. They were discovered and soundly defeated before they could extricate themselves.[51]

Coastal dwellers also sought to control the movement of canoes along their shores. Lagoons were dangerous during hostilities. Canoes on lagoons were caught between potentially hostile shores and fringing reefs punctuated by only a few passages. Pursuing foes could close rapidly as their rivals attempted to escape the lagoon by beaching their canoes or crowding through reef passages. Canoes traveling in narrow lagoons were particularly vulnerable to interference from shore. One village on the east coast of Palau's Babeldoab Island was able to exploit its narrow lagoon to control coastal travel by building a 150-fathom-long stone pier from shore to reef. Coastal dwellers occasionally tried to block the passage of outsiders beyond the reef. In 1860 a boat carrying Dyson was intercepted just beyond the breakers in Samoa. As he passed a particular reef opening, he noticed

> a large boat after us—16 or 18 young men on it—come with evil intentions—turn our boat to meet them—along side each other—they look cool & salute us. We return it—A leading chief says he knew us not—mistook us—thought we were an Atua boat—begs pardon for having chased us.[52]

Dyson noted that his pursuers had axes, clubs, swords, and spears onboard. When a Woleai canoe was blown off-course to the Ralik chain in the Marshalls, locals came from Kili Atoll and attacked them at sea.[53]

A significant amount of fighting took place at sea. Its nature varied between localities. Yapese traditions refer to battles between fleets of canoes on the lagoon and canoe raids on enemy territory.[54] Palauans constructed large canoes specifically for naval operations. These canoes were up to 58 feet long, and equipped with an outrigger platform to accommodate paddlers and warriors.[55] The only accounts of fighting at sea by atoll dwellers in Micronesia come from the Marshalls, where combatants used grappling hooks to lock their canoes together, and then engaged in hand-to-hand combat. An account of a battle against Ngatik claims that as many were killed at sea as on land.[56] Reefs served as battlegrounds on rare occasions. In the early 1800s the forces of the rival Marshallese chiefs Jemaluit and Letalju fought on the reefs and beaches of Ebon.[57] Some time in the late 1700s, the inhabitants of Ulong Island in Palau formed their battle line along Ikesakes Reef to defend their island from attack. They were defeated and forced from their island.[58]

Naval warfare in western Polynesia was most developed in Fiji. Fijian nautical technology was well suited to the pursuit of naval power. Huge double-hulled *drua* and outriggers known as *camakau* carrying hundreds of men each served as troop transports. Other canoes were designed specially for fighting at sea. Known as *tabilai*, they combined hulls tipped with several feet of solid wood at either end to enable ramming, with wind-driven speed and maneuverability.[59] Smaller canoes were also used in war, and are even recorded attacking much larger vessels. William Lockerby was onboard a *drua* carrying two hundred men when it was attacked by five small canoes carrying ten men each.[60] Samoans and Tongans did not develop or modify canoes specifically for naval warfare until the middle of the nineteenth century. The new designs were essentially a response to Western artillery and longboats. Prior to this, battle at sea in Samoa was decided by hand-to-hand combat between crews, or between champions stationed at the front of normal canoes. There are a number of accounts of Tongans pursuing the canoes of rivals, but only one that refers to combat. It occurred in the late 1790s when Toogahowe (Tuku-'aho) sailed ahead of his own fleet and routed his Vavau'an enemies single-handedly.[61]

Fijian naval battles were on the whole bloodier than land operations, which tended to be directed against fortified villages. Unless the village could be taken by surprise, the prospect of a long and indecisive siege loomed. Fleet movements were coordinated by commanders in canoes distinguished by battle flags flown from the mast. The other vessels followed the lead of the commander's canoe. Naval tactics usually consisted of attempts to run down or ram opponents to sink or disable them. Once this was achieved, the victors would board and finish off the occupants of the disabled canoe, or kill the survivors in the water. Approaching an enemy vessel from the windward side was crucial, as it exposed their outrigger. The enemy crew could not venture onto the outrigger to defend it without the risk of capsizing their vessel. This allowed attackers to seek to bring down the rigging by chopping the masthead. Vessels caught downwind were not totally exposed. Lockerby saw portable breastworks erected on a *drua* for protection against projectiles and attempts at boarding.[62]

Naval warfare in eastern Polynesia aimed to kill enemy personnel rather than disable their canoes. Naval operations in Hawai'i mostly involved transporting troops and supplies, although there were other types of activity. In a comprehensive survey of Hawaiian traditions, Hommon found three references to major naval battles, one on Moloka'i where an O'ahu force was attacked from the sea and the mountains simultaneously, and one to the successful repulse of a landing on O'ahu. Fighting at sea consisted of exchanges of projectiles followed by attempts to board. Hawaiians spent much time training in their canoes, and were highly proficient in handling them. After the introduction of Western artillery, some double-hulled canoes were modified to carry cannon.[63]

Tahitian battle fleets in the 1770s consisted of specialist war canoes supported by sailing canoes in transport roles. The main fighting vessel was a double canoe with high hulls and bulky fronts for ramming. It was propelled by paddlers, and had a raised fighting stage in the front.[64] In the mock battles witnessed by the members of Cook's expedition, canoes came head to head and warriors fighting on the raised platforms decided the issue.[65] Henry claims that Tahitians developed a long pike called a *tao* specifically for this type of fighting.[66] Presumably its length allowed warriors to strike their enemies without leaving their own stage. Each canoe carried eight to ten warriors. Cook's Tahitian informant Tupaia suggested that only one or two warriors fought on the platform at any time, being relieved or replaced as they became tired or were struck down.[67] This implies that canoes were little more than elaborate stages for individual combat. Certainly some land battles were decided by duels.

There is reason to doubt this interpretation. Morrison noted that paddlers on these vessels were armed with slings, and that in times of war the war deck was filled with baskets of sling-stones.[68] Cook never actually saw a naval battle in Tahiti. He was uncertain whether the whole fleet moved in a concerted fashion or if battle simply deteriorated into a series of uncoordinated tussles between paired canoes.[69] Traditions suggest that the former was more usual. Tahitian accounts refer to fleets fighting in coordinated battle lines, with canoes sometimes lashed together to provide a more stable platform and to prevent retreat. Traditions also refer to battles outside of the reef, despite war canoes being poorly designed for open sea conditions.[70]

Sea Power in Oceanic History

Very little has been written on indigenous sea power in Oceania. Early European visitors were impressed with Islanders' naval prowess, yet most modern studies depict naval operations as being of minor importance. In contrast, the concept of sea power is deeply embedded in European historiography. The literature on sea power in the Atlantic contains useful concepts for exploring the influence of sea power in the Pacific. In essence, sea power is "the ability to ensure free movement on the sea for oneself and to inhibit, if need be, a similar capacity in others."[71] For much of European history effective domination of the sea was not obtainable. Technical and logistical limitations restricted the incidence of battles at sea and confined most operations close to shore. Most actions consisted of low-level harassment of enemy shipping or raids against coasts or ports. In both cases, the sea-borne aggressors enjoyed the advantage of mobility, but their actions rarely resulted in political dominion.[72]

These characteristics may not apply to Oceania. Most European seafaring regions could draw upon the resources of large hinterlands. However, this situation could also distract them from developing their naval power. The Pacific environment of islands with comparatively small populations and resource bases, often separated by long stretches of ocean, may well have generated quite different configurations of naval power.

Despite limited populations and resources, many island communities deployed impressive naval forces. By the late eighteenth century, Hawaiians could assemble fleets capable of transporting armies of up to 10,000 men between islands. A fleet witnessed by the trader Joseph Ingraham in the 1790s was estimated to contain 700 canoes.[73] Another a few years later was said to have numbered 1200.[74] Although these fleets were not made up solely of war canoes, it is still remarkable that they were raised from just one island—Hawai'i. Population estimates for the island of Hawai'i range from 90,000 to 340,000.[75] In the 1770s Cook witnessed a Tahitian fleet of 160 large war canoes and 170 sailing canoes. He estimated that the fleet carried over 7000 men.[76] This was a significant achievement given that the total population of the coalition contributing to it probably numbered in the tens of thousands.[77] Lockerby sailed with a Bauan expedition in 1809 that transported almost 3000 men in 136 canoes.[78] In 1855 the English scientist William Harvey was in Lakeba to see a Tongan fleet of 35 canoes carrying 2000 people.[79]

Fleet sizes elsewhere were significantly smaller. The Fanui people on Borabora and Tahaa had risen to dominate the Leeward Islands with fleets as small as 10 canoes.[80] Porter believed that most Marquesan chiefs could only put around 300 warriors to sea, in fleets averaging 10 canoes.[81] Information on atoll fleet sizes comes from Ha'apai in Tonga and the Ratak chain in the Marshalls. In the early 1800s, Finau 'Ulukalala of Ha'apai invaded neighboring Vava'u with 5000 men, accompanied by 1000 women. The entire expedition was transported in a fleet of 50 large canoes. Such a force was unusual for atolls. The Ha'apai people had access to canoe timber from Fiji, while the size of the army suggests it included more than just Ha'apai men.[82] The fleet assembled by the northern Ratak ruler Lamari to invade the southern atoll of Majuro in 1817 numbered only 40 vessels. Noting that up to 10 people sailed on each canoe, Kotzebue estimated Lamari's force at 400 people. This was a significant commitment for the drought-prone atolls that constituted Lama-ri's sphere of influence.[83]

Do these fleet sizes mean that naval warfare was the predominant form of fighting? Cook certainly believed most battles in Tahiti were fought at sea. Sea battles were more decisive than those on land, as the vanquished party lacked the option of fleeing to safe havens like the mountain refuges used on land.[84] The large fleet witnessed by Cook was intended for use against neighboring Mo'orea Island so all the coalition's forces had to be transported by canoe. When war was conducted against opponents on the same island, combined land and sea operations tended to occur. The emphasis on land versus sea forces depended on the relative strength of the protagonists on land and sea, the distance to be traveled, and the ease of land (and particularly sea) communication.

The Hawaiian archipelago seems unsuited to naval warfare. It has dangerous channels between islands, and large sections of coast lack sheltered lagoons. Because the prevailing winds blow across the chain rather than along it, storms blow canoes out into the empty oceans. Despite these hazards, Hawaiians were enthusiastic and skilled seafarers who conducted naval operations along the length of their isolated archipelago. Traditions suggest that major inter-island expeditions were launched as early as the sixteenth century.[85] By the 1770s, Hawaiians conducted naval expeditions in sailing canoes up to 70 feet long with double hulls connected by a platform.[86] Most naval operations merely transported forces and provisions between islands. Military engagements and operations generally took place on land.

Samoans conducted combined land and sea operations. The usual strategy was to divide forces into coastal contingents that pinned the enemy down and smaller canoe-borne or inland forces that delivered surprise flank attacks.[87] In contrast, Palauans conducted both land and sea operations, but rarely launched combined operations. Palau was divided into territorially discrete polities known as *beluu,* the largest of which had populations numbering a few thousand. *Beluu* lacked the resources to launch combined operations, while much of the landmass consists of small rugged islands, which curtailed large-scale land operations.[88]

Political and geographical fragmentation extended beyond Palau. Throughout Oceania efforts to concentrate power were constrained by the nature of political power, as well as the demands of living in a sea of islands. All over the world the emergence of centralized power required the breakup of kin-based affiliations and their replacement with associations based on territory. There also needed to be a transition from personalized leadership to institutionalized offices of government to ensure continuity beyond the lifetime of a single ruler.[89] These processes had begun in some island polities, notably those in Hawai'i, by the late eighteenth century.[90] For most of the region, however, leadership remained personal, with loyalties still based on kin affiliations.

Kin-based loyalties present problems to rulers seeking to consolidate or expand power. Initially, a new paramount chief's kin support base would not be much larger than the more powerful chiefs in the polity. Unless frequent visits were made to areas away from the paramount chief's power base, local rulers might be tempted to assert their independence or even challenge the paramount chief. These dangers were enhanced by communication problems. Most land routes consisted of narrow trails, vulnerable to disruption by bad weather. Sea travel was also determined by the weather, especially in the absence of fringing reefs. These problems were exacerbated in larger polities. Political expansion increased the resource base, but ran the risk of overextending the realm. More resources might be needed to maintain coherence than were gained through expansion.[91]

The structure held together, in part, because the ruler's demands did not intrude too deeply into parochial worlds. Entrenched local kin-based power was not the only barrier. Logistical problems and individual displays of prowess in battle for chiefly and warrior prestige all worked against the formation of a full-time army loyal to the ruler. Dietary staples could be preserved in a relatively compact and transportable form to feed the armies. The problem was that economies were geared to the needs of a dispersed population. For most of the year, warriors needed to be scattered throughout the polity to rely on food from their own kin. Chiefly rights of expropriation were based on their sacred status, and could not be pushed too far without putting that status at risk. The problem was not production, but supply. To increase their military capacity, rulers needed to get enough food to their army for sustained periods in an essentially dispersed economy without placing too high a burden on any locality.[92]

These characteristics shaped the role of naval power. In an island with poor overland communications and no beasts of burden, sea power conferred mobility. Canoes were the only bulk carriers of men and supplies. With a fleet, the center became less remote in perception and reality to those contemplating rebellion. Those with naval forces could harass enemy coasts at will if not met by naval forces of comparable strength. While an army could contest landings, canoe-borne opponents could soon outdistance them and move on to attack unguarded coasts.

Unmatched naval power also made inshore waters dangerous for the weaker side. The dominant side did not have to maintain a permanent presence there to overawe the local community. In effect, these waters became a no-man's-land. This situation placed a severe strain on the defensive polity and eroded the *mana* of the ruler. When Hawaiian chiefs Kahekili and Kaeokulani conceded naval hegemony to Kamehameha in the early 1790s, for example, they then felt obliged to maintain a fully mobilized army on Maui for three years out of fear of sea-borne invasion. This exhausted the resources of Maui, and also the neighboring islands of Lanaʻi and Molokaʻi.[93]

The inhabitants of Peleliu in Palau came to fear sea raids from Koror to such an extent that they moved their settlements inland.[94] In the first decade of the 1800s the numerically inferior coral islanders of Haʻapai were able to force the larger population of Tongatapu onto the defensive through superior canoe numbers and seamanship. Tongatapuans paid a high price for being "better cultivators than seamen."[95] The 70-mile voyage from Haʻapai to Tongatapu could be completed in half a day with the right winds. Haʻapai forces could strike at will, and then retire to their canoes or offshore islands. Although they were unable to dominate on land, night raids were enough to persuade Tongatapuans to lock themselves up in fortified villages and neglect cultivations away from the immediate vicinity of settlements.[96] To the people of Tongatapu, Haʻapai men were truly *kakai me tahi*, a people from the sea.[97]

Political fragmentation meant that the arrival of even one or two canoe loads of warriors could have a significant impact on the balance of power. While they were not able to dominate local politics,[98] newcomers could tip the balance of power. This was particularly apparent in western Polynesia. Eastern Fiji's role as a gathering place for young Tongans seeking adventure or trade goods, or for defeated parties seeking refuge, has been noted.[99] Those who tired of their overseas adventures, or felt strong enough to challenge their rivals at home, returned to Tonga. English missionaries on Tongatapu recorded the arrival of a canoe from Fiji on March 16, 1799, followed by eight or nine more over the next four days. The canoes were manned by Tongans forced to flee to Fiji a decade earlier when supporters of Tukuʻaho defeated their party.[100] In 1803 and 1804 canoe loads of Tongans returned from eastern Fiji, drawn back by mounting tensions.[101] The unheralded return of these contingents, now with enhanced resources and military experience, made Tongan politics unstable.

Contingents of overseas warriors were not always a cause of instability. Astute rulers occasionally used them to consolidate or enhance their position. In the early nineteenth century warriors from the Society Islands' Leeward group came to play a prominent role in the affairs of Tahiti Nui, the main island of the Windward group. After 1800 the Pomare family of Tahiti Nui used kinship and marriage links to gain the support of Leeward rulers in their struggles with rivals on Tahiti Nui. Ra'iatean and Huahinean warriors became an important part of the Pomare's forces, particularly from 1808 until Pomare II's final victory at Fei Pi in 1815.[102] The vagaries of the sea passage rarely prevented Leeward Islanders from answering Pomare's call. One fleet even survived a violent storm mid-passage without the loss of a single canoe. Leeward flotillas occasionally lost canoes in bad weather, but the vast majority arrived to support their Windward ally.[103]

The fragmentation of power meant that quite small polities with naval capacity could exercise significant influence. They were often based on small islands off large islands, and included groups distinguished as "sea people." Bau, Manono, Borabora, Anaa, and Puluwat were good examples. Other small islands close to major islands were not as prominent, and formed part of larger polities. Examples included Kayangel Atoll off the northern cost of Babeldoab, Ni'ihau off Kaua'i, and Lana'i off Maui.

Sahlins has argued that Fijian polities were conceived of as unions between externally derived rulers with warrior followers and local cultivators of the land. These foreign warriors included *kai wai dina* (sea people), who were renowned for ferocity and skill as assassins.[104] Outside groups continued to move between polities as their fortunes waxed and waned, so that *vanua* (Fijian polities) consisted of a variety of kin groups.[105] The tiny island of Bau was the *vanua* most clearly associated with sea people. Half a mile off the east coast of Viti Levu, Bau is only 20 acres in extent. It was founded in the 1750s, and rose to become Fiji's leading naval power by the 1840s. Its war canoes were feared throughout the archipelago.

Bau's initial strength was based on an alliance between the founding chiefly line from the interior of Viti Levu and the seafaring inhabitants of Bau—the Butoni. Other seafaring people joined later. When disputes arose, the Butoni and Soso migrated to various localities around the eastern islands of Fiji. They retained links with Bau, however, which strengthened Bau's influence in the east. Bauans were able to gain greater access to *vesi* wood of the southern Lau group for their canoes. Bauans also extended their influence through marriage, although ultimately their influence rested on the power of their fleet.[106]

The sea people of Bau were also fishers of men, much feared for their cruelty and ferocity. The Levuka, the Butoni, and especially the Lasakau were prominent in this role. Lasakau means "at home on a spear." They resided at Bau, but spent most of their time in their canoes. They secured human sacrifices for Bau when required.[107] One such occasion was the launching of war canoes.[108] A Western observer who met the leader of the Lasakau in the 1850s described him as "a noted Cannibal & cruel & wily villain. He is mentioned in Mr. Young's 'Southern World' as the person who kidnapped the women on the reef & took them to be killed and eaten at the Heathen feast at Bau." His companions were described as "a very wild looking crew."[109] Jaggar noted that after Bau stormed Verata, Lasakau warriors burned the town and tied Veratan children to the masts of their canoes. The children were blown about by the wind as the canoes sailed home so that they were eventually beaten to death against the masts.[110] Bau was not alone in relying on sea people as the nucleus of its naval and military forces. Groups such as the Macui of Verata, the Vutia, Nukui and Nasilai fishermen of Rewa, and the Navatu people of Cakaudrove filled similar roles.[111]

The island of Manono in Samoa was also famous for its sea power. Off the western end of Upolu, but within its fringing reef, Manono is strategically placed between Upolu and Savai'i. A strong fleet gave Manono control of the seas between the two islands, as well as access to allies in Tonga and Samoa.[112] Its people were greatly feared for their ability to launch surprise raids by sea.[113] To other Samoans, the Manono people were *'Aiga i le tai* (the family in the sea).[114] Manono's naval strength was reinforced by its control of the neighboring island of Apolima, which formed a near impregnable refuge. Apolima is a drowned volcanic crater whose seaward coast consisted of 200- to 300-foot cliffs with only one narrow, easily defended entrance into its sheltered anchorage. The interior slopes were fertile and well watered. Although the Manono people were forced to leave Manono on a number of occasions, they were never conquered because of their ability to regroup on Apolima.[115]

The Fanui people of Borabora were infamous for their raids on neighboring islands. The reputation of Borabora among Tahitians was reflected in such titles as "Porapora of the fleet that consumes two ways," "Porapora the destroyer of fleets," and "Porapora of the muffled paddle."[116] The latter title was a reference to the tactic of launching raids with small fleets using muffled paddles.[117] Borabora had risen from relative obscurity to dominate the Leeward Islands sometime shortly before the arrival of Cook in 1769. Huahine men told a member of Cook's expedition that

Borabora warriors descended on Huahine "every month or six weeks taking away their things and killing all that Oppose them."[118] When Cook returned to Tahiti in the 1770s he found that many considered the Boraborans to be invincible. He was told that Borabora warriors

> never fly in battle, and that they always beat an equal number of the other islanders. But, besides these advantages, their neighbours seem to ascribe a great deal to the superiority of their god, who they believed detained us at Ulietea by contrary winds, as being unwilling that we should visit an island under his special protection.[119]

For part of the late eighteenth century, the *ari'i* (chief) Puni ruled over Ra'iatea and Huahine from Borabora through deputies.[120] The sudden rise of the Fanui on Borabora may have been assisted by recent arrivals. Sydney Parkinson noted that in the recent past the chiefs of Tahiti and a number of adjacent islands had banished thieves and other criminals to Borabora.[121] Instead of isolating undesirable elements, the move may have concentrated them. Now they were returning to take vengeance under the cover of muffled paddles.

Some atolls also influenced large areas through coercive means. Anaa dominated the entire Tuamotu chain in the early 1800s. While the archipelago is largely drought-prone and resource-poor, Anaa could sustain a much larger population than other atolls because of its rich coconut groves. Anaa's population was approximately 2000 in the 1840s out of an estimated 6500 people in the entire chain. The Anaa people used their 60 large double canoes to raid their neighbors. They were careful to destroy crops and coconut trees on these raids, enhancing their relative strength.[122] The inhabitants of Puluwat in the central Carolines dominated not only their immediate neighbors Pulap and Pulusuk, but also influenced affairs on several high islands in Chuuk Lagoon. Puluwatese influence was based on their seafaring ability and large number of sailing canoes that enabled them to deliver warriors swiftly and without warning to the locality of their choosing. In this way they could gain a local advantage despite their small population. While the Puluwatese lacked the manpower to control islands in Chuuk, they were valued as allies because of the highly factionalized nature of Chuukese society.[123]

Some sea people improved their effectiveness in battle by incorporating elements from the sea into their weaponry and apparel. The inhabitants of Kiribati and Hawai'i fitted sharks' teeth to their spears and daggers. Warriors in Kiribati wore full suits of armor made from coconut

sennit to protect themselves from the slashing wounds that these weapons could inflict.[124] The people of Mataia (Mehetia) went even further.
Cook records how

> the men of Mataia also wear their hair very long; and when they fight,
> cover their arms with a substance which is beset with sharks teeth, and
> their bodies with a sort of shagreen, being skin of fishes. At the same time,
> they are ornamented with polished pearl shells, which make a prodigious
> glittering in the sun; and they have a very large one that covers them
> before, like a shield or breastplate.[125]

The appearance of the warriors of Mehetia was clearly designed to set
them apart. While other sea people did not dress as distinctly, they were
still readily recognized. Their ferocity and arrogance also set them apart.
Tuamotuans called Anaans *Parata,* after a large ferocious man-eating
shark.[126] These intruders were also a fact of life as spheres of influence
and zones of control waxed and waned, while social networks brought
more welcome visitors from beyond the horizon. Pacific historians have
been slow to take account of the extent to which external influences
affected communities on the eve of sustained Western contact. Any
attempt to evaluate the impact of Western influence must view the arrival
of these new sea people in the context of existing expectations and patterns of behavior toward elements from beyond the horizon.

Across the Horizon:
Interactions with
the Outside World

MOST ISLANDERS expected intrusions from beyond the horizon. Some devastated entire communities. Expectations and realities led to the development of behavior and protocols to deal with unheralded arrivals from across the sea. The world beyond the horizon was also seen as one filled with opportunity, as it had been for generations. This was a world of long-term cultural continuities, punctuated by periods of rapid change. The expansive world of the people of the sea meant that few localities were totally isolated. External influences could dramatically alter local worlds.

Europeans became increasingly prominent in this process from the late eighteenth century. The flow of Western influence up to 1870 and beyond needs to be viewed alongside the continuing intrusion of preexisting elements from beyond the horizon. In this chapter European and Islander intrusions are examined together, particularly those that affected maritime life. These human elements are examined alongside meteorological intrusions, to present a more complex perspective on Islanders' interactions with the outside world. Islanders were far more expectant of outside influences than has generally been acknowledged. This outlook made them better able to respond to influences from beyond the horizon.

Perceptions of the World beyond the Horizon

Samoans and Tongans referred to Europeans as *papālangi* (sky bursters). Some infer that this was because the radically different appearance and behavior of these strangers led Islanders to believe that they had literally burst through the dome of heaven that marked the limits of the known world. They had come from another world. To the Samoans and Tongans, at least, the known world was a complete universe of sea and lands, contained by the dome of the sky and divided into invisible layers containing the living places of gods. Below the sea was the realm of Pulotu, entered by the spirits of the aristocratic dead through an entrance under the sea, off the westernmost shore of the islands.[1]

As the horizon in most of Oceania occurs where the sky appears to meet the sea, gods and ancestral spirits were described as coming from the sea or from beyond the horizon.[2] Hocart noted that the Fijian term for spirits *(kalou)* also carried an association with a distant place.[3] Strangers with remarkable technology from beyond the horizon would naturally be seen as gods or spirits.

Most societies divide their worlds into the near and familiar, and the more distant and unusual.[4] In Remote Oceania, the border between these two zones usually lay at some ill-defined point on the sea's surface. The realms of the familiar and the strange transcended this border, however. Pacific spaces consisted of multiple, parallel worlds—familiar seas close to home were infused with supernatural elements. Seas beyond the horizon were believed to harbor more supernatural elements and dangers than seas closer to home, but these existed side by side with familiar elements; old lands vaguely remembered, new lands, new people, and new opportunities.

Chapter 2 traced the Hawaiian names for the sea's zones radiating out from shore as far as *kai hi aku,* the seas of the outermost fishing expeditions. Beyond this lay a zone known as *kai kohala,* where whales and monsters were found. The sea then passed into *moana* (the deep ocean) that extended all the way to *Kahiki moe* (the utmost bounds of the ocean).[5] Hawaiians first encountered gods on *moana* off Keʻei in South Kona when two fishermen named Kuheleimoana and Kuheleipo saw the spirit forms of the gods Kane, Kanaloa, and Haumea coming over the surface from Kahiki.[6] The gods of Kapingamarangi also made themselves visible to their worshippers at sea, as some monster of the deep, particularly an eel or a squid. Their appearance was a sign that a *tapu* had been broken.[7]

Sea monsters of fearsome size inhabited these distant seas. A Tahitian chant about a voyage to Hiti-Poto (short border or Mangareva) recorded on Borabora in 1825 mentions a mid-ocean encounter with the sea serpent Ahifa tu moana. This was followed by struggles with the wave spirits Are mata roroa (long wave) and Are mata popoto (short wave), and a giant tridacna shell. The voyagers reached Hiti Poto safely and pressed on to

Hiti au rereva (Pitcairn).[8] The fact that the voyage succeeded was important. These tales inspired rather than deterred voyaging. Māori, however, had ceased to venture far from the coasts of Aotearoa by 1770. The Southern Ocean was a place of danger, the lair of *taniwha*, frightening and unpredictable spirits. The rise and fall of the tide was the breath of Te Parata, son of Tangaroa, who took the form of a giant monster that lived in the deepest part of the ocean. Humans were creatures of Tane, who controlled the land. They were the enemies of his rival Tangaroa, lord of the sea. Men attacked the sea by fishing, and the sea retaliated by sinking their canoes.[9]

Like most other Islanders, Hawaiians conceived of their islands as existing within a dome of the sky that enclosed multiple dimensions. The border where the sky met the ocean was *kukulu-o-ka-lani* (the walls of heaven).[10] Tahitians also believed that the sky joined the sea at the horizon, or just beyond it.[11] They believed that the sun sank into the sea every evening and passed through a submarine passage, to rise the next morning. No one had ever seen the sun plunge into the sea, but some on Bora-bora and Maupiti, the westernmost inhabited islands of the chain, claimed to have heard hissing as it made contact with the ocean.[12]

Objects occasionally came into the Islanders' worlds from beyond the horizon. Logs drifted to Hawai'i from North America, and into the Carolines from New Guinea, flushed out to sea by rains in the headwaters of great rivers like the Columbia and Sepik.[13] Large drift logs were reported even farther from the continental margins. One of Kotzebue's officers found large logs that resembled oaks on an atoll in the Marshalls.[14] These may have come from the Americas, as Kotzebue's expedition was told about a beam with an iron band that had drifted from the northeast.[15] Water-borne pumice also occasionally fetched up on island shores. A large amount came to the Marshalls in 1884 as a result of the eruption of Krakatoa in 1883.[16] Driftwood and pumice did not necessarily indicate land beyond the horizon. Satawalese believed that the driftwood brought north by storms came from Yuweyuweyéér, an area of sea controlled by resident spirits.[17] Most Islanders believed that flotsam was a gift from the gods, sent from the sacred ocean in which they dwelt.[18]

Hawaiians acknowledged that humans also passed through the wall of heaven. The annual *makahiki* celebration was a reminder. *Makahiki*, or *ma-tahiti*, referred to a voyage from a distant place, and celebrated the journey of the god Lono to Hawai'i.[19] Hawaiians said little about encountering the wall of heaven themselves. When Lutké asked a Mortlock Islander what lay west of Pelly (Palau), the man "drew a line and indicated very clearly with gestures that the sky leans on the sea there, and that you have to crawl under it."[20] Tahitians conceived the world beyond as a series of domed worlds just like their own, where the world of humans existed alongside that of gods, spirits, and monsters. They believed that Marquesans, Tongans, British, and Spanish all lived within such worlds, each of which had a distinct atmosphere.[21]

Islands floated throughout these distant seas and parallel dimensions. One must take care to distinguish different types of islands in traditions and legends. Some were spirit isles that existed in a parallel dimension as the home of spirits and the final destination of souls. On occasion they were visible to humans, who were rarely able to reach them. The legend of Kane-huna-moku (Kane's hidden land) tells how Kane was banished to a floating land inhabited by dwarfs, for desecrating a garden. He was informed that his land was sacred and could only be seen by humans during certain *kapu* periods in July and August, when it was seen to hover near Haena on Kaua'i. At this time, it was near the floating island of Kaonohiula, a beautiful residence of Kane and Kanaloa. Floating islands moved on the wind at night.[22] Perhaps the most famous in Hawaiian legend was Paliuli, the paradise of the gods, which floated above the clouds or rested upon the earth at the will of its keeper. In ancient times it was associated with the deep seas, but later it was identified with an area of upland forest between Hilo and Puna on Hawai'i. A mortal, Nauahi of Hilo, once chanced upon Paliuli, but when she brought others back to see it the gods hid it.[23] Kuaihelani (supporting heaven) was the land most often mentioned in legends about visits to the heavens or to lands distant from Hawai'i. It lay 40 days sailing west of Hawai'i, where the sun set into the deep blue sea, but in another dimension.[24]

Marshallese believed that particularly attractive spirit beings called *muniak* lived on islands near their own. *Muniak* and their islands were normally invisible to humans. Only women desired by *muniak* and the offspring of their unions with *muniak* were able to see *muniak* and their world.[25] The souls of the dead lived on two islands to the west. Those of the good lived contentedly on Juirik, while the souls of evil people were condemned to suffer on Laulib. The souls' journey to these islands went through Narikerik Island near Mille Atoll, where they prepared provisions for the journey from *nin,* a slimy creeper growing on the beach.[26] Spirit paths to their eventual resting-places were a feature of the cultural landscapes and seascapes of most Islanders. They culminated in leaping places, where souls sought to enter the afterlife. Many were on hills overlooking the sea, the most notable being the pohutakawa tree that clung to a cliff above Te Reinga (the leaping place) in Muriwhenua.[27] From here, the soul left the realm of humans and entered the world of the spirits. Hawaiian spirits needed the guidance of their ancestral spirits to make this transition. Those denied this assistance were condemned to wander in desolate isolation on earth, or to dwell in *milu,* the place of endless darkness.[28]

Floating islands were not necessarily mythical. Discovered islands were described as fish tethered by vine, rope, or fishhook to the bottom of the sea so that they did not drift away. Navigational knowledge was the vine that secured them and prevented them from drifting into oblivion. Oʻahu, for example, was once a floating island, *he ʻaina lewa o Oʻahu,* until it was secured by fishhooks.[29] Islands described as floating and drifting, or being hidden from view by the gods, may well have been real. Details of their location may have been lost with the death of navigators, or simply have faded from the collective memory as contacts waned.

The legend of Pulotu is particularly germane. Western Polynesians believed Pulotu to be their original homeland. Descriptions of it contain many of the elements cited above, such as its ability to float and its elusive quality. It was often smelled on the wind, but rarely seen. It was also believed to be the paradise where the souls of chiefs went. Treating Polynesian legends as stories built around a factual core, Paul Geraghty interprets this to mean that Pulotu was the homeland of the most recent ruling chiefs of the region. He proposes that the legends of Pulotu refer to a location in southern Lau, most probably the island of Matuku.[30] Matuku became the center for the lucrative *kula* (red parrot feather) trade around 2000 BP, after other stocks were depleted. Linguistic evidence suggests that its fame spread throughout Polynesia (with the exception of isolated Rapanui) as Fanuakula (Golden Land).[31] Eventually the two polities of Burotu and Babajea on Matuku went to war to control declining stocks of *kula.* The war resulted in migrations. The migrants' martial skill enabled them to impose their control on a number of localities, including Tonga and Samoa.[32] When Matuku's *kula* was depleted, the trade moved to other locations such as Kadavu. Matuku faded from prominence, and Burotu became a mythical disappearing island peopled only by females, full of valued items and the source of all things exotic. The reference to a disappearing island may also be to a natural disaster involving inundation. This area is subject to tsunami and tectonic disturbances, both of which could inundate the coast. As the importance of Matuku declined, the exact location of Burotu faded from the memory of the migrants' offspring. Eventually it became Pulotu, an abode of departed spirits and the source of exotic goods.[33]

Early European accounts of navigators' knowledge of islands beyond their normal sailing range demonstrate how memories of islands remained after regular contact ceased. Some were remembered as detailed sailing directions, while the memory of others faded to become the distant and elusive homes of gods and spirits. Perhaps the best example was the testimony of the Tahitian priest and navigator Tupaia,[34] who named seventy-four islands for Cook, including islands 1400 miles west of Tahiti in western Polynesia. The only Polynesian groups not referred to seem to have been Aotearoa, Hawai'i, and the Gambier group.[35] After initially claiming to have sailed to all these islands, Tupaia conceded that he had only visited twelve. Nine were in the Society group, while the other three were Mehetia, Rurutu, and 'Manua.' Dening believes that Tupaia's Manua is the small Cook Island atoll of Manuae, three days' sail northeast of Rurutu. Others claim that it refers to Manu'a in Samoa.[36] While the former is more consistent with the sailing range of the other eight islands, Gunson notes that the chiefly families of Manu'a and the Cook Islands were linked by marriage.[37] The remaining islands were part of the pool of knowledge passed down from generation to generation by navigators. Tupaia frequently referred to information given to him by his father and grandfather.[38]

Intrusions from across the Sea

Geraghty's interpretation of Pulotu is consistent with Islander political and social philosophy, which centered on the idea of melding local and exotic elements. Gavan Daws, for example, notes that power in Hawai'i was "always violent, always usurping, came from the outside, and belonged to strangers. But authority was always legitimate, always came from within, belonged to those born with it, belonged to natives."[39] Hawaiians referred to their chiefs as sharks that walked on land—wild elements that needed controlling. History taught that strangers came to overthrow rulers. They then married the highest-born local women to gain legitimacy, as they rarely had sufficient numbers to sustain their position without local cooperation.[40] Relations might be tense and filled with suspicion, but there was little alternative. Rulers who offended their people could not rely on their support when the next usurper arrived, and might even face a challenge from within.[41]

Europeans may also have seemed usurping strangers arriving to challenge local rulers, as had been the pattern since the dawn of time.[42] Most scholars suggest that Europeans were radically different than previous intruders.[43] Prior to their arrival, most outsiders had broadly similar appearance and ways of behaving, regardless of whether they were drift voyagers or visiting kin. Even hostile invaders usually came from the known world of the communities they attacked. Other Islanders might not speak the same language, but they generally acted in ways that made sense to those encountering them.

Between 1770 and 1870 there are few instances of encounters between total strangers involving only Islanders. The one detailed reference located is worth recounting in detail. Around 1870 a large fleet was scattered in a storm between Ebon and Majuro in the Marshalls. A number of canoes managed to keep together and eventually drifted to the remote atoll of Kapingamarangi. The locals were of Polynesian origin, and found the Marshallese sufficiently different to emphasize their appearance.[44] German ethnographers in the early 1900s were told how a number of big canoes had arrived with many men and women:

> They looked like the people here, but others say they were black (dark owing to sunburning). The men carried spears with shark's teeth, but they had no bows. The women were clothed in pandanus mat aprons decorated with black patterns. The men's hair was compressed into a tuft over the crown of the head, the women's was tied together in the nape of the neck. The men were tattooed on the chest, lines running from the nipples and meeting on the belly (Whether their backs were tattooed the teller could not say for sure). They said that their home was Maturu and Japon (Maturu = Majuro; Japon = Ebon; both belong to the Marshall Islands group).[45]

Their behavior shocked the Kapinga people. They showed little respect from the outset. Landing on the islet of Hale, they helped themselves to coconuts without asking permission. Once they had recovered from their voyage they attacked the natives of Hale and other islets, killing men, women, and children indiscriminately. The inhabitants offered little resistance as their sacred leader, Takau, and their secular chief, Tikoro, were slain. Property was left intact, apart from the cult house on Touhou, which was burned to the ground. The slaughter eventually ended, and the survivors settled down to an uneasy coexistence with their tormentors. A number of women were forced to live with Marshallese men. Estimates of the relative strength of the Kapinga population and their Marshallese tormenters vary. The Kapinga probably never numbered more than 450. Many had perished in a severe drought around 1850, so they may still have not recovered when the Marshallese arrived. The population was recorded as only 150 in 1883. The Marshallese numbers are merely stated at between three and eight canoe loads.[46] The misery of Kapingamarangi eventually ended when the schooner *Matautu* picked up the castaways in 1872 and took them home. The Kapinga were left bewildered, explaining this episode as punishment from their god for neglect of ritual by Tikoro.

Europeans had an uneven impact before 1870. Māori were the only group in Remote Oceania to become a minority in their own land before 1870. Elsewhere, Western settlement was limited to a few thousand people concentrated around one or two port towns, or a handful of beachcombers. In many locations, contacts were limited to visits from naval and trading vessels manned by crews of five to a few hundred men.[47] Few were able to impose their will without naval support. Even then, naval expeditions soon had to move on. Most local economies were able to meet the demand for provisions from visiting vessels, providing they did not outstay their welcome.[48] Most localities hosted larger groups than these in the course of their normal social relations. The desire for Western goods did cause some communities to alter production. This was perhaps most notable in growing food to cater to Western palates around ports like Honolulu for whaling fleets and trading vessels, and Māori growing flax to trade for muskets.[49]

Pacific history has led the way in examining the cultural logic behind the exchange of items and ideas between Europeans and Islanders. Island beaches are portrayed as transformative spaces and processes where objects, ideas, and individuals move between cultures, mediated by power relations and acculturation.[50] Cultural differences are portrayed as a driving force behind the "sickening cycle of friendly welcomes, misunderstandings, sullen retreats, occasional reconciliations, robberies and killings"[51] that typified much of this interaction.

Not all scholars subscribe to this perspective. Campbell points out that Pacific history has vacillated between explanations of culture contact that emphasize differences in cultural understanding, and those that opt for explanations based on desires to advance one's interests in terms of power, material possessions, and physical comforts. Campbell takes issue with the idea that most conflicts occurred in contact situations because Islanders did not share the European belief about private property. Europeans often took offense when Islanders took goods without asking permission. Campbell notes that W. H. Pearson's influential thesis that Islanders believed they had the right as hosts to take visitors' goods is based on one reference to the reception of Kau Moala in Futuna. It is not clear that this was the practice elsewhere. Campbell demonstrates that there was a clear distinction between open attempts to take goods off Western vessels and efforts to conceal them. He demonstrates that Polynesians had the concept of property rights and punished theft severely.[52]

Campbell suggests that these situations reveal not a clash of two cultures, but the moderation of cultural practices to suit what both sides realized was an unusual situation. The result was a culture of contact, where unusual patterns of behavior occurred in response to the unfamiliarity and uncertainty present. Polynesians would initially apply rituals and practices normally used to greet strangers, but they might also practice unusual behavior, such as giving their women for material gain and to placate the foreigners. Similarly, Europeans sometimes overlooked theft in the name of maintaining peace.[53] Campbell also suggests that references to Europeans as *papālangi, papaa,* or *etua* was not a mark of respect associating them with the gods, but a temporary label denoting anything unfamiliar and yet to be understood.[54] The equivalent today would be the term *UFO.* Gunson notes that *papaa* was simply the word for foreigner in eastern Polynesia, while *papālangi* was translated as the "land of strangers" in some early European sources and as "cloth from the sky" (European manufactures) in others.[55]

Some associated these strangers with the spirit world. These beliefs persisted in places. Sahlins points out that beachcombers in Fiji were still being asked if they were spirits decades after they arrived.[56] Islanders eventually came to realize that these strangers were merely men with extraordinary capabilities. As outsiders, they were also a means by which ambitious chiefs could circumvent convention. Chiefs such as Naulivou of Bau employed musket-armed beachcombers to violate the sacred immunity of Fijian chiefs in battle. It was perhaps this tactic, rather than the muskets used to achieve it, which gave beachcombers such a decisive impact. These new outsiders altered the balance between internal legitimacy and external usurping force, tipping the scales in favor of the latter.[57] Campbell notes that while Islanders initially believed that Westerners' capabilities derived from their gods, they soon realized that these skills could be emulated. Campbell also detects cultural chauvinism in Polynesian attitudes toward Westerners and their ways, which was only questioned in times of self-doubt such as during virulent epidemics.[58]

Introduced diseases were the element of Western contact that Island communities were least able to counteract. The fatal impact thesis is most often associated with the trauma caused by introduced diseases. Fatal impact was brought into question in the 1960s and 1970s, as many estimates of death rates were lowered and significant variation in the demographic history of individual islands and communities was recognized.[59] The idea of Western contact as fatal has experienced a resurgence in the past two decades with the advent of environmental histories that include disease among the exotic invaders.[60] These decades have also seen the rise of a body of literature that seeks to reexamine the impact of European colonialism from the perspective of indigenous people. These works often include significant upward revisions of populations at contact. Such revisions require far higher death rates to reach the population figures recorded later in the nineteenth century. This perspective has been most forcefully articulated in David Stannard's works on the demographic collapse of the Hawaiian population.[61]

There is a good deal of evidence to show that epidemics introduced by Western vessels struck the islands from the time of Cook's expedition onward. Possibly the most dramatic was that which ravaged Oʻahu in 1804.[62] It seems probable that venereal disease was also introduced early, and contributed to population decline in a less dramatic way by causing infertility. Hawaiian histories certainly attribute most of the population decline to loss of fertility from sexual diseases acquired in liaisons with sailors. This infertility is ranked ahead of epidemics, wars, and infanticide as the leading cause of the Hawaiian population's decline in the fifty years following Cook's arrival.[63] The technical details concerning the demographic impact of Western diseases remain far from resolved. The social impact is also unclear. It may have been a major factor behind the rejection of the old ways that was so apparent among many *aliʻi* in the first decades of the nineteenth century. There is little evidence of a crisis of confidence. Agricultural production increased in some areas after 1800 in response to Western trade.[64] In the first decade of the century, Campbell found the population of the western part of the island of Hawaiʻi numerous and industrious.[65] The situation had changed dramatically by the middle of the nineteenth century. Infertility was now so widespread that Hawaiians began to wonder if their race would become extinct.[66]

Epidemics and rising infertility were a traumatic and regular part of life for many of the region's inhabitants between 1770 and 1870. Other destructive forces from beyond the horizon also took their toll. Few Islanders reached old age without experiencing the destructive forces of nature. While the overall death toll from natural disasters was probably well below that caused by disease, they could be equally devastating on specific localities. Rarely a decade passed without some community being leveled. Although these episodes are important indicators of Islanders' capacity to deal with disruption and population loss, they have received little attention from scholars.

Introduced and natural hazards occasionally combined to produce what must have seemed truly apocalyptic conditions. In the first decade of the nineteenth century Fiji experienced a total eclipse of the sun in 1803, the passage of a comet across the heavens in either 1805 or 1807, an epidemic of dysentery, a hurricane, and the inundation of many coastal areas as a result of either a tsunami or cyclonic storm waves.[67] Similar calamities occurred in the early 1840s that were later seen as portents of the bloody struggle between the rival powers Bau and Rewa. On February 25, 1840, a violent storm struck the archipelago. Flooding of much of the Rewa Delta followed. Then on August 2, 1841, there was a total eclipse of the sun. The Lau Islands were struck by a severe hurricane in late January 1842. The portents ended with a comet that crossed the skies during March 1843.[68] Guam fared even worse in the late 1840s. The island was struck by three typhoons in 1847, another in June 1848, followed by a super-typhoon in August. The next year brought no respite as a whaling ship introduced influenza, followed by a major earthquake on January 25, 1849. Finally, a plague of worms devoured most crops in July and August.[69]

These periods were abnormal. Records suggest that individual islands in Remote Oceania experience, at most, five to six typhoons per generation. Typhoons vary in intensity. The most destructive are super-typhoons, which usually only occur once a century in any locality and are capable of destroying communities totally. Even if people survive the high winds and storm waves, they face starvation in the wake of the destruction of flora and fauna. High winds blow over trees, and defoliate those that remain standing. Breadfruit trees are particularly susceptible to wind damage. Salt from sea spray and storm waves destroys crops and delays regeneration by altering the soil chemistry and biology. A "dry" typhoon will still generate the high winds that cause wind damage and inundation, but not the rains associated with "wet" typhoons, which dilute the salinity resulting from the invasion of the sea. Regeneration also depends on how many trees are blown down. Saplings fare better than more mature trees because of their low height and more flexible structure. Trees begin to recover by putting out new leaves to resume photosynthesis, before they produce fruit and flowers.[70]

Buzacott left a chilling account of a hurricane that battered Rarotonga on March 16–17, 1846. He noted that strong winds buffeted the island from the east during the 16th, increasing in violence until 1:00 A.M. on the 17th. Then a lull descended as the eye of the storm passed over. The respite was short-lived:

> a rumbling sound was heard in the distance in an almost opposite direction, W.N.W., like thunder, and swept over the island. The night was of the most awful description. Though only a few days after the full of the moon, it was pitch dark. The only light was that afforded by incessant and vivid flashes of lightning. The rain descended in torrents. The trees shivered to pieces or torn up by the roots, houses blown to fragments, and their foundations swept away by the sea. Every inhabitant of our settlement was exposed to the pitiless storm from 10 P.M. till the morning dawned, except a few who managed to shelter in our house, and two cottages in the settlement which escaped destruction.[71]

Buzacott had to pile furniture against his door to keep it closed. He only opened the door to admit those begging for shelter. All told of being washed out of their homes by the seas that had broken over the reef and were sweeping over the coastal lowlands. The sound of neighboring houses being torn apart and windblown debris thudding against the house punctuated the night. Two windows were shattered, allowing the wind to blow in. The heavy rainfall caused a cascade of water to pour off the mountains onto the inundated coastal plain. The rush of water down the slope destroyed a stone wall at the rear of Buzacott's house, forced in his back door, and flowed through the house. Soon water was also pouring through the saturated thatch roof. He went outside with some Rarotongan parishioners for a few minutes to clear away rubbish blocking the outflow of water from his house, and described the experience as "like standing under a cataract." A desolate scene greeted survivors the next morning:

> A few headless cocoa-nut trees are the only conspicuous objects in the universal waste. Our beautiful stone school-house lies in a mass of ruins, broken down by the united force of sea and wind. The streets are impassable from the heaps of large pieces of coral left by the receding waves.[72]

It takes months, or even years, before vegetation recovers from storms of this magnitude.[73] Meanwhile, birds, insects, and animals that depend on leaves and fruit may perish.[74] Storm waves can also smash the living coral communities of fringing reefs, reducing the number of fish they can support.[75] Famine is a real possibility. Buzacott recorded how a hurricane destroyed most crops on Rarotonga in December 1831. At this time of the year the fruit was still not ripe. Fruit trees had either been torn up by the roots, or denuded, so that the only fruit remaining lay bruised and saturated with saltwater where it had fallen. Taro pits were inundated. The survivors gorged themselves on the green fruit and salty taro before it began to rot. Within two weeks they were living off roots and any fish they could catch. It would be years before crops and trees would again provide an adequate supply of food. In their weakened state the people became even more vulnerable to disease.[76] Starvation was not necessarily the most worrying legacy. Boddam-Whetham found that in the wake of a hurricane that struck Rotuma in the early 1870s, "the loss of the bones of their ancestors which were swept off by the sea was a great grief to the natives, who regarded it as a greater calamity than the impending famine."[77]

Typhoons are particularly destructive on coral islands. Some generate 20-foot waves that break up coral on the seaward face of the reef and wash it onto the reef flat and beaches. They also wash beach sand inland as they surge over low-lying islands. The vegetation that survives is saturated with saltwater, as is the groundwater that it depends on. A few hardy plants that colonize the shoreline tolerate salinity, but most food crops and larger trees cannot. The salt in the soil and groundwater attracts water, reducing that available to plants. Salt deposited on surviving vegetation pulls water out of them by osmosis, effectively creating drought. If severe typhoons occur more frequently than the five to seven years required for flora to recover, only hardy wind- and salt-tolerant species may recolonize the land.[78]

Islanders developed strategies to deal with these conditions. Buzacott noted that Rarotongans planted papaw after the devastation of their preferred crops, as it was the fastest species to yield edible fruits.[79] If social order was maintained, the survivors could be mobilized to gather what food remained. The anthropologist Tomoya Akimichi describes how chiefs on Satawal organized society after a typhoon in 1958. They initiated relief measures known collectively as *yammenaw* (to give life). Fallen coconuts were collected and stored, while fallen breadfruit was preserved in *ma* pits before it rotted. Taro from inundated pits was either consumed before it rotted or transplanted to drier ground. Food was shared equally regardless of whose land it came from. Food exchanges were made between men and women to maximize access to all foods and enhance the sense of solidarity needed for survival. Finally, broken trees were felled to

CATEGORY	NAME	MAXIMUM SUSTAINED WIND MPH [KPH]	PEAK GUSTS MPH [KPH]	POTENTIAL DAMAGE
Tropical storm 1	Strong tropical depression/weak tropical storm	30–49 [48–79]	40–64 [64–103]	Minor damage to bananas and agricultural crops; little or no penetration of waves across reefs.
Tropical storm 2	Severe tropical storm	50–73 [80–118]	65–89 [105–143]	Moderate damage to bananas and most crops; large dead limbs, ripe coconuts blown from trees.
Typhoon 1	Weak typhoon	74–90 [119–144]	91–115 [146–185]	Major damage to crops; some young trees downed; less than 10% defoliation of trees; some live branches broken.
Typhoon 2	Moderate typhoon	91–110 [146–177]	116–130 [187–209]	Bananas totally destroyed; 10–20% defoliation of trees; many palm fronds damaged and limbs of other trees broken off; some trees blown down.
Typhoon 3	Strong typhoon	111–130 [179–209]	131–160 [211–257]	Major damage to trees and shrubbery; up to 50% of palm fronds bent or blown off; a few palms decrowned; some ironwood trunks snapped; 30–50% defoliation for most trees, up to 70% for tangantangan; considerable beach erosion.
Typhoon 4	Severe typhoon	131–155 [211–249]	161–190 [259–306]	Shrubs and trees 50–80% defoliated, tangantangan 100%; many trees downed; extensive beach erosion; inundation likely to 10 ft. elevation; many well-built wooden structures severely damaged or destroyed.
Typhoon 5	Extreme typhoon (equivalent to super-typhoon)	156–190 [251–305]	191–230 [307–370]	Shrubs and trees up to 100% defoliated; up to 100% palm fronds bent or broken off; numerous palms decrowned and other trees toppled; inundation likely to 12–15 ft.; severe beach erosion; only concrete buildings survive, some structural damage.

TABLE 1 Relative destructive force of tropical cyclone. (Lobban and Schefter, 110, after Guard and Lander)

allow others to grow in their place. As most sailing canoes had been destroyed by the typhoon, more effective use had to be made of near-shore fisheries. Chiefs organized large-scale fishing operations such as communal fish drives, and directed the distribution of fish to make sure everyone received a share. Canoes were repaired to allow the resumption of offshore fishing. Continuous fishing expeditions were allowed for one month, with crews being spelled to keep them fresh.[80]

Post-typhoon recovery measures had their limits. Ultimately, survival depended on how much food remained. If the typhoon had caused too much damage, survivors had to seek sustenance elsewhere, or perish. Social and political links forged and maintained through regular visits meant that refuge was usually near at hand. These links had to be wide-ranging, however, as some major typhoons could devastate whole archipelagos. When Typhoon Owen crossed the western Carolines in November and December 1990, the atolls of the Hall Islands, Namonuito, Pulap, Satawal, Lamotrek, Elato, Ifalik, and Woleai all lost over 90 percent of their dwellings and food crops, while Faraulep, Ulithi, and Chuuk had up to 30 percent of their human infrastructure destroyed.[81]

A typhoon of similar magnitude seems to have hit the eastern Carolines sometime between 1775 and 1780. Traditions about it were recorded in the middle of the nineteenth century on Kosrae, Pingelap, Mwaekil, and Pohnpei.[82] These four islands lie in a straight line marking the path of the typhoon. Kosraen legends record how the typhoon destroyed the island of Kiol, and the sea wall and western end of Leluh, the great artificial settlement built out into Leluh harbor. Almost half of Kosrae's population lived at Leluh at the time. Many lives and all food crops were lost. Famine raged as the survivors fought each other for food left in the forests and parties scoured the reef. This typhoon is remembered as Man Sisik—the typhoon that destroyed Kosrae. European visitors in the early 1800s were informed that Leluh was now a mere remnant of its former self.[83] Records are less clear for Pohnpei. Man Sisik may have been the legendary typhoon that stripped the island down to naked earth, and caused a prolonged famine that lasted until the breadfruit began to bear again.[84]

The two islands most affected were the atolls of Mwaekil and Pingelap. The typhoon destroyed virtually all food plants on Mwaekil, causing a severe famine. Only twenty-five to thirty people survived the typhoon and famine. Most were children; only three men and their wives survived. Many older traditions and customs died with the majority of the population. Older forms of communal land ownership disappeared as the survivors parcelled up land. The atoll's society had to be rebuilt, both demographically and culturally. Migration from surrounding atolls helped, but the atoll's political history remained troubled for much of the nineteenth century as groups vied to fill the vacuum.[85] Pingelap suffered a similar loss of life in the typhoon and famine, but recovered more successfully. By 1859 its population was between four hundred and five hundred, and traditions make little reference to infighting.[86]

Less severe storms could still have a significant impact. A typhoon that hit the atoll of Ujelan in 1870 killed all but 20 of the population. The missionary Gulick estimated Ujelan's population at 1000 in 1860. The survivors sought shelter on their relatively unaffected neighbor Jaluit. In 1878 there were only 6 people living on Ujelan, its immediate future uncertain.[87] Faka'ofa's domination of the Tokelau chain of atolls ended abruptly in 1846, when strong winds destroyed most of its coconut trees. Faced with starvation, a number of residents set off for neighboring atolls, but many were dispersed en route by adverse winds. Peruvian slavers abducted others in the early 1860s. As a result, Faka'ofa's population declined from an estimated 800 to 1000 in 1841 to only 200 in 1868.[88] Many lives were lost on Hikueru in the Tuamotus during a hurricane in January 1903 that destroyed much of the atoll. The usually sparsely populated atoll was then occupied by hundreds of people from neighboring atolls for the pearling season. A French source claims that 78 men, 82 women, and 102 children from Hao were among those who drowned on Hikueru.[89]

Responses to the Outside World

Islanders sought to control forces from beyond the horizon by every means available. They were always wary, but nonetheless ready to seize opportunities. These expectations were reflected in two institutions that were central to island cultures: prophecy and rituals of reception. Prophecy played a central role in Islander religion.[90] It induced a "sociopsychological preparedness"[91] that could soften the shock of the unexpected in times of change and uncertainty, created in part by the ongoing infusion of people, objects, and natural disturbances from beyond the horizon.

Islanders made general predictions about the imminent arrival of outsiders in strange ships. These simply expressed a reality of island life. They hark back to experiences when gods and usurping strangers intruded into island life. Other traditions derived from the fact that Islanders learned of approaching influences through their links with other communities. Tahitian prophecies about the imminent arrival of strangers in outriggerless canoes could be explained as attempts to incorporate knowledge of earlier European arrivals in the neighboring Tuamotus.[92] Islanders sometimes remembered European encounters unknown to later visitors and scholars. Cheyne was shown evidence of a now forgotten visitor to Palau in the form of papers in a bottle in the Rock Islands that included the words "July 16th 1763 onboard the Bayne many H . . . "[93] At other times, drift voyagers brought word of new elements. Rarotongans knew about Europeans long before they met any, because of tales told by Tahitian castaways.[94]

More precise predictions had particular efficacy in this island world because of the unheralded speed with which vessels and natural disasters arrived. Prophecy may have been more empirically grounded than modern commentators are willing to concede. Westerners noted that Islanders were aware of approaching vessels well before they saw them. Just after the Pacific War, Weckler described how the inhabitants of Mwaekil knew about the imminent arrival of a ship well before it docked. Vessels were spotted as soon as they appeared on the horizon, and word was immediately spread by a high-pitched, two-syllable cry that traveled the length of the island. Even vessels that arrived at 3:00 or 4:00 A.M. and lay offshore until daylight were detected, as night fishing meant that keen eyes scanned the horizon continually.[95] The idea that maritime people have extraordinary long-distance vision is not limited to the Pacific. Edwin Dunkin, of the Royal Observatory, observed that the eye could be trained to distinguish certain objects at great distance "by constant practice." He found that port officials at Portreath in Cornwall could not only spot vessels on the horizon "several hours before people with ordinary sight," but they could also, "nine times out of ten, announce her name, and frequently the place to which she was bound." Dunkin was present when the vessels arrived to confirm the accuracy of their claims.[96]

Some predictions went beyond the range of extended eyesight. The German ethnographer Wilhelm Müller recorded a Yapese tradition about the accurate prediction of a vessel arriving nine days after the sudden emergence of a large coral rock from the sea.[97] Such predictions could possibly be explained by knowledge of the sailing time between islands, combined with the fact that regular visits occurred soon after the resumption of favorable winds. Thomas Trood, however, believed that the noted ability of Islanders to predict arrivals might simply relate to their powers of observation. Islanders could detect signs of small islands well before they came into sight by observing the clouds. Trood argued that the same was possible for vessels. He conducted his own experiments in Samoa, and concluded that clouds reflected vessels as well as islands. This reflection might only occur for a few minutes at some indeterminate time of the day, but the resulting pattern was clear and distinct. He noted that in January 1862

> I perceived an anomaly in the clouds—a resemblance though in but a slight degree, to a schooner away to the eastward. Two days after, she arrived, and proved to be the "Mathew Vasa," from Tahiti, and was, according to her log-book, 180 miles distant on the day I first saw her indications in the clouds. Other vessels were also seen by me at about the same distance during the month (January 1862), all of which vessels duly arrived in this port [Apia].[98]

The possibility of making out a vessel's outline in clouds at such a distance cannot be explained through modern studies of Islander navigation, which suggest that even the larger shape of islands cannot be discerned on the underside of clouds at this distance. Islander sources are silent on this subject; the prophet ceases to be a prophet when his or her skills are known.

Islanders were certainly attuned to signs of approaching storms, but they could only be detected a few days beforehand. When navigators of the Marshall Islands saw a bank of southern stratus clouds, they knew that heavy weather would arrive in three or four days. Any maritime task of more than a few days' duration therefore ran the risk of being caught at sea. Particularly stormy times of the year were associated with certain configurations of stars. The Marshallese believed that if the Pleiades rose shortly before dawn at the beginning of July, storms were on their way.[99] Short of refusing to sail at all during these seasons, Islanders could only seek to minimize risk. Typhoons could only be anticipated by a few days also. What Europeans detected as a drop in barometer pressure, Islanders could perceive as a change in the feel of the air, accompanied by unusual behavior of wildlife.

The causes and solutions to natural disasters lay within society. Gods angered by local behavior were believed to be a cause of storms, as were chiefs employing sorcerers to wreak havoc on people who offended them.[100] In other words, they occurred because of breakdowns in social relations or neglect of ritual. These causes also explained invasions.[101] Predicting and averting intrusions from beyond the horizon involved the maintenance of community harmony. If this did not prevent intrusions, it at least made the community better equipped to deal with them.

Maintaining correct relations with other communities was also important. The arrival of outsiders from across the sea differed from those overland because there were fewer intermediaries to warn of their approach. Visitor protocol usually consisted of signaling one's friendly intentions and acknowledging the sovereignty of the host. This often took the form of approaching the shore with sails lowered, and reporting to the local ruler immediately.[102] Voyagers visiting Chuuk were required to leave their sails with the local chief until they left. By this act, they surrendered themselves to the ruler's protection, as their means of leaving was removed. In return, actual or designated kin treated the visitors hospitably. They were well fed and entertained.[103] Visits by more powerful groups without blood ties were usually tense affairs characterized by mutual suspicion, thinly cloaked in protocol.

The treatment of unexpected arrivals such as drift voyagers varied enormously. The Futunans' generous treatment of Kau Moala's party was by no means universal. Weak and vulnerable drift voyagers might be attacked, or taken in and looked after. Some were given assistance to sail home.[104] Those possessing useful skills were adopted by their host community. Others were unfortunate enough to arrive when the community could not accommodate them. When people from Mejit were washed ashore on Likiep in the 1840s during a post-typhoon famine, they were promptly dispatched so that they did not become additional mouths to feed.[105]

Not all encounters occurred on the beach. Cultural boundaries may be seen as encounters with "otherness" rather than fixed lines in space. The border of any seafaring people also lies where their vessels carry them. From 1770 vessels themselves became zones of encounter, as Islanders took the opportunity to travel on Western ships. What began as a trickle of invited guests in the late 1700s and early 1800s became a flood as Islanders eagerly sought employment on commercial vessels.[106] Hawaiians, Tahitians, and Māori were particularly prominent because of their islands' popularity as ports of call. By the late 1840s as many as three thousand Hawaiians at a time were working on whaling vessels or in the fur trade in the Pacific Northwest. Chappell estimates that Hawaiians may have comprised 20 percent of the entire American whaling fleet in the 1840s.[107] Most Islanders traveling on these vessels spent their time within the sea of islands, with occasional visits to ports on the Pacific Rim such as Sydney and Valparaiso. Some sailed into the Indian and Atlantic oceans.[108]

Travel exposed them to Western ship culture, the cultures of the crew, and those of the islands they sailed to. The maritime culture of the European world was truly international by this time. Islanders mixed with a variety of other Islanders, various European and American nationals, as well as Chinese and Indians. Pacific whalers were plagued with high rates of desertion, and captains were always eager to replace their losses.[109] The skills that European captains praised were usually the general skills possessed by most Islanders, rather than those of maritime specialists like *pelu*. Island seamen were noted for their ability at swimming and diving, endurance in tropical conditions, and handling small boats in difficult surf.[110]

Islanders' ability to learn the skills to sail Western vessels varied. Many were initially unwilling or unable to learn, and were particularly unenthusiastic about going aloft. Recruits who remained usually overcame their reticence and became skilled and enthusiastic seamen. A few excelled and were rewarded with promotion, although individuals such as the literate Māori chief mate of the Australian whaler *Earl Stanhope* were rare.[111] One reason may have been language problems in such a multicultural, multilingual context. Communication was even a problem between groups of Polynesians. During one voyage, a Tahitian's ability to give orders was compromised by the apparent inability of even his Hawaiian charges to understand him, while at other times the safety of vessels was put at risk because of failures of communication between senior European crew members and Islander sailors.[112]

Some Islanders did not make good sailors. Many were terrified by storms, and some suffered dreadfully from seasickness. Chappell speculates that this may have been because of the different ways canoes and Western vessels responded to ocean swells.[113] It is also worth recalling Williams's distinction between Fijian seamen who handled rough seas well and *kai vanua* passengers, who were reduced to clinging to the deck. Not all Islanders were regular travelers on the open seas. The ship's diet was also an alien experience. The regular diet was salted meat, hard biscuit, and boiled potatoes supplemented with vegetables and fruit whenever the vessel made a landfall. Not only was this diet very different from their usual diet, it also had to be endured for much longer periods than was the norm in indigenous voyaging. Islander crew members took every opportunity to improve their diet through fishing, devouring their catch raw or by whatever method of preparation was open to them.[114]

Islanders traveled out of a sense of curiosity and adventure, or a desire to free themselves from constraints at home. They hoped to return with their reputations enhanced through tales and goods. In some communities "shipping out" became almost a rite of passage for young men, to the extent that Hawaiian and Rotuman chiefs voiced concerns about the loss of so many overseas. Most seem to have intended returning home, although many spent years traveling on Western vessels, including periods on shore as beachcombers. There were reported to be four hundred Hawaiian beachcombers in Tahiti in 1846.[115]

The career of the Woleai navigator Kadu encapsulates many features of the sea world around this time. He had risen in status on Woleai through his role as emissary for the chief of Woleai to other islands in the western Carolines. This required navigational skills, which helped him and three others survive a storm-blown passage to the Marshalls. Although he arrived as a drift voyager, his martial prowess, knowledge of the outside world, and the iron he carried with him elevated his status in the eyes of his hosts. He was taken in by the chief of Aur Atoll, married into the community, and fought in their wars. Kadu used his secondhand knowledge of Westerners to act as intermediary between his Marshallese hosts and the Kotzebue expedition in 1817.[116]

He leapt at the opportunity to travel on the *Rurick* with Kotzebue when it sailed for the northern Pacific. Kadu's travels with the Russians provide valuable insights into the spirit of exploration and inquiry still evident in Islanders. He exhibited immense curiosity. He attentively observed the position and passage of the stars as the *Rurick* moved north out of familiar seas.[117] At Unalaska he spent his time collecting nails, glass, and discarded iron along the harbor shore for his friends in the Marshalls, as well as tide-washed rocks that would make good whetstones. He observed all that was new, and was particularly fascinated by cattle, following them around every day. He was most excited by a herd of sea lions and ursine seals. A degree of alienation can also be detected in Kadu's reaction to this bleak and barren land. He urged the Russians to plant coconuts to make it more suited for human settlement, and while observing the cattle grazing in the meadows would sing songs of the Marshall Islands and Woleai.[118] Kadu mixed easily with Hawaiians when the *Rurick* called there, and again went about collecting useful and unusual objects such as Hawaiian manufactures, seedlings, and plants.[119]

When Kadu returned after nine months on the *Rurick*, he distributed gifts to his adopted kin, and regaled the community with tales of his journey. His audience listened to him with excitement and enthusiasm.[120] Kadu's reception in the Marshalls was typical. Island communities enjoyed learning about foreign lands and cultures. Other Pacific Islands were eyed as possible resource areas. Floyd, for example, noted of Murilo that

> these inhabitants in general enjoy talking very greatly; their evenings are ordinarily spent in telling stories or the adventures of those who have made distant voyages; they also talk with pleasure of the new or unknown islands they have visited or seen, of their inhabitants, their products, of the way they were received by the natives, of what they noticed in the Spanish colonies, particularly the vessels they saw and the place they saw them. Their conversations on these different subjects are continued until well into the night. It is by means of these conversations that the knowledge is maintained of the location of the various islands that make up the Caroline Archipelago. It is a truly surprising thing, the exactness with which they are able to indicate the direction in which they are found, the number of days necessary to get there, the chiefs to whom they belong, the amount of fresh water these islands contain, as well as the number of inhabitants, canoes etc.[121]

By contrast, tales of Western lands focused on strange and exotic elements, rather than opportunities. These were lands to marvel at. Fijian *talanoa vahavalangi* (white people's country stories) were renowned for their tendency to exaggerate. Jackson detected a degree of cynicism in an audience at Rewa toward a *talanoa vahavalangi*. Similar tales occurred throughout the sea of islands. Ports like Canton and London became filled with ships the size of islands, and ships were so numerous their masts resembled a forest.[122] With the exception of Ellis's comments on the Tahitian view of the world beyond the horizon as a series of island-centered domes, sources are silent on how this information was integrated into existing conceptions. Presumably London, Sydney, and Canton became new domed worlds, separated by unknown seas that Islanders had only passed through on Western vessels, rather than explored and mapped in their own ways.

Knowledgeable travelers were assets to their communities in dealings with the increasing Western presence. In many ways, they became the new prophets, forewarning their communities of what to expect. Many were unable to settle back into their home communities, however. A number had left to free themselves from restrictions. Tales of Islanders abandoning traditional *tapu* as soon as they were on Western vessels are common.[123] Travel also changed them. Many shipped out again, never to return. Others never made it home. Chappell found that at least a quarter of the 298 Islanders he was able to identify lived out their lives overseas.[124]

Fascination with tales of distant lands should not be equated with unquestioned acceptance of new ideas and objects. The mere presence of outsiders in ports of call did not necessarily ensure change. Nor did the mere diffusion of ideas result in innovation and change. Prior to 1870 Westerners were in no position to force change on communities. The adoption of new ideas and objects was driven by internal factors. Lieber notes that the Kapinga regard innovation with great ambivalence. The innovator is usually greeted with ridicule until his or her creation proves useful or superior to existing methods or objects. There were only two exceptions to Kapinga's usual initial mistrust. The first was locals who had been singled out early in life as gifted by the gods, and the other was externally derived innovations. The latter were still regarded with skeptical reserve until their efficacy was proven. Lieber concluded that "the more powerful, prestigious, and further removed from the atoll X is, the less likely people are to denigrate the innovator."[125] The openness of Kapinga to ideas and objects from beyond the horizon as long as practical benefit could be demonstrated epitomizes the views of Islanders throughout the region.

As seafaring people, Islanders were particularly interested in maritime technology and practices. Concepts of navigation were less readily adopted than more tangible aspects of seafaring such as boat designs. Islanders continued to rely on traditional navigational practices beyond 1870. They expressed interest in compasses and maps, but did not adopt them.[126] They were more open to lessons that could be taken from the design and operation of Western vessels. Kotzebue described how Samoan fishermen's

> attention was strongly attracted to the ship. They examined her closely from the holds to the mast-head, and made many animated remarks to each other on what they saw. If they observed any manoeuvres with the sails or tackle, they pointed with their fingers towards the spot, and appeared to watch with the most eager curiosity the effect produced . . . It was evident that this people, sailors by birth, took a lively interest in whatever related to navigation.[127]

Many Islanders attempted to adapt or adopt practices that enhanced their seafaring technology. Kotzebue found his experience in Samoa repeated in the Marshalls, where a local ruler measured all the ship's dimensions with a piece of string, then climbed the mast and measured the yards and the sails.[128] Western boat building drew even more interest, for here the secrets of construction were revealed rather than just the capabilities of the finished product. The construction of boats by foreigners inevitably elicited a request to build similar vessels for local rulers, or at least to leave behind boat builders or their tools.[129]

Reactions to Western maritime technology varied enormously. Western vessels sometimes totally replaced traditional canoes, or existed side by side with them, some influenced the design of traditional craft without replacing them, while others had no impact at all.[130] The mix of technology that emerged depended on social and political circumstances, the efficacy of existing canoe designs, local resources, and the degree of Western presence. Fijian and Hawaiian reactions to Western maritime technology represent the two ends of the continuum. Both Fiji and Hawai'i experienced revolutionary changes in their technology, but these were influenced by different factors, and resulted in very different configurations by 1870.

Drua were only developed in Fiji in the late eighteenth century. Although made in Fiji, their appearance owed much to skills and ideas developed elsewhere. Their design and handling techniques came from Tonga and Uvea, while their fore-and-aft rig was Micronesian, probably introduced by way of Kiribati. The craftsmen who built the *drua* were from Tonga and Samoa. The Lemaki, a clan of plank-building specialists from Manono brought to Lau by Tongans in the second half of the eighteenth century, built the first *drua* in Fiji.[131] They eventually settled permanently on Kabara.[132] These craftsmen were notable for their method of joining and fastening planks so that no lashings or perforations showed on the outside of the hull. The staggered joins were so tightly fitted that they were difficult to detect on the outside of the hull. When caulked with breadfruit sap, these joins were far more waterproof than those formed by the previous Fijian method of binding the join by means of lashings threaded through multiple holes drilled in the hull, and sealed with a putty made from the *mākita (Parinari glaberrima)* fruit.[133]

These improved hull designs allowed far bigger hulls to be constructed, which in turn increased carrying capacity. The new sails, rigs, and reversible hulls gave them greater maneuverability than previous canoes. The old designs faded in the late 1700s as the new technology arose.[134] These new canoes facilitated travel within western Polynesia, allowing Tongans to play an increasing role in the politics of Fiji, and making Tongan exiles in Fiji an important factor in Tongan politics.[135] Samoan canoes based on the design of *drua* replaced the Samoan *va'a tele* canoe by the 1830s, although this does not appear to have led to an increase in voyaging as it did in Tonga.[136]

In contrast, the increasing presence of Westerners did little to influence Fijian maritime technology. Fijians learned how to use oars from observing Europeans, but most inter-island traffic continued to be carried on *drua* and *camakau*.[137] Indeed, *drua* continued to be developed, with the largest ever built by the Lemaki clan being constructed in the 1870s.[138] Schooners were built in Fiji and New Zealand to serve the needs of European settlers from the 1830s. They were generally small fore-and-aft rigged vessels, ideally suited to the needs of the Western community in Fiji. They were seaworthy enough and large enough to carry passengers and cargo between islands, yet small enough to negotiate reef passages and shallow lagoons.[139] Although Cakobau ordered a schooner built overseas to enhance his *mana*,[140] Fijians generally did not take to Western vessels. Owning a schooner did not engender the same pride as the construction of a great *drua*. *Drua* and *camakau* also fulfilled their transport needs. One European noted that a large *drua* once transported twelve head of cattle in her holds for a distance of 120 miles and another carried a cargo of maize sufficient to fill a 50-ton Western vessel.[141]

The indigenous nautical revolution in western Polynesia did not reach Hawai'i,[142] where another transformation took place. From the 1790s, Hawaiians rapidly adopted vessels based on Western designs. This change was accompanied by the gradual decline in the use of the double-hulled canoes that had served them so well for inter-island voyaging. The first Western vessel was built in the early 1790s with the assistance of craftsmen from the Vancouver expedition. The vessel was named *Beretane* (Britain), and was promptly incorporated into the battle fleet of the local chief Kamehameha.[143] Kamehameha went on to conquer most of the archipelago by 1795. Kaua'i and Ni'ihau were only saved by the destruction of Kamehemeha's invasion fleet in a storm mid-passage in 1796.[144] Kamehameha responded by building a new fleet of 800 war canoes. Unlike the usual double canoe, *pelelu* were shorter, broader, and able to carry far more men.[145]

In the first years of the nineteenth century Kamehameha supplemented his fleet of *pelelu* with sloops and schooners equipped with cannon. By 1810 Kamehameha possessed over thirty Western vessels. Most were under 40 tons and constructed by Hawaiian carpenters under the direction of an English resident. Hawaiians made up most of their crews, although the majority of the captains were Westerners. As no naval threat existed within the archipelago, most of these vessels were hauled up on Waikiki beach in boat sheds, with their spars laid alongside and their rigging and cables under cover. Only ten or twelve were anchored in Honolulu harbor, and only one was regularly used for inter-island voyages. The magnificent *pelelu* fleet, drawn up on the beach, slowly fell into disrepair.[146]

When Kamehameha died in 1819 he left his son Liholiho a fleet of 5 brigs of 90 to 100 tons each, 5 schooners of 60 to 70 tons, and about 10 20-ton cutters. Many were equipped with cannon, although their main function continued to be transport between islands. Some had been made by the king's own carpenters, while others were purchased overseas.[147] Liholiho also inherited over 170 canoe makers. Western visitors in 1819 were still confronted by hundreds of canoes just as Cook had been 40 years earlier.[148] The next 20 years saw the rise of Western influence as missionaries and other foreigners settled, and whaling ships visited in increasing numbers.

Despite the steady decline of the population, Hawaiians remained enthusiastic inter-island travelers. In 1840, a British visitor to Honolulu reported that the local canoes were

> merely trees hollowed out generally from 20 to 30 feet in length & capable of holding 2 to 8 persons—they seldom exceed 1 1/2 foot in breadth & to give them stability 2 spars are rigged out on one side, with a third across. They are frequently upset but the people are almost amphibious & care little for such accidents.[149]

Some Hawaiians still sailed in outrigger canoes as late as 1856, although most travelers were using Western vessels by then. This did not overcome the dangers of the archipelago's waters. Over six hundred people were lost at sea on inter-island voyages from 1841 to 1858. A number of problems occurred because Hawaiian captains and crew lost their bearings.[150]

By the 1860s inter-island canoe travel was declining as steamers became a serious possibility, and more and more of the Hawaiian economy became geared to supplying the U.S. sugar market. Europeans dominated the Hawaiian sugar industry. A new group of usurping strangers had settled on the land.[151] It would be another two decades before they overthrew the Hawaiian monarchy. In the meantime they exercised influence through their economic power and links to their homeland. Few married Hawaiians. Most continued to consider themselves American rather than Hawaiian. Upon seizing power in 1893, one of their first moves was to seek the integration of Hawai'i into the United States. The history of the sea of islands became a history of expanding horizons. It is to that history that we now turn.

Connected by the Sea:
Toward a Regional History of
the Western Caroline Islands

THE WESTERN Caroline Islands are a particularly appropriate region in which to explore the maritime dimension of Pacific history. Many of its smaller islands remained relatively free from colonial influence, allowing traditional seafaring to flourish well into the twentieth century. This is also a crowded sea, full of islands and open sea markers. The history of the western Carolines is as much a history of interactions along sea routes as histories of individual communities. There are a number of excellent histories of individual islands, but few regional histories. The latter focus on the intrusion of Europeans and pay little attention to indigenous interactions. Natural hazards are also sidelined, and are depicted as underlying structural constraints rather than specific events that alter the course of history.[1]

This chapter argues that the history of this region between 1770 and 1870 is best understood as a story of interactions between four distinct, yet interconnected worlds. These were the three high island complexes of Yap, Palau, and the Mariana Islands, and one consisting of the twenty atolls and two raised coral islands between Yap and Chuuk.[2] The chapter begins by reviewing the annual *sawei* exchange between Yap and the coral islands to the west, before demonstrating how this coexisted with a relationship between Yap and Palau. Each introduced different goods into Yap that were used by rivals to extend their influence. The focus then moves to the coral islands, and challenges depictions of them as peaceful, coherent entities unified by the *sawei* relationship. Both continuity and change are visible in their relationships between 1770 and 1870. The chapter concludes with the colonization of the northern Marianas by Carolinians fleeing natural disasters and military threat, and their impact on relations between coral islands and the *sawei*. By adopting this regional perspective, the western Carolines may be seen as a more dynamic place,

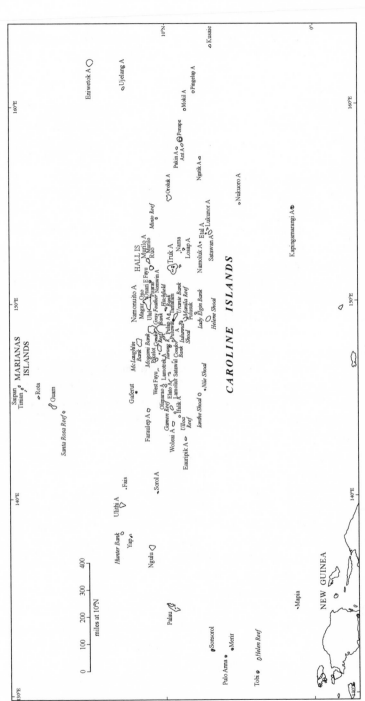

MAP 7　The Caroline Islands region. (RSPAS Cartography, adapted from Riesenberg, "Navigational Knowledge," following 24)

with Europeans just one of many groups of outsiders to influence communities. Indigenous history becomes more prominent, and the sea becomes
an integral part of that history.

The *Sawei* System

The only published studies of indigenous interactions in the western Carolines that adopt a regional perspective are postwar anthropological studies of the *sawei* system. This exchange relationship centered on Yap is still
in existence. It extends 900 nautical miles east to Namonuito Atoll, and
consisted of regular and lengthy visits from low island fleets to Yap to
present tribute and exchange goods. The majority of studies focus on the
reception of the low island fleet on Yap, and emphasize structural continuities rather than historical disruptions.[3]

The delivery of the *sawei* tribute occurred annually or every two to
three years.[4] The tribute fleet contained representatives of all islands from
Ulithi to Namonuito. They delivered their tribute to Gachpar Village in
the Gagil district of Yap.[5] The fleet set out from Namonuito and went
from island to island in a set order, picking up representatives. The fleet
increased in size the farther west it sailed until it numbered ten or more
canoes. The islands of Lamotrek, Wottagai on Woleai, Fais, and Mogmog
on Ulithi had higher status than the others, and served as focal points for
the fleet. Each led the fleet west from their island to the next high-status
island. In other words, status within the *sawei* increased farther west and
closer to Yap.

The fleet set sail during the season of the northeast winds between
December and June, and remained in Gachpar for a few months until the
winds changed to the southwest to allow a relatively easy passage home.
Three distinct forms of tribute were presented: religious tribute (known
as *mepel* on the coral islands and *magbil* on Yap), presented to Yongelap,
the great god worshipped throughout the Carolines; canoe tribute (*pitigil
tamol* on the coral islands and *kapitalwa* on Yap), presented to the chiefs
of Gachpar; tribute of the land (known as *sawei* on the coral islands and
on Yap), presented by individual outer island lineages to their Yapese lineage hosts. During their stay on Yap, outer island "children" were also
required to show their Yapese "parents" respect. In return, their hosts
were obliged to take care of them, and give them gifts when they left.
Informal trading was also conducted during the stay.

There has been much speculation over what sustained this relationship. Five different reasons have been proposed: religious affiliations; Yapese military prowess; fear of Yapese magic; mutual economic benefits; and the political benefits it conferred on Gachpar. The prominence of tribute dedicated to Yongelap has led to speculation that his cult bound the *sawei* together. Most Carolinians claimed Yongelap as their founding ancestor. Yongelap came from Yap, and elevated the status of Yapese. Failure to recognize this primacy might lead to disaster. Yap was believed to control the hook that fished up Fais, as well as the axe with which Ulithi was hewn from the sea. If the Yapese chose to dig up either of these sacred items, those islands would sink.[6]

Did low islanders believe these charters, or did they merely rationalize an imbalance of power in favor of the Yapese? Historian Mark Berg asserts that the modern overbearing and exploitative reputation of the Yapese toward their *sawei* tributaries may be a legacy of the colonial era. Colonial policy put outer islanders at a disadvantage by forcing them to work on colonial projects in Yap.[7] There are indications that this relationship existed prior to the colonial era, however. Nineteenth-century visitors commented on outer islanders' fear of Yapese ferocity and skill in warfare. Arago talked to a navigator from the low islands who stated that the "natives of Yapa [Yap], an island situated near Manilla, are very ferocious; that they have muskets (pac), powder, and carry on war against their neighbours."[8] Arago noted that he "spoke of them with terror," and added, "he was unable to inform us if they had already ventured as far as his own country."[9] There is no evidence of Yapese expeditions against any of the islands that participated in the *sawei* after 1770, although fear of Yapese may have harked back to previous interventions.[10] These fears were probably justified. Tetens found the hundred Yapese he took with him on a trading voyage in 1867 to be ferocious warriors, carrying all before them in confrontations in New Guinea, Losap, Nama, and Ulithi.[11]

Yapese sorcerers were believed to be able to inflict illness and typhoons on those who offended them. The threat was powerful in an area plagued by storms. The Russian explorer Adelbert von Chamisso noted:

> The people of Eap [Yap] are notorious because of their magical arts. They know how to conjure up the wind, to conjure the storm so that it becomes silent, and in calm to evoke the wind from a favourable direction. They know how, by casting a plant into the sea with appropriate incantation, to agitate the waves and cause endless storms. The capsizing of many vessels from Mogemug [Mogmog] and Feis [Fais], as well as the gradual depopulation of the latter island, are ascribed to this.[12]

Outer islanders received tangible benefits from participating in *sawei* fleets, receiving more than they gave in the tribute and trading exchanges in Gachpar.[13] Yapese also fed and sheltered them. Although Alkire claims that the difference in resource use between high islands and low islands is more one of scale and emphasis than kind,[14] exchanges during the time in Gagil consisted largely of items that were scarce in the recipients' areas. Outer islanders brought woven banana fiber loincloths *(thu)*, sennit twine, turtle and coconut shell, mother of pearl shell, and spondylus shell. Yapese also occasionally purchased canoes from Woleai. In return, the Yapese gave turmeric (used as a cosmetic skin paste in the Carolines), red earth pigment, tridacna shell, whetstones, orange wood used in ancestral altars, and Polynesian chestnuts. Occasionally they also contributed wood for canoes and European goods procured from visiting traders.[15]

Why did Yapese continue this apparently uneven exchange? The *sawei* link was particularly valued for the political influence it conferred on the chiefs of Gachpar. They enhanced their status by having overseas' tributaries,[16] and could expand alliances by distribution of outer island tribute to potential allies on Yap.[17] Yap was divided into two rival camps during the nineteenth century. Broadly speaking, the districts of Tomil and Rull were allied against Gagil. In more precise terms, Gagil chiefs were prominent among the *vaani pagal* (young men's party), while the chiefs of Tomil and Rull dominated the *vaani pilung* (chiefs' party). These groups cut across district boundaries, and constantly sought to maintain and extend their alliances.[18] Spondylus shell from the outer islands was particularly valued by Yapese. This shell was made into much sought after *gau* (shell money). Spondylus shell was only available on Eauripik Atoll, Udot Island in Chuuk, and Etal Atoll in the Mortlock Islands.

The *vaani pilung*'s overseas links extended south to Palau rather than to the east. In this case, however, Yapese were guests rather than hosts. They traveled there to quarry Palauan aragonite for use as *fei* (stone money).[19] *Fei* was also distributed on Yap to cement alliances, fulfilling the same role that *gau* did for the *vaani pagal*. Yapese were not in a position to dictate terms, and had to act respectfully and humbly to their hosts. They were willing to do this because Palauan aragonite was of much higher quality than Yapese.[20]

The *vaani pilung* could use Palauan *fei* because Yap's southern district of Rull had a strong seafaring base. Its navigation schools and sailing skills were still very evident in the latter part of the nineteenth century.[21] They were needed for the 454-kilometer sea gap between Palau and Yap.

Canoes could make the crossing in five days in good weather. *Fei* measured a meter or more across, so that even the largest Yapese canoe could only carry one large *fei* at a time. Yapese used large bamboo rafts called *fofoot* towed behind canoes to carry *fei*. The dangers of maneuvering these heavy vessels in the open sea only enhanced the value of *fei*.[22] Alkire, however, claims the sailing skills of Yapese atrophied. He speculates that one of the reasons Gagil may have been willing to continue its costly exchanges with outer islanders was to utilize their seafaring skills. By using outer island canoes they increased their access to more of the region's resources. Certainly all the Yapese navigational chants recorded by Müller in 1917 were in the language of Ulithi. Chamisso also noted that Yapese sought canoes from Woleai.[23]

Coral Islanders were not the only outsiders that Yapese and Palauan rulers sought to use. Western traders also came to play an important role in Palauan and Yapese politics in the nineteenth century. The rulers of Koror were quick to realize the advantages of courting Western traders. When the *Antelope* was shipwrecked in Palau in 1783 the English crew found the *Ibedul* of Koror a willing host. They discovered a shipwrecked Malay seaman already serving the *Ibedul* after finding refuge there from less amiable hosts elsewhere in Palau.[24] A succession of beachcombers followed the Malay in gravitating toward Koror. The *Ibedul* also welcomed visiting vessels seeking *bêche-de-mer*. Koror's control of the sheltered harbor of Malakal added to its attractiveness. Koror virtually monopolized Western trade goods within Palau, including firearms.[25]

Traders gradually came to pose problems for the *Ibedul,* however. In the middle of the nineteenth century captains such as Cheyne and Woodin acted against the interests of the *Ibedul.* Woodin established a commercial station in Ngerard, elevating the importance of a district that had been secondary to Koror and Melekeok. In 1860 Ngerard was able to fend off an attack from Koror.[26]

Cheyne's position in both Palau and Yap became increasingly fragile. While he traded muskets with the Yapese,[27] he still mistrusted them. He constantly feared attack, and learned that the *Ibedul* was offering payment for his death. On July 17, 1864, for example, he met five canoe loads of Yapese at the northern end of Babeldaob awaiting favorable winds for a passage back to Yap. They told him

that the Coroar people have instructed them to cut off any vessel at Yap should I again go there; that no Coroar men will go in the ship, and that they will give the Yap men plenty of muskets for doing so, and that if they do not obey the Coroar chiefs instructions, they will not get any more stone money.[28]

Relations between Cheyne and the *Ibedul* declined. Cheyne was increasingly insulting to the *Ibedul*, who reacted by slowing down supplies of *bêche-de-mer* and other items. Cheyne soon learned that the *Ibedul* was also intimidating other tribes into not trading with him. By September 1865 he felt the only way to overcome the *Ibedul*'s hindrance was "to arm the other tribes, so as to make them independent of Oreor [Koror]."[29] He then began trading muskets and ammunition with Koror's rivals, contravening an 1843 agreement in which the *Ibedul* facilitated Cheyne's trade access to Palau and Yap in return for Cheyne agreeing to trade only with Koror.[30] The chiefly council of Koror ordered his execution. Cheyne was killed in Palau in 1866.[31]

The killing of Cheyne was only a temporary reprieve. In 1867 the British warship *Perseus* sailed to Palau to seek the murderers of Cheyne. Palauans had to execute the *Ibedul* to satisfy British demands for justice.[32] By the 1860s their ability to resist Westerners and their weapons was already eroding as introduced diseases decimated the population. In 1862 Semper estimated the total population of Palau was only 10,000. Estimates at the time of Captain Wilson's enforced sojourn 70 years earlier vary from 20,000 to 50,000.[33] Yapese hostility to outsiders reduced the number of visits from potential carriers of disease before 1870. Nevertheless, Cheyne still noted outbreaks of influenza during his visits to Tomil in the 1860s.[34]

Continuity and Change within the Sea of Atolls

The coral islands of the *sawei* system were also subject to visits from Western traders and explorers from the 1790s. They found the inhabitants eager to trade, particularly for iron. Few Westerners sought to establish permanent stations on the coral islands, however, as their commercial potential was limited.[35] The influence of the outside world was felt less directly here than in Palau and Yap, as its inhabitants sailed out and sought Westerners and their goods elsewhere. These new connections caused some disruption and reorientation of coral island life, although most relationships between the coral islands of the *sawei* system continued. There has been little attempt to examine the *sawei* system's place within the totality of inter-island relations west of Yap. As a result, the *sawei* takes on more importance than it perhaps had outside Yap. The voyages of the *sawei* fleet were significant events among the coral islands of the western Carolines, but they were also just one of many regular exchanges.

The close proximity of most atolls, and the wealth of reefs and shoals between islands to serve as navigational markers allowed relatively easy passages. There are twenty shoals and banks between 5 and 10 degrees north latitude in this region. Some cover large areas. Mogami and Gray Feather Banks, for example, are 30 and 50 miles in diameter. They are only one mile apart, and combine to form a large sea marker 50 miles west of Namonuito Atoll. The people of Namonuito referred to Gray Feather Bank as Mannaijeu.[36] Puluwat and Pulusuk were the emergent ends of much larger reefs, known respectively as the Uranie and Manila Banks. Some of these open sea features were also sailing hazards. The Puluwatese did not sail directly to Pulusuk, 42 miles southeast, but sailed around an intervening reef to avoid the dangerous seas that broke over it. The extended route was 50 miles long, but eliminated the danger of Maihun, the "Reef of Spirits that Eats Canoes."[37] Northern and southern equatorial currents flow strongly westward through the region, separated by the equally powerful equatorial countercurrent. The width of the currents could vary by as much as 100 miles at different times, but these currents were also markers.[38]

Locals considered any distance of less than 150 miles to be one day's sail in good conditions.[39] Only a few sea gaps exceeded this distance: Woleai to Sorol, Woleai to Fais, and Faraulep to Fais.[40] Most other gaps were around half this distance, with routes punctuated by reefs and shoals to serve as markers. The eastern part was particularly crowded with coral islands, reefs, and shoals. As one sailed west, the number of coral islands and markers declined. Woleai and Eauripik marked the western limit of the crowded sea.[41] Lutké was told that the passage from Woleai to Fais took two days with good winds, or three days in light winds. The return voyage took four days. Ulithi and Yap lay one and two days, respectively, west of Fais.[42] The high islands of Chuuk Lagoon lay just west of this crowded sea, and western atolls like Puluwat had much more interaction with Chuuk than they did with Yap. Linguistic relations mirrored geographical relations. Linguists categorize these coral islands into three groups, whose internal coherence reflects the fact that each lies within a day's sail of its neighbors. The western group consists of Ulithi, Fais, Ngulu, and Sorol. The middle group takes in Eauripik, Faraulep, Woleai, Ifalik, Elato, Lamotrek, and Satawal. The eastern group consists of the string of atolls that circle Chuuk: Pulusuk, Puluwat, Pulap, Namonuito, Murilo, Losap, Nama, and the Mortlock Islands.[43]

The configuration of coral islands promoted inter-island ties. The sea was conceived of as named sea lanes between specific destinations and *metau*, open sea outside sea lanes.[44] The navigators of Lamotrek referred to the sea lane between Lamotrek and Satawal as Uoirekh, for example. To travel to Ifalik they sailed along Hapilerap, and to reach West Fayu they used Lekarakh.[45] Kin links were regularly maintained by visits along the sea lanes throughout the region. Many clans had members on a number of atolls they could call on. The clans of Pulusuk sought wives from related kin groups on Puluwat and in Chuuk.[46] Similarly, women from Fais married into related clans in Ulithi and Woleai.

When Lutké visited Woleai for the second time in 1828, he provided an insight into the mobility of Carolinian chiefs that he had met previously. He noted that

> among other natives, we met a tamol [chief] whom we had seen in the spring at Elato, and he told us that the tamol Oralitaou, whom we had met at Guahan [Guam], had returned from there to his own country. During our absence the old Rooua had died; his brother Roouameun, who was now in Namourrek [Lamotrek], had succeeded him. Tapeligar had gone to Fais and to Mogmog [Mogmog in Ulithi], and Aman to Farroilap [Faraulep].[47]

These links served as a safety net in case of drought, war, or storms. Each coral island's potential carrying capacity generally exceeded its actual population during optimum conditions, enabling refugees to be accommodated.[48]

A highly seasonal pattern of inter-island visits took place. The northeast trade winds (November and June) favored visits to islands to the west, while the southwest winds (June to October) facilitated travel to the east.[49] The southwest winds coincided with the season of plenty, when the breadfruit became ripe and fishing was good. Large inter-island exchanges occurred during the first few months of this season. Lutké recorded one such occasion in June 1828, when Islanders from Satawal, Pulusuk, Puluwat, and Pulap visited Fananu for a dance festival.[50] However, September and October were noted for strong winds and typhoons, so that travel was avoided whenever possible. The *sawei* fleets departed for Yap toward the end of the northeast trade wind season in February or March. While these winds facilitated travel to Yap, it was a poor time for voyaging in other respects. Just as today, a series of high-pressure systems reached into the region from the Asian mainland. The doldrums belt moved south, and strong northeast trade winds gave rise to huge waves that made sailing difficult. Stocks of preserved breadfruit were running low, the new season's crop was not yet ripe.[51] The arrival of the *sawei* fleet during this season placed strains on the Gachpar economy, although it would not be long before the winds changed and the homeward journey could be made.

The value of items obtained from the Yapese must be gauged against the full range of goods exchanged. The *sawei* exchanges formed a significant part of the total goods obtained. Other exchanges were more limited. Tobacco grown on Fais was much sought after in Ulithi and Yap. Both Ulithi and Fais obtained canoes from Woleai, while Fais received shell ornaments and belts from the coral islands to the east. Ulithi also had contact with Ngulu and the coral islands southwest of Palau.[52]

The central islands drew upon the resources of both the eastern and western coral islands, as well as from their own area. Woleai traded for shell valuables from Eauripik, Sorol, Ngulu, and Fais. According to Kadu,

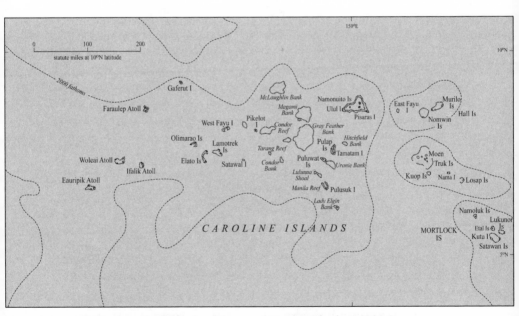

MAP 8 Islands, reefs, and banks of the central Caroline Islands. (RSPAS Cartography after Gladwin, *East is a Big Bird,* 158–59; Risenberg, "Navigational Knowledge" following 24; and Ridgell et al., 96)

the navigators of Woleai sailed west to Palau and the Southwest Islands and as far east as Satawal. Satawalese were more oriented to the west, making annual visits to Chuuk, as well as regular visits to Puluwat. They obtained valuables from as far afield as Eauripik, Woleai, Truk, and the Mortlock Islands.[53]

The western coral islands had relatively limited interaction with the coral islands to the east beyond their involvement in the *sawei*. Seafarers from Puluwat and Pulusuk sailed east as far as Woleai to trade and visit kin, although much of their seafaring was oriented toward atolls surrounding Chuuk such as Pulap, Namonuito, Murilo, and the Mortlocks. Puluwatese visited Chuuk twice a year to trade and renew social ties. The quality of the turmeric from Chuuk was much higher than that of Yapese turmeric obtained through the *sawei*.[54]

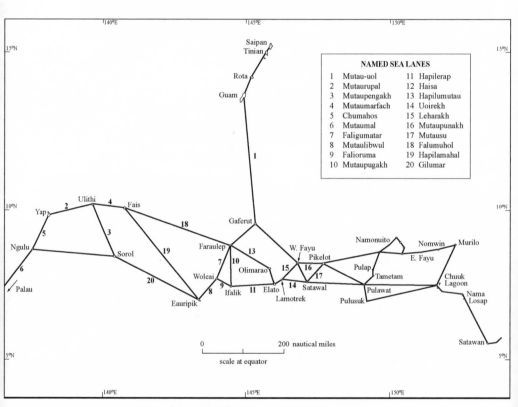

MAP 9 Sea lanes of the western Caroline Islands. (RSPAS Cartography, adapted from Alkire, *Lamotrek*, 125; Ridgell et al., 96; and Farrell, 191).

The *sawei* was not the only tributary relationship in these islands. The *hu* was a system of semiannual exchanges between Lamotrek, Elato, and Satawal, in which the others acknowledged the senior status of Lamotrek. Lamotrek received turtles from Elato, and *mar* (fermented breadfruit paste) and ripe coconuts from Satawal, in return for the right to forage on the uninhabited coral islands to the north controlled by Lamotrek. They also had the right to ask for food from Lamotrek when they were in need.[55]

All these exchanges were regular and well ordered. European visitors noted the passive nature of low Islanders. Lutké compared them favorably with the inhabitants of high islands:

> Among the inhabitants of the different kinds of islands which make up the archipelago of the Carolines, there reigns quite a considerable difference in manners and customs. While those of the high islands with the single exception of Ualan [Kosrae], are engaged in everlasting wars with their neighbours, we behold those of the low islands enjoying the most perfect peace; they busy themselves only with cultivation of the soil, with commerce and also with industrial labours.[56]

He qualified this, however, by noting that although they appeared to dislike war, it

> is by no means unknown to them; they even derive an advantage from the dissensions of their neighbours by providing them with the arms they lack. The most beautiful lances and the best clubs are manufactured in the low islands, they are made of the hardest part of the trunk of the coconut palm, and the workmanship is carefully done, they are much in demand and are very dear.[57]

This image of relative peace and stability among the atolls has persisted.[58] Alkire even suggests that the development of the *sawei* system helped to reduce conflict.[59] He concluded that traditions of wars of conquest by Ifalik occurred in the distant past. In these, Ifalik conquers and then colonizes its neighbors.[60] Alkire may be correct that warfare had diminished, but traditions show that it was still a reality for many low Islanders in the nineteenth century.[61] In a comprehensive survey of conflict on Ifalik, Laura Betzig and Santus Wichimai show that conflict occurred at all levels: from interpersonal violence within kin groups, to disputes over land between lineages, to inter-island disputes. The small atoll of Eauripik even produced military specialists who were used by other Islanders.[62]

Puluwat began to play an increasingly dominant role in the western isles from the middle of the nineteenth century. In the era of chief Jämŭt, Puluwat launched a number of attacks on its neighbors. All were recorded in Puluwat traditions as responses to unprovoked attacks on its seafarers or on Puluwatese allies. The inhabitants of Namonuito seem to have particularly incurred the wrath of the Puluwatese. Wars against Namonuito ended when Puluwat inflicted a heavy defeat and peace was restored.[63]

Soon Puluwat dominated most of the western isles. Damm noted that

> the natives of Polowat have always had a reputation among the Central Carolinians of being a particularly martial people. They consider themselves masters of quite a number of the Central Caroline Islands (as far as Onoun) and received tribute from some of them as late as 1910.[64]

The Puluwatese received tribute from Pulusuk, Pulap, Tametam, Olul (Ulul), Piseras, Magur, and Ulalu (Unanu), and also intervened in Chuukese disputes to assist their allies.[65] Puluwatese still participated in the *sawei* fleets and obeyed status protocols within them. Outside the *sawei*, however, they seem to have become less willing to acknowledge the privileged status of Lamotrek. Damm recorded how "Pigelot [Pikelot] used to belong to the Lamotrik [Lamotrek] people, but then Bunuluk of Polowat [Puluwat] claimed it and today only the Polowat natives and no other islanders fish there."[66] However, Krämer was under the impression that the Puluwatese still required the permission of Lamotrek to visit Pikelot, so that this ascendancy may have only been temporary.[67]

Sailing North to the Islands of Opportunity

There is still one vital link missing from our analysis—the Mariana Islands. These northern islands became increasingly important to Carolinians from the early 1800s. When natural disasters struck the low islands, their inhabitants turned north to the Marianas for relief, rather than westward toward Yap. As these connections were forged, old connections within the Carolines were altered and redefined.

In 1788 canoes from Lamotrek under the direction of the navigator Luito sailed to the Spanish colony of Guam in search of iron.[68] Luito had never been to Guam, but knew how to sail there and about the Spanish and their goods. Luito was not the first Carolinian to visit the Marianas.

A Spanish census of Guam in 1727 listed three Carolinians among the population of 2780. These three were drift voyagers from Ulithi who were cared for by authorities on Guam in the early 1720s.[69] Spanish priests had followed up this encounter with an ill-fated mission to Ulithi in 1730–31, which disappeared without a trace. A follow-up expedition received a less than friendly welcome, prompting the Spanish to withdraw from the Carolines.[70] In 1756–57 another Carolinian canoe was blown to Guam.[71] Links between the two archipelagos were older, however. Prior to the bloody conquest of the Chamorro by the Spanish in the last three decades of the seventeenth century, Carolinians had maintained regular contact with the Marianas. They ceased their visits after learning of Spanish brutality from Chamorro refugees.[72]

Luito's voyage restored the old links along Mutau-uol, a seaway between Gaferut and Guam remembered in a navigational chant.[73] Luito reached the old landfall of Talofofo Bay on Guam's southwest coast without difficulty. The Spanish received his party warmly. Luís de Torres, a young Guam-born *sargento mayor*, was particularly welcoming. Torres ensured that the Carolinians obtained iron and other trade goods, and encouraged them to return. Luito's party sailed home with word of the new opportunity. He voyaged to Guam again in 1789, but his fleet was lost at sea on the return leg. His relatives on Lamotrek feared that he had become a victim of Spanish brutality, and voyages to Guam were suspended.[74]

Torres rose to become vice governor of Guam, and continued to ponder the absence of the Carolinians. In 1804 he chartered an American vessel and sailed south to investigate. He touched at Woleai, Faraulep, West Fayu, and Pikelot, assuring all he met that no harm had befallen Luito on Guam, and promising them a warm welcome and trade if they returned.[75] Word of Torres's invitation spread, and Carolinian visits were resumed the following year when a fleet from Woleai, Lamotrek, and Satawal landed on Guam.[76] Annual trading voyages were made along Mutau-uol from 1805. Although the size of the fleet varied, Chamisso records it as eighteen *proa* in 1814.[77] Even the Chuukese were lured to Guam in search of trade goods. They unfortunately arrived off the coast at night during a festival, and were so perturbed by the display of fireworks that they returned to Chuuk.[78]

The Carolinian fleets would gather each April in Namonuito, Lamotrek, and Faraulep, and proceed to Gaferut. This uninhabited atoll was the closest island in the archipelago to Guam, and the starting point for the open sea passage. May was chosen because the prevailing northeast wind was at its weakest, so that it was easier to sail before the wind. They sailed due north to Guam, keeping the North Star on their bow, and taking account of drift caused by winds and currents from the east. It took two days to sail from Lamotrek to Gaferut, and three days to make the 756-kilometer passage from Gaferut to Guam. In adverse winds the journey could take up to two weeks.[79]

The Marianas are a relatively easy target for skilled navigators. The chain consists of high islands, most of which are separated by less than 50 miles of ocean and heavily populated with land-based sea birds. They thus formed a near-continuous screen of navigational signs extending north to south for hundreds of miles across the path of the predominant winds.[80] The Carolines presented a long east to west screen of signs to navigators approaching from the north in the form of atolls, underwater reefs, and daily flight patterns of shore-based sea birds.[81] Gaps appeared in this screen the farther west one aimed. The fleet returned south again in May to avoid the western monsoon in June–July. This also allowed navigators to return for the season of inter-island visits within the sea of atolls. In this way, Western goods and information about the Spanish and the northern islands were disseminated throughout the area.

Caroline Islanders sought iron, copper, colored cloth, tobacco, and ornaments in return for shell, indigenous cloth, *proa*, and sennit rope.[82] Guam soon occupied a prominent position in the minds of the low Islanders. Lesson noted "Caroline Islanders call the island of Guam Waghal, and look upon it as a great country, where there are plenty of cattle, iron and other riches."[83] Trade goods from Guam were soon circulating within inter-island networks, enhancing the status and influence of those who sailed north to obtain them. Iron was particularly sought, and soon ranked alongside *proa*, cloth, and turmeric as the most valued items of indigenous trade.[84] Particular islands seized the initiative to become centers for redistribution. Pulusuk, for example, traded knives and axes from Guam as far west as Woleai, and eastward as far as Chuuk.[85]

Carolinians were of great use to the Spanish on Guam. Their seafaring skills were particularly sought after. By 1819 Guam was largely isolated from the outside world. Although the Spanish governor had a brigantine of around 40 tons to maintain communications with Manila, contact was infrequent and few Western vessels visited the Marianas.[86] Virtually none of the Spanish on Guam were accomplished seafarers. Lutké noted that while his expedition was visiting Guam, the governor's schooner was even unable to reach Saipan, such was the state to which "the sailing compatriots of Magellan [have] been reduced."[87] The Chamorro population had also lost their connection with the sea after a century of colonial rule. A visitor in the early 1600s had commented that the Chamorro were such accomplished swimmers and sailors "that one would think that they had a treaty with wind and water."[88] As late as 1742 Chamorro *proa* still sailed between Guam and Tinian on missions for the Spanish.[89] Yet by 1817 Chamisso lamented how "the present inhabitants no longer know the sea, are not sailors, not swimmers anymore, and they have ceased to build boats."[90]

Carolinians began conducting inter-island traffic for the Spanish within the Marianas in return for trade goods. Seafarers from Elato were particularly prominent. They were primarily employed to ferry vegetables from Rota, and dried beef and pork from Tinian to feed Guam.[91] One legacy of the violent seizure of power by the Spanish was that almost the entire population had been concentrated on Guam. The majority of the 5389 inhabitants lived on Guam, while just a few hundred lived on Rota and Tinian.[92] These duties made Carolinians aware that the northern islands were largely unoccupied. Saipan, the largest island north of Guam, particularly drew their attention. Large, fertile, and unoccupied, it was a tempting opportunity to inhabitants of the small, typhoon-prone coral islands to the south. The low islands of the *sawei* system were all vulnerable to typhoons. The typhoon that hit Woleai in 1907 killed two hundred people.[93]

In the second decade of the nineteenth century Saipan became a storm refuge for the low Islanders. Carolinian traditions record that Saipan was used within a decade of the resumption of trade voyages to Guam in 1805, when the Pulusuk navigator and chief Piwamwan gathered a group of navigators and sailed there to collect coconuts and other food for Pulusuk and neighboring islands devastated by a typhoon.[94] Another typhoon in 1815 was severe enough to convince many low Islanders to relocate to Saipan. According to Arago, over nine hundred people gathered at Lamotrek and set sail in 120 canoes. Most of the fleet was lost in another terrible storm.[95] The impact of this loss on inter-island relations is hard to gauge. It is uncertain whether the influence of the feared Yapese storm magicians was enhanced by two destructive typhoons in successive years. It is also unclear if this was seen as a signal that the Yapese or Yongelap were unhappy with the new relationships being forged outside of the *sawei*.

What does appear certain is that the people of Lamotrek suffered significant casualties, and perhaps erosion of status. A few years later Chamisso commented that Woleai seemed to have risen past Lamotrek to become the dominant island in the region:

> In Cantova's time, the islands comprising his Second Province were divided between the two states of Ulea [Woleai] and Lamureck [Lamotrek]. Today however those islands recognize the tamon [tamol] or prince of Ulea as their exclusive ruler. This chief, whose name is Toua, is also recognized in several other, more easterly islands.[96]

Woleai enhanced its position by embracing trade opportunities with Guam. Kadu claimed that the status of Woleai was particularly acknowledged in Chuuk. Chuukese desired iron and Woleai people traded *proa* for iron on Guam. Toua himself came to Guam in 1817 to seek iron. Chuukese did not participate in the annual trading fleets to Guam, but traded cloth for iron with Woleai seafarers visiting Chuuk. Torres believed that the ascendancy of Woleai was temporary, and would not last beyond the death of Toua.[97] His prediction proved to be correct.

New opportunities continued. When the Spanish authorities on Guam learned of the Carolinian fleet's disaster, they requested permission from the governor general of the Philippines to resettle low islanders in the Marianas. The request was granted in 1818, and the Spanish gave the Carolinians permission to settle on Saipan, providing they embraced Christianity.[98] Although Freycinet states that the initial group of settlers consisted of a hundred Islanders from Lamotrek, Carolinian traditions claim otherwise. They name two groups arriving to settle Saipan: one from Elato led by Chief Nguschul, and a second, larger group from Satawal under the command of Chief Agrub. They met at Lamotrek and sailed to Guam. After meeting the Spanish on Guam, they sailed north and established settlements on the shores of Saipan's broad eastern lagoon.

The site chosen by Nguschul was named Ppiyol Oolng (view of the sand and sky). Agrub established another village nearby named Arabwal, after the green vine that grew there and on Satawal. The two villages eventually merged and were known collectively as Arabwal.[99] The sites were chosen because they fronted a wide sheltered lagoon, had sandy beaches and swampy areas just east of the beach for taro cultivation, and provided easy access to the ocean through reef passages.[100] In other words, the colonists sought to re-create the best aspects of their home islands. Another group from Lamotrek and one from Tametam soon joined them.[101]

Arabwal became a permanent Carolinian settlement. Agrub ended his days there. His body was committed to the sea off a reef due west of Managaha Island in a weighted mat. Through the act of naming locations, and daily use of the sea for burial, fishing, sailing, and recreation, a foreign sea became a familiar sea.[102] The colonists remained distinctly Carolinians, practicing their old lifestyle for the remainder of the century. They referred to themselves as *Falawasch,* Carolinians in their own language.[103] Visitors to Saipan in 1840 found the inhabitants living chiefly off fish and turtle, and cultivating plots of taro and yam.[104] Sánchez y Zayas's account of their seafaring has already been described. He also mentioned being entertained by traditional dancing, and noted that they had barely any notion of Christianity.[105]

Cultural continuity was aided by limited contacts with the Spanish on Guam. Most communication with Guam continued to be conducted on Carolinian *proa.* Carolinians visited Guam as they pleased, while the Spanish only established a presence on Saipan in 1835. This presence was hardly intrusive, consisting of a solitary, resident Chamorro official. Few Western vessels stopped at Saipan beyond the occasional whaling ship.[106] The Carolinian community continued to maintain annual links with their home islands.[107] Oral traditions suggest that Nguschul died of old age on Elato.[108] Settlers continued to come to Saipan as storms battered the low islands. In 1839 more typhoon victims arrived at Guam seeking refuge. Spanish government documents from the time record how just over a hundred inhabitants from the "Islands to the South" were settled on Saipan, at about the same time as the leper colony on Guam was moved there.[109] More refugees arrived as a succession of natural disasters wreaked havoc on Satawal and Lamotrek between 1847 and 1849. Three typhoons hit the atolls in 1847, another hit in June 1848, followed by a super-typhoon in August 1848. The latter resulted in at least three boatloads of refugees sailing north to the Marianas.[110]

On January 25, 1849, a severe earthquake hit Guam. A tsunami resulted that inundated Satawal and Lamotrek. In April refugees arrived at Guam describing how the tsunami caused death and destruction. In August three more canoe loads of asylum seekers arrived from Satawal and Lamotrek. A report to the governor general of the Philippines outlined their plight:

> their migration had come about because of a great earthquake, which was followed immediately by a flood that caused the islands to disappear for several hours, destroying all plantings and most of the trees. These people

and a few others, having remained [on the island] for lack of boats, had saved their lives by climbing trees. Many people had perished when the waters swept across [the islands]. Others, less fortunate than they, who had also climbed into the trees, were swept away by the waves.[111]

Once they had recovered their strength, the refugees intended to sail back to their home islands, collect the other survivors, and abandon their islands forever and settle on Saipan. The majority of the population of the low islands did not relocate, however. In 1851 there were only 267 people on Saipan.[112] Chiefs such as Agrub of Satawal, Toua of Woleai, and Jämŭt of Puluwat had seized upon the myriad opportunities offered through contacts with the northern isles to advance themselves, but old patterns persisted. The links forged with the Marianas added to existing relationships, rather than replaced them.

Natural disasters were not the only reason for resettlement. A new wave of Carolinians came to the northern Marianas in the late 1860s. Most were brought as laborers to develop new plantations. Carolinian traditions relate how a Captain Dororou came in the 1860s and took many people to Luta (Rota).[113] Records from the Marianas identify the entrepreneur as George Johnston, who traveled in his schooners *Ana* and *Aguila*. He initially hired 265 Carolinians from Pulusuk in 1865. Over the next four years he hired another 1234 from Namonuito.[114] Here the two archipelagos' histories interlink. All the workers were hired from islands under threat of raids and tribute demands from Puluwat. Puluwat's rising prominence during the reign of Jämŭt may have been due in part to the weakening of Lamotrek's influence after losses caused by storm devastation and outmigration to the north. One source also claims that guns acquired in trade with Guam assisted Puluwat in its wars in Chuuk. Puluwat gained a relatively easy victory in Chuuk through possession of two rifles traded from Saipan, "as was the case on other islands."[115] They encountered the unfortunate Chuukese offshore, where there was no place to hide.

In 1868 Arabwal was devastated by a powerful typhoon. Most of the buildings were destroyed as storm waves nearly 3 meters high washed over the village. With the luxury of high island resources, the community quickly recovered and Arabwal was rebuilt in the same location.[116] By 1869 the population of Saipan consisted of 331 Carolinians. But life did not return to normal for Saipan's *Falawasch*. In the late 1860s they faced a new factor from beyond the reef. The Chamorro population of Saipan rose from nine in 1865 to 128 in 1869, aided by regular shipping services between Guam and Saipan. They established themselves in a separate section of the settlement. There was little mixing between *Falawasch* and Chamorro and the future of *Falawasch* autonomy became uncertain. Arabwal was renamed San Isidro de Garapan, and the Christian church was rebuilt to symbolize the faith of the new residents and the power of the colonial authorities.[117] Once more, the people of the sea had to come to terms with a new force from across the water.

Conclusion:
Reclaiming the Sea

A SECOND settlement of Carolinians was established on Saipan in 1889. It consisted of Ulul islanders from Namonuito who had been working plantations on neighboring Tinian. They founded the village of Tanapag 8 kilometers north of Garapan. They represented a new era on Saipan. Many converted to Catholicism on Tinian, and married Chamorro on Saipan.[1] By 1902 Chamorro outnumbered Carolinians in the northern isles. Saipan's population consisted of 967 Chamorro, 621 Carolinians, and 43 "foreigners," while only 750 of the 2264 people living north of Guam were Carolinians.[2] *Falawasch* remained distinct, but their unique character began to fade as links with the home isles weakened.

By 1902 all the western Carolines were under colonial rule. Germany ruled until 1914, when Japan seized the islands. German activity was largely limited to copra plantations, so that only a few Germans moved into the region. Nevertheless, punitive measures were threatened against anyone who disobeyed the laws of the administration. In 1908, Puluwatese took advantage of the temporary absence of the German resident trader Kobelt to raid Pulap for questioning their right to harvest coconuts there. They confiscated canoes as punishment, but stopped short of killing anyone, as they knew Kobelt would soon return. When the Germans learned about the raid, they sent a warship to Puluwat and exiled sixteen men to Saipan.[3]

Japanese continued to develop a plantation economy, as well as recruiting or forcing young Islanders to labor for them in phosphate mines on Fais, Angaur, or Yap. They also forbade long-distance canoe travel in the name of safety. The *sawei* system was the main casualty of this policy, although tribute was occasionally sent to Yap on trading vessels. The development of regular inter-island shipping services reduced low Islanders' reliance on kin for disaster relief. German and Japanese colonial authorities used government vessels to ferry supplies to storm-ravaged areas or to evacuate refugees.[4]

Colonial prohibitions on inter-island canoe travel were widespread— from the British Gilbert Islands to French Polynesia.[5] Arbitrary colonial boundaries divided the Pacific into spheres of European interest, while policies eroded Islanders' means of independent travel. Hau'ofa sees this as one of the greatest legacies of the colonial era:

> Nineteenth-century imperialism erected boundaries that led to the contraction of Oceania, transforming a once boundless world into the Pacific Island states and territories that we know today. People were confined to their tiny spaces, isolated from each other. No longer could they travel freely to do what they had done for centuries. They were cut off from their relatives abroad, from their far-flung sources of wealth and cultural enrichment. This is the historical basis of the view that our countries are small, poor and isolated. It is true only insofar as people are still fenced in and quarantined.[6]

Hau'ofa is only partly correct. Access to seas was contested prior to colonial rule, while regular Western shipping services and the peace imposed by colonial authorities provided new opportunities to travel. The wanderlust of young men continued, leading to a chronic shortage of manpower on Rotuma that forced the British to impose restrictions on outmigration.[7]

Increased access to Western technology had a profound effect on vessels, seafaring skills, and fishing practices. Traditional designs persisted but incorporated new materials. On Kapingamarangi, Japanese throwing nets replaced many traditional netting practices, and by the 1970s they in turn had been supplanted by spear guns and snorkeling gear. In the late 1980s the Kapinga range of fishing techniques was less than a third of what it had been around 1900. Western sailcloth replaced heavier pandanus matting on some canoes, while the people of Kiribati went as far as importing timber for canoe hulls. These materials were paid for by the sale of copra or work in mines or on plantations. Steel tools lessened the time taken to construct canoes. All this made the acquisition of seagoing vessels a possibility for more Islanders than had been the case. As a result, the acquisition and use of canoes became less of a cooperative venture. This was most notable in near-shore fishing, as colonial legislation restricted their use on the open sea.

The use of motorized vessels threatened to make many seafaring skills redundant. Ships' engines operated independently of wind and current, while the compass provided another means of determining direction. Traditional canoes and skills continued to be used as reliable backups when modern technology failed or was unavailable. Some communities that abandoned traditional seafaring for modern shipping and air services found themselves more isolated than before when these services fell victim to commercial realities. On larger islands, jet travel led to massive outmigration.[8]

Fijian *drua* were still being built as late as 1943, and pockets of Islander seafaring survived the colonial era reasonably intact—especially on small, isolated islands. *Proa* were still being built and navigators trained in the traditional manner on Micronesian coral islands in the 1970s as the United States signaled its intention of giving Micronesians greater control over their own affairs.[9] These oases of traditional knowledge enabled a voyaging revival to take place. In the late 1960s and early 1970s, Satawalese and Puluwatese *pelu* using traditional navigation made a number of canoe voyages between the western Carolines and Marianas along Mutau-uol. In 1976, the Carolinian navigator Mau Piailug navigated the *Hōkūleʻa*, a reconstructed Hawaiian double-hulled canoe, 2500 miles from Hawaiʻi to Tahiti using traditional methods. The same year, a recently constructed *baurua* (voyaging canoe) from Kiribati was sailed to Fiji, a distance of 1500 miles. Unlike Hawaiʻi, Kiribati had maintained its seafaring tradition, although this voyage was much longer than usual.[10]

The voyage of the *Hōkūleʻa* captured the imagination of many, and inspired a voyaging renaissance. Other Islanders followed the Hawaiian example and relearned the lost art, reconstructed voyaging canoes based on early European accounts, and sailed along old sea lanes to ancestral homes. This renaissance reached its peak at the 1992 Pacific Festival of the Arts in Rarotonga, when reconstructed canoes from across the region converged to celebrate the theme of canoe voyaging. It was designed to unify Islanders with a sense of pride in their ancestral achievements. Hauʻofa's "Sea of Islands" reflected the spirit of these times.

Other, more cautious voices were sounded. Finney noted that these experimental voyages included their share of dangers and near disasters, although this was probably in keeping with historical patterns.[11] The prominent place of *waka* (canoes) in ceremonies to usher in the new millennium in New Zealand was followed by a debate in the media about whether occupants of ceremonial *waka* should have to wear life jackets. Some argued that this was culturally inappropriate, while others considered it common sense in light of the drowning of a member of a capsized *waka* on Lake Rotorua.[12] A further reminder of what had been lost occurred in February 2000 when *Te Aurere,* the double-hulled voyaging *waka* that sailed to Rarotonga in 1992, had to be towed into Wellington Harbor for a third time when its boom broke. This occurred almost within sight of the scene of the ancestral hero Māui's victory over the giant octopus he had pursued from Hawaiki.[13]

While many academics celebrate Hauʻofa's vision of Oceania to counter the negative MIRAB image, few believe it offers any way of addressing contemporary problems. Islanders now conduct most of their activities on land, and the main problems are rural poverty and those marginalized on the urban fringe.[14] Most Islanders' interactions with the sea have dramatically declined since 1870. Ellis's comment on Hawaiians' ability in water was still appropriate in 1870. The great Duke Kahanamoku won gold medals in swimming at the 1912 and 1920 Olympic Games, but since then modern coaching and training regimes have pegged back Islanders' "natural advantage."[15] Hawaiʻi is now more famous for surfing than swimming. Hawaiians figure prominently, but do not dominate the sport. They are no longer as closely connected to the sea. Finney comments that

> not everyone in Hawaiʻi benefits from its unique marine recreation heritage. By no means can it be said today that all the children of Hawaiʻi are amphibious. Many do not know how to swim, a lot never go to the beach, and still more never experience the thrill of sailing in a canoe or any other craft. Difficulty of access to the sea from underprivileged urban areas; lack of funds to buy surfing equipment, much less a small catamaran or even a windsurfer; a lingering continental, land-orientated world view that affects both personal preferences and government priorities; and a market-dictated land-development syndrome combine to keep an entire range of the population from achieving that joyful communion with the sea that is the Polynesian maritime heritage.[16]

Hawaiians also live under laws that promote the Western concept of sea tenure. Modern fisheries are dominated by 200-mile exclusive economic zones (EEZS), instituted under the protocols of the 1982 United Nations Convention of the Law of the Sea (UNCLOS III). Nations are entitled to exercise sovereign rights over resources 200 miles from their shores as long as they allow free air and sea passage.[17] Access rights within EEZS vary. In Hawaiʻi, vested near-shore rights such as *konohiki* fishing rights are recognized, but the claimant must prove this in an American court. Meanwhile, state and federal lawyers argue over control of the waters farther offshore within the 200-mile EEZ.[18] New Zealand

Māori have received better treatment in the courts, with a quota of the EEZ fishery set aside for them.[19] Islanders in independent Pacific nations have more interaction with the sea and more control over near-shore fisheries than Māori and Hawaiians. There is considerable debate over the compatibility of traditional marine tenure and government control using modern scientific fisheries management techniques.[20] Island nations have more trouble controlling offshore territorial waters, however. [21]

Modern fishing is big business. Corporations employ fleets and factory ships, sonar, and spotter planes. Tuna fishing vessels cost over $12 million, use $5000 worth of fuel a day, and may catch 150,000 fish in a single set of the net. The Pacific tuna fishery produces hundreds of millions of dollars' worth of raw product each year, which translate into value-added sales well in excess of $1 billion each year. Island nations see little of this money and consume little of the catch. They lack the capital to develop such huge enterprises, or even to patrol fishing in their own waters. With limited natural resources on land, demand for manufactured goods, and a pressing need to develop infrastructure, most gladly accept several million dollars in annual rent for fishing rights to their EEZs and use of harbor facilities from corporations like Ting Hong. Island nations probably only receive around 5 percent of the market value of the reported catch from these agreements. In addition, most commercial fishers almost certainly under-report their catch. Governments cannot press too hard for increased rents as most deep-water fleets operate from countries that are also significant aid donors.[22]

These stark realities animate the sense of loss that pervades Hau'ofa's vision. Critics accuse Hau'ofa of presenting a romantic image of the pre-colonial past. This study adopts a different stance. It criticizes his lack of evidence for his claim that colonial rule severely restricted Islanders' interactions and perceptions of their region, but argues that his vision is closer to reality than other scholars admit. Few Island communities were restricted to one island. They often traveled by sea, and knew or suspected worlds beyond their usual voyaging range. Expectations of forces from beyond the horizon were deeply embedded in their worldviews long before the tall ships sailed into view. Centuries of experience had taught them that new lands, new opportunities, and new and old threats hovered just beyond the walls of heaven.

Hau'ofa's other vision of Islanders' deep affinity with the sea is also borne out by this study. It has detailed a variety of ways in which the oceanic environment shaped Islander societies and Islanders shaped the sea. Most felt at home in the water. The waters of the Pacific were cultural seascapes rich in symbolic meaning, crowded with navigational markers, symbols of tenure, fishing and surfing sites, and reminders of gods and spirits in the form of maritime familiars and sites of their exploits. These seascapes altered as territories changed hands, navigational knowledge expanded and contracted, and storms and climate affected reef and shore configurations and the distribution of species.

This study attempts to integrate aspects of Islanders' interaction with the sea into a coherent overview. To truly understand Islanders' relationship with the sea it is necessary to look at all maritime activities: swimming, diving, fishing, seafaring and navigation, boat building, religion and ritual, naval warfare, and strategies for dealing with familiar outsiders and unexpected intrusions. Although this study draws on examples from across the region, there is enough material to apply its thematic model to a number of areas. The western Carolines case study could be repeated for western Polynesia and central eastern Polynesia. Even smaller areas have enough material to merit investigation: Palau, the Marshalls, Kiribati, Hawai'i, Aotearoa, Tahiti, Fiji, Tonga, Samoa, Tokelau, and Tikopia. There is much scope for comparative studies, particularly between localities with similar environments in Polynesia and Micronesia to explore the influence of environment on culture. Alkire has already conducted such a comparison for coral island communities.[23] This work suggests a number of maritime themes that Micronesia and Polynesia have in common.

The broad agenda outlined and the conclusions of the western Carolines case study have significant implications for Pacific history, anthropology, and archaeology. The prominence of the sea in Islanders' thoughts and actions means that works seeking Islander perspectives should pay more attention to maritime activities and scientific literature on ocean ecosystems. When maritime themes are emphasized for the western Carolines, indigenous agency is prominent in a period whose historiography is usually dominated by European activities. Expectations of natural disasters and human intruders led to extended and flexible social organization to accommodate newcomers and refugees. Irwin also urges exploration of the sea as a space rather than just a time passage between islands. There were many seascapes: the sea was important for livelihood and sustenance, social networks, and assertions of chiefly and community *mana*. It also shaped identity, as for most the familiar world ended and new worlds began at sea. Islanders left by sea and outsiders came by sea, and both were transformed.

The second implication is that there must be a sharper focus on regional studies to reflect the reality of the island world. Calls made twenty years ago to end monograph myopia have largely gone unheeded. While there is still merit in culturally specific studies, these risk projecting colonial boundaries back into the past, obscuring highly localized identities within wider, regional zones of interaction. A high degree of mobility meant that identities were also fluid and dynamic. There was a great deal of movement between island groups in the western Carolines and western Polynesia. Marshallese, I Kiribati, and Tuamotuans were also mobile, but largely within their own archipelagos. Inter-island sailing also occurred on a regular basis in central eastern Polynesia, but declined toward the margins of eastern Polynesia as distances between islands increased.

Variation in seafaring range supports the third contention of this study —the need for greater emphasis on variation across time and between localities. The openness of the island world meant that outside influences often resulted in periods of rapid change. The sea has many moods, and its more violent ones influenced the course of history. Mwaekil and Kosrae took decades to recover from the destruction and loss of life caused by the typhoon Man Sisik in the 1770s. Natural hazards and Islander interlopers disrupted communities well after Europeans made their presence felt. The 1770–1870 period saw dramatic changes in seafaring technology and voyaging, only some of which were due to Europeans. While some high Islanders' seafaring gradually atrophied, that of others rose and fell according to circumstances. Seafaring required a significant investment, yet navigation and canoe building remained restricted professions, leaving them vulnerable to natural disaster or disease. We need to move away from debates about change versus continuity, toward recognition that change was a constant. What mattered was how societies coped with change. As the anthropologist Alexander Spoehr noted:

> Change of itself need not imply instability. Change is always present in greater or lesser degree in every culture and society. Stability is not. Stability lies in orderly change and finds expression in a continuing successful adaptation to habitat and in non-violent shifts in the pattern of social organization.[24]

The degree of change between 1770 and 1870 has important implications for archaeology. Most works on seafaring draw heavily on modern studies of accomplished navigators from coral islands in the western Carolines and accounts of nautical technology from the early years of Western contact. This material is often used to speculate on the initial colonization of the Pacific, implying a continuity of technology and knowledge not supported by this study. Emphasis is given to accounts of drift voyages and computer simulations based on modern environmental data and the capabilities of the best canoes available in the late eighteenth century. By focusing on technology, they neglect the social and political organization required to sustain seafaring. The modern navigators Mau Piailug and Hipour represent the height of their profession, not the average. Navigational knowledge was partial, varied between locations and groups, and was vulnerable to intergenerational loss. Those hoping to understand initial colonization need to examine these issues and historical accounts of Islander colonization like those for Saipan and Sawana.

The study's emphasis on the importance of inter-island contacts between 1770 and 1870 also has implications for archaeological models of sociopolitical evolution in Remote Oceania. Archaeological opinion is currently divided over the extent to which Kirch and Green's phytogenetic evolutionary model measuring cultural divergence from a common ancestral base among Polynesian societies is compromised by postsettlement interactions between these communities. Kirch and Green recently maintained that differences in Polynesian cultures noted at European contact reflect predominantly internally driven divergence from a common ancestral base. They argued that inter-island voyaging declined over time in more remote Polynesian societies like Hawai'i and Aotearoa, while voyages in the main areas of inter-island communication at European contact, western Polynesia, and central eastern Polynesia were of limited frequency, involved a small percentage of the population, and really only had an impact on elite sections of society. They suggest this level of interaction was insufficient to lead to the dissolution of patterns of Polynesian homologous traits as some of their critics had suggested. They cite linguistic and genetic divisions within Polynesia to support their claims that external factors were not a major influence.[25]

Despite repeatedly emphasizing that history cannot be left out of the equation, Kirch and Green cite few works by Pacific historians. This study challenges their claims about the limited scale and influence of inter-island voyaging and external influences. While this does not necessarily invalidate Kirch and Green's approach, it does suggest sources and methodologies employed by Pacific historians could significantly enhance Pacific archaeology. This work has portrayed Islander communities as highly localized in their affinities, expansive, even regional in their interactions, and subject to rapid and significant changes resulting from external influences. The question we need to ask is whether the pattern of movement and interaction portrayed here is the exception rather than the rule over the centuries. If not, how did Tongans, Samoans, Puluwatese, and other inhabitants of Remote Oceania develop and maintain their cultural distinctiveness despite this fluidity of residence and movement? Such issues of cultural construction and cultural resilience require collaboration between archaeologists, anthropologists, *and* historians.[26]

There are exceptions to the neglect of history by archaeologists. Athol Anderson is also a skilled historian, and recently questioned many of these assumptions. He notes that most theories assume that colonizers possessed craft with the best aspects of technology used in the 1770s, and that twentieth-century climate and ocean data are applicable to the initial colonization period. Reconstruction of the initial language in Remote Oceania and radiocarbon dates from the earliest discovered sites are used to argue for a continuous trend of eastward exploration and settlement. But none ask the obvious question of why colonizers did not find islands earlier, if the right conditions were in place. Anderson speculates that the answer lies in a pattern of bursts of exploration followed by inertia brought about by climatic variation and inadequacies in nautical technology. He supports this by noting the relatively late introduction of *drua* to Fiji, and that eastern Polynesian canoes were often paddled and performed relatively poorly into the wind.[27]

The fourth implication of this study is that research on social and political organization must investigate how the requirements of seafaring and confronting external forces influenced the practice of political power. To what degree were strong kin links and chiefly power a response to natural hazards? Did the needs of seafaring promote the consolidation of chiefly power to enhance maritime logistics? If so, then why did some chiefs restrict the seafaring base to consolidate political power? This study suggests that sea power was an important means of maintaining access to sea travel and fisheries, as well as the coherence of multi-island polities. Significant struggles for domination centered on naval battles: Kamehameha against Kahekili in the 1790s, Bau versus Rewa in the 1840s, and the defeat of Manono and Tongan naval forces in Samoa in the 1850s.[28] More attention also needs to be placed on relations between the maritime environment and power in the colonial context. Movement should have been easier to control on sea than on land because it was concentrated in a few vessels. Vessels were easy to destroy, whereas a host of pathways were open to pedestrians. On the other hand, the colonial presence was limited, and seafaring specialists were always a restless, uncontrollable factor. The marginalization of specialist seafaring communities in the colonial era has yet to be studied.

Since independence, thousands of Islanders have migrated to new "islands" on the Pacific Rim for better employment and education. From Carson City to Canberra they forge new lives while maintaining links with their home islands. Outmigration is just one response to the economic restrictions of small island states. Hau'ofa has been criticized for not offering practical solutions to the problems of Pacific Islands—their small size, remoteness, lack of resources, and dependence on external funding. This response views the solution in terms of natural resources rather than attitudes. The reality is that many problems cannot be solved with the resources available, but there is much that can be changed, and here lessons can be learned from the past. Hau'ofa attempts to reshape attitudes. His call for Islanders to return to seeing themselves as unified by the Pacific mirrors the administrative reality of the Forum Fisheries Agency, in which Islanders unite to achieve concessions from fishing nations on the Pacific Rim. Their EEZs also create a coherent legal entity stretching over much of the western and central Pacific. Power and wealth still lie with outsiders, but Islanders' strength is enhanced through unity.

While Hau'ofa is correct in asserting that his ancestors saw the Pacific as a sea of opportunity, there are other lessons. This study departs from his in proposing that Islander voyaging was also restricted prior to colonial rule. The many requirements for seafaring were hard to maintain, and communities were always vulnerable to forces from beyond the horizon and beyond their control. Islander societies needed flexibility and adaptability to deal with external influences. Survival in the sea of islands also involved a high level of organization. Islanders should not only have pride in the achievements of their ancestors, but also learn from them.

Smallness is a weakness in the modern world, but it can also be a source of strength. In 1999 I attended a talk by the Cook Islands High Commissioner to New Zealand, Jon Jonassen, in which he compared microstates with canoes at sea. His address centered on a Cook Island Māori chant that translates into English as "The Magic of Buoyancy." Buoyancy is the capacity to float over even the most threatening waves. It is not a matter of size or resources. Small canoes can have this capacity as can small nations. Five areas are critical for maintaining canoe buoyancy: effective leadership, discipline, personal responsibility, forward planning, and adaptability.[29] It is worth recalling that Carolinians attribute disaster to social divisions, while recovery from natural disasters focuses on maintaining social cohesion. The chant offers a similar perspective:

Te enua mamaiti, mei te vaka   Microstates are like a canoe in the
   nui rai.   wide-open sea,
Tere maʻora ua na te vaka   It can sail freely or be navigated
   rangatira e toʻu.   with purpose.
Ko tei kite i te natura, ka ora   It survives only if one has learned
   uatu.   nature's challenges.
Matakite ra, ko te vare i te   However, watch out for the wrath
   tuputupua karape.   of the trickster giant.
Maʻara e kaʻore te atupaka o te   Remember that canoe size matters
   vaka e puʻapinga.   not to safety.
A tetaʻi tuatau, teitei roa atu   For there will come a time when the
   te ngaru: waves are bigger:
E kitea ei te tomoʻanga ruku,   Bigger than even the canoe to surely
   no te mea te ora,   sink it because life
Tei te manamana o te paunu,   Depends not on canoe size,
Kaore e ko to-na nunui.   but on the magic of buoyancy.[30]

Small polities are not necessarily more coherent than large ones. Two thousand years of political and social fission fueled much of the colonization of the Pacific. However, the societies that succeed and survive troubled times are coherent. They are also ready to respond to challenges and opportunities from beyond the horizon. There is no other way for a people of the sea.

APPENDIX:
THE MARITIME HISTORIOGRAPHY
OF OCEANIA

THE FRAGMENTED nature of published sources on maritime aspects of the history of Remote Oceania was noted in chapter 1. This appendix briefly outlines the main works thematically and highlights lacuna that this work has sought to address. It concludes with a brief overview of the best primary sources for maritime topics located.

Interlopers, from ships' captains to academics, have always been fascinated by how Islanders could locate and settle the islands scattered across the vast Pacific. From the time of Pedro Fernandez de Quiros onward they speculated and investigated how this feat might have been achieved.[1] Andrew Sharp's *Ancient Voyagers in the Pacific* rekindled modern academic interest. Sharp argued that colonization must have been accidental, as Polynesians lacked the ability to conduct deliberate return voyages to hitherto unknown destinations.[2] This theory ran counter to the high regard that most European explorers held for Islanders' seafaring ability.

Sharp's ideas generated a comprehensive response from his generally unsympathetic contemporaries. Computer simulation of wind patterns and ocean currents showed that canoes could not have reached all the islands that have evidence of pre-European settlement merely by drifting at the mercy of winds and currents.[3] A number of scholars scoured the historical record to catalogue deliberate versus accidental voyages.[4] Others investigated navigational techniques still practiced in some parts of the Pacific. David Lewis and Thomas Gladwin participated in open sea voyages by indigenous navigators without the aid of Western instruments and techniques.[5] Ben Finney headed a team that reconstructed a pre-European voyaging canoe from late eighteenth-century European drawings, and successfully sailed it between Hawai'i and Tahiti relying only on traditional navigational techniques. The voyage inspired a voyaging revival in a number of Pacific communities.[6]

The most recent and sophisticated work in this vein is by Geoff Irwin. A keen yachtsman himself, Irwin argues that Oceania was settled by a deliberate strategy of sailing into the prevailing trade winds. Navigational skills and maritime technology improved as early mariners moved into the Pacific. It was a gradual learning process.[7]

There were flaws in the logic underlying a number of these investigations, however. Do they really disprove Sharp's theories? The application of twentieth-century "traditional" skills to seafaring achievements from preceding centuries rests on the questionable assumption that navigational skills and vessel designs were relatively unchanging. Only a fragment of the traditional seafaring skills of most Pacific communities remained when these investigations began. The fragment was not necessarily typical of Remote Oceania as a whole.

Richard Feinberg's *Seafaring in the Contemporary Pacific Islands* surveys ethnographic studies since Lewis's time. While he acknowledges diversity in practices, he again proposes a broadly similar cultural pattern. Much of the diversity is explained away as a result of different colonial experiences.[8] The communities studied tend to be small and isolated like those studied in the 1960s, but most of the region's population lives on larger islands where navigational skills have long since fallen into disuse. Only by going back to the historical record before European activity disrupted seafaring on larger islands can a more representative picture be established. By focusing on master navigators, the ethnographers of the 1960s and 1970s inadvertently created an artificially optimistic view of traditional seafaring. Such men did not necessarily typify the abilities of all navigators. Surveys of voyages in the historical period suggest that most were successfully completed, but they also record troublesome voyages and disasters resulting from poor judgment or miscalculation.[9]

There is a trove of historical and scientific sources on these subjects, particularly for the two centuries since sustained European contact. Despite this, there has been no comprehensive investigation of variation in navigational practice across time, space, and community.

Maritime technology is particularly well documented. The standard secondary work is still Haddon and Hornell's classic *Canoes of Oceania*. A good updated and succinct summary of the diversity of canoe designs across Australasia and the Pacific is found in Douglas Oliver's 1989 work, *Oceania*.[10] Most of the information in these surveys is based on the observations of early European visitors. Modern speculation about voyaging craft in the era of initial colonization largely derives from these accounts, in conjunction with terms related to maritime technology from reconstruction of the language of the first colonizers. Given this implied continuity, it is surprising that few scholars have studied the rate and extent of change to maritime technology in the historically documented era. While there have been a number of articles on the long-term, ongoing evolution of the means of canoe propulsion, at least one commentator has suggested that the most appropriate designs for oceanic conditions were developed early. After that, canoe designs were relatively unchanging, particularly in Micronesia, where the swift *proa* held sway.[11]

The few surveys of changes in maritime technology in Remote Oceania suggest that change could be rapid and dramatic. There have been a number of works on the construction of Western-style schooners and other vessels.[12] This process usually began within a few decades of the first appearance of these vessels. Articles by Hiroa and Neich detail short-term changes to canoe technology in Polynesia during the period under review.[13] While the changes chronicled by Neich arise from Samoan adaptations of Western designs, Hiroa attributes changes on Mangareva and the Chatham Islands to internal factors. Recently, Ian Campbell built upon an innovative paper on maritime technological change by Gordon Parsonson to suggest that major changes occurred relatively late in Polynesia as a result of new, indigenous influences.[14] Not all change had to be inspired by Western contact.

Seafaring is about more than technology and seafaring skills. Activities at sea need to be viewed in their wider social context. Voyaging is a social process that also involves onshore infrastructure to provide logistical and organizational needs, as well as training and motivational influences. Although Irwin has made this point, neither he nor any other archaeologist who deals with the initial settlement of the Pacific has examined historically documented cases of colonization by Islanders. Enough detail exists to replace speculation with documentation of the infrastructure required. Gladwin and Feinberg discuss how both the high status assigned to navigators and the sociopolitical organization of the community help to facilitate modern inter-island voyaging.[15] Leiber similarly demonstrates how many aspects of social organization on Kapingamarangi deliberately or inadvertently help to optimize fishing practices.

The role of women in maritime pursuits has been neglected. The sea has generally been viewed as a space dominated by male activities. Recent studies suggest that the amount of maritime food collected by women often matches or exceeds that contributed by the men in some communities.[16] All this research was conducted within the living memory of the current generation. Dye's work on the decline of fishing in the Marquesas Islands proves that it is still possible to use such an approach to convey a sense of historical process for periods before the ethnographic present.

There have been many studies of Islanders' fishing techniques, equipment, and knowledge of marine biota. Anthropologists and archaeologists have been particularly interested in these topics. Good comparative overviews exist of fishing practices throughout the region.[17] There are also detailed case studies on specific communities in Remote Oceania.[18] Most discuss the seasonal cycle of marine activities and the related issue of how closely traditional knowledge of the marine environment matched modern Western scientific conceptions. Most studies conclude that indigenous knowledge about species' temporal and spatial behavior is detailed and accurate, although others have noted inconsistencies and inaccuracies in this body of knowledge.[19] A number of studies emphasize the different rationales underlying indigenous and Western classifications of sea species. While the Linnaean classification is based on physical features, some Islander classifications are based on the location of a species or its supernatural affiliations.[20]

This literature rarely incorporates the increasingly expansive scientific research on marine environments and ecosystems outlined in chapter 1. Although historians take account of anthropological studies of economic activity, they have been slow to use the works of geographers. While anthropologists tend to seek the social implications of subsistence activities, geographers are more concerned with human-environment relations. The work of Tim Bayliss-Smith is particularly impressive.[21] He sought to quantify the economies of Pacific communities in terms of the relative contribution of marine and terrestrial flora and fauna to the diet. Components such as shellfish and specific crops are plotted in terms of energy and nutrient cycles and exchanges. For example, so many hours of near-shore gathering by humans will produce so many units of fish and shellfish, which in turn absorbed so many units of energy from the sun and nutrients from the environment. Some nutrients are washed out to sea as a result of agriculture. In this way, humans become part of the ecosystem, delivering both energy and nutritional inputs, and harvesting outputs.

The reconceptualization of marine ecosystems as dynamic, open systems challenges most studies of marine tenure. It is usually assumed that marine tenure is based on a stable and known distribution of near-shore resources. Sea tenure and maritime knowledge in Remote Oceania are well documented for this region in comparison to other seafaring regions such as island Southeast Asia.[22]

Marine tenure is particularly well documented for Micronesia. A wide variety of islands and offshore environments have been studied. Margie Falanruw and Mary McCutcheon produced detailed studies of offshore tenure for two villages on Yap and Palau, respectively.[23] Lessa and Ushijima describe sea tenure on the atoll of Ulithi in great detail, while Alkire does the same for Lamotrek Atoll.[24] All these studies are on coastlines bounded by coral reefs. For this reason, Rubinstein's discussion of sea tenure around the reefless island of Fais is of particular value.[25] There is also a body of work that discusses sea tenure across Micronesia. Sudo, in particular, makes a fascinating comparison of sea tenure across a variety of environments, and concludes that social organization rather than environmental factors determined the form of sea tenure practiced.[26]

Polynesian marine tenure is also well documented. While Micronesian tenure studies are mainly based on postwar ethnography, those in Polynesia rely heavily on material from the eighteenth and nineteenth centuries. Hawai'i is particularly well served, as a great deal of indigenous marine lore was recorded in Hawaiian-language publications the century before last.[27] These fragments are crucial to our understanding of indigenous marine tenure, as colonial regimes were generally unreceptive to indigenous concepts. In the colonial era Western courts generally defined indigenous tenure as land-based, ending at the high water mark. Anything seaward of this was defined as the property of the Crown.[28]

The few studies of naval warfare in Oceania treat the sea as an environment to fight on, rather than to fight for. Naval warfare is portrayed merely as a seaward extension of clashes on land. Rarely is sea power seen as decisive. The only areas where naval activity is generally acknowledged to have involved more than merely the transport of forces are Tahiti and Fiji. Oliver and Ferdon present comprehensive reviews of Tahitian naval warfare in the late eighteenth century, while Gunson discusses how Western vessels facilitated the extension of Pomare II's inter-island sphere of influence in the 1800s.[29] At least four works emphasize naval aspects of the war between the Fijian polities of Bau and Rewa in the middle of nineteenth century. Most assign a significant role to sea power, although all conclude that the outcome was decided on land.[30]

Island communities had a long history of facing powerful new influences from across the sea. Despite this, the majority of works in Pacific history focus upon local responses to the presence of Europeans. While a number also chronicle relations between indigenous communities, interactions with Europeans are rarely considered alongside the extensive inter-island exchanges of the island world. There is now a sizeable body of published information on indigenous interaction between islands to allow a study of all external contacts from 1770 to 1870. The western Carolines, western Polynesia, and central eastern Polynesia are particularly well served.

There was a great deal of overlap between the Islander and European maritime worlds. While there is a rich body of literature on European beachcombers, much less has been written on Islanders who lived outside their familiar cultural world in this period.[31] Scholars have only recently begun to investigate this subject in detail. Particular attention has been paid to the significant presence of Islanders on Western vessels plying the Pacific and beyond. In the past decade Chappell, Binney, and Howard have written on this subject.[32] However, only Howard has given even passing attention to the seafaring and traveling heritage of these mariners. No one has sought to compare indigenous seafaring with the conditions and experiences of crewing Western vessels. No one has explored what the behavior of Islanders on Western ships reveals about the context from which they came. All existing studies treat this experience as one where Islanders engaged with the European world.

Cultural familiarity was important in this multicultural world. Few works examine Islander conceptions of the world beyond their familiar sphere of travel and interaction. In the 1980s, Driessen and Langdon argued over Tahitians' ability to predict elements from beyond the horizon.[33] A few years later, Sahlins suggested why such skills might be valued when he proposed that external groups who periodically usurped power from local rulers were part of the Polynesian mindset.[34] Echoing a more general sentiment among human cultures, Goodenough and Alkire claimed that the Carolinian world was considered increasingly supernatural and dangerous the farther one went from the near and familiar world of everyday life.[35] Distance from home is portrayed as the main cultural influence on attitudes to the world. It does not seem to have mattered that in most parts of Oceania the sky merged with the sea, and not the land. As in so many other respects, the sea remains a void.

The sea was not a featureless void to Islanders. There are a number of studies on local attitudes toward the sea. All physical environments contain culturally specific, symbolic markers that are only apparent to people versed in those cultures. Landscapes that incorporate such elements are known as cultural landscapes. Hviding makes a convincing case for the need to construct cultural seascapes.[36] Only a few modern works hint at the extent to which the sea could figure in the thoughts of its inhabitants. Modern research into traditional navigation in the Carolines involves studies on spatial perceptions at sea and cognitive mapping of seaways.[37] But there are few published works on indigenous perceptions of the sea according to culturally specific criteria. Minerbi has constructed such a model for Hawai'i based largely on the writings of Malo.[38] Alkire has done the same for certain western Carolinian atolls.[39] Both roughly conform to the near and familiar versus the distant and alien dichotomy proposed above.

Recent articles by Gunson and Geraghty cast doubt on the near/familiar–distant/sacred schema. Using a wealth of primary material they suggest that this continuum is an oversimplification. Rather, they suggest the world of Islanders consisted of parallel, overlapping spheres containing both sacred and secular elements.[40] Islander categories and associations do not conform to those of Western science. For example, a number of works explore ritual links between land crops and marine fauna. Links were also perceived between certain human kinship groupings and particular marine species.[41] Multiple overlapping spheres are more the norm than rigid, discrete categories. This point is particularly well documented in an article by Luomala on the diverse ways that the people of Kiribati perceive and interact with sharks.[42]

The range and quality of primary sources pertaining to maritime topics varies between island societies. The most useful for specific localities examined in this study were Kahaulelio, Kamakau, and Malo for Hawai'i; Henry and Morrison for Tahiti; Mariner for Tonga; Williams, Jackson, and Thomson for Fiji; Sánchez y Zayas, Floyd, von Kotzebue, and Chamisso for the western Carolines; and Keate, Semper, and Kubary for Palau. At a more general level, the journals of the members of Cook's expedition offer a wealth of detail on most Polynesian cultures, while the work of Damm and Sarfert contained in the volumes resulting from the German Südsee expedition stand out for the Caroline Islands.

NOTES

INTRODUCTION

1. For more detail, see R. C. Green, "Near and Remote Oceania—Disestablishing Melanesia in Culture History," in *Man and a Half: Essays in Pacific Anthropology and Ethnobiology in Honour of Ralph Bulmer,* ed. Andrew Pawley (Auckland: Polynesian Society, 1991), 491–502. The term Oceania is usually used to refer to all islands in the Pacific within the cultural areas defined as Melanesia, Micronesia, and Polynesia. The geographical boundaries of these areas are defined in chapter 1. In this study it refers to Remote Oceania.

2. The terms *Islanders* and *island communities* will be used henceforth to refer collectively to the inhabitants of Remote Oceania.

3. The terms *European* and *Western* are used here as umbrella terms for all Western cultures that sailed into the Pacific from the Atlantic.

CHAPTER 1: THE OCEANIC ENVIRONMENT

1. See K. R. Howe, *Nature, Culture, and History: The "Knowing" of Oceania* (Honolulu: University of Hawai'i Press, 2000).

2. Jocelyn Linnekin, "Contending Approaches," in *The Cambridge History of the Pacific Islanders,* ed. Donald Denoon (Cambridge: Cambridge University Press, 1997), 3–36, 6.

3. This scheme is most elegantly argued in P. V. Kirch, *The Evolution of the Polynesian Chiefdoms* (Cambridge: Cambridge University Press, 1984), 71–216. For a concise overview on the evolution of theory in Oceanic prehistory, see P. V. Kirch, "Prehistory," in *Developments in Polynesian Ethnology,* eds. Alan Howard and R. Borofsky (Honolulu: University of Hawai'i Press, 1989), 13–46.

4. D. L. Oliver, *Ancient Tahitian Society,* 3 vols. (Honolulu: University of Hawai'i Press, 1974), vol. 2, 1122.

5. K. R. Howe, "Pacific Islands History in the 1980s: New Directions or Monograph Myopia?" *Pacific Studies* 3 (1979): 81–90, 81.

6. O.H.K. Spate, "The Pacific as an Artefact," in *The Changing Pacific: Essays in Honour of H. E. Maude,* ed. Niel Gunson (Melbourne: Oxford University Press, 1978), 32–45, 34.

7. Howe, "Monograph Myopia," 86–89.

8. Geoffrey Irwin, *The Prehistoric Exploration and Colonisation of the Pacific* (Cambridge: Cambridge University Press, 1992), 204. For an early exploration of this concept, see P. V. Kirch, "Exchange Systems and Inter-island Contact in the Transformation of an Island Society: The Tikopia Case," in *Island Societies: Archaeological Approaches to Evolution and Transformation,* ed. P. V. Kirch (Cambridge: Cambridge University Press, 1986), 33–41.

9. This topic will be discussed in detail in chapter 3.

10. I. C. Campbell, *A History of the Pacific Islands* (Christchurch: University of Canterbury Press, 1989), 36.

11. Epeli Hau'ofa, "Our Sea of Islands," *The Contemporary Pacific* 6, no. 1 (1994): 148–61, 153–54.

12. These issues are discussed in Karen Nero, "The End of Insularity," in *The Cambridge History of the Pacific Islanders,* ed. Donald Denoon (Cambridge: Cambridge University Press, 1997), 439–67, 441.

13. Irwin, *Prehistoric Exploration,* 136.

14. Epeli Hau'ofa, "The Ocean in Us," *The Contemporary Pacific* 10, no. 2 (1998): 392–410, 405.

15. R. E. Johannes, *Words of the Lagoon: Fishing and Marine Lore in the Palau District of Micronesia* (Berkeley: University of California Press, 1981); Michael D. Lieber, *More Than a Living: Fishing and the Social Order on a Polynesian Atoll* (Boulder, Colo.: Westview Press, 1994); Edvard Hviding, *Guardians of Marovo Lagoon: Practice, Place, and Politics in Maritime Melanesia* (Honolulu: University of Hawai'i Press, 1996).

16. Hviding, xiii.

17. Linnekin, "Contending Approaches," 7. Discussions of these three areas as cultural entities can also be found in K. R. Howe, *Where the Waves Fall: A New South Sea Islands History from First Settlement to Colonial Rule* (Sydney: Allen & Unwin, 1984): 44–66; Campbell, *A History,* 11–27; and Nicholas Thomas, "The Force of Ethnology: Origins and Significance of the Melanesia/Polynesia Division," *Current Anthropology* 30, no. 1 (1989): 27–41. See also Map 1.

18. Bronwen Douglas, "Rank, Power and Authority: A Reassessment of

Traditional Leadership in South Pacific Societies," *Journal of Pacific History* 14 (1979): 2–27.

19. Linnekin, "Contending Approaches," 9.

20. Green, especially 493–95. See Map 1.

21. Excluding the Santa Cruz group 352 kilometers to the east of the main chain. See Map 1.

22. G. J. Irwin, "The Colonisation of the Pacific Plate: Chronological, Navigational and Social Issues," *Journal of the Polynesian Society* 107, no. 2 (1998): 111–43, 125.

23. William H. Alkire, *Coral Islanders* (Arlington Heights, Ill.: AHM Publishing Corporation, 1978), 65–69.

24. Hviding, 5–6, 8.

25. For the legend of Paikea riding on a whale, see Margaret Orbell, *The Illustrated Encyclopedia of Māori Myth and Legend* (Christchurch: Canterbury University Press, 1995), 130.

26. Hviding, 27, 369, 371.

27. Tom Dye, "The Causes and Consequences of a Decline in the Prehistoric Marquesan Fishing Industry," in *Pacific Production Systems: Approaches to Economic Prehistory*, ed. D. E. Yen and J.M.J. Mummery (Canberra: Occasional Papers in Prehistory no. 18, Department of Prehistory, RSPAS, ANU, 1990), 70–84; and P. V. Kirch and Marshall Sahlins, eds., *Anahulu: The Anthropology of History in the Kingdom of Hawai'i*, 2 vols. (Chicago: University of Chicago Press, 1992).

28. See I. Cameron, *Lost Paradise: The Exploration of the Pacific* (Boston: Salem House, 1987), 24; William L. Thomas Jr., "The Pacific Basin: An Introduction," in *Peoples and Cultures of the Pacific: An Anthropological Reader*, ed. A. P. Vayda (Garden City, N.Y.: The Natural History Press, 1968); and James Hamilton-Paterson, *Seven-Tenths: The Sea and Its Thresholds* (London: Vintage, 1993), 167.

29. See Lester C. King, *Wandering Continents and Spreading Sea Floors on an Expanding Earth* (London: John Wiley & Sons, 1983), 168–70; Douglas L. Oliver, *Oceania: The Native Cultures of Australia and the Pacific Islands*, 2 vols. (Honolulu: University of Hawai'i Press, 1989), vol. 1, 1–6; and Cameron, 19–24.

30. On the distribution of islands, see Thomas, "Pacific Basin," 5–8, and Cameron, 19–24. See also Map 1.

31. P. V. Kirch, *Feathered Gods and Fishhooks: An Introduction to Hawaiian Archaeology and Prehistory* (Honolulu: University of Hawai'i Press, 1985), 25.

32. R. F. McLean, "Spatial and Temporal Variability of External Physical Controls on Small Island Ecosystems," in *Population-Environment Relations in Tropical Islands: The Case of Eastern Fiji*, ed. H. C. Brookfield (Paris: Man and Biosphere Technical Notes 13, UNESCO, 1980), 149–76, 170.

33. The most devastating eruption in the region between 1770 and 1870 seems to have been that of Kīlauea in Hawai'i in the early 1790s. Clouds of poisonous gas billowed forth, asphyxiating a sizable section of a passing army. See S. M. Kamakau, *Ruling Chiefs of Hawai'i* (Honolulu: Kamehameha Schools Press, 1961), 152.

34. On tsunami, see Harold V. Thurman, *Essentials of Oceanography* (Columbus, Ohio: Charles E. Merrill Publishing Co., 1983), 155–61.

35. For example, see Lieber, 52, and Johannes, 49, 54–56. Nineteenth-century accounts are discussed in more detail in the following chapter.

36. For a good succinct summary, see Oliver, *Oceania*, vol. 1, 409–12.

37. Typhoons and hurricanes are different terms for the same phenomenon. The term *typhoon* comes from *tai fung*, a Cantonese term that loosely translates as "intense storm." Hurricanes are named after the wrathful Taino Indian god *Huracan*. The Taino were Arawakan Indians who lived in the Caribbean. See Christopher S. Lobban and Maria Schefter, *Tropical Pacific Island Environments* (Mangilao, Guam: University of Guam Press, 2001), 347 note 4.

38. On typhoons, see Lobban and Schefter, 108ff.; Matthias Tomczak and J. Stuart Godfrey, *Regional Oceanography: An Introduction* (Oxford: Pergamon, 1994), 115–18; and Irwin, *Prehistoric Exploration*, 11–12.

39. On seasonal wind patterns and their variability, see Oliver, *Oceania*, vol. 1, 411; Irwin, *Prehistoric Exploration*, 119–20; Robert A. Muller and Theodore M. Oberlander, *Physical Geography Today: A Portrait of a Planet*, 2nd ed. (New York: Random House, 1978), 122–24; and Ben Finney, Paul Frost, Richard Rhodes, and Nainoa Thompson, "Wait for the West Wind," *Journal of the Polynesian Society* 98, no. 3 (1989): 261–302, especially 265–67, 272–73.

40. Oliver (1989), 15–17.

41. Good discussions of tidal patterns are found in Harold J. Wiens, *Atoll Environment and Ecology* (New Haven: Yale University Press, 1962), 207–15; William A. Anikouchine and Richard W. Sternberg, *The World Ocean: An Introduction to Oceanography* (Englewood Cliffs, N.J.: Prentice Hall, 1973), 133–38; and Thurman, 152–56.

42. This discussion of Pacific currents is based on information drawn from Thurman, 125–35; Anikouchine and Sternberg, 96–117; Wiens, 188–90; Tomczak and Godfrey, 118–31; and Oliver, *Oceania*, vol. 1, 7–8.

43. Otto von Kotzebue, *A Voyage of Discovery into the South Sea and Behring's Straits, in search of a North-east passage, Undertaken in the Years 1815, 16, 17, and 18 in the ship Rurick*, 3 vols. (Amsterdam: N. Israel and New York: Da Capo Press, 1967; Bibliotheca Australiana reproduction of 1821 original edition), vol. 2, 91.

44. For example, see Rudolf S. Scheltma, "Long-distance Dispersal by Planktonic Larvae of Shoal-water Benthic Invertebrates among Central Pacific Islands," in *A Natural History of the Hawaiian Islands: Selected Readings II*, ed. E. Alison Kay (Honolulu: University of Hawai'i Press, 1994), 171–86, especially 178–79.

45. This overview is based on Thurman, 261–62; Eugene M. Rasmusson, "El Niño and Variations in Climate," *American Scientist* 73, no. 2 (1985): 168–77; David B. Enfield, "Historical and Prehistorical Overview of El Niño/Southern Oscillation," in *El Niño: Historical and Paleoclimatic Aspects of the Southern Oscillation*, ed. Henry F. Diaz and Vera Markgraf (Cambridge: Cambridge University Press, 1992), 95–117; Tomzcak and Godfrey, 363–74; Lobban and Schefter, 103–7; and Tom Spencer, "Changes in the Global Environment: Uncertain Prospects for the Pacific," in *Environment and Development in the Pacific Islands*, ed. Ben Burt and Christian Clerk (Canberra: National Centre for Development Studies, ANU, 1997), 243–63, especially 253–54. See also Figure 1 and Map 2.

46. Good overviews of global weather patterns associated with the ENSO phenomenon are found in Enfield, 100–102; Tomzcak and Godfrey, 364–67; and Rasmusson, 168–69. A re-creation of historical ENSO patterns using such data is attempted by William H. Quinn, "A Study of Southern Oscillation-related Climatic Activity for A.D. 622–1990 Incorporating Nile River Flood Data," in *El Niño: Historical and Paleoclimatic Aspects of the Southern Oscillation*, ed. Henry F. Diaz and Vera Markgraf (Cambridge: Cambridge University Press, 1992), 119–49.

47. Wiens, 155.

48. McLean, 170.

49. Kenneth P. Emory, *Kapingamarangi: Social and Religious Life of a Polynesian Atoll* (Honolulu: BPBM, 1965), 41–43, 66.

50. Lobban and Schefter, 104–6.

51. Ibid., 105.

52. McLean, 170–71.

53. Neville Nicholls, "Historical El Niño/Southern Oscillation Variability in the Australasian Region," in *El Niño: Historical and Paleoclimatic Aspects of the Southern Oscillation*, ed. Henry F. Diaz and Vera Markgraf (Cambridge: Cambridge University Press, 1992), 151–73, especially 160–65.

54. See especially M. Yamaguchi, "Sea Level Fluctuations and Mass Mortalities of Reef Animals in Guam, Mariana Islands," *Micronesica* 11 (1975): 227–43.

55. Good overviews of the distribution of terrestrial flora and fauna in the Pacific Islands are contained in E. Alison Kay, *Little Worlds of the Pacific: An Essay on Pacific Basin Biogeography*, Harold L. Lyon Arboretum Lecture no. 9, May 9, 1979 (Honolulu: Lyon Arboretum, 1980); Oliver, *Oceania*, vol. 1, 15–25; Lobban and Schefter, 224–30; and Peter Crawford, *Nomads of the Wind: A Natural History of Polynesia* (London: BBC Books, 1993), 109–10, 122–23, 139–44. For current thinking on factors shaping the Pacific's west-east biodiversity gradient, see Ronald H. Karlson, Howard V. Cornell, and Terence P. Hughes, "Coral Communities are Regionally Enriched along an Oceanic Biodiversity Gradient," *Nature* 429 (June 24, 2004): 867–70.

56. See Kay, *Little Worlds*, 25, 33; B. Salvat, "The Living Marine Resources of the South Pacific: Past, Present and Future," in *Population-Environment Relations in Tropical Islands: The Case of Eastern Fiji*, ed. H. C. Brookfield (Paris: Man and Biosphere Technical notes 13, UNESCO, 1980), 131–48, especially 134–35; Thurman, 232–36, 288–90; and Anikouchine and Sternberg, 222ff.

57. On ocean food chains, see Salvat, 132–33; Thurman, 258–60; Anikouchine and Sternberg, 235–39; and Taivo Laevastu and Herbert A. Larkins, *Marine Fisheries Ecosystem: Its Quantitative Evaluation and Management* (Farnham, Surrey: Fishing News Books Ltd., 1981), 20–21.

58. For discussions on the optimal conditions for fisheries, see G. D. Sharp, "Fish Populations and Fisheries: Their Perturbations, Natural and Man–Induced," in *Ecosystems of the World 27: Continental Shelves*, ed. H. Postma and J. J. Zijlstra (Amsterdam: Elsevier, 1988), 155–202, especially 172; Anikouchine and Sternberg, 214ff.; Thurman, 224, 264; David Sopher, *The Sea Nomads: A Study of the Maritime Boat People of Southeast Asia* (Singapore: National Museum of Singapore, 1977), 22–25, 31, 34; Hamilton-Paterson, 202–3; and T. Stell Newman, "Man in the Prehistoric Hawaiian Ecosystem," in *A Natural History of the Hawaiian Islands: Select Readings*, ed. E. Alison Kay (Honolulu: University of Hawai'i Press, 1972), 559–603, especially 577.

59. See particularly Laevastu and Larkins, 6, 98–100; and Arthur F. McEvoy, *The Fisherman's Problem: Ecology and Law in the California Fisheries, 1850–1980* (Cambridge: Cambridge University Press, 1986), 7–9.

60. Sharp, "Fish Populations," 167.

61. McEvoy, 7–8.

62. Sharp, "Fish Populations," 156.

63. Ibid., 157.

64. The following discussion is limited to regimes seaward of the low tide mark rather than intertidal regimes such as mangrove forests. On lagoon-reef ecosystem productivity, see Sequoia Shannon and Joseph R. Morgan, "Management of Insular Pacific Marine Ecosystems," in *Ocean Yearbook 10,* ed. Elisabeth Mann Borgese, Norton Ginsburg, and Joseph R. Morgan (Chicago: University of Chicago Press, 1993), 196–213, especially 199–200; Salvat, 140; Asahitaro Nishimura, "Fishing in Indonesia from the Marine Ethnological Viewpoint with Respect to Wallace's Line," in *The Fishing Culture of the World: Studies in Ethnology, Culture and Folklore,* 2 vols., ed. Béla Gunda (Budapest: Akadémiai Kiadó, 1984), vol. 2, 677–703, 696–97; and Johannes, *Words of the Lagoon,* ix, x.

65. Gilbert David, "Dynamics of the Coastal Zone in the High Islands of Oceania: Management Implications and Options," in *The Margin Fades: Geographical Itineraries in a World of Islands,* ed. Eric Waddell and Patrick Nunn (Suva: Institute of Pacific Studies, University of the South Pacific, 1993), 189–214, especially 190–92.

66. The neritic and oceanic zones are contrasted in Anikouchine and Sternberg, 231–33; and Thurman, 228–32. Interesting observations about the oceanic province's relative stability and its consequences for marine species are made by John E. McCoster, in "Fish," in *The Encyclopedia of the Earth: Oceans and Islands,* ed. Frank H. Talbot (London: Merehurst, 1991), 36–39.

67. Peter Dillon, *Narrative of La Pérouse's Expedition,* 2 vols. (Amsterdam: N. Israel and New York: Da Capo Press, 1972; Bibliotheca Australiana reproduction of 1829 original edition), vol. 2, 206.

68. Sharp, "Fish Populations," 170. Wiens, 247–49, describes flying fish entering Kapingamarangi Lagoon at dusk to feed, and returning to the open sea at dawn.

69. Wiens, 249.

70. Good discussions of scientific conceptions of coral reef ecosystems are found in Richard W. Grigg and Steven J. Dollar, "Natural and Anthropogenic Disturbance on Coral Reefs," in *Ecosystems of the World 25—Coral Reefs,* ed. Z. Dubinsky (Amsterdam: Elsevier, 1990), 439–52, especially 438–40, and Karlson et al.

71. Wiens, 184–86; Grigg and Dollar, 440–42, 448; and Lobban and Schefter, 102–3.

72. A. Krämer, "Zentralkarolinen, Part I (Lamotrek Gruppe, Oleai, Feis)," in *Ergebnisse der Südsee-Expedition 1908–1910,* vol. II, B, x, I, ed. G. Thile-

nius, 1–413, 204 (HRAF 1013, 223) (Hamburg: Friederichsen, De Gruyter & Co., 1937).

73. Spencer, 255–57, and T. P. Hughes et al., "Climate Change, Human Impacts, and the Resilience of Coral Reefs," *Science* 301, no. 5635 (2003): 929–33, 930.

74. Grigg and Dollar, 441–42.

75. On the circulation of ocean water within lagoons, see William J. Kimmerer and Ted W. Walsh, "Tarawa Atoll Lagoon: Circulation, Nutrient Fluxes, and the Impact of Human Waste," *Micronesica* 17, no. 1 (1981): 161–79, especially 163, 167, 171, and Wiens, 216–17. Arthur Grimble, *A Pattern of Islands* (London: John Murray, 1952), 134–36, describes a large congregation of lagoon and ocean fish attracted by plankton washed into a lagoon by spring tides.

76. John L. Culliney, *Islands in a Far Sea: Nature and Man in Hawai'i* (San Francisco: Sierra Club Books, 1988), 64.

77. Newman, 575, and Philip Helfrich and Sidney J. Townsley, "The Influence of the Sea," in *Man's Place in the Island Ecosystem: A Symposium,* ed. F. R. Fosberg (Honolulu: Bishop Museum, 1963), 39–53, 47.

78. Sharp, "Fish Populations," 169, and Wiens, 249.

79. See Culliney, 64–65, 99, and Johannes, *Words of the Lagoon,* 34–36, 48–49.

80. Johannes, *Words of the Lagoon,* 36.

81. Ibid., 44–45.

82. Culliney, 66.

83. McCoster, 37–38; Thurman, 307; John E. Bardach and Penelope J. Ridings, "Pacific Tuna: Biology, Economics, and Politics," in *Ocean Yearbook* 5, ed. Elisabeth Mann Borgese and Norton Ginsburg (Chicago: University of Chicago Press, 1985), 29–57, especially 33; and Alex Wild and John Hampton, "A Review of the Biology and Fisheries for Skipjack Tuna, *Katsuwonus pelamis,* in the Pacific Ocean," in *Interactions of Pacific Tuna Fisheries,* 2 vols., ed. Richard S. Shomura, Jacek Majkowski, and Sarah Langi (Rome: Fisheries Technical Paper 336/1 and 2, FAO, 1994), vol. 2, 1–51, especially 1–2.

84. Lorimer Fison, *Tales from Old Fiji* (London: The De La More Press, 1907), 162–63.

85. R. A. Derrick, *A History of Fiji,* vol. 1 (Suva: Government Press, 1968; reprint of 1950 revised edition), 37 note 1.

86. Max W. de Laubenfels, "Ocean Currents in the Marshall Islands," *Geographical Review* 40, no. 2 (1950): 254–59, especially 258.

CHAPTER 2: LOCAL WORLDS

1. S. Boyden, *Biohistory: The Interplay between Human Society and the Biosphere Past and Present* (Paris: UNESCO and Park Ridge, N.J.: The Parthenon Publishing Group, 1992), 29–39.

2. Hamilton-Paterson, 5.

3. Thomas Farber, *On Water* (Hopewell, N.J.: The Ecco Press, 1994), 48–49.

4. Ibid., 49.

5. For information on atoll settlement patterns, see Alkire, *Coral Islanders,* 41–46; William A. Lessa, *Ulithi: A Micronesian Design for Living* (New York: Holt, Rinehart and Wilson, 1966), 16–17; John L. Craib, "Settlement on Ulithi Atoll, Western Caroline Islands," *Asian Perspectives* 24, no. 1 (1981): 47–56, 49; Thomas Gladwin, *East is a Big Bird: Navigation and Logic on Puluwat Atoll* (Cambridge, Mass.: Harvard University Press, 1970), 8; H. Damm, P. Hambruch, and E. Sarfert, "Inseln um Truk (Polowat, Hok, Satowal)," in *Ergebnisse der Südsee-Expedition 1908–1910,* vol. II, B, VI, ii, ed. G. Thilenius, 1–288, 125, 128 (HRAF 1011, 108–9), (Hamburg: Friederichsen De Gruyter & Co., 1935); Tom Dye, "Archaeological Survey and Test Excavations on Arno Atoll, Marshall Islands," in *Marshall Islands Archaeology,* ed. Tom Dye (Honolulu: BPBM, December 1987), 271–399, 280; David V. Burley, "Settlement Pattern and Tongan Prehistory: Reconsiderations from Haʻapai," *Journal of the Polynesian Society* 103, no. 4 (1994): 379–411, 390.

6. Craib, 53.

7. Palauan settlement patterns are described in Richard J. Parmentier, *The Sacred Remains: Myth, History, and Polity in Belau* (Chicago: University of Chicago Press, 1987), 56–57, and W. Bruce Masse, David Snyder, and George J. Gummerman, "Prehistoric and Historic Settlement in the Palau Islands, Micronesia," *New Zealand Journal of Archaeology* 6 (1984): 107–27, especially 112–14.

8. For overviews of settlement patterns on Yap, see Sherwin G. Lingenfelter, *Yap: Political Leadership and Culture Change in an Island Society* (Honolulu: University of Hawaiʻi Press, 1975), 77, 86; Rosalind L. Hunter-Anderson, *Yapese Settlement Patterns: An Ethnoarchaeological Approach* (Guam: Pacific Studies Institute, June 1983), 20; and Ross Cordy, *Archaeological Settlement Pattern Studies on Yap* (Saipan: Office of Historic Preservation, Trust Territory of the Pacific Islands, August 1986), vi.

9. William H. Alkire, *An Introduction to the Peoples and Cultures of*

Micronesia, 2nd ed. (Menlo Park, Calif.: Cummings Publishing Company, 1977), 59.

10. For a good overview of Tahitian settlement patterns in this era, see Oliver, *Tahitian Society,* vol. 1, 44–45.

11. L. A. Milet-Mureau, *A Voyage Round the World, performed in the years 1785, 1786, 1787, and 1788 by J.F.G. de La Pérouse,* 3 vols. (London: J. Johnson Printer, 1798), vol. 2, 37–38.

12. H. D. Tuggle, "Hawai'i," in *The Prehistory of Polynesia,* ed. Jesse D. Jennings (Canberra: ANU Press, 1979), 167–99, 181.

13. For Tonga in general, see E. W. Gifford, *Tongan Society* (Honolulu: BPBM, 1929), 5–8, and Edwin N. Ferdon, *Early Tonga as the Explorers Saw it, 1616–1810* (Tucson: University of Arizona Press, 1987), 13, 207–9. Most of these general accounts focus on Tongatapu. For descriptions of the other parts of Tonga, see William Wales in J. C. Beaglehole, ed., *The Journals of Captain James Cook on His Voyages of Discovery,* 3 vols. (Cambridge: Cambridge University Press, vol. 2, 1961), 807, 810–11, for Eua; Burley, 379, 384–85, 403, for Ha'apai; and Janet M. Davidson, "Preliminary Report on an Archaeological Survey of the Vava'u Group, Tonga," in *Cook Bicentenary Expedition in the South-west Pacific,* Royal Society of New Zealand Bulletin 8 (1971): 29–40, for Vava'u.

14. John Jackson, "Narrative by John Jackson of his residence in the Feejees," in John Elphinstone Erskine, *Journal of A Cruise Among the Islands of the Western Pacific* (London: Dawsons of Pall Mall, 1967, reprint of 1853 edition), 411–77, 431.

15. Esther and William Keesing-Styles, eds., *The Journal of Thomas James Jaggar: Feejee 1838–1845* (Auckland: Solent Publishing, 1988), 63. On the inland peoples of Fiji in general, see Thomas Williams, *The Islands and their Inhabitants,* vol. 1 of George Stringer Rowe, ed., *Fiji and the Fijians,* 2 vols. (Suva: Fiji Museum, 1982, reprint of 1858 edition), vol. 1, 94.

16. Derrick, *History of Fiji,* 93, 108 note 3.

17. Russell Robertson, "The Caroline Islands," *Transactions of the Asiatic Society of Japan* 5 (1877): 41–63, 51, and F. W. Christian, *The Caroline Islands: Travel in the Sea of the Little Lands* (London: Frank Cass and Co., Ltd, 1967, new impression of 1st edition, 1899), 21.

18. Martin Dyson, Journal, May 16, 1861, microfilm copy in Hocken Library, Dunedin, of journal and papers held in Mitchell Library, Sydney. For a more general survey, see J. M. Davidson, "Settlement Patterns in Samoa before 1840," *Journal of the Polynesian Society* 78 (1969): 44–82.

19. See Dillon, vol. 2, 94–95; C. F. Wood, *A Yachting Cruise in the South*

Seas (London: Henry S. King and Co., 1875), 24; and Litton Forbes, *Two Years in Fiji* (London: Longman, Green, and Co., 1875), 231.

20. William Ellis, *Polynesian Researches: Hawai'i* (Rutland, Vt.: Charles E. Tuttle Co., Publishers, 1969, reprint of new edition, 1842), 369.

21. Captain David Porter, *Journal of a Cruise made to the Pacific Ocean,* 2 vols. (Upper Saddle River, N.J.: The Gregg Press, 1970, reprint of 1822 edition), vol. 2, 109.

22. Frederick W. Beechey, *Narrative of a Voyage to the Pacific and Beering's Strait, 1825–1828,* 2 vols. (Amsterdam: N. Israel and New York: Da Capo Press, 1968; Bibliotheca Australiana reproduction of 1831 edition), vol. 1, 45.

23. Mifflin Thomas, *Schooner to Windward: Two Centuries of Hawaiian Interisland Shipping* (Honolulu: University of Hawai'i Press, 1983), 32, citing a report in *The Polynesian* of August 21, 1852, 48.

24. Porter, 140.

25. Ibid., 180.

26. Basil Thomson, *The Fijians: A Study of the Decay of Custom* (London: Dawsons of Pall Mall, 1968), 316.

27. Ibid., 317–18.

28. Dillon, vol. 2, 100–101.

29. J. Arago, *Narrative of a Voyage Around the World* (Amsterdam: N. Israel and New York: Da Capo Press, 1971; Bibliotheca Australiana reproduction of 1823 edition), Part 2, 20.

30. For a good discussion of Pacific Islanders working as divers for Europeans, see David A. Chappell, *Double Ghosts: Oceanic Voyagers on Euroamerican Ships* (Armonk, N.Y.: M. E. Sharpe, 1997), 11, 38–39, 49–51.

31. On the Yapese, see Alfred Tetens, *Among the Savages of the South Seas: Memoirs of Micronesia, 1862–1868* (English translation by Florence Mann Spoehr) (Stanford: Stanford University Press, 1958), 20, 67–69; and Frédéric Lutké, *Voyage Autour du Monde, 1826–1829,* 3 vols. (Amsterdam: N. Israel and New York: Da Capo Press, 1971; Bibliotheca Australiana reproduction of 1835 edition), vol. 1, 123. For Rotumans, see Thomson, *The Fijians,* 317, and William Allen, "Rotuma," *Report of the Australasian Association for the Advancement of Science* 8 (1895): 556–79, especially 565–79. On Raivavaens, see David Branagan, ed., *Science in a Sea of Commerce: A day–by–day account of an 1820s south seas trading venture, based on the journal of Samuel Stutchbury, a scientific observer* (Northbridge, NSW: David Branagan, Publisher, 1996), 103.

32. Thomson, *The Fijians,* 317–18.

33. Branagan, 103–4, and 173 notes 718 and 719.

34. On the use of the sea for childhood and adult leisure, see Ben R. Finney, "The Ocean and the Quality of Life," in *The Emerging Marine Economy of the Pacific*, ed. Chennat Gopalakrishnan (London: Butterworths, 1984), 187–92, especially 189; David Malo, *Hawaiian Antiquities: Moolelo Hawai'i*, 2nd ed. (English translation by Nathanial B. Emerson) (Honolulu: BPBM, 1951), 223–24, 233; Dorothy Bàrrere, ed., *Fragments of Hawaiian History*, by John Papa Ii (English translation by Mary Kawena Pukui) (Honolulu: BPBM, 1983), 131–33; Ellis, *Hawai'i*, 369–72; Teuira Henry, *Ancient Tahiti* (Honolulu: BPBM, 1928), 278–79; Edwin G. Burrows and Melford E. Spiro, *An Atoll Culture: Ethnography of Ifaluk in the Central Carolines*, 2nd ed. (New Haven: HRAF, 1957), 263.

35. Bàrrere, *Fragments*, 133–35. The definitive book on Hawaiian surfing remains Ben R. Finney and James D. Houston, *Surfing: The Sport of Hawaiian Kings* (Rutland, Vt.: Charles E. Tuttle Company, 1966).

36. Philip Houghton, *People of the Great Ocean: Aspects of Human Biology of the Early Pacific* (Cambridge: Cambridge University Press, 1996), 13, 21, 56–61.

37. Houghton, 61–76, 80–86; Irwin, *Prehistoric Exploration*, 210.

38. Irwin, *Prehistoric Exploration*, 210; Houghton, 99.

39. King in Beaglehole, *Captain Cook*, vol. 3:1, 611.

40. Chappell, *Double Ghosts*, 104.

41. Ibid., 121 citing Harlan Page, *A Memoir of Thomas H. Patoo of the Marquesas Islands* (Andover, Mass.: American Tract Society, 1825), 8–11.

42. Damm, 25 (HRAF 1011, 19).

43. P. Salesius, *Die Karolinen-Insel Jap* (Berlin: MS, c. 1906), 22 (HRAF 1963, 32).

44. Damm, 25 (HRAF 1011, 19).

45. Frédéric Lutké, *Voyage Autour du Monde Exécuté par ordre de sa Majesté l'Empereur Nicholas Ier*, 3 vols. (Paris: Firmin Didot, 1836), vol. 3, 170 (HRAF 1319, 39).

46. Te Rangi Hiroa, *Arts and Crafts of Hawai'i* (Honolulu: BPBM, 1957), 285.

47. Gordon R. Lewthwaite, "Man and the Sea in Early Tahiti: Maritime Economy through European Eyes," *Pacific Viewpoint* 7, no. 1 (1966): 28–53, 34, citing J. R. Forster, *Observations made during a Voyage round the World* (London: G. Robinson, 1778), 440–41.

48. Some of the better accounts are Lewthwaite, "Early Tahiti"; Anderson in Beaglehole, *Captain Cook*, vol. 3, 942–43; Cook in Beaglehole, *Captain Cook*, vol. 3:169; and Edwin N. Ferdon, *Early Tonga as the Explorers Saw it,*

1616–1810 (Tucson: University of Arizona Press, 1987), 103–4, 106, 108, on Tonga; Thomson, *The Fijians,* 334–36, on Fiji; Robert Craig, ed., *The Palau Islands in the Pacific Ocean* by Karl Semper (English translation by Mark Berg) (Guam: University of Guam, 1982), 44, for Palau; Dennis Kawaharada, ed., *Hawaiian Fishing Traditions* (Honolulu: Kalamaku Press, 1993), xi, and Kirch, *Feathered Gods,* 199, for Hawai'i. Accounts of the destruction of crops by rats and ants can be found in Cook in Beaglehole, *Captain Cook,* vol. 3:1, 120; Craig, 163; and James Wilson, *A Missionary Voyage to the Southern Pacific Ocean 1796–1798* (London: Praeger, 1968; reproduction of 1799 original edition), 239.

49. For an overview of the methods used to preserve fish, see F. M. Reinman, *Fishing: An Aspect of Oceanic Economy. An Archaeological Approach* (Chicago: Fieldiana Anthropology 56(2), Field Museum of Natural History, March 1967), 192–93. Good accounts of fish preservation are found in George Keate, *An Account of the Pelew Islands, situated in the Western Part of the Pacific Ocean, composed from the journals and communications of Captain Henry Wilson, and some of his officers, who, in August 1783, were there shipwrecked, in the Antelope, A Pocket belonging to the Honorable East India Company,* 2nd ed. (London: G. Nicol, 1788), 190–91, 305; and Cook in Beaglehole, *Captain Cook,* vol. 3:1, 279.

50. For a discussion of the use of salt as a dietary supplement, see Ferdon, *Early Tonga,* 109, and as a medicine, see Dorothy B. Bàrrere, ed., *Ka Po'e Kahiko: The People of Old,* by S. M. Kamakau (Honolulu: BPBM, 1964), 113. *'Uala* is the Hawaiian name for *kumara,* the sweet potato.

51. T. P. Bayliss-Smith, "Population Pressure, Resources and Welfare: Towards a More Realistic Measure of Carrying Capacity," in *Population-Environment Relations in the Tropical Islands: The Case of Eastern Fiji,* ed. H. C. Brookfield (Paris: Man and Biosphere Technical Notes 13, UNESCO, 1980), 61–94, especially 77–79, and T. P. Bayliss–Smith, *The Ecology of Agricultural Systems* (Cambridge: Cambridge University Press, 1982), 61–62.

52. Béla Gunda, "Introduction," in *The Fishing Culture of the World—Studies in Ethnology, Culture and Folklore,* 2 vols., ed. Béla Gunda (Budapest: Akadémiai Kiadó, 1984), vol. 1, 11–26, 15.

53. Chamisso in Kotzebue, *Voyage 1815–18,* vol. 3, 181.

54. Thomson, *The Fijians,* 335–36.

55. Ibid., 335, notes that periods of stormy weather were the only time that the inshore fishery failed to meet daily needs. Hiroa, *Hawai'i,* 286, notes that Hawai'i's rainy winter season disrupted the inshore fishery through the increased runoff of mud and silt into the sea, forcing fishermen to fish beyond

the inundated reefs and turbid near-shore waters. This occurred when winter storms made the open sea dangerous.

56. Good discussions of ciguatera are found in Lobban and Schefter, 192; and Wiens, 291–95.

57. For examples of this division of the fishing calendar, see Lieber, 51, for Kapingamarangi; Johannes, *Words of the Lagoon,* 42–43, for Palau; and Lewthwaite, "Early Tahiti," 35–36, for Tahiti. The following discussion is based on Lewthwaite.

58. See Henry, 311, for example, on Tahitian knowledge of fish behavior in relationship to the phases of the moon and wind patterns.

59. Alkire, *Micronesia,* 7, 14–15.

60. Craib, 47; and Burrows and Spiro, 26.

61. Johannes, *Words of the Lagoon,* 1–2, and Masse, "Settlement in the Palau Islands," 87.

62. Alkire, *Coral Islanders,* 27, and Krämer, "Zentrolkarolinen," 334 (HRAF 1013, 363).

63. On Lamotrek, see William H. Alkire, *Lamotrek Atoll and Inter-Island Socioeconomic Ties* (Urbana: University of Illinois Press, 1965), 148; on Satawal, see Ken-Ichi Sudo, "Social Organisation and Types of Sea Tenure in Micronesia," in *Maritime Institutions in the Western Pacific,* ed. Kenneth Ruddle and Tomoya Akimichi (Osaka: National Museum of Ethnology, 1984), 203–20, 208–10, and Robert Gillett, *Traditional Tuna Fishing: A Study at Satawal, Central Caroline Islands* (Honolulu: Bishop Museum Bulletin in Anthropology no. 1, BPBM, 1987), 4–6; on Ifalik, see William H. Alkire, "Cultural Adaptation in the Caroline Islands," *Journal of the Polynesian Society* 69 (1960): 123–50, 129–30; and for Tobi, see Johannes, *Words of the Lagoon,* 85–87.

64. Dillon, vol. 2, 134.

65. Dye, "Marquesan Fishing," 78–79.

66. King in Beaglehole, *Captain Cook,* vol. 3:1, 611. *Maka'ainana* were common people below chiefly rank.

67. The Hawaiian diet is discussed in detail in E.S.C. Handy and E. G. Handy, *Native Planters of Old Hawai'i: Their Life, Lore, and Environments* (Honolulu: BPBM, 1972), 75–101. For the nutritional value of this diet, see Emile Massal and Jacques Barrau, *Food Plants of the South Sea Islands* (Noumea: South Pacific Commission Technical Paper no. 42, 1956), 7–9, and J. W. Purseglove, *Tropical Crops: Volume One—Monocotyledons 1* (London: Longmans, 1972), 64. Human nutritional needs are outlined in Konrad B. Krauskopf and Arthur Beiser, *The Physical Universe,* 5th ed. (New York: McGraw Hill, 1985), 419–26.

68. Lewthwaite, "Early Tahiti," 31, citing Joseph Banks from J. C. Beaglehole, ed., *The Endeavour Journal of Joseph Banks, 1768–1771*, 2 vols. (Sydney: Angus and Robertson, 1962), vol. 1, 342; and Andia y Varela, "Narrative 1774–5," in Bolton Glanvill Corney, *The Quest and Occupation of Tahiti by Emissaries of Spain During the Years 1772–1776* (London: The Hakluyt Society, 1913, 1915, 1919), vol. II (1915), 83, 280.

69. Keate, 305.

70. Cook in Beaglehole, *Captain Cook*, vol. 3:1, 279.

71. Lewthwaite, "Early Tahiti," 32–33, citing John Turnbull, *A Voyage Round the World in the Years 1800–1804* (Philadelphia: Benjamin and Thomas Kite, 1810), 285.

72. Lutké, *Voyage par ordre*, vol. 3, 166 (HRAF 1319, 37).

73. Hawaiian fishponds are discussed in detail in Kirch, *Feathered Gods*, 211–13, and Robert J. Hommon, *Use and Control of Hawaiian Inter-island Channels—Polynesian Hawai'i: A.D. 1400–1794* (Honolulu: Office of the Governor of Hawai'i, 1975), 114.

74. Henry, 281.

75. For a general review of fishing *tapu* in Oceania, see Reinman, 191–92.

76. For example, see Porter, 21–22; Margaret Orbell, *The Natural World of the Māori* (Auckland: David Bateman Ltd, 1996), 77–78, 80; and Fergus Clunie, *Yalo i Viti—Shades of Viti: A Fiji Museum Catalogue* (Suva: Fiji Museum, 1986), 159–61.

77. Keate, 234, 314; Tetens, 75; and Dorothy Shineberg, ed., *The Trading Voyages of Andrew Cheyne 1841–1844* (Canberra: ANU Press, 1971), 239.

78. For example, see Dillon, vol. 2, 103, on rare shells that were obtained from Vaitapu that were highly valued on Rotuma. The political and economic ramifications of the regional distribution of rare shells in the western Caroline Islands will be discussed in detail in chapter 7.

79. Malo, 78–79.

80. There have been numerous studies of fishing methods in Oceania. This overview of Remote Oceania is based on Reinman. His conclusion about the predominance of inshore fishing (181) is supported by most modern scholars. See Alkire, "Cultural Adaptation," 139; David, 192–94; Johannes, *Words of the Lagoon*, 63; Oliver, *Oceania*, vol. 1, 249; and Salvat, 145. Certain works stand out among the many detailed primary sources on fishing techniques and equipment in the region. In particular, Henry, 280–81, and James Morrison, *Journal* (London: Golden Cockerel Press, 1935), 154ff., on Tahiti; A. D. Kahaulelio, "Fishing Lore from Ka Nupepa Kuokoa" (in 13 installments—February 28, March 7, 14, 21, 28, April 4, May 2, 16, 23, 30, June 20, 27, July 4, 1902), English translation by Mary Kawena Pukui (Honolulu: photo-

copy of typescript in Library of Hawai'i Institute of Marine Biology, University of Hawai'i, n.d.), and Malo, 78–79, 208–13, on Hawai'i; Anderson in Beaglehole, *Captain Cook,* vol. 3:1, 939–40, on Tonga; Bruce W. Masse, "A Millennium of Fishing in the Palau Islands, Micronesia," in *Traditional Fishing in the Pacific,* ed. Athol Anderson (Honolulu: Pacific Anthropological Records 37, BPBM, 1986), 85–117, 85–92, on Palau; and Lutké, *Voyage par ordre,* vol. 3, 169–78 (HRAF 1319, 39–44), on the beachcomber Floyd's testimony about fishing practices on Murilo and Fananu.

81. On fishing techniques, see Reinman, 121–40.

82. This discussion of species-specific fishing techniques is based on Shannon and Morgan, 201; David, 200; and Foss Leach and Graeme Ward, *Archaeology on Kapingamarangi Atoll* (Dunedin: Studies in Prehistoric Anthropology, vol. 16, University of Otago, 1981), 99–100.

83. See Reinman, 118; Newman, 583; Hommon, 123.

84. *Aku* are identified in Mary Kawena Pukui and Samuel H. Elbert, *Hawaiian Dictionary: Hawaiian–English English–Hawaiian,* revised and enlarged edition (Honolulu: University of Hawai'i Press, 1986), 15, and *mahimahi,* 219. The most thorough reviews of offshore pelagic fisheries in this period are Hommon, 123ff., for Hawai'i, and Lewthwaite, "Early Tahiti," 44–46, for Tahiti.

85. See Hommon, 142; Archibald Campbell, *A Voyage Round the World from 1806 to 1812* (Honolulu: University of Hawai'i Press, 1967, facsimile reproduction of the 3rd edition of 1822), 140–42; and Patricia Price Beggerly, "Hawaiian Initial Settlement—A Possible Model," in *Micronesian and Polynesian Voyaging: Three Readings* (Honolulu: Pacific Islands Program Miscellaneous Work Papers, University of Hawai'i at Mānoa, 1976), 53–140, 99.

86. Pukui and Elbert, *Hawaiian Dictionary,* 270 *(noio),* 156 *(ko'e),* 374 and 362 *('uwae'u).*

87. Pukui and Elbert, *Hawaiian Dictionary,* 229.

88. Yellowfin tuna, ibid., 7.

89. Silversides, ibid., 93.

90. Kahaulelio, 11–13.

91. Reinman, 120–21, 139–40, 180–81; David Lewis, *The Voyaging Stars: Secrets of the Pacific Island Navigators* (Sydney: Collins, 1978), 66.

92. Henry, 394.

93. Gifford, *Tongan Society,* 288.

94. H. G. Cummins, "Tongan Society at the Time of European Contact," in *Friendly Islands: A History of Tonga,* ed. Noel Rutherford (Melbourne: Oxford University Press, 1977), 63–89, 71.

95. Richard Moyle, ed., *The Samoan Journals of John Williams, 1830 and 1832* (Canberra: ANU, 1984), vol. II, 196.

96. Martha Warren Beckwith, "Hawaiian Shark Aumakua," *American Anthropologist* 19, no. 4 (1917): 503–17, 508.

97. Henry, 386–92.

98. Ernest Sabatier, *Astride the Equator: An Account of the Gilbert Islands* (English translation by Ursula Nixon) (Melbourne: Oxford University Press, 1977), 56–57.

99. Bàrrere, *The People of Old*, 79.

100. Craig, 151.

101. Gifford, *Tongan Society*, 312–14.

102. Colman Wall, "Dakuwaqa," *Transactions of the Fiji Society for the Year 1917* (1918): 39–46, especially 45–46; Shelley Ann Sayes, "Cakaudrove: Ideology and Reality in a Fijian Confederation" (Ph.D. thesis in history, RSPAS, ANU, 1982), 37–47. Similar tales are related in Bàrrere, *The People of Old*, 83–84.

103. Henry, 389–91.

104. Mary Kawena Pukui, E. W. Haertig, and Catherine Lee, *Nana i Ke Kumu: Look to the Source* (Honolulu: Hui Hanai, 1972), vol. 1, 36–37, Bàrrere, *The People of Old*, 82.

105. 'Aumakua is the Hawaiian term for ancestral spirits. See Gifford, *Tongan Society*, 295–301; Henry, 389; Bàrrere, *The People of Old*, 74; Martha Beckwith, *Hawaiian Mythology* (Honolulu: University of Hawai'i Press, 1970), 128; and W. E. Russell, "Rotuma Its History, Traditions and Customs," *Journal of the Polynesian Society* 51, no. 4 (1942): 229–55, 248–49.

106. Henry, 389 (Moe) and 192 (Ra'iatea). The missionary Ellis and Tyerman and Bennet record that Tamatoa of Ra'iatea claimed that this had happened to him (Henry, note 55). Tyerman and Bennet were part of a deputation of home churchmen visiting LMS stations (Niel Gunson, pers. com., May 3, 2000).

107. Wall, "Dakuwaqa," 44–45.

108. Beckwith, *Mythology*, 140–41.

109. Ibid., 132–33.

110. Parmentier, *Sacred Remains*, 143.

111. Johannes, *Words of the Lagoon*, 35.

112. Parmentier, *Mythology*, 130.

113. Malo, 234–37, 239.

114. E. Sarfert, "Kusae," in *Ergebnisse der Südsee-Expedition 1908–1910*, vol. II, B, IV, ed. G. Thilenius, 416 (Hamburg: Friederichsen & Co., 1932), (HRAF 1007, 138).

115. See William H. Alkire, "Porpoises and Taro," *Ethnology* 7, no. 3 (1968): 280–89, and Katharine Luomala, "Porpoises and Taro in Gilbert Islands' Myths and Customs," *Fabula* 18, no. 1 (1977): 201–11.

116. D.K.B. Born, "Einigo Bemerkungen ubor Musik, Dichtkunst und Tanz der Yaploute," *Zeitschrift fur Ethnologie* 25, 134–42, 1903, 137 (HRAF 1186, 5).

117. The following account of Hawaiian conceptions of the sea is based on Malo, 25–27, and Luciano Minerbi, Davianna McGregor, and Jon Matsuoka, eds., *Native Hawaiian and Local Cultural Assessment Project: Phase 1 Problems/Assets Identification* (Honolulu: University of Hawai'i Press, June 1993), 89–90.

118. Aaron Buzacott, *Mission Life in the Islands of the Pacific* (Suva: Institute of Pacific Studies, 1985; reprint of 1866 edition), 16.

119. This knowledge is comprehensively reviewed by Hommon, 145–46.

120. Kahaulelio, 24–25.

121. Bàrrere, *The People of Old*, 73–74.

122. On the legend of 'Ai'ai, see Beckwith, *Mythology*, 22–23; Kawaharada, 2, 14–15. The *pahoehoe* formation at Leho'ula is depicted in Figure 2.

123. Williams, *The Islands*, 89.

124. Takashy Chipen, comp., *Uruon Chuk: A Resource of Oral Legends, Traditions and History of Truk*, 2 vols. (Saipan: Omnibus Program for Social Studies—Cultural Heritage, Trust Territory of the Pacific Islands, July 1979, copy in Micronesian Seminar Library, Kolonia, Pohnpei), vol. 1, 241.

125. Emory, 197–98, 228.

126. Burrows and Spiro, 48.

127. Russell, "Rotuma," 231, 249–50. See Map 3.

128. See, for example, Gillett, 43; Luomala, "Porpoises and Taro," 206; and Raymond Firth, "Sea Creatures and Spirits in Tikopia Belief," in *Polynesian Culture History: Essays in Honor of Kenneth P. Emory*, ed. G. A. Highland et al. (Honolulu: BPBM, 1967), 539–64, 548–49.

129. Chipen, 173.

130. Henry, 5.

CHAPTER 3: COMMUNICATION AND RELATIVE ISOLATION IN THE SEA OF ISLANDS

1. See Paul Bahn and John Flenley, *Easter Island Earth Island* (London: Thames and Hudson, 1992), and Jared Diamond, "Twilight at Easter," *New York Review of Books*, March 25, 2004, 6–10.

2. G. Forster, *A Voyage round the World in His Britannic Majesty's Sloop, "Resolution"*. . . *1772–1775*, 2 vols. (London: B. White, 1777), vol. 1, 601, cited in Greg Dening, "The Geographical Knowledge of the Polynesians and the Nature of Inter-Island Contact," in *Polynesian Navigation*, 3rd ed., ed. Jack Golson (Wellington: A. W. and A. H. Reed, 1972), 102–31, 108.

3. See Gordon R. Lewthwaite, "Geographical Knowledge of the Pacific Peoples," in *The Pacific Basin: A History of Its Geographical Exploration*, ed. H. R. Friis (New York: American Geographical Society, 1967), 57–86; G. S. Parsonson, "The Settlement of Oceania: An Examination of the Accidental Voyage Theory," in *Polynesian Navigation*, 3rd ed., ed. Jack Golson (Wellington: A. W. and A. H. Reed, 1972), 11–63, 28–32; Dening, "Geographical Knowledge," 121–25; Oliver, *Oceania*, vol. 1, 397ff.; and Irwin, *Prehistoric Exploration*, 211–13.

4. David Lewis, *From Maui to Cook: The Discovery and Settlement of the Pacific* (Lane Cove, New South Wales: Doubleday, 1977), 29; Ben R. Finney, "Voyaging," in *The Prehistory of Polynesia*, ed. Jesse D. Jennings (Canberra: ANU Press, 1979), 324–51, 349–50; and Irwin, *Prehistoric Exploration*, 213–14. These areas are outlined in Maps 4 and 5 that follow, and Maps 7, 8, and 9 in chapter 7.

5. Jeffrey C. Marck, "Micronesian Dialects and the Overnight Voyage," *Journal of the Polynesian Society* 95, no. 1 (1986): 253–58, especially 253, 256.

6. Branagan, 113. For other accounts, see Alkire, *Coral Islanders*, 103; Parsonson, "Settlement of Oceania," 28; Beechey, 198–199, 205, 207, 212; and E. Lucatt, *Rovings in the Pacific from 1837 to 1849: by a merchant long resident at Tahiti*, 2 vols. (London: Longmans, 1851), vol. 1, 258.

7. For example, see William H. Alkire, "Systems of Measurement on Woleai Atoll, Caroline Islands," *Anthropos* 65 (1970): 1–73, especially 6–7, 66–67, and Alkire, *Coral Islanders*, 119–20.

8. Damm, 37 (HRAF 1011, 28).

9. On the shells from Tonga, see Wood, 25–26. Wood identifies these shells as *Cypraea ovula*. For the Vaitapu shells, see Dillon, vol. 2, 103.

10. Alkire, *Coral Islanders*, 102.

11. Lewthwaite, "Early Tahiti," 51.

12. See chapter 7 for more detail.

13. On Tahiti, see Lewthwaite, "Early Tahiti," 51. For the Marquesas, see Dening, "Geographical Knowledge," 121–22, and Porter, 52.

14. This review of exchanges in the Society group is based on Lewthwaite,

"Early Tahiti," 48, 51, and Ferdon, *Early Tahiti,* 225. *Pahi* were a type of ocean-going canoe.

15. On Samoa, see Oliver, *Oceania,* vol. 1, 569; and Janet M. Davidson, "Western Polynesia and Fiji: The Archaeological Evidence," *Mankind* 11, no. 3 (1978): 383–90, especially 385.

16. Thomson, *The Fijians,* 280.

17. A. D. Couper, "Indigenous Trading in Fiji and Tonga: A Study of Changing Patterns," *New Zealand Geographer* 24, no. 1 (1968): 50–60, 51–52.

18. There is a wealth of primary material on exchanges between Tonga and Fiji in this period. The best overviews are Ferdon, *Early Tonga,* 234, and Alexander Philip Lessin and Phyllis June Lessin, *Village of Conquerors, Sawana: A Tongan Village in Fiji* (Eugene: Department of Anthropology, University of Oregon, 1970), 3.

19. Alkire, *Micronesia,* 72; Mason, *Economic Organization,* 22–24; and Leonard Mason, *Arno: Story of an Atoll* (Honolulu: Typescript draft held in Pacific Collection, Hamilton Library, University of Hawai'i at Mānoa, 1957), 32, 35–37.

20. Chamisso in Kotzebue, *Voyage 1815–18,* vol. 3, 163.

21. William Lay and Cyrus M. Hussey, *A Narrative of the Mutiny onboard the whaleship Globe* (New York: Corinth Books, 1963; reprint of 1828 original), 83–84.

22. Rev. L. H. Gulick, "Micronesia—of the Pacific Ocean," *The Nautical Magazine and Naval Chronicle* 31, no. 6 (1862): 298–308, 306–7. *Proa* are sailing canoes.

23. William A. Lessa, *More Tales from Ulithi Atoll: A Content Analysis* (Berkeley: University of California Press, 1980), 42–43. Alkire, *Lamotrek,* 29, 154, refers to the clan as the Mongalifach clan.

24. Burrows and Spiro, 131.

25. Alkire, *Lamotrek,* 154–55, and Damm, 43, 80 (HRAF 1011, 33, 74).

26. Krämer, "Zentrolkarolinen," 200 (HRAF 1013, 217) citing Lutké, *Voyage par ordre,* vol. 3, 144.

27. For a good discussion of this phenomenon, see Alkire, *Lamotrek,* 29, 154–60.

28. Lutké, *Voyage par ordre,* vol. 2, 343 (HRAF 1318, 138).

29. Lutké, *Voyage par ordre,* vol. 3, 180 (HRAF 1319, 46).

30. Lutké, *Voyage par ordre,* vol. 3, 180–87 (HRAF 1319, 46–50); Damm, 264–65 (HRAF 1011, 207–9).

31. See Parmentier, *Sacred Remains,* 56, on village sites, and 67, on migra-

tions. Another detailed discussion is found in Machiko Aoyagi, "The Geo-graphical Recognition of Palauan People," in *Islanders and their Outside World: A Report of the Cultural Anthropological Research in the Caroline Islands of Micronesia in 1980–1981,* ed. Machiko Aoyagi (Tokyo: Committee for Micronesian Research, St. Paul's [Rikkyo] University, March 1982), 3–33, especially 18–23.

32. On links between villages, see Parmentier, *Sacred Remains,* 56ff and 90ff. See also Craig on men's clubs (29–30) and women's clubs (56–57).

33. This relationship is discussed in chapter 7. Information on Kubary's visit is contained in William H. Alkire, "Technical Knowledge and the Evolu-tion of Political Systems in the Central and Western Caroline Islands of Micronesia," *Canadian Journal of Anthropology* 1, no. 2 (1980): 229–37, especially 234. Other good accounts are found in M. L. Berg, "Yapese Politics, Yapese Money and the Sawei Tribute Network before World War 1," *Journal of Pacific History* 27, no. 2 (1992): 150–64, especially 150–54, and Inez de Beauclair, "The Stone Money of Yap Island," *Bulletin of the Institute of Ethnology, Academia Sinica* 16 (1963): 147–60.

34. On *malaga* and other village interactions, see Oliver, *Oceania,* vol. 1, 568. For information on the size of *malaga* parties, see J. P. Sunderland, letter of July 23, 1847, *SSL 20,* LMS (Dunedin: Pacific Manuscript Bureau Microfilm copy in Hocken Library).

35. Aaron Buzacott, "Manners, Customs Language Religion etc of the Samoans," *SSL*—Box 8, Folder 113—Cook Islands 1836–1837, May 30–March 10, Rarotonga to Navigator Islands, 1837, LMS (Dunedin: Pacific Manuscript Bureau Microfilm copy in Hocken Library).

36. On *solevu* in general, see Thomson, *The Fijians,* 280–81. A good account of a *solevu* held at Natewa in the middle of the nineteenth century is found in John Elphinstone Erskine, *Journal of A Cruise Among the Islands of the Western Pacific* (London: Dawsons of Pall Mall, 1967; reprint of 1853 edition), 269.

37. The most thorough study of these connections is Niel Gunson, "The Tonga–Samoa Connection 1777–1845," *Journal of Pacific History* 23, no. 2 (1990): 176–87. See especially 176–77 on the scale and nature of these exchanges.

38. See Cummins, 68, and Gifford, *Tongan Society,* 140–41, 148–50, on the role of *muli* in Tonga.

39. William Diapea, *Cannibal Jack: The true Autobiography of a White Man in the South Seas* (London: Faber and Gwyer Ltd, 1948), 111–12.

40. John Martin, *Tonga Islands, William Mariner's Account,* 4th ed.,

2 vols. (Tonga: Vavaʻu Press, 1981), vol. 1, 183–96, relates Kau Moala's adventures in detail.

41. Martin, *Tonga Islands,* vol. 1, 69, outlines Tuihalafatai's career. Good discussions of the impact of Tongan chiefs in Fiji are found in Lessin and Lessin, 3–4, and Clunie, *Yalo i Viti,* 178.

42. This discussion on touring and visiting within the Society Islands is based on Oliver, *Tahitian Society,* vol. 1, 343–48.

43. This discussion is based on Oliver, *Tahitian Society,* vol. 2, 914–28, 1106–8. Oliver estimates that the *Arioi* constituted 20 percent of the population at most (1106). The best primary account is Henry, 237–41.

44. See discussions in Greg Dening, *Islands and Beaches: Discourse on a Silent Land, Marquesas 1774–1880* (Honolulu: University of Hawaiʻi Press, 1980), 83–84, and Dye, "Marquesan Fishing," 77. See also Greg Dening, ed., *The Marquesan Journal of Edward Robarts, 1797–1824* (Honolulu: University of Hawaiʻi Press, 1974), 331–33. Dening, *Islands and Beaches,* 49, notes that *tuhuna* was a term applied to those with specialist knowledge.

45. Good overviews of *ahupuaʻa* are found in Kirch, *Feathered Gods,* 2; Hommon, 15–17; and Handy and Handy, 48–49. *Makaʻainana* social interactions are discussed in Jocelyn Linnekin, "Statistical Analysis of the Great Mahele: Some Preliminary Findings," *Journal of Pacific History* 22, no. 1 (1987): 15–33, especially 22–23; Caroline Ralston, "Hawaiʻi 1778–1854: Some Aspects of Makaʻainana Response to Rapid Cultural Change," *Journal of Pacific History* 19, no. 1 (1984): 21–40; and Marshall Sahlins, *Islands of History* (Chicago: University of Chicago Press, 1985), 22–25.

46. Handy and Handy, 274, 510–11.

47. King in Beaglehole, *Captain Cook,* vol. 3:1, 561, 618.

48. Archibald Menzies, *Hawaiʻi Nei 128 Years Ago* (Honolulu: T. H. Press, 1920), 67.

49. For example, see Abraham Fornander, *An Account of the Polynesian Race* (Rutland, Vt.: Charles E. Tuttle Company, 1969; reprint of the 1879 edition), vol. 2, 200–201.

50. Sahlins, *Islands of History,* 20–21. These blood links are plotted in Fornander, endpaper.

51. Fornander, 296.

52. On Tongan canoe-building colonies in Fiji, see Diapea, 114; Martin, *Tonga Islands,* 293–303; W. T. Pritchard, *Polynesian Reminiscences* (London: Chapman Hall, 1866), 383–84; Derrick, *History of Fiji,* 121; A. C. Haddon and James Hornell, *Canoes of Oceania,* 3 vols. (Honolulu: BPBM, 1936, 1937, 1938), vol. 1 (1936), 329–30, citing Coleman Wall, *Catalogue of the Fiji Museum* (Suva: Fiji Museum, 1916); and Lessin and Lessin, 5.

53. See Deryck Scarr, "Cakobau and Maʻafu: Contenders for Pre-eminence in Fiji," in *Pacific Island Portraits,* ed. J. W. Davidson and Deryck Scarr (Canberra: ANU Press, 1970), 95–126.

54. Derrick, *History of Fiji,* 81.

55. On the environment of Sawana, and the initial setting up of the colony, see Lessin and Lessin, 6ff. and 33–35.

56. Ibid., 109–10.

57. Ibid., 10, 33.

58. Ibid., 18–23.

59. Parsonson, "Settlement of Oceania," 31, and Oliver, *Oceania,* vol. 1, 399, discuss this form of punishment in Oceania.

60. Lutké, *Voyage par ordre,* vol. 3, 162–63 (HRAF 1319, 351).

61. Rev. J. Waterhouse, *The King and People of Fiji* (London: Wesleyan Conference Office, 1864), 19–20; Fison, 1–17; Thomson, *The Fijians,* 23; and R. A. Tippett, "The Survival of an Ancient Custom relative to the Pig's Head, Bau, Fiji," *Transactions and Proceedings of the Fijian Society for the Years 1955 to 1957* 6, no. 1 (1958): 30–39, especially 31–33, 38–39.

62. Thomson, *The Fijians,* 355–64, especially 362.

63. On the Marshall Islands, see A. Tobin, *Land Tenure in the Marshall Islands,* revised edition (Washington, D.C.: The Pacific Science Board, Atoll Research Bulletin 11, June 1956), 34–35. James D. Nason, "The Strength of the Land: Community Perception of Population on Etal Atoll," in *Pacific Atoll Populations,* ed. Vern Carroll (Honolulu: University of Hawaiʻi Press, 1975), 117–59, especially 121, has a good discussion on the perception of the land being strengthened by residents.

64. Alkire, *Lamotrek,* 172.

65. J. E. Weckler, "Land and Livelihood on Mokil, an Atoll in the Eastern Carolines," *Coordinated Investigation of Micronesian Anthropology 1947–1949* (Los Angeles: University of Southern California), 11, no. 1 (1949): 42. The rendition *Mwaekil* is preferred here as it is more in keeping with local pronunciation. See David Damas, *Bountiful Island: A Study of Land Tenure on a Micronesian Atoll* (Waterloo, Ont.: Wilfred Laurier University Press, 1994), 213.

66. Weckler, 8, 48.

67. Ibid., 74.

68. Alkire, *Coral Islanders,* 28–29.

69. Michael J. Levin and L. J. Gorenflo, "Demographic Controls and Shifting Adaptive Constraints on Eauripik Atoll," *Isla* 2, no. 1 (1994): 103–45, especially 106.

70. Shineberg, 338.

71. Andrew Cheyne, *Journal of a Voyage to the Islands of the Western Pacific in the Brigantine "Acis"* A. *Cheyne Commander* (log I 28/11/63–14/12/64 and 10/2/65–6/2/66), (MS copy in possession of Dorothy Shineberg) September 28, 1864, October 11, 1864.

72. Levin and Gorenflo, 109.

73. Laura Betzig and Santus Wichimai, "A Not so Perfect Peace: A History of Conflict on Ifaluk," *Oceania* 61, no. 3 (1991): 240–56, 244.

74. Levin and Gorenflo, 109.

75. Berg, 150–53.

76. Dening, *Robarts,* 121–33, 274–75.

77. Captain James Cook and Lieutenant James King, *A Voyage to the Pacific Ocean undertaken by the command of his majesty, for making discoveries in the Northern Hemisphere . . . in the Years 1776, 1777, 1778, 1779, and 1780 – in 3 volumes* (vols. 1–2 Cook, and vol. 3 King), (London: G. Nicol, 1784), vol. 3, 26.

78. Porter, 132.

79. Ibid., 51–52, 93.

80. On Rotuma, see Lucatt, vol. 1, 235. For Futuna, see J. W. Boddam-Whetham, *Pearls of the Pacific* (London: Hurst and Blackett, Publishers, 1876), 260–61.

81. The history of 'Ata is outlined in Gifford, *Tongan Society,* 278–83.

82. This episode is discussed in detail in chapter 7.

83. G. Vason, *An Authentic Narrative of Four Year's Residence at Tongataboo* (London: Longman, Hurst, Rees, Orme, 1810), 10.

84. See Davidson, "Vava'u," 35–36, for Vava'u, and Burley, for Ha'apai.

85. Handy and Handy, 470, 489–90.

86. On inland trails, see Ferdon, *Early Tahiti,* 228–29, and Morrison, *Journal,* 141, for Tahiti; and Samwell in Beaglehole, *Captain Cook,* vol. 3:2, 1166, for Hawai'i. Such trails were also dangerous to travel on because enemy forces could easily conceal themselves alongside them. See Bàrrere, *Fragments,* 3–4, on an ambush on a trail in Hawai'i.

87. Dyson (n.d.), May 3, 1861.

88. Oliver, *Tahitian Society,* vol. 1, 15, 194.

89. Ibid., 194, 210–11, and Cook in Beaglehole, *Captain Cook,* vol. 1, 107.

90. Janet M. Davidson, "Auckland," in *The First Thousand Years: Regional Perspectives in New Zealand Archaeology,* ed. Nigel Pricett (Palmerston North: The Dunmore Press, 1982), 28–48, 28. Muriwhenua is the Māori name for the northern part of the North Island, which is known as Te Ika a Māui (the fish of Maui) to Māori.

91. Jackson, 471.

92. See Ferdon, *Early Tahiti,* 229, and Ferdon, *Early Tonga,* 237–38.

93. Martin, *Tonga Islands,* vol. 1, 132–34, 135, 139.

94. Otto von Kotzebue, *A New Voyage Round the World in the Years 1823, 24, 25 and 26,* 2 vols. (London: Colburn and Bentley, 1830), vol. 1, 276.

95. Sunderland (1847), Dyson (n.d.), October 4, 1860.

96. Alkire, *Lamotrek,* 93–94, 131–32.

97. Burrows and Spiro, 69–71.

98. On the dangers of lagoon travel at low tide, see Parmentier, *Sacred Remains,* 97; Craig, 46, 54, 119; Boddam-Whetham, 204; and Dyson (n.d.), May 23, 1862.

99. See Hviding, 186–88.

100. Keate, 135.

101. J. S. Kubary, *Ethnograpische Beitrage zur Kenntnis des Karolinen—archipels* (Leiden: P.W.M. Trap, 1896), 149.

102. Thomson, *The Fijians,* 230.

103. Kotzebue, *Voyage 1815–18,* vol. 2, 16–18.

104. For example, see Dyson (n.d.), May 17, 1861.

105. See particularly Parsonson, "Settlement of Oceania," 57–58, and Dening, "Geographical Knowledge," 119–20.

106. W. H. Harvey, letter of December 15, 1856 [1855], Sydney, New South Wales, in Sophie C. Ducker, ed., *The Contented Botanist: Letters of W. H. Harvey about Australia and the Pacific* (Carlton, Victoria: Melbourne University Press, 1988), 263. See also Pritchard, 402–3.

107. Damm, 96 (HRAF 1011, 88).

108. Gladwin, *East is a Big Bird,* 63 (Puluwat); Hommon, 161–70 (Hawai'i); and Parsonson, "Settlement of Oceania," 33, citing A. Aitken, *Ethnology of Tubuai* (Honolulu: BPBM, 1930), 45.

109. Kotzebue, *Voyage 1815–18,* vol. 2, 240–41; Chamisso in Kotzebue, *Voyage 1815–18,* vol. 3, 111.

110. Arago, Part 2, 12.

111. For 1830 and 1860, see Haddon and Hornell, vol. 1, 374, citing Captain Winkler, "On Sea Charts Formerly Used in the Marshall Islands," *Smithsonian Institute, Annual Report for 1899* (1901): 487–508.

112. Lewis, *Voyaging Stars,* 16.

113. See, for example, Diapea, 125–36.

114. Pritchard, 406, praised the survival skills of Islanders on drift voyagers. Finney, "Voyaging," 350, acknowledges this ability, but still believes large numbers of people were lost at sea.

115. See particularly Parsonson, "Settlement of Oceania," 33–34; and Dening, "Geographical Knowledge," 130.

116. Oliver, *Oceania*, vol. 1, 404. Pritchard, 406, also mentions the use of old coconuts carried on all sea trips, and the capturing and eating of sharks, as two ways in which fluid intake was maintained on drift voyages.

117. See Parsonson, 35, for a good discussion of survival problems at sea.

118. Lucatt, vol. 2, 40–41.

119. Parsonson, "Settlement of Oceania," 34, citing G. Turner, *Nineteen Years in Polynesia* (London: John Snow, 1861), 386–92.

120. The reception of drift voyagers will be reviewed in chapter 6.

121. Raymond Firth and Rosemary Firth, "Tikopia Songs of the Sea," in *Man and a Half: Essays in Pacific Anthropology and Ethnobiology in Honour of Ralph Bulmer,* ed. Andrew Pawley (Auckland: Polynesian Society, 1991), 405–12, 411–12.

122. Raymond Firth, *The History and Traditions of Tikopia* (Wellington: Polynesian Society Memoir 32, 1961), 139.

CHAPTER 4: SEAFARING IN OCEANIA

1. The prerequisites for voyaging are discussed in Thomas Gladwin, "Canoe Travel in the Truk Area: Technology and its Psychological Correlates," *American Anthropologist* 60, no. 5 (1958): 893–99, 893.

2. Gladwin, *East is a Big Bird,* 56.

3. The idea of song lines across the sea first occurred to me after reading about how Australian Aborigines sang routes across the land in Bruce Chatwin, *The Songlines* (London: Picador, 1988), and how Pacific Islanders also recorded their navigational information in songs in William H. Davenport, "Marshall Islands Navigational Charts," *Imago Mundi* 15 (1960): 19–26, 20.

4. Marshallese canoe songs are discussed in William H. Davenport, "Marshallese Folklore Types," *Journal of American Folklore* 66 (1953): 219–37, 236–37. Other examples include the partial English translation by Elizabeth Murphy of A. Krämer and Hans Nevermann, *Ralik–Ratak, (Marshall–Inseln),* in *Ergebnisse der Südsee-Expedition 1908–1910,* vol. II, B, ii, ed. G. Thilenius (Hamburg: Friederichsen De Gruyter & Co., 1932), (Honolulu: Typescript held in Pacific Collection, Hamilton Library, University of Hawai'i at Mānoa, 1985), 98–99, and J. Frank Stimson, "Songs of the Polynesian Voyagers," *Journal of the Polynesian Society* 41, no. 163 (1932): 181–201.

5. To the open sea.

6. Navigational indicator. The song recorded by Mason is reproduced in Davenport, "Folklore Types," 236–37. Mason's annotations are reproduced here as footnotes, although Davenport included them in the text.

7. A kind of bird that is never seen close to land.

8. This is a rhetorical question, for the *kalo* is never seen to land anywhere.

9. The name of an indicator.

10. Place names.

11. Reference to a story.

12. Three places on Likiep.

13. The chorus has some reference to calming the ocean and making haste. It is intoned with a quavering voice, not used in the verses, rising in pitch to the *o* and *e* syllables, then falls slowly and unevenly.

14. A short distance offshore for a certain kind of fishing.

15. Actually refers to a vague distance downward into the earth.

16. Into another realm even.

17. Kind of bird.

18. This infers that the canoe is far from land, for this bird alights far from land.

19. Name of a current.

20. A navigational indicator that is way to the north, thus suggesting the canoe is too far northward.

21. Suggesting the wind dies.

22. The word used for pillow refers to a woman's pillow on which one will go to sleep easily if he isn't careful. This phrase is a warning to use a man's pillow, a polished coconut shell instead, so that if the navigator dozes, his head will fall off and he will wake up and be ready to keep the canoe from capsizing if the wind suddenly strikes. The reference to a woman's pillow also makes an analogy with the calm sea reference just before.

23. Calm sea is suggested here by the use of a name for a specific kind of smooth wave pattern that is reflected from a certain kind of atoll formation.

24. A small fish, but also the name of a countercurrent that runs under the surface, from the land seaward.

25. Irwin, *Prehistoric Exploration,* 45.

26. Oliver, *Oceania,* vol. 1, 407.

27. The best overview of these signs is found in Oliver, *Oceania,* vol. 1, 406–22.

28. Lewis, *Voyaging Stars,* 45.

29. Oliver, *Oceania,* vol. 1, 418–19. Cheyne, *Acis,* February 24–25, 1865, noted that shoals at sea were detectable as lighter, discolored water, which

contrasted sharply with the normal clear, deep blue appearance of the sea mid-ocean.

30. Dening, "Geographical Knowledge," 115, citing H. Carrington, ed., *The Discovery of Tahiti: A journal of the second voyage of H.M.S. "Dolphin" round the World* by G. Robertson (London: The Hakluyt Society, 1948), 106.

31. John R. Hunter et al., *The Dynamics of Tuna Movements: An Evaluation of Past and Future Research* (Rome: FAO Fisheries Technical Paper 277, FAO, 1986), 25–29.

32. Wiens, 181; Tomczak and Godfrey, 129; and Thurman, 250. Crawford, 101, notes that the Tonga Trench, and other boundaries of tectonic plates located in the open ocean, are also nutrient-rich zones of upwelling.

33. Culliney, 124, and Gillett, 25.

34. Wood, 142.

35. Adelbert von Chamisso, *A Voyage Around the World with the Romanov Exploring Expedition in the Years 1815–1818 in the Brig Rurik, Captain Otto von Kotzebue*, (English translation by Henry Kratz) (Honolulu: University of Hawai'i Press, 1986), 201. See also Kotzebue, *Voyage 1815–18*, 225–28.

36. See Steven S. Amesbury and Michelle Babin, "Ocean Temperature Structure and the Seasonality of Pelagic Fish Species near Guam, Mariana Islands," *Micronesica* 23, no. 2 (1990): 131–38, especially 132–34, and Helfrich and Townsley, 41–42.

37. On the use of winds, see Oliver, *Oceania*, vol. 1, 409–11; David Lewis, *We, the Navigators: The Ancient Art of Landfinding in the Pacific* (Canberra: ANU Press, 1973), 74; and Lewis, *Voyaging Stars*, 44, 76. For swell patterns, see Oliver, *Oceania*, vol. 1, 413–14, and especially Herb Kawainui Kane, *Voyage* (Honolulu: Island Heritage Limited, 1976), 107.

38. See Figures 3 and 4. The basic principles of star navigation in the Pacific are reviewed in Oliver, *Oceania*, vol. 1, 417–18; Lewis, *Voyaging Stars*, 32–33, 45, 75; Irwin, *Prehistoric Exploration*, 75, 219–20; Kane, 106; and Davenport, "Navigational Charts," 20.

39. Don Eugenio Sánchez y Zayas, "The Mariana Islands: The Caroline Islanders," *The Nautical Magazine and Naval Chronicle* 35, no. 5 (1866): 253–66, 259–60. Two other notable accounts of navigational techniques are Andia y Varela, 284–86, for Tahiti, and Damm, 86–92 (HRAF 1011, 81–92), for Puluwat.

40. Sánchez y Zayas, 263–64.

41. Gladwin, *East is a Big Bird*, 144, discusses dead reckoning. See also Davenport, "Navigational Charts," 20.

42. For reviews of the *etak* system, see Howe, *Waves,* 20, and Oliver, *Oceania,* vol. 1, 419–21.

43. Krämer, "Zentralkarolinen," 272 (HRAF 1013, 291–92).

44. Oliver, *Oceania,* vol. 1, 407.

45. On cloud formations over islands, see Oliver, *Oceania,* vol. 1, 408–9, and Lewis, *Navigators,* 173–80.

46. On sea bird behavior as a navigational aid, see Oliver, *Oceania,* vol. 1, 408; Kane, 109; and Lewis, *Navigators,* 162–72.

47. Oliver, *Oceania,* vol. 1, 409.

48. See Figures 5 and 6. Oliver, *Oceania,* vol. 1, 408–9, has a good discussion of the interaction of swells and islands, and Davenport, "Navigational Charts," has a comprehensive review of Marshallese stick charts.

49. Adrian Horridge, "The Austronesians Conquest of the Sea—Upwind," in *The Austronesians: Historical and Comparative Perspectives,* ed. Peter Bellwood, James Fox, and Darrell Tryon (Canberra: Department of Anthropology, RSPAS, ANU, 1995), 135–51, 149, and Dening, "Geographical Knowledge," 116.

50. Oliver, *Oceania,* vol. 1, 407.

51. See Figure 7. On the design and capabilities of *proa,* see Sánchez y Zayas, 262–63; Gladwin, *East is a Big Bird,* 70ff.; and Peter Bellwood, *Man's Conquest of the Pacific: The Prehistory of Southeast Asia and Oceania* (Auckland: Collins, 1978), 297. Good accounts of Oceanic sails are contained in Oliver, *Oceania,* vol. 1, 380–82, and Kane, 111–14.

52. Bellwood, 298, and Kane, 111.

53. Cook in Beaglehole, *Captain Cook,* vol. 2, 408.

54. See Cook in Beaglehole, *Captain Cook,* vol. 2, 401, and Oliver, *Tahitian Society,* vol. 1, 207–9, on Tahiti; and Clerke in Beaglehole, *Captain Cook,* vol. 3:1, 598, King in Beaglehole, *Captain Cook,* vol. 3:1, 626, and Samwell in Beaglehole, *Captain Cook,* vol. 3:2, 1183–84, on Hawai'i.

55. Tacking involves steering the boat around to realign the sails with the wind.

56. This point is made by Bellwood, 298. For descriptions of *drua,* see Williams, *The Islands,* 73–76. Figure 8 is an illustration of a *drua* taken from Williams.

57. Oliver, *Oceania,* 393, makes this observation.

58. Arago, Part 1, 259.

59. See, for example, Sánchez y Zayas, 262–63, and Gladwin, *East is a Big Bird,* 60.

60. An excellent discussion of command onboard *proa* is given in Gladwin, *East is a Big Bird,* 57.

61. Sánchez y Zayas, 256.

62. The use of the crew as ballast is described in Chamisso, *Voyage,* 133, and Gladwin, *East is a Big Bird,* 99ff.

63. Lutké, *Voyage par ordre,* vol. 2, 342 (HRAF 1318, 138).

64. Gladwin, *East is a Big Bird,* 2.

65. Firth and Firth, "Tikopia Songs," 406–7.

66. Beechey, 231–32.

67. Chamisso in Kotzebue, *Voyage 1815–18,* vol. 3, 98.

68. See, for example, Lewis, *Voyaging Stars,* 177, and Diapea, 116.

69. See Ferdon, *Early Tonga,* 7, and Robert Langdon, *The Lost Caravel* (Sydney: Pacific Publications, 1975), 179. Langdon's evidence comes from Bellinghausen. See Frank Debenham, ed., *The Voyages of Captain Bellinghausen to the Antarctic Seas 1819–1821,* 2 vols. (London: Hakluyt Society, 1945), vol. 1, 237, 244, 249, 256.

70. William Ellis, *Polynesian Researches: Society Islands, Tubuai Islands, and New Zealand* (Rutland, Vt.: Charles E. Tuttle Co., Publishers, 1969; reprint of new edition, "originally published in the early nineteenth century"), 164.

71. Diapea, 126. On the experience of sailing the large double canoes of western Polynesia last century, see Williams, *The Islands,* 86–89; Jackson, 439, 470; Thomson, *The Fijians,* 293; Harvey in Ducker, 263; and Diapea, 126–30.

72. Williams, *The Islands,* 88. Harvey in Ducker, 263, also expressed doubts about the safety of *drua* in heavy seas.

73. Jackson, 470.

74. Diapea, 129–34.

75. On the handling of sails in high winds, see Kane, 113–14, and Gladwin, "Canoe Travel," 894–95.

76. Arago, Part 1, 266. See also Bàrrere, *Fragments,* 130–31, for Hawai'i. Sánchez y Zayas, 256, was highly impressed with Carolinians' ability at righting overturned canoes.

77. Andia y Varela, 286–87.

78. Damm, 106 (HRAF 1011, 92).

79. For discussions of sailing seasons as indicated by star alignments, see Gladwin, *East is a Big Bird,* 39, and Lutké, *Voyage par ordre,* vol. 2, 340 (HRAF 1318, 136).

80. On the advantages and disadvantages of sailing in convoys, see

Gladwin, *East is a Big Bird*, 58–59. Rev. Thomas West, *Ten Years in South-Central Polynesia* (London: James Nisbet & Co., 1865), 222–23, contains a good account of a convoy of four canoes scattered by a storm.

81. Krämer and Nevermann in Murphy, 98–99.

82. Henry, 123.

83. For example, see Chamisso in Kotzebue, *Voyage 1815–18*, vol. 3, 193; Cheyne, *Acis*, January 7, 1863, July 17, 1863; and Franz Hernsheim, *Südsee-Erinnerungen (1875–1880)* (Berlin: A. Hofmann, 1884), 19–20 (HRAF 1330, 3–93, 13). Hernsheim notes that the canoes traveled in a line to extend their front in a manner similar to that described by Krämer and Nevermann for the Marshallese.

84. Sabatier, 108–9.

85. Williams, *The Islands*, 89.

86. Ellis, *Society Islands*, 164.

87. Damm, 113–14 (HRAF 1011, 100–101).

88. Henry, 178–79.

89. Damm, 114, 208–9 (HRAF 1011, 100–101, 197–98).

90. Arago, Part 1, 269.

91. Damm, 208 (HRAF 1011, 197).

92. Chipen, 204, recounts the story of Saretam, a woman of the Katamak clan of Puluwat, who used her ability to call up the winds to sink an enemy canoe from Pulusuk.

93. Damm, 114 (HRAF 1011, 101).

94. For discussions of voyaging food, see Gladwin, *East is a Big Bird*, 50–51; Lutké, *Voyage par ordre*, vol. 2, 341–42 (HRAF 1318, 137); Gulick, no. 6, 303; Krämer, "Zentralkarolinen," 271–72 (HRAF 1013, 290–91); and Ferdon, *Early Tahiti*, 63, 191, citing S. Parkinson, *A Journal of a Voyage to the South Seas in His Majesty's Ship, the "Endeavour"* (London: C. Dilly and J. Phillips, 1784), 45–46.

95. Lutké, *Voyage par ordre*, vol. 3, 194 (HRAF 1319, 56).

96. Lutké, *Voyage par ordre*, vol. 3, 196–97 (HRAF 1319, 57).

97. This account of the preservation of pandanus is based on the description of the method used in the Marshall Islands by Admiral Sir Cyprian Bridge, *Some Recollections* (London: John Murray, 1918), 292–93.

98. Lewis, *Voyaging Stars*, 137, 177, discusses the storage of voyage provisions.

99. On cooking onboard canoes, see Lutké, *Voyage par ordre*, vol. 2, 342 (HRAF 1318, 137), and Diapea, 115–16.

100. Gulick, no. 6, 413.

101. Arago, Part 2, 16.

102. Gladwin, *East is a Big Bird,* 45–46, contains a very good account of how the social relationships developed in canoe houses facilitate voyaging.

103. Bàrrere, *The People of Old,* 74–75.

104. Ferdon, *Early Tonga,* 71, makes this observation, citing Anderson's list of maritime deities on Tongatapu in Beaglehole, *Captain Cook,* vol. 3:2, 949, and Mariner 1817, vol. 2, 106–8 (see Martin, *Tonga Islands,* 303–4) for the northern islands. A list of Ha'apai gods is also presented in Gifford, *Tongan Society,* 304–9. The different emphasis in the worship of Tangaloa is noted by Niel Gunson, "Great Families of Polynesia: Inter-island Links and Marriage Patterns," *Journal of Pacific History* 32, no. 2 (1997): 139–52, 141–44, especially 144.

105. Jackson, 439; Williams, *The Islands,* 85; and Thomson, *The Fijians,* 320–21, 366–67, 384.

106. Gladwin, *East is a Big Bird,* 127–28.

107. The most detailed accounts of the learning process come from the western Carolines. See Damm, 84–85 (HRAF 1011, 79–80); Gladwin, *East is a Big Bird,* 128–32; and Alkire, "Technical Knowledge," 231.

108. Excellent discussions of techniques used to enhance the retention of oral navigational knowledge are found in Alkire, "Technical Knowledge," 231, and Ward H. Goodenough and Stephen D. Thomas, "Traditional Navigation in the Western Pacific: A Search for Pattern," *Expedition* 29, no. 3 (1987): 3–14, 12.

109. Lewis, *Voyaging Stars,* 21–22.

110. Gladwin, *East is a Big Bird,* 132.

111. Alkire, "Technical Knowledge," 231.

112. Damm, 85 (HRAF 1011, 79).

113. Goodenough and Thomas, "Traditional Navigation," 11–12, and Krämer, "Zentralkarolinen," 271 (HRAF 1013, 290).

114. Irwin, *Prehistoric Exploration,* 220, citing Stephen D. Thomas's evaluation of the contemporary Micronesian navigator Mau Piailug in *The Last Navigator* (London: Hutchinson, 1987), 83.

115. Sánchez y Zayas, 259.

116. Alkire, "Technical Knowledge," 231.

117. Alkire, "Technical Knowledge," 231, and 'Okusitino Māhina, "The Poetics of Tongan Traditional History, Tala-ē-fonua: An Ecology-centred Concept of Culture and History," *Journal of Pacific History* 28, no.1 (1993): 109–21, especially 116.

118. The restricted dissemination of navigational knowledge within Mar-

shall Islands' society is outlined in Krämer and Nevermann, "Ralik–Ratak," 73, 75; Krämer in Leonard Mason, comp., *Select Writings on the Marshall Islands* (drawn from HRAF English translations) (Honolulu: Department of Anthropology, University of Hawai'i at Mānoa, 1947), 76; and Davenport, "Navigational Charts," 23–24.

119. Gifford, *Tongan Society*, 38, 142–43. Lewis, *Voyaging Stars*, 71, 73, lists the three main navigator families as Akau'ola, Ula, and Tuita. This apparent contradiction is resolved in Gifford, 143, where it is stated that the gods of Haa Vakatolo brought about the elevation of Ula. In other words, Ula and Fakatulolo are two names for the same group.

120. See Lewis, *Voyaging Stars*, 80, on Kau Moala, and Sione Latukefu, "King George Tupou of Tonga," in *Pacific Island Portraits*, ed. J. W. Davidson and Deryck Scarr (Canberra: ANU Press, 1970), 55–75, 58, on Taufa'ahau.

121. Lewis, *Voyaging Stars*, 75–77.

122. Lewthwaite, "Early Tahiti," 29, citing J. R. Forster, *Observations*, 441.

123. Dening, "Geographical Knowledge," 103, citing G. Forster, *Voyage*, vol. 2, 148, 155.

124. Damm, 84–86 (HRAF 1011, 79–80), and Gladwin, *East is a Big Bird*, 19.

125. Krämer and Nevermann, "Ralik–Ratak," 73, note that a woman called Libe had been a teacher in the Ebon school of navigation in the Marshall Islands. Lewis, *Voyaging Stars*, 78, 127, discusses *Kiribati* women navigators. Sabatier, 108–9, relates the traditions about Baintabu.

126. A general discussion of woods used to construct ocean-going canoes on high islands can be found in Edward Dodd, *Polynesian Seafaring* (New York: Mead and Co., 1972), 100. See also Dyson (journal) May 21, 1859, for Samoa, and Oliver, *Tahitian Society*, vol. 1, 199–201, for Tahiti.

127. The qualities of breadfruit timber are outlined in Dodd, 100, Krämer in Mason, *Select Writings*, 69, and Finsch in Mason, *Select Writing*, 75. *Teredo navalis* are actually bivalve mollusks with greatly reduced shells.

128. See Sánchez y Zayas, 127, for *proa* built at Saipan. Alkire, "Systems of Measurement," 25–27, discusses canoe construction and woods used on Woleai.

129. Lutké, *Voyage par ordre*, vol. 3, 191 (HRAF 1319, 55).

130. There are a number of detailed accounts of the canoe-building process from the period. These include Damm, 112–13 (HRAF 1011, 98–99), for Puluwat; Lutké, *Voyage par ordre*, vol. 3, 191–99 (HRAF 1319, 54–59),

for Murilo; Henry, 146–47, and Morrison, *Journal,* 205–6, for Tahiti; and Malo, 126–31, for Hawai'i.

131. All sources on canoe building place as much emphasis on ritual aspects of the construction process.

132. Henry, 146–47.

133. Ibid., 180–82.

134. Sánchez y Zayas, 261.

135. Damm, 110 (HRAF 1011, 98).

136. Martin, *Tonga Islands,* 294–95, and Gifford, *Tongan Society,* 143–44.

137. Williams, *The Islands,* 71, and Fison, 27, 30–31.

138. Henry, 146; Morrison, *Journal,* 165; Oliver, *Tahitian Society,* vol. 1, 200–201.

139. See Cook in Beaglehole, *Captain Cook,* vol. 1, 153–54, and Oliver, *Tahitian Society,* vol. 1, 200, on Ra'iatea; and Cook in Beaglehole, *Captain Cook,* vol. 2, 396, on Tu's "dock yards."

140. For discussions of the care taken with canoes, see Mason, *Economic Organization,* 55; Conrad Bentzen, "Land and Livelihood on Mokil, an Atoll in the Eastern Carolines" (Los Angeles: *Coordinated Investigation of Micronesian Anthropology 1947–1949* 11, no. 2, June 1949), 86; Cook in Beaglehole, *Captain Cook,* vol. 1, 154; and Ferdon, *Early Tahiti,* 243–44.

141. Reilly Ridgell, Manny Ikea, and Isaoshy Uruo, "The Persistence of Central Carolinian Navigation," *Isla* 2, no. 2 (1994): 181–206, 195–96.

142. See Oliver, *Tahitian Society,* vol. 2, 998, for a discussion of the resources individuals had to be able to muster to commission the construction of large canoes.

143. Rev. A. R. Tippett, *Fijian Material Culture: A Study of Cultural Context, Function, and Change* (Honolulu: BPBM, 1968), 85, 97.

144. Morrison, *Journal,* 205–6.

145. Damm, 113 (HRAF 1011, 99).

146. Derrick, *History of Fiji,* 81.

147. Malo, 77.

148. Gladwin, *East is a Big Bird,* 46, 50–51.

149. Parsonson, "Settlement of Oceania," 61.

150. See Gladwin, *East Is a Big Bird,* 45–46, and Damm, 120 (HRAF 1011, 104), for discussions of canoe house and kin group support networks.

151. Henry, 179–80.

152. Kenneth Brower, *Micronesia: The Land, the People and the Sea* (Singapore: Mobil Oil Micronesia Inc., 1980), 29. Similar perspectives are

expressed in Alkire, *Micronesia,* 14; Ward H. Goodenough, "Sky World and This World: The Place of Kachaw in Micronesian Cosmology," *American Anthropologist* 88, no. 3 (1986): 551–68, 555; and Ridgell, 197–200.

153. Goodenough, "Sky World," 554–55, and Marck, 253ff.

154. Chamisso in Kotzebue, *Voyage 1815–18,* vol. 3, 192–93.

155. See Lewis, *Voyaging Stars,* 129, and Ridgell, 186.

156. Michael McCoy, "A Renaissance in Carolinian–Marianas Voyaging," in *Pacific Navigation and Voyaging,* ed. Ben Finney (Wellington: Polynesian Society Memoir 39, 1976), 129–38, 138.

157. The 1910 figure comes from Damm, 83 (HRAF 1011, 76).

158. See Lutké, *Voyage par ordre,* vol. 3, 192–93 (HRAF 1319, 55), on canoe builders in Murilo, vol. 3, 197–98 (HRAF 1319, 58), on Rua's navigators, and vol. 3, 195–96 (HRAF 1319, 56–57), on the importance of trade with Chuuk.

159. Krämer, "Zentralkarolinen," 368–69 (HRAF 1013, 413–15).

160. Lutké, *Voyage par ordre,* vol. 2, 309 (HRAF 1318, 117).

161. Chamisso, *Voyage,* 273.

162. Wood, 15.

163. Ibid., 25.

164. Dillon, vol. 2, 103–4.

165. Alan Howard, "Rotuman Seafaring in Historical Perspective," in *Seafaring in the Contemporary Pacific Islands: Studies in Continuity and Change,* ed. Richard Feinberg (DeKalb: Northern Illinois University Press, 1995), 114–43, 118, citing Robert Jarman, *Journal of a Voyage to the South Seas, in the Japan, Employed in the Sperm Whale Fishery, under the Command of Capt. John May* (London: Longman and Co. and Charles Tilt, 1838), 183–84.

166. David Arthur Chappell, "Beyond the Beach: Periplean Frontiers of Pacific Islanders aboard Euroamerican Ships, 1768–1887" (Ph.D. thesis in history, University of Hawai'i at Mānoa, 1991), 180, citing the log of the *Emerald,* March 5, 1834.

167. See Dening, "Geographical Knowledge," 108, and Te Rangi Hiroa, "The Disappearance of Canoes in Polynesia," *Journal of the Polynesian Society* 51, no. 3 (1942): 191–99, 195.

168. See Williams, *The Islands,* 71; Thomson, *The Fijians,* 292–93; and Tippett, *Fijian Material Culture,* 110–11.

169. For an example of fleet sizes in the 1770s, see Cook in Beaglehole, *Captain Cook,* vol. 2, 385–86.

170. Morrison, *Journal,* 171.

171. Wilson, *Missionary Voyage,* Appendix—section XII "Canoes," 376.
172. Ibid., 200.

CHAPTER 5: FLUID FRONTIERS

1. See, for example, King in Beaglehole, *Captain Cook,* vol. 3:2, 1381; Kotzebue, *Voyage 1815–18,* vol. 2, 102; and McCutcheon, 46.

2. Lessa, *Ulithi;* 12–13; Sudo, 218–19; and Iwao Ushijima, "The Control of Reefs and Lagoons: Some Aspects of the Political Structure of Ulithi Atoll," in *Islanders and their Outside World: A Report of the Cultural Anthropological Research in the Caroline Islands of Micronesia in 1980–1981,* ed. Machiko Aoyagi (Tokyo: Committee for Micronesian Research, St. Paul's [Rikkyo] University, March 1982), 35–75. Sudo's map of lagoon and reef tenure in Ulithi is reproduced in Map 6.

3. Tobin, 57.

4. Lieber, 104, 113–27, has a particularly good analysis of this dimension of fishing on Kapingamarangi Atoll.

5. See Lessa, *Ulithi,* 46; Ushijima, 50–59, and Sudo, 218, on Ulithi; and Damm, 55 (HRAF 1011, 45–46), on this practice in Puluwat.

6. See Tobin, 58. Historical sources confirm this was a long-standing practice. For example, it was mentioned by Kotzebue, *Voyage 1815–18,* vol. 3, 154–55.

7. Tobin, 56–59.

8. See Lewthwaite, "Early Tahiti," 31–32, on Tahiti; Māhina, 111 note 25, on Tonga; Minerbi, 123–24, and Kawaharada, xvi–xvii, on Hawai'i. Historical records confirm this. See Cook in Beaglehole, *Captain Cook,* vol. 3:1, 141, for Tahiti; Vason, 136, Martin, *Tonga Islands,* 180, and Gifford, *Tongan Society,* 103, for Tonga; and Kamakau, 77, 105, 203, for Hawai'i.

9. See Oliver, *Tahitian Society,* 309–11, on Tahiti; Melody Kapilialoha Mackenzie, *Native Hawaiian Rights Handbook* (Honolulu: Native Hawaiian Legal Corporation, 1991), 174, 224, for Hawai'i; and McCutcheon, 45–46, 115–17, for Palau.

10. Henry, 70–71.

11. Karen Louise Nero, "A cherechar a lokelii: Beads of History of Koror, Palau, 1783–1983" (Ph.D. thesis, University of California, 1987), 124.

12. Parmentier, *Sacred Remains,* 198 note 1.

13. Thomson, *The Fijians,* 384–85.

14. Kingdom of Hawai'i, Laws of 1845–1846, chapter VI, article V, section 8, cited in Mackenzie, 174, 188 note 15, and Minerbi, 124, 126.

15. Colin Newbury, *Tahiti Nui: Change and Survival in French Polynesia 1767–1945* (Honolulu: University Press of Hawai'i, 1980), 45, citing LMS Transactions, 1818, 305.

16. AJHR, "Report of the Select Committee on the Thames Sea Beach Bill" (Wellington: *Appendices to the Journals of the House of Representatives 1869*, vol. II, F–7, 1867), 1–18, 6–7.

17. See Hommon, 183–97, and Mackenzie, 174, on Hawai'i; and Newbury, *Tahiti Nui*, 45, on Tahiti.

18. Thomas G. Thrum, ed., *Collection of Hawaiian Antiquities and Folk-lore* (6 vols.) by Abraham Fornander (Honolulu: BPBM, 1916–19), vol. 6 (1919), 186–87.

19. Dorothy B. Bàrrere, ed., *The Works of the People of Old: Na Hana a ka Po'e Kahiko,* by Samuel Kamakau (Honolulu: BPBM, 1976), 78–79.

20. Kahaulelio, 22, and Hommon, 128–30.

21. Dillon, vol. 2, 110–11.

22. Hommon, 96–98, 100–101, 183–97.

23. See, for example, Kamakau, 107, and Fornander, 218.

24. Islander perceptions of the world beyond the horizon are discussed in the next chapter. A good overview is Goodenough, "Sky World."

25. See Map 8 and chapter 7.

26. Gladwin, *East is a Big Bird,* 27.

27. Damm, 50, 56 (HRAF 1011, 40, 47).

28. Alkire, *Lamotrek,* 147–48, 154.

29. Sudo, 226–27.

30. Ibid., 205.

31. For example, see John Keegan, *The Price of Admiralty: War at Sea from Man of War to Submarine* (London: Arrow Books, 1990), 13–21.

32. A. Krämer, "Inseln um Truk (Zentralkarolinen Ost, Lukunor, Namoluk, Losap, Nama, Lomarafat, Namonuito, Pollap-Tamatam)," in *Ergebnisse der Südsee-Expedition 1908–1910,* vol. II, B, vi, I, ed. G. Thilenius (ed.), 1–291, 93 (Hamburg: Friederichsen, De Gruyter & Co., 1935), (HRAF 1010, 103).

33. Hommon, 113–14, citing Curtis Lyons, "Land Matters in Hawai'i," *Islander* 1, nos. 18, 19, 20 (1875): 103–19, 111.

34. Kubary, "Karolinen-archipels," 148 (HRAF 1179, 47).

35. AJHR, 7, testimony of James Mackay.

36. Fornander, 282.

37. Cheyne, *Acis,* February 21, 1864.

38. Boddam-Whetham, 227. He dates this incident to c. 1837. However,

Gunson, "Tonga–Samoa," 181 dates this to c. 1827. He also maintains that the dispute most probably concerned control of the paramountcy (pers. com., April 2000).

39. Alkire, *Micronesia,* 69.

40. McCutcheon, 115.

41. Sahlins, "Return of the Event," 65, citing the Fijian Native Land Court testimony of Bau, VQ 284–88.

42. Damm, 55 (HRAF 1011, 46).

43. Malo, 172–73.

44. Dening, *Islands and Beaches,* 56, and Greg Dening, "Institutions of Violence in the Marquesas," in *The Changing Pacific: Essays in Honour of H. E. Maude,* ed. Niel Gunson (Melbourne: Oxford University Press, 1978), 134–41, 134.

45. Craig, 147, and Cheyne, *Acis,* June 25, 1865, provide examples of raiding parties concealing themselves in mangrove thickets to ambush unwary enemy canoes.

46. John Thomas, "History of Tonga" (Dunedin: Typescript copy in Hocken Library of manuscript held in the Mitchell Library, n.d.), 188–90. The typescript was made by G. S. Parsonson.

47. Weckler, 56.

48. Cheyne, *Acis,* October 15, 1864.

49. Examples of village warriors mobilizing in response to the approach of canoes can be found in Craig, 166–68, 173, and Cheyne, *Acis,* July 22, 1864. For examples of Palauan village defenses, see Craig, 32, on Aibukit, and 267–68, on Ngetkeuang.

50. Keate, 141.

51. Parmentier, *Sacred Remains,* 272–75.

52. Dyson, journal, June 26, 1860.

53. Krämer and Nevermann, "Ralik–Ratak," 50.

54. Accounts contained in Yapese historical traditions are related in Lingenfelter, 171–72, while Cheyne, *Acis,* February 21, 1864, and October 15, 1864, details incidents that occurred while he was in Yap.

55. Naval operations in these canoes are described in Craig, 32, and Tetens, 59. Palauan warfare in general is discussed in Parmentier, *Sacred Remains,* 79, 82–86.

56. Krämer and Nevermann, "Ralik–Ratak," 50.

57. Leonard Mason, *Land Rights and Title Succession in the Ralik Chain, Marshall Islands* (Kolonia, Pohnpei: Final report on research for Iroij Lablab Kabua Kabua, Typescript M.S. held in Micronesian Seminar Library, n.d.), 9.

58. Parmentier, *Sacred Remains,* 288.

59. Details of the vessels used in Fijian naval warfare can be found in Williams, *The Islands*, 72–75, and Fergus Clunie, *Fijian Weapons and Warfare* (Suva: Fiji Museum, 1977), 22.

60. E. Imthurn and L. C. Wharton, eds., *The Journal of William Lockerby* (London: Hakluyt Society and Cambridge University Press, 1922), 41.

61. Traditional naval warfare in Samoa is mentioned in Rev. John B. Stair, *Old Samoa or Flotsam and Jetsam from the Pacific Ocean* (London: The Religious Tract Society, 1897), 245–46. For Tuku'aho, see Wilson, *Missionary Voyage*, 248.

62. Naval tactics are outlined in Imthurn and Wharton, 41–42; Clunie, *Fijian Warfare*, 21–23; Tippett, *Fijian Material Culture*, 28–29; and Derrick, *History of Fiji*, 51. On the relative decisiveness of sea warfare compared to land warfare, see Clunie, *Fijian Warfare*, 21–23 (naval) and 23–32 (land), and Derrick, *History of Fiji*, 48–52.

63. Hommon, 176–78. One of these accounts refers to a naval battle in the 1790s, when Hawaiian forces repulsed an invading force from neighboring islands in the early 1790s. Victory was assisted by the deployment of Western ordnance mounted on some of their vessels. See Kamakau, 161–62. Hawaiian naval tactics and canoe exercises prior to the introduction of cannon are outlined in Ellis, *Hawai'i*, 155. On Hawaiian paddle training and proficiency at canoe maneuvering, see Bàrrere, *Fragments*, 130–31, and W. Kaye Lamb, ed., *The Voyage of George Vancouver 1791–1795*, 4 vols. (London: The Hakluyt Society, 1984), vol. 3, 811–12.

64. For descriptions of Tahitian naval canoes and battle fleets, see Cook in Beaglehole, *Captain Cook*, vol. 2, 385, 390, 406, and vol. 3:1, 213 note 1; Morrison, *Journal*, 199–203; and Oliver, *Tahitian Society*, vol. 1, 400–401.

65. Cook in Beaglehole, *Captain Cook*, vol. 2, 406, and vol. 3:1, 212–13.

66. Henry, 299.

67. Cook in Beaglehole, *Captain Cook*, vol. 2, 406–7.

68. Morrison, *Journal*, 200.

69. Cook in Beaglehole, *Captain Cook*, vol. 3:1, 212–13.

70. Henry, 317, and Oliver, *Tahitian Society*, vol. 1, 406.

71. Warren Tute, "War at Sea," in *The Commanding Sea: Six Voyages of Discovery*, ed. Claire Francis and Warren Tute (London: Book Club Associates, 1981), 175–85, 175.

72. Keegan, 13–21.

73. Mark D. Kaplanoff, ed., *Joseph Ingraham's Journal of the Brigantine Hope on a Voyage to the Northwest Coast of North America 1790–1792* (Barre, Mass.: Imprint Society, 1971), 86.

74. Michael Roe, ed., *The Journal and Letters of Captain Charles Bishop*

on the North-west coast of America in the Pacific and in New South Wales
1794–1799 (London: Cambridge University Press for the Hakluyt Society,
1967), 141. Bishop's source was the knowledgeable and respected European
resident John Young, who served the Hawaiian ruler Kamehameha I from
1790 onward.

75. Hawai'i is the largest island in the chain. The estimates above are for
1779. The lower figure comes from R. C. Schmitt, "New Estimates for the
Pre-censal Population of Hawai'i," Journal of the Polynesian Society 80, no. 2
(1971): 237–43, 242. The higher estimate is from David Stannard, Before the
Horror: The Population of Hawai'i on the Eve of Western Contact (Honolulu: Social Science Research Institute, University of Hawai'i, 1989), 54.

76. Cook in Beaglehole, Captain Cook, vol. 2, 385–86, and Oliver,
Tahitian Society, vol. 1, 30–33.

77. Oliver, Tahitian Society, vol. 1, 405.

78. Lockerby in Imthurn and Wharton, 41–42, cited in Clunie, Fijian
Warfare, 22.

79. Harvey in Ducker, 261.

80. Cook, vol. 1, 132. The Fanui people of Borabora and Tahaa were the
dominant house on Borabora at the time (Niel Gunson, pers. com., April 23,
2000).

81. Porter, 101.

82. Martin, Tonga Islands, 120. Gifford, Tongan Society, 9, estimates the
total population of Ha'apai at only four thousand in 1840. Even allowing for
depopulation due to Western disease in the intervening years, Mariner's figure
of six thousand people on the expedition still seems far more than the group
was capable of committing.

83. Kotzebue, New Voyage, vol. 1, 316–17.

84. Cook in Beaglehole, Captain Cook, vol. 3:1, 212–13.

85. Hommon, 177–80.

86. Clerke in Beaglehole, Captain Cook, vol. 3:1, 598, King in Beaglehole,
Captain Cook, vol. 3:1, 626, and Samwell in Beaglehole, Captain Cook, vol.
3:2, 1183–84.

87. Stair, 246, and G. Turner, Samoa: A Hundred Years Ago and Long
Before (London: Macmillan, 1884), 194–95.

88. Parmentier, Sacred Remains, 79ff.

89. See Timothy Earle, How Chiefs Come to Power: The Political Econ-
omy in Prehistory (Stanford: Stanford University Press, 1997). P. C. Lloyd,
"The Political Development of West African Kingdoms," review article in
Journal of African History 9, no. 2 (1968): 319–29, especially 324–27, and

Henri J. M. Claessen and Peter Skalnik, "The Early State: Models and Real-ity," in *The Early State,* ed. Henri J. M. Claessen and Peter Skalnik (The Hague: Mouton Publishers, 1978), 637–50, also offer impressive analysis of this topic.

90. The process of centralization in Hawai'i was the major focus of my earlier research. See Paul D'Arcy, "Warfare and State Building in Hawai'i" (M.A. thesis, University of Otago, 1982), especially 138ff., and 198–201. See also "Warfare and State Formation in Hawai'i: The Limits on Violence as a Means of Political Consolidation," *Journal of Pacific History* 38, no. 1 (2003): 29–52.

91. Good discussions can be found in Campbell, *A History,* 47, and Mark Elvin, "Three Thousand Years of Unstable Growth: China's Environment from Archaic Times to the Present," *East Asian History* 6 (1993): 7–46, especially 18.

92. For example, see Fornander, 200–201, on the mobility of chiefly courts in Hawai'i.

93. Fornander, 244, and Vancouver in Lamb, vol. 2, 452–54, vol. 3, 853, 855–56, 858, 860–61, 870.

94. Craig, 231–33.

95. La Pérouse in Milet-Mureau, 139. This observation was made in December 1787.

96. See Thomas, "Tonga," 186–87; Vason, 145, 162, 172, 187–90; and Martin, *Tonga Islands,* 75.

97. Hau'ofa, "Sea of Islands," 153.

98. See, for example, Chamisso in Kotzebue, *Voyage 1815–18,* vol. 3, 208.

99. As discussed in chapter 3. See also Thomas, "Tonga," 75, 279–80, and A. C. Reid, "The Fruit of Rewa: Oral Traditions and the Growth of the Pre-Christian Lakeba State," *Journal of Pacific History* 12, no. 1 (1977): 2–24, especially 17–18.

100. J. Buchanan, S. Kelso, and J. Wilkinson, "Journal," 1798–1799 (*SSJ,* LMS, typescript in the possession of G. S. Parsonson), 1.

101. Thomas, "Tonga," 181–82, 184–85.

102. The best overview of the Leeward-Windward alliance is Colin Newbury, "Te Hau Pahu Rahi: Pomare II and the Concept of Inter-island Government in Eastern Polynesia," *Journal of the Polynesian Society* 76, no. 4 (1967): 477–514.

103. Robert Thomson, "History of Tahiti," 3 vols. (typescript of unpub-lished manuscript in the LMS Archives in the possession of G. S. Parsonson, n.d.), vol. 3, 23, 27–29.

104. Marshall Sahlins, "The Stranger-King, or Dumezil among the Fijians," *Journal of Pacific History* 16, no. 3 (1981): 107–32, 129.

105. See Lessin and Lessin, 47–53.

106. On the early history of Bau, see Derrick, *History of Fiji,* 30, 54, 58, and Sayes, 223–24.

107. On Bau's sea peoples, see Waterhouse, 15; Sahlins, "Stranger-King," 129; Rev. A. R. Tippett, "The Nature and Social Function of Fijian War," *Transactions and Proceedings of the Fijian Society for the Years 1951 to 1954* 5, no. 4 (1955): 137–55; and Tippett, *Fijian Material Culture,* 98, 101.

108. Jackson, 454–55, discusses the use of human sacrifices to launch great canoes, and the role of the Lasakau in obtaining these sacrifices. See also Jaggar in Keesing-Styles, 15.

109. Harvey in Ducker, 264.

110. Jaggar in Keesing-Styles, 37. I am indebted to Vicki Lukere for alerting me to this example of Lasakau terror.

111. The Macui are mentioned in Marshall Sahlins, "The Discovery of the True Savage," in *Dangerous Liaisons: Essays in Honour of Greg Dening,* ed. Donna Marwick (Melbourne: History Department, University of Melbourne, 1994), 41–96, 68, and 90 note 93. Thomson, *The Fijians,* 366–67, discusses the sea people of Rewa, while the reference to the Navatu of Cakaudrove comes from Sayes, 196.

112. Tui Atua Tupua Tamasese, "Tamafaigā—Shaman, King or Maniac? The Emergence of Manono," *Journal of Pacific History* 30, no. 1 (1995): 317–27.

113. For example, see Pritchard, 54. See Map 5.

114. J. W. Davidson, *Samoa mo Samoa: The Emergence of the Independent State of Western Samoa* (Melbourne: Oxford University Press, 1967), 26, and R. P. Gilson, *Samoa, 1830–1900: The Politics of a Multi-Cultural Community* (Melbourne: Oxford University Press, 1970), 52 note 27.

115. On Apolima, see John Williams, *A Narrative of Missionary Enterprises in the South Sea Islands* (London: John Snow, 1838), 485–86, and Boddam-Whetham, 217–20.

116. Henry, 461. See Map 4.

117. Henry, 461 note 26.

118. Pickersgill in Beaglehole, *Captain Cook,* vol. 1, 143 note 1.

119. Cook, vol. 2, 133–34.

120. Cook in Beaglehole, *Captain Cook,* vol. 2, 224, 429–30, and Newbury, "Inter-island Government," 493.

121. Parsonson, "Settlement of Oceania," 31–32, citing Parkinson, 73, note.

122. Anaa's population and resource base are discussed in Lucatt, vol. 1, 239. The population figure for the Tuamotu chain as a whole comes from Alkire, *Coral Islanders,* 103. On Anaa's domination of the chain, see Alkire, *Coral Islanders,* 107; Dening, "Geographical Knowledge," 110; and Branagan, 113.

123. Puluwat's regional influence will be dealt with in more detail in chapter 7. See Gladwin, *East is a Big Bird,* 16; Ridgell, 203; and Damm, 20 (HRAF 1011, 15). Puluwat's population seems to have been three hundred to four hundred people since records have been kept.

124. Alkire, *Micronesia,* 79, and Katharine Luomala, "Sharks and Shark Fishing in the Culture of Gilbert Islands, Micronesia," in *The Fishing Culture of the World: Studies in Ethnology, Culture and Folklore,* 2 vols., edited by Béla Gunda (Budapest: Akadémiai Kiadó, 1984), vol. 2, 1202–52, 1243, discuss integration of sharks' teeth into Kiribati weaponry. Hawaiian weaponry is outlined in Clerke in Beaglehole, Captain Cook, vol. 3:2, 1322, and J. Feher, *Hawai'i: A Pictorial History* (Honolulu: BPBM, 1969), 116–19.

125. Cook, vol. 2, 174.

126. J. F. Stimson and D. S. Marshall, *A Dictionary of Some Tuamotuan Dialects of the Polynesian Language* (The Hague: Martinus Nijhoff, 1964), 369–70, and Langdon, *Lost Caravel,* 177 note 24, citing John Davies, "Public Journal, 21 August 1807–22 November 1808" (*SSJ* 31, LMS Archives, London, AJCP mfm M2).

CHAPTER 6: ACROSS THE HORIZON

1. Malama Meleisea and Penelope Schoeffel, "Discovering Outsiders," in *The Cambridge History of the Pacific Islanders,* ed. Donald Denoon (Cambridge: Cambridge University Press, 1997), 119–51, 119.

2. Ibid., 121.

3. A. M. Hocart, *The Life-Giving Myth and Other Essays,* Second Impression (London: Tavistock, 1973), 82, cited in Marshall Sahlins, "True Savage," 75, 93 note 131.

4. The universality of this theme is explored in Mary W. Helms, *Ulysses' Sail: An Ethnographic Odyssey of Power, Knowledge and Geographical Distance* (Princeton: Princeton University Press, 1988).

5. Malo, 26.

6. Bàrrere, *The People of Old,* 67–68.

7. Emory, 200.

8. Henry, 468ff., especially 471–72.

9. Orbell, *Natural World,* 75.

10. See Malo, 10–12, for Hawaiian beliefs on this subject. Similar beliefs can be found in Ellis, *Society Islands,* 168–69 (Tahiti); Niel Gunson, "Tongan Historiography: Shamanic Views of Time and History," in *Tongan Culture and History: Papers from the 1st Tongan History Conference held in Canberra 14–17 January 1987,* ed. Phyllis Herda, Jennifer Terrell, and Niel Gunson (Canberra: RSPAS, ANU, 1990), 12–20, 16–18 (Tonga); and Goodenough, "Sky World," 557–58, and Damm, 191–92 (HRAF 1011, 173–75) (Central Caroline Islands).

11. Ellis, *Society Islands,* 168.

12. Ibid., 170.

13. See Vancouver in Lamb, vol. 3, 1207, for driftwood east of Hawai'i, and 886–87 for a Hawaiian canoe made from North American driftwood. See Wood, 142, for driftwood north of New Guinea.

14. Kotzebue, *Voyage 1815–18,* vol. 2, 25.

15. Ibid., 63.

16. Krämer and Nevermann, "Ralik–Ratak," chapter 2, 15. See also E. W. and D. S. Gifford, *Archaeological Excavations in Yap* (Berkeley: University of California Press, Anthropological Records 18, no. 2, 1957), 160–61.

17. Tomoya Akimichi, "Conservation of the Sea: Satawal, Micronesia," in *Traditional Fishing in the Pacific,* ed. Athol Anderson (Honolulu: BPBM, Pacific Anthropological Records 37, 1986), 15–33, 20.

18. See Emory, 275, on Kapinga beliefs about beached whales.

19. Gavan Daws, "The Death of Captain Cook," *Pacific Islands Monthly* (April 1984), 15–17, (May 1984), 51–53, 16, and Greg Dening, *Performances* (Melbourne: Melbourne University Press, 1996), 64.

20. Lutké, *Voyage par ordre,* vol. 2, 48 (HRAF 1318, 32).

21. Ellis, *Society Islands,* 168.

22. Beckwith, *Mythology,* 70–72. For another perspective, see Goodenough, "Sky World," 558, on the central Carolines.

23. Beckwith, *Mythology,* 72.

24. Ibid., 78–80.

25. Knappe in Mason, *Select Writings,* 16–17.

26. Ibid., 5–6, and Krämer and Nevermann, "Ralik–Ratak," 37.

27. A good account of spirit paths is Orbell, *Natural World,* 44–45. Spirit paths are mapped in John T. Parry, *The Sigatoka Valley: Pathway into Prehistory* (Suva: Bulletin of the Fiji Museum 9, 1987), Figures 6A and 6B, End Pocket. Te Reinga is discussed in Orbell, *Natural World,* 43–45. Similar leaping places in Hawai'i are described in Bàrrere, *The People of Old,* 48, and Beckwith, *Mythology,* 155–56.

28. Bàrrere, *The People of Old,* 28–29, 47–53.

29. Ibid., 38–39. See also Katharine Luomala, *Voices on the Wind* (Honolulu: BPBM, 1955), 25, on Aitutaki.

30. Paul Geraghty, "Pulotu, Polynesian Homeland," *Journal of the Polynesian Society* 102, no. 4 (1993): 343–84, 365, reviews nineteenth-century sources on Pulotu. His own theory is summarized on 370.

31. Ibid., 363.

32. Ibid., 346–47, 366. Geraghty bases much of this aspect of his theory on Samoan legends recorded in Turner, *Samoa,* 222–23.

33. Geraghty, 362–63. Parsonson, "Settlement of Oceania," 60, interprets comments that Pulotu/Burutu lay out of reach because its air caused a speedy death in mortals as a reference to the malaria-ridden climates of Melanesia. It may be a reference back to their immediate origins, or to subsequent voyages back to Melanesia from western Polynesia.

34. Cook in Beaglehole, *Captain Cook,* vol. 1, 156–57. Tupaia's geographical knowledge is discussed in Gordon Lewthwaite, "The Puzzle of Tupaia's Map," *New Zealand Geographer* 26 (1970): 1–18; Parsonson, "Settlement of Oceania," 47–48; and Dening, "Geographical Knowledge," 102–6.

35. Dening, "Geographical Knowledge," 103.

36. Parsonson, "Settlement of Oceania," 47–48, and Dening, "Geographical Knowledge," 106.

37. Gunson, "Great Families," 142–44.

38. Dening, "Geographical Knowledge," 105.

39. Daws, "Captain Cook," 16.

40. Sahlins, "True Savage," 63–65, 69.

41. See, for example, Goodenough, "Sky World," 553, on Pohnpei; Fornander, 201–2, 229, and Kamakau, 143, on Hawai'i.

42. Dening, *Performances,* 64–65, and Daws, "Captain Cook," 16.

43. For example, Meleisea and Schoeffel, 120–21.

44. The following account is based on Emory, 53–55, and Leach and Ward, 3–8.

45. Emory, 53.

46. Ibid., 42–43, 53, 66, and Leach and Ward, 3–8.

47. On ships' complements, see Lamb, vol. 3, 819. Crew numbers on British naval vessels ranged from 70 to 115 men.

48. See, for example, Ross Cordy, "The Effects of European Contact on Hawaiian Agricultural Systems—1778–1819," *Ethnohistory* 19, no. 4 (1972): 393–418, especially 400–403.

49. See Cordy, "Agricultural Systems," 402, 407, 411–12, and Kamakau,

190, on Hawai'i; and James Belich, *Making Peoples: A History of the New Zealanders from Polynesian Settlement to the End of the Nineteenth Century* (Auckland: Penguin, 1996), 152, on Aotearoa.

50. A good example of this approach is Dening, *Islands and Beaches,* 3, 157–61, especially 159.

51. J. W. Davidson, "Lauaki," 267–99, 267, and O.H.K. Spate, *The Pacific Since Magellan,* vol. 1, *The Spanish Lake* (Canberra: ANU Press, 1979), 129, quoted in Meleisea and Schoeffel, 122.

52. I. C. Campbell, "European-Polynesian Encounters: A Critique of the Pearson Thesis," *Journal of Pacific History* 29, no. 2 (1994): 222–31, especially 223–25, 229.

53. Ibid., 230–31. See also W. H. Pearson, "The Reception of European Voyagers on Polynesian Islands, 1568–1797," *Journal de la Société des Océanistes* 26 (June 1970): 121–50.

54. I. C. Campbell, "Polynesian Perceptions of Europeans in the Eighteenth and Nineteenth Centuries," *Pacific Studies* 5, no. 2 (1982): 64–80, especially 67–69.

55. Niel Gunson, "The Coming of Foreigners," in *Friendly Islands: A History of Tonga,* ed. Noel Rutherford (Melbourne: Oxford University Press, 1977), 90–113, 93, and 259–60 note 34.

56. Sahlins, "True Savage," 75.

57. Ibid., 72.

58. Campbell, "Polynesian Perceptions," 75–79.

59. See in particular, Norma McArthur, *Island Populations of the Pacific* (Canberra: ANU Press, 1967). This overview of the historiography of disease in the Pacific Islands is based on Victoria Lukere, "Mothers of the Taukei: Fijian Women and 'the Decrease of Race'" (Ph.D. thesis, RSPAS, ANU, 1997), 5–13.

60. Most notably Alfred W. Crosby, *Ecological Imperialism: The Biological Expansion of Europe, 900–1900* (Cambridge: Cambridge University Press, 1986).

61. See particularly Stannard.

62. Kamakau, 189, and Gavan Daws, *Shoal of Time: A History of the Hawaiian Islands* (Honolulu: University of Hawai'i Press, 1968), 42–43.

63. Dorothy Kahananui, ed., *Ka Moolelo Hawai'i* (Honolulu: University of Hawai'i Press, 1984), 232–33.

64. Cordy, "Agricultural Systems," 408–9, notes increased production in some localities, although Kirch, *Feathered Gods,* 178, 314, suggests that production may have fallen elsewhere.

65. Campbell, *Voyage,* 87.

66. Daws, *Shoal of Time,* 168–69.

67. Thomson, *The Fijians,* 26, and Derrick, *History of Fiji,* 75.

68. Derrick, *History of Fiji,* 75–76.

69. Robert F. Rogers, *Destiny's Landfall: A History of Guam* (Honolulu: University of Hawai'i Press, 1995), 98–99.

70. See Lobban and Schefter, 98; Alkire, *Coral Islanders,* 37; and Table 1.

71. Buzacott, *Mission Life,* 93–94.

72. Ibid., 95.

73. Lobban and Schefter, 103, cite 6 to 10 years as the time needed for vegetation to make a full recovery, while Alkire, *Coral Islanders,* 14, 17, puts the recovery time at 5 to 7 years. Emory, 133, notes that breadfruit trees take 20 years to reach their full fruit-bearing stage, when they can produce 100 to 200 fruits per picking for many years to come.

74. Lobban and Schefter, 99–100.

75. Ibid., 102–3.

76. Buzacott, *Mission Life,* 88–89.

77. Boddam-Whetham, 266.

78. Lobban and Schefter, 105–7, and Alkire, *Coral Islanders,* 37.

79. Buzacott, *Mission Life,* 110.

80. Akimichi, 21.

81. Lobban and Schefter, 108. See Map 7.

82. Weckler, 42, and William, A. Lessa, "An Evaluation of Early Descriptions of Carolinian Culture," *Ethnohistory* 9, no. 4 (1962): 313–403, 340.

83. Sarfert, 26, 423–24 (HRAF 1007, 23, 146–47).

84. Paul Hambruch and A. Eilers, "Ponape Part II," in *Ergebnisse der Südsee-Expedition 1908–1910,* vol. II, B, VII, II, ed. G. Thilenius, 348–49 (Hamburg: Friederichsen De Gruyter & Co., 1932), (HRAF 1005, 279).

85. Weckler, 42–43, 48, 51, and Leonard Mason, "Suprafamilial Authority and Economic Process in Micronesian Atolls," in *Peoples and Cultures of the Pacific: An Anthropological Reader,* ed. A. P. Vayda (Garden City, N.Y.: The Natural History Press, 1968), 199–329, 309–10.

86. Damas, 20–21, 23, 26.

87. Dirk H. R. Spennemann, *Population Control Measures in Traditional Marshallese Culture: A Review of 19th Century European Observations* (Alele Museum, Majuro, report presented to the Population Co-ordination Committee, 1990—MS copy held in Micronesian Seminar Library, Kolonia, Pohnpei), 1.

88. Alkire, *Coral Islanders,* 102.

89. See *L Illustration,* 11 Avril 1903, 239–40. This information was supplied to me by Niel Gunson (pers. com., March 5, 2000).

90. H.A.H. Driessen, "Outriggerless Canoes and Glorious Beings: Precontact Prophecies in the Society Islands," *Journal of Pacific History* 17, no. 1 (1982): 3–28, 4, citing John Davies, *Journal,* December, 10, 1805, *SSJ,* LMS (Held in School of Oriental and African Studies Library, University of London, n.d.). For other accounts of the influence of prophets, see Cheyne, *Acis,* July 20, 1864, and Parmentier, *Sacred Remains,* 74, on Palau; Lingenfelter, 111, on Yap; Damm, 213 (HRAF 1011, 201), on Puluwat; and Krämer and Nevermann, "Ralik–Ratak," chapter 5, 30–32, on the Marshalls.

91. Driessen, "Outriggerless Canoes," 11.

92. Ibid., 17–23, and Robert Langdon, "Of Time, Prophecy and the European Ships of Tupaia's Chart," *Journal of Pacific History* 19, no. 4 (1984): 239–47, 240–45.

93. Cheyne, *Acis,* August 4, 1865.

94. Williams, *Missionary Enterprises,* 169–72.

95. Weckler, 7–8. Islanders' vision at sea has been noted in chapter 4.

96. E. Dunkin, "Far–off Vision," *The Leisure Hour,* 1866, 512. I am indebted to Niel Gunson for material from *The Leisure Hour* on ship prediction.

97. Wilhelm Müller, "Yap," in *Ergebnisse der Südsee Expedition, 1908–1910, II: Ethnographie: B: Mikronesien,* 2, ii, ed. G. Thilenius, pt. 1, 347 (Hamburg: Friederichsen, de Gruyter, 1917), cited in Amanda Morgan, "Mystery in the Eye of the Beholder: Cross-Cultural Encounters on 19th Century Yap," *Journal of Pacific History* 31, no. 1 (1996): 27–41, 31.

98. Thomas Trood, "Far-off Vision," *The Leisure Hour* (1866): 485–86, 486.

99. Krämer and Nevermann, "Ralik–Ratak," chapter 4, 83.

100. See Chamisso in Kotzebue, *Voyage 1815–18,* vol. 3, 168, on the Marshall Islands, and David M. Schneider, "Typhoons on Yap," *Human Organization* 16, no. 2 (1957): 10–15, 11.

101. For example, see Emory, 53–55, and Kamakau, 89.

102. For example, see Chamisso in Kotzebue, *Voyage 1815–18,* vol. 3, 207, and Lessa, *Ulithi,* 17–18, 45–46.

103. Chamisso in Kotzebue, *Voyage 1815–18,* vol. 3, 212, and Lutké, *Voyage par ordre,* vol. 3, 159 (HRAF 1319, 32).

104. See Parsonson, "Settlement of Oceania," 32, and Dening, "Geographical Knowledge," 137ff.

105. Spenneman, 9–10.

106. A good overview of this process is contained in Chappell, *Double Ghosts,* 28–40.

107. Ibid., 158–63, and Chappell, "Beyond the Beach," 175, 437–39, 221 note 380.

108. Chappell, *Double Ghosts,* chapters 5, 6, and 7, and Chappell, "Beyond the Beach," 309–13, 331.

109. Chappell, *Double Ghosts,* chapters 4 and 5.

110. Chappell, "Beyond the Beach," 171–72, 175–76, and Chappell, *Double Ghosts,* 52–56.

111. Chappell, *Double Ghosts,* 56–59.

112. Ibid., 51, 58; Chappell, "Beyond the Beach," 172, 177–78; and J. W. Davidson, "Peter Dillon: The Voyages of the *Calder* and *St. Patrick,"* in *Pacific Island Portraits,* ed. J. W. Davidson and Deryck Scarr (Canberra: ANU Press, 1970), 9–30, 22–23.

113. Chappell, "Beyond the Beach," 141–42, 144, and Chappell, *Double Ghosts,* 46.

114. Chappell, "Beyond the Beach," 160–61, 168.

115. Ibid., 221 note 380, citing *The Polynesian* of August 8, 1846. See also Chappell, *Double Ghosts,* 93–97, 160–61. On Rotuman concerns about the loss of their young men overseas, see Wood, 10, 16–17, and Howard, 130. Similar concerns were expressed in Hawai'i. See Richard A. Greer, "Wandering Kamaainas: Notes on Hawaiian Emigration Before 1848," *Journal of the West* 6, no. 2 (1967): 221–25, 224, cited in Chappell, "Beyond the Beach," 445.

116. Information on Kadu's life is contained in Chamisso, *Voyage,* 129, 181–86, 195–97, 267–68, 270–71; Kotzebue, *Voyage 1815–18,* vol. 2, 124, 132, 211–20, vol. 3, 97–99, 105–6; and Kotzebue, *New Voyage,* vol. 1, 306–10.

117. Chamisso, *Voyage,* 160.

118. Ibid., 169, and Chamisso in Kotzebue, *Voyage 1815–18,* vol. 3, 103–4.

119. Chamisso, *Voyage,* 181–86, 267–70, and Kotzebue, *Voyage 1815–18,* vol. 2, 188–99.

120. Lutké, *Voyage par ordre,* vol. 2, 147, cited in Chappell, "Beyond the Beach," 240.

121. Floyd in Lutké, *Voyage par ordre,* vol. 3, 163–65 (HRAF 1319, 35).

122. Jackson, 474–75. A good general review of travelers' tales about the lands of Europeans is Chappell, *Double Ghosts,* 168–74.

123. See, for example, Richard A. Cruise, *Journal of a Ten Months'*

Residence in New Zealand (London: Longman, 1823), 129, on Māori break-ing tapu the moment they stepped on Western vessels, and Sahlins, *Historical Metaphors*, 53–55, on a similar process among Hawaiians.

124. Chappell, *Double Ghosts*, 159–61.

125. Lieber, 141.

126. See, for example, Cruise, 196, and Chamisso, *Voyage*, 160.

127. Kotzebue, *New Voyage*, vol. 1, 269.

128. Ibid., 312–13.

129. For example, see Keate, 124, 246.

130. An example of the enthusiastic adoption of Western vessel designs occurred in the Leeward Islands of the Society group in the 1820s and 1830s. See Newbury, "Inter-island Government," 487; Niel Gunson, "Pomare II of Tahiti and Polynesian Imperialism," *Journal of Pacific History* 4 (1969): 65–82, 70–71; and Branagan, 85. For an example of the purchase of Western vessels that were used alongside traditional vessels, see J. R. Elder, ed., *The Letters and Journals of Samuel Marsden, 1765–1838* (Dunedin: A. H. Reed, 1932), 399. This relates to Hongi Hika's purchase of a ship's longboat for war. New Samoan boat designs inspired by Western designs are discussed in Roger Neich, "Samoan Figurative Carvings on Samoan Canoes," *Journal of the Polynesian Society* 93, no. 2 (1984): 191–97, and "Samoan Figurative Carvings and Taumualua Canoes: A Further Note," *Journal of the Polynesian Society* 100, no. 3 (1991): 317–27. The atolls of the Caroline Islands retained their traditional *proa* until well into this century because of their effective-ness, a lack of direct Western influence, and a lack of resources for alternatives.

131. Clunie, *Yalo i Viti*, 15.

132. Ibid., 171 note 142.

133. The method of binding joins is outlined in Clunie, *Yalo i Viti*, 144–45, and Diapea, 112–13.

134. This "nautical revolution" is outlined in Gordon S. Parsonson, "The Nautical Revolution in Polynesia" (Dunedin: Typescript copy held in the Hocken Library, 1975), 71–73, and Campbell, *A History*, 37–38. See also Williams, *The Islands*, 76, and Thomson, *The Fijians*, 295.

135. Clunie, *Yalo i Viti*, 15.

136. Haddon and Hornell, vol. 1, 241.

137. Tippett, *Fijian Material Culture*, 112.

138. Clunie, *Yalo i Viti*, 143.

139. John Young, "Sailing to Levuka: The Cultural Significance of the Island Schooners in the Late 19th Century," *Journal of Pacific History* 28,

no. 1 (1993): 36–52, especially 36, 39–40, 42–45, and Derrick, *History of Fiji*, 93.

140. Derrick, *History of Fiji*, 105–6.

141. Haddon and Hornell, vol. 1, 326, citing Wall, *Catalogue.*

142. Campbell, *A History*, 37.

143. Vancouver in Lamb, vol. 3, 1178–80.

144. Kamakau, 173, and Broughton, 71.

145. Kamakau, 187; W. D. Alexander, *A Brief History of the Hawaiian People* (New York: American Book Co., 1891), 150–51; and Thomas, Schooner, 10, 12.

146. Campbell, *Voyage*, 111; Bàrrere, *Fragments*, 103, 105, 109, 113; and Daws, *Shoal of Time*, 43.

147. M. Kelly, ed., *Hawai'i in 1819: A Narrative Account by Louis Claude de Saules de Freycinet* (Honolulu: BPBM, 1978), 86–87, 91.

148. Freycinet in Kelly, 86–87, 91.

149. Captain Henry Byam Martin, *The Polynesian Journal of Captain Henry Byam Martin . . . August 1846 to August 1847* (Canberra: ANU Press, 1981), 27.

150. Thomas, *Schooner*, 29–30. The report of the 1856 canoe passage appeared in the *Pacific Commercial Advertiser*, Honolulu, August 13, 1856, 2. The figure of six hundred people being lost on voyages was made in the Hawaiian-language newspaper, *Hae Hawai'i*, Honolulu, June 2, 1858, and was quoted in the *Pacific Commercial Advertiser*, June 10, 1858, 2.

151. Thomas, *Schooner*, 13, citing Laura Fish Judd, *Honolulu* (Chicago: R. R. Donnelly and Sons, 1966), 41–42, on an inter-island voyage she made in a canoe in 1828, and *Pacific Commercial Advertiser*, Honolulu, August 13, 1856, 2, on inter-island canoe voyages in 1856.

CHAPTER 7: CONNECTED BY THE SEA

1. In particular, see Francis X. Hezel, *The First Taint of Civilization: A History of the Caroline and Marshall Islands in Pre-Colonial Days, 1521–1885* (Honolulu: University of Hawai'i Press, 1983). A shorter version of this chapter was published under the same title in *Journal of Pacific History* 36, no. 2 (2001): 163–82. I am grateful to the journal's publishers, Taylor and Francis, for allowing me to reproduce it here.

2. This region is depicted in Map 7.

3. See William A. Lessa, "The Place of Ulithi in the Yap Empire," *Human Organization* 9 (1950): 16–18; William A. Lessa, "Myth and Blackmail in

the Western Carolines," *Journal of the Polynesian Society* 65 (1956): 67–74; Lessa, *Ulithi*, 35–39; Alkire, *Micronesia,* 50–52; Alkire, *Coral Islanders,* 122–24; Lingenfelter, 147–53; Ushijima, 68–73; and Rosalind L. Hunter-Anderson and Yigal Go'ospan Zan, "Demystifying the Sawei, A Traditional Interisland Exchange System," *Isla* 4, no. 1 (1996): 1–45. The details about the structure and process of the *sawei* related in the next two paragraphs are based on the consistent analysis contained in these sources. Additional footnotes are only included when sources diverge in their details.

4. Alkire, *Coral Islanders,* 122, states that the *sawei* was an annual undertaking, but Lessa, "Place of Ulithi," 42, claims that it took place every 2 to 3 years. Hunter-Anderson and Zan, "Sawei," 41 note 5, claim that while Ulithi maintained annual links, atolls farther east participated in the *sawei* less frequently.

5. Both Gachpar and the contiguous village of Wonyan hosted the *sawei* fleet. Gachpar is the village most usually associated with the *sawei,* however.

6. On Yongelap and the religious aspects of the *sawei,* see Inez de Beauclair, "On Religion and Mythology of Yap Island, Micronesia," *Bulletin of the Institute of Ethnology, Academia Sinica* 23 (1967): 23–36, especially 34; Lessa, "Myth and Blackmail," 67–71; Ushijima, 54, 67; Tetens, 66; K. Sapper et al., *Jap. Deutches Kolonial—Lexikon II* (Leipzig: Quallo and Meyer, 1920), 5 (HRAF 1181, 125–27, 126); Damm, 198–99 (HRAF 1011, 184); and Krämer, "Zentralkarolinen," 348 (HRAF 1013, 385).

7. Berg, 162.

8. Arago, Part 2, 13–14. Lessa, "Myth and Blackmail," 72–73, also discusses the possible role of coercion in ensuring low Islander participation in the *sawei.*

9. Arago, Part 2, 14.

10. Berg, 159, and Betzig and Wichimai, 243, both relate traditions about the extension of Yapese influence into the low islands through military action that seem to date to the 1600s.

11. Tetens, 78 (Admiralty and Hermit Islands), 93 (Ulithi), and 94–95 (Losap and Nama).

12. Chamisso, *Voyage,* 291. Yapese sorcery is cited as a major influence on low Islanders' actions by Lessa, "Myth and Blackmail," 71–72; Alkire, *Micronesia,* 52; Ushijima, 67; Berg, 157; Hunter-Anderson and Zan, "Sawei," 4; Betzig and Wichimai, 242; and Schneider, 11–12.

13. See, for example, Lessa, "Myth and Blackmail," 71–72; Alkire, "Technical Knowledge," 232; and Hunter-Anderson and Zan, "Sawei," 4.

14. Alkire, *Micronesia,* 14–15.

15. For a comprehensive review of item exchanges, see Hunter-Anderson and Zan, "Sawei," 4; Lingenfelter, 147; Alkire, "Technical Knowledge," 234; Ushijima, 72–73; and Krämer, "Inseln um Truk," 345 (HRAF 1013, 378–79). The information about the purchase of canoes from Woleai comes from Chamisso in Kotzebue, *Voyage 1815–18*, vol. 3, 193.

16. Hunter-Anderson and Zan, "Sawei," 33, believe this to be the key factor behind Gachpar's hosting of the *sawei* fleet. Ridgell, 198–99, and Alkire, "Technical Knowledge," 234, also emphasize the importance of this factor.

17. On the role of *gau* in Yapese politics, see Berg, 154–56. *Gau* consisted of discs of Spondylus shell about 3 millimeters thick and one centimeter in diameter, bored through the center, and strung along a cord (Berg, 150).

18. On Yapese politics, see Lingenfelter, 153, and David Labby, *The Demystification of Yap: Dialectics of Culture on a Micronesian Island* (Chicago: University of Chicago Press, 1976), 106.

19. *Fei* were huge wheels of aragonite with holes bored in the center, with diameters of one or more meters. The form and role of *fei* are discussed by Berg, 150; de Beauclair, "Stone Money," 153–54; and Hernsheim, 20 (HRAF 1330, 13).

20. De Beauclair, "Stone Money," 153, notes the different quality of Palauan and Yapese aragonite. The subordinate role of Yapese quarrying communities on Palau is outlined in Alkire, "Technical Knowledge," 234; de Beauclair, "Stone Money," 155–56; Aoyagi, 25–27; Berg, 150–54; and Muller, "Yap," 27. Tetens, 10, noted that Yapese greatly feared Palauans.

21. Hunter-Anderson and Zan, "Sawei," 11–12, 39.

22. On the transporting of *fei* to Yap, see de Beauclair, "Stone Money," 155–56; Cheyne, *Acis,* May 9, 1864; Hernsheim, 19–20 (HRAF 1330, 13); and Salesius, 96–97 (HRAF 1027, 104).

23. Alkire, "Technical Knowledge," 235–36. He cites Müller, "Yap," 287, in reference to Ulithian navigational influence. Others detected a withering of Yapese seafaring in the nineteenth century, and a corresponding increased reliance on their (i.e., Gagil's) low Island "children" to fulfill their seafaring requirements. For example, see Christian, 258–59; Lessa, *Ulithi,* 47; William Lessa, "The Portuguese Discovery of the Isles of Sequeira," *Micronesica* 11, no. 1 (1975): 35–70, 64–65; and Lessa, *More Tales,* 31.

24. Keate, 24–25.

25. Nero, "Beads of History," 272–73, and Parmentier, *Sacred Remains,* 42–46, 187–91. See also Rev. John Pearce Hockin, *A Supplement to the Account of the Pelew Islands* (London: G. & W. Nicol, 1803), 54, on the reception of beachcombers at Koror. On the development of Malakal as a

roadstead for Western shipping, see Shineberg, 232, 324, and Tetens, 2–3, 58–59. The *bêche-de-mer* industry in Palau is discussed in detail by Craig, 37–43.

26. Cheyne 1862, September 9, 1862, noted that Woodin was arming Ngerard to resist Koror. See also Craig, 30–31.

27. For example, see Cheyne, *Acis,* March 31, April 4, 8, May 4, 12, 16, June 3, 9.

28. Ibid., July 17, 1864.

29. Ibid., September 27, 1865.

30. Parmentier, *Sacred Remains,* 191.

31. For indigenous reasons for killing Cheyne, see ibid., 192–93, and especially Karen Nero, "Linkages between Yap and Palau: Towards Regional Histories" (Kolonia, Pohnpei: unpublished paper held in Micronesian Seminar Library, n.d.), 13–14.

32. Tetens, 103, and Nero, "Beads of History," 289–95.

33. Craig, 289–90, 292; Nero, "Beads of History," 199–201; and Parmentier, *Sacred Remains,* 46.

34. An outbreak of influenza in Tomil is described in Cheyne, *Acis,* March 28 and April 5, 1864.

35. See Lessa, "Early Descriptions," 338, and Hezel, *First Taint,* 82–108, especially 99ff.

36. Wiens, 29–30, and Map 8 outline the seascape of this area. The Namonuito name for the Gray Feather Bank comes from Lutké, *Voyage par ordre,* vol. 2, 107 (HRAF 1318, 68).

37. Lewis, *Voyaging Stars,* 137.

38. Ibid., 166.

39. Lutké, *Voyage par ordre,* vol. 2, 340 (HRAF 1318, 136).

40. Lewis, *Navigators,* 227; Alkire, *Coral Islanders,* 114–15; and Lutké, *Voyage par ordre,* vol. 2, 339–40 (HRAF 1318, 135–36).

41. Ridgell, 202.

42. Lutké, *Voyage par ordre,* vol. 2, 359 (HRAF 1318, 135–36).

43. Marck, 254–56.

44. Alkire, *Lamotrek,* 124–25, and Glynn Barratt, *Carolinian Contacts with the Islands of the Marianas: The European Record* (Saipan: Micronesian Archaeological Survey report no. 25, Division of Historic Preservation, Department of Community and Cultural Affairs, Commonwealth of the Northern Mariana Islands, August 1988), 6–7.

45. Alkire, *Lamotrek,* 125. Indigenous Carolinian sea lanes are depicted in Map 9.

46. Damm, 159ff. (HRAF 1011, 136ff.).

47. Lutké, *Voyage par ordre,* vol. 2, 300 (HRAF 1318, 110–11).

48. Alkire, *Coral Islanders,* 36–37.

49. See Gladwin, *East is a Big Bird,* 40–44; Alkire, *Coral Islanders,* 55; and Alkire, *Micronesia,* 6, for information on seasonal weather patterns.

50. Lutké, *Voyage par ordre,* vol. 3, 180–87 (HRAF 1319, 46–50), and Damm, 264–65 (HRAF 1011, 207–9).

51. The winter months were a season of scarcity, particularly March. See Lutké, *Voyage par ordre,* vol. 3, 216–17 (HRAF 1319, 71), and vol. 2, 127–28 (HRAF 1318, 81), for Lamotrek; vol. 3, 194, 196 (HRAF 1319, 56–57), for Murilo; and Gladwin, *East is a Big Bird,* 24, for Puluwat.

52. On the trade with Woleai for canoes, see Chamisso in Kotzebue, *Voyage 1815–18,* vol. 3, 192–93. The trade in tobacco from Fais is discussed in Hunter-Anderson and Zan, "Sawei," 7; Lessa, *More Tales,* 38–39, *Ulithi,* 39, and "Early Descriptions," 372; Lutké, *Voyage par ordre,* vol. 2, 309 (HRAF 1318, 116–17); and Krämer, "Zentralkarolinen," 345 (HRAF 1013, 378). Krämer, "Zentralkarolinen," 322 (HRAF 1013, 350), discusses the sources of belts.

53. Woleai's external contacts and trade partners are outlined in Chamisso in Kotzebue, *Voyage 1815–18,* 97, 196, and Krämer, "Zentralkarolinen," 214 (HRAF 1013, 234–35). For Ifalik, see Burrows and Spiro, 174–75, and for Satawal, Damm, 37–41, 55 (HRAF 1011, 28–31, 46).

54. Damm, 55–56, 82, 107, 155–58, 185 (HRAF 1011, 46, 75, 92–93, 131–36, 165); Gladwin, *East is a Big Bird,* 37–39, 43, 62–63.

55. Alkire, *Lamotrek,* 145–46.

56. Lutké, *Voyage par ordre,* vol. 3, 144–45 (HRAF 1319, 22).

57. Ibid.

58. The tendency of Western historiography to downplay the prevalence of conflict in this region is outlined in Betzig and Wichimai, 240.

59. Alkire, *Coral Islanders,* 116.

60. William H. Alkire, "Central Carolinian Oral Narratives: Indigenous Migration Theories and Principles of Order and Rank," *Pacific Studies* 7, no. 2 (1984): 1–14, especially 4–7. Some of these traditions are also reproduced in Lessa, *More Tales,* 131–33. Berg, 159, suggests that the wars of Ifalik against its neighbors related in these traditions may refer to historical events in the sixteenth and seventeenth centuries when Yapese families moved into the area in an attempt to gain control of sources of *gau.*

61. See an overview in Lessa, "Early Descriptions," 354–57.

62. Betzig and Wichimai, 241, 244, 250.

63. Damm, 182–84 (HRAF 1011, 161–65). See also Chipen, 209.

64. Damm, 138 (HRAF 1011, 109).

65. Damm, 171, 180 (HRAF 1011, 145, 158); Gladwin, *East is a Big Bird,* 16; and Ridgell, 203.

66. Damm, 55–56 (HRAF 1011, 46). Bunuluk died c. 1905, according to Damm, 185 (HRAF 1011, 165).

67. Krämer, "Zentralkarolinen," 82, 123, cited in Saul H. Riesenberg, "Tables of Voyages Affecting Micronesian Islands," in R. T. Simmons, J. J. Graydon, D. C. Gajdusek, and Paul Brown, "Blood Group Genetic Variations in Natives of the Caroline Islands and in Other Parts of Micronesia," *Oceania* 36, no. 2 (1965): 132–70 (Riesenberg, 155–68), 161.

68. Chamisso in Kotzebue, *Voyage 1815–18,* vol. 3, 111–12, and Kotzebue, *Voyage 1815–18,* vol. 2, 240–41.

69. These numbers are in Document No. 1, AHN, Codices: 1727, 1787, 1828, ff. 60–61 [Population], held in the Spanish Documents Collection of the MARC, Guam, reproduced in *Carolinians in the Mariana Islands in the 1800s,* ed. Marjorie G. Driver and Omaira Brunal-Perry, 2 (Guam: MARC and Division of Historic Preservation, Department of Community and Cultural Affairs, Commonwealth of the Northern Mariana Islands, 1996). Information on these drift voyagers comes from Don A. Farrell, *History of the Northern Mariana Islands* (Saipan: Public School System, Commonwealth of the Northern Mariana Islands, 1991), 194, and Barratt, 20. Farrell's information came from a Carolinian historian on Saipan, Dr. Benusto Kaipat. These traditions are particularly valuable as much of the archive relating to Carolinian traditions was destroyed in a fire in the CNMI Archive on Saipan (Scott Russell, Division of Historical Preservation, CNMI, Saipan, pers. com.).

70. Chamisso in Kotzebue, *Voyage 1815–18,* vol. 3, 93–94, and Ibáñez y García, 171–72.

71. Barratt, 23, citing Louis de Freycinet *Voyage autour de monde . . . exécuté sur les corvettes de S.M. l'Uranie et la Physicienne, pendant les années 1817, 1818, 1819, et 1820,* 5 vols. (Paris: Pillet Aine, 1824–44), Vol. 2, Part 2, Historique, 84.

72. Barratt, 4–8; Farrell, 193; Kotzebue, *Voyage 1815–18,* vol. 2, 240, 244; de Beauclair, "Stone Money," 152 note 2; and V. M. Golovin, *Around the World on the Kamchatka, 1817–1819* (English translation by Ella L. Wisnell) (Honolulu: University of Hawai'i Press, 1979), 231. The Spanish conquest of the Marianas is outlined in Rogers, 70–73.

73. Alkire, *Lamotrek,* 125, and Barratt, 7. Mutau-uol is rendered as Metawal Wool, "the sea route to the north," in Farrell, 192.

74. Two canoes came in May 1787, and four in 1788. According to Kaipat, Lamotrek, Satawal, Elato, and Woleai, each contributed one canoe to the 1788 fleet led by Luito. Luito is rendered Luwito in Farrell.

75. Barratt, 24; Hezel, *First Taint*, 104; Kotzebue, *Voyage 1815–18*, vol. 2, 241–42; and Chamisso in Kotzebue, *Voyage 1815–18*, vol. 3, 111–14.

76. Rogers, 89.

77. Chamisso in Kotzebue, *Voyage 1815–18*, vol. 3, 115. Later in the century, Christian, 20, recorded that the fleet consisted of eighteen to twenty canoes.

78. Barratt, 27, and Kotzebue, *Voyage 1815–18*, vol. 3, 116.

79. This information on Metau-uol is based on discussions in Farrell, 192, 197; Riesenberg, "Ghost Islands," 19–20; and Scott Russell, *From Arabwal to Ashe: A Brief History of Garapan Village: 1818 to 1945* (Saipan: Micronesian Archaeological Survey Report no. 19, Office of Historic Preservation, CNMI, June 1984), 10. Information on this sea route is also found in Kotzebue, *Voyage 1815–18*, vol. 2, 242–43; Chamisso in Kotzebue, *Voyage 1815–18*, vol. 3, 114–15; and R. P. Lesson, *Voyage autour du monde entrepris par ordre du gouvernement sur la corvette "La Coquille,"* 4 vols. (Bruxelles: N. J. Gregoir, V. Wouters & Co., 1839), vol. 2, 122 (HRAF 1324, 2). Farrell states that fleets sailed northeast to take account of the Pacific current, which sweeps due west at latitude 150 degrees until longitude 9 degrees 13 minutes, where it moderates to a west-northwest current south of the Marianas.

80. Lewis, *Navigators*, 218–19.

81. Ibid., 220–21. Lewis sailed this route in a traditional canoe, where the navigators aimed for Pikelot rather than Gaferut.

82. Arago, Part 2, 10–11.

83. Lesson, vol. 2, 122 (HRAF 1324, 2).

84. Chamisso in Kotzebue, *Voyage 1815–18*, vol. 3, 193.

85. Damm, 83 (HRAF 1011, 76).

86. Freycinet, vol. 2, 460–61 (HRAF 1410, 146).

87. Lutké, *Voyage par ordre*, vol. 2, 124–25 (HRAF 1318, 79).

88. This statement was made by Fr. Juan de Medina on a visit to the Mariana Islands in 1610, and is reproduced in *History of Micronesia: A Collection of Source Documents*, vol. 3, *First Real Contact 1596–1637*, ed. Rodrique Lévesque (Gatineau, Quebec: Lévesque Publications, 1993), 331.

89. Rogers, 80.

90. Chamisso in Kotzebue, *Voyage 1815–18*, vol. 3, 83, discusses the Chamorro's loss of maritime skills.

91. Chamisso in Kotzebue, *Voyage 1815–18*, vol. 3, 83, 116; Lutké, *Voyage par ordre*, vol. 2, 122–24 (HRAF 1318, 77–79); and Amanda A. Morgan,

"Mystery in the Eye of the Beholder: Cross-Cultural Encounters in the Western Caroline Islands with a Special Focus on Yap, 1525–1886" (M.A. thesis, University of Hawai'i at Mānoa, August 1994), 67, citing F. H. von Kittlitz, *Denkwurdigkeiten einer Reise nach dem russischen Amerika, nach Mikronesien und durch Kamtschatka,* 2 vols. (Gotha: J. Perthes, 1858).

92. Rogers, 91.

93. Alkire, *Coral Islanders,* 50.

94. Farrell, 198. Piwamwan was also known as Faillelon, or Failūūlōl— "rock of the deep sea."

95. Arago, Part 2, 12; Krämer, "Zentralkarolinen," 127 (HRAF 1013, 139); Barratt, 42, citing Adelbert von Chamisso, *Werke, Bd. 1: Reise um die Welt mit der Romanoffischen Entdeckungs—Expedition in den Jahren 1815–18...: tagebuch. Bd.11: Bemerkungen und Anisichten* (Leipzig: Weidmann'sche Buchhandlung, 1836), vol. 2, 187; and Russel, "Arabwal," 13.

96. Chamisso, *Werke,* vol. 2, 187, cited in Barratt, 42.

97. Kotzebue, *Voyage 1815–18,* vol. 2, 233; Chamisso, *Werke,* vol. 2, 187, cited in Barratt, 42; and Chamisso in Kotzebue, *Voyage 1815–18,* 115, 193.

98. Arago, Part 2, 12, and Farrell, 201. Although traditions cited in Farrell claim the Carolinians settled Saipan in 1815, Hezel, *First Taint,* 106, documents that permission for the settlement was not received from Manila until after this date.

99. One version is presented by Hezel, *First Taint,* 106, citing Freycinet (1825–44), Part 2, vol. 2 (1829), 88. The Carolinian version occurs in Farrell, 199. Farrell renders Agrub as Agurubw, and Nguschul as Ngushull. My translation Ppiyol Oolng combines Farrell's "beach view sky" with Russell's, "Arabwal," 1, "view of the sand" translation of Pien Olong.

100. Scott Russell, "Roots of the Falawasch" (Guam: unpublished MS paper, MARC Library, University of Guam, n.d.), 5.

101. Farrell, 201.

102. Ibid.

103. Russell, "Falawasch," 1.

104. D. Parker Wilson, *Log of the Gypsy, kept by D. Parker Wilson, ship's surgeon, 23 Oct. 1839–19 mar. 1843* (Canberra: M198, Records Room, Department of Pacific History, ANU, 1839–42), entry for August 30, 1840, cited in Hezel, *First Taint,* 106–7.

105. Sánchez y Zayas, 260–61, 264–65.

106. Driver and Brunal-Perry, 292. Saipan's relative isolation from the Western world is commented on in Sánchez y Zayas, 265; Russell, "Arabwal,"

14; and Farrell, 219. Driver and Brunal-Perry, 62–64, produce Spanish records of payments for inter-island transport services rendered by *Falawasch* in the 1850s.

107. Krämer, "Zentralkarolinen," 195 (HRAF 1013, 206).

108. Farrell, 201.

109. Document No. 3, PNA, Marianas, Bundle 5(1), Expediente, 3, ff. 1–6, 1839–40, Settlements, letter dated July 1, 1839, held in the Spanish Documents Collection of MARC, Guam, reproduced in Driver and Brunal-Perry, 6–7.

110. Rogers, 98.

111. Document no. 4. PNA, Marianas-2, Bundle 25, Memorias, Perez, f. 29a, 1849, Settlements, held in the Spanish Documents Collection, MARC, Guam, reproduced in Driver and Brunal-Perry, 12–13.

112. Alexander Spoehr, *Saipan: The Ethnology of a War-Devastated Island* (Chicago: Fieldiana: Anthropology, vol. 41, Chicago Natural History Museum, February 11 1954), 71, citing *Diccionario Geografico Estadistico de las Filipinas—Historico 1851* (Madrid, 1851).

113. Damm, 182–83 (HRAF 1011, 161–62).

114. Farrell, 220–22.

115. Damm, 180–81 (HRAF 1011, 158).

116. Russell, "Arabwal," 15–16, citing Aniceto Ibáñez del Carmen et al., *Chronicle of the Mariana Islands* (translated by Marjorie G. Driver) (Mangilao, Guam: MARC, University of Guam, 1976), 20–21.

117. Farrell, 223. Government documents relating to the granting of a lease to Johnston to set up enterprises in the northern islands are reproduced in Driver and Brunal-Perry, 95ff. (Document no.16, PNA Marianas, Bundle 33, Expediente 72, ff. 1–39, 1877, Economic Development).

CONCLUSION

1. Ibáñez del Carmen, 64.

2. Scott Russell, ed., *The Chamorro: A History and Ethnography of the Marianas* by Georg Fritz (English translation by Elfriede Craddock) (Saipan: Division of Historic Preservation, 1984), 18.

3. Damm, 186–87 (HRAF 1011, 167–68).

4. Alkire, *Lamotrek,* 149; Alkire, *Coral Islanders,* 140–41; and Damm, 186–87 (HRAF 1011, 167–68).

5. Lewis, *Voyaging Stars,* 93.

6. Hau'ofa, "Sea of Islands," 155.

7. Howard, 131.

8. Ward H. Goodenough and Richard Feinberg, "Epilogue: Seafaring in the Pacific, Past and Present," in *Seafaring in the Contemporary Pacific Islands: Studies in Continuity and Change,* ed. Richard Feinberg (DeKalb: Northern Illinois University Press, 1995), 219–30, 226–27, and Lieber, 11.

9. Lewis, *Voyaging Stars,* 108–10.

10. Ibid., 187–90; Finney, "Voyaging," 335–43.

11. Finney, "Putting Voyaging Back," 372–73.

12. Sarah Catherall, "Waitangi Day Worries over Waka Safety—Training to Follow Tragedy," *Sunday Star Times,* January 6, 2000, A6.

13. *The Dominion,* Wellington, February 25, 2000, 1. On Māui, see Orbell, *Maori Myth and Legend,* 124.

14. Teresia Teaiwa, review of Eric Waddell et al., eds., *A New Oceania: Rediscovering Our Sea of Islands* (Suva: School of Social and Economic Development, University of the South Pacific, 1993), in *The Contemporary Pacific* 8, no. 1 (1996): 214–17, 214.

15. Finney, "The Ocean," 191–92.

16. Ibid.

17. Karen Nero, "The Material World Remade," in *The Cambridge History of the Pacific Islanders,* ed. Donald Denoon (Cambridge: Cambridge University Press, 1997), 359–396, 368.

18. Alan Murakami, "*Konohiki* Fishing Rights and Marine Resources," in *Native Hawaiian Rights Handbook,* ed. Melody Kapilialoha MacKenzie (Honolulu: Native Hawaiian Legal Corporation, 1991), 173–95, 185–88, and Minerbi, 125–29.

19. See Paul Moon, "The Creation of the 'Sealord Deal,'" *Journal of the Polynesian Society* 107, no. 2 (1998): 145–74, and Waitangi Tribunal, Department of Justice, *Report of the Waitangi Tribunal on the Muriwhenua Fishing Claim, Wai–22* (Wellington: Department of Justice, 1985).

20. R. E. Johannes, "Traditional Law of the Sea in Micronesia," *Micronesica* 13, no. 2 (1977): 121–27, 125–26.

21. One of the most comprehensive reviews of marine policy options in the independent Pacific is Roniti Teiwaki, *Management of Marine Resources in Kiribati* (Suva: University of the South Pacific, 1988).

22. Lobban and Schefter, 274–77; Nero, "Material World Remade," 377–78; Bardach, 43; Gillett, 1.

23. Alkire, *Coral Islanders.*

24. Spoehr, 210.

25. Patrick Vinton Kirch and Roger C. Green, *Hawaiki, Ancestral Polynesia: An Essay in Historical Anthropology* (Cambridge: Cambridge University

Press, 2001), especially 86–89. Recent criticism of Kirch and Green's approach can be found in J. E. Terrell, T. L. Hunt, and C. Gosden, "The Dimensions of Social Life in the Pacific: Human Diversity and the Myth of the Primitive Isolate," *Current Anthropology* 38 (1997): 155–96.

26. These issues are discussed in more detail in Paul D'Arcy, "Cultural Divisions and Island Environments since the Time of Dumont d'Urville," *Journal of Pacific History* 38, no. 2 (2003): 217–35. This article was part of a special issue on the legacy of d'Urville involving archaeologists, anthropologists, and historians that demonstrated the potency of such collaboration.

27. Athol Anderson, "Slow Boats from China: Issues in the Prehistory of Indo-Pacific Seafaring," in *East of Wallace's Line: Studies of Past and Present Maritime Cultures of the Indo-Pacific Region*, ed. Sue O'Connor and Peter Veth (Rotterdam: Modern Quaternary Research of Southeast Asia 16, Balkema, 2000), 1–34. The author kindly gave me an advance copy of his article in July 2000.

28. Sahlins, "Return of the Event," and Tippett, *Fijian Material Culture*, discuss the Bau-Rewa wars and Tamasese discusses Manono. Only Tippett, 98–99, explores the significance of naval power. For Hawai'i, see D'Arcy, "Warfare and State Formation," and "Limits on Violence," 40, 46–47.

29. Jon Jonassen, "Diplomacy and Politics of Culture—The Case of Voyaging Canoes," paper presented at Victoria University, Wellington, May 18, 1999, 8.

30. The chant is reproduced in Cook Island Maori and English in Jonassen, 15. It is a proverbial chant recited by Ti'avaru Mata-ka-vau-a-Pa on Aitutaki, sometime around the 1920s.

APPENDIX

1. For overviews of Western theories on the colonization of Oceania, see Bellwood, 303–11; Campbell, *A History*, 28–35; and Irwin, *Prehistoric Exploration*, 13–16.

2. Andrew Sharp, *Ancient Voyagers in the Pacific* (London: Penguin, 1957). See also Andrew Sharp, *Ancient Voyagers in Polynesia* (Auckland: Paul's Book Arcade, 1963).

3. M. Levison, R. G. Ward, and J. W. Webb, *The Settlement of Polynesia: A Computer Simulation* (Minneapolis: University of Minnesota Press, 1973).

4. Dening, "Geographical Knowledge," 102–31; Parsonson, "Settlement of Oceania," 11–63; Saul H. Riesenberg, "Tables of Voyages," 155–68.

5. David Lewis, *Navigators*, and *Voyaging Stars*; and Gladwin, *East is a Big Bird*.

6. See Finney, "Voyaging," 324–51.

7. Irwin, *Prehistoric Exploration,* 7–8.

8. Richard Feinberg, ed., *Seafaring in the Contemporary Pacific Islands: Studies in Continuity and Change* (DeKalb: Northern Illinois University Press, 1995). His "Introduction: Theme and Variation in Pacific Island Seafaring," 3–15, presents a good overview of the approaches contained within this edited collection.

9. See note 4.

10. Oliver, *Oceania,* vol. 1, 361–86.

11. On the evolution of propulsion, see David Lewis, "The Pacific Navigators' Debt to the Ancient Seafarers of Asia," in *The Changing Pacific: Essays in Honour of H. E. Maude,* ed. Niel Gunson (Melbourne: Oxford University Press, 1979), 46–66; Adrian Horridge, "The Evolution of Pacific Canoe Rigs," *Journal of Pacific History* 21, no. 1 (1986): 83–99; and I. C. Campbell, "The Lateen Sail in World History," *Journal of World History* 6, no. 1 (1995): 1–23. For a recent assertion of the idea of design continuity, see Horridge, "Austronesians," 135–51.

12. Young, and Clifford W. Hawkins, "The Passage of Sail: European Sailing Ship Building in the South West Pacific," *The Great Circle* 5, no. 2 (1983): 87–97.

13. Hiroa, "Disappearance of Canoes," 191–99; and Neich, "Samoan Canoes" and "A Further Note."

14. Campbell, *A History,* 37–39. The paper Campbell refers to is Parsonson, "Nautical Revolution."

15. Gladwin, *East is a Big Bird;* and Richard Feinberg, *Polynesian Seafaring and Navigation: Ocean Travel in Anutan Culture and Society* (Kent, Ohio: Kent State University Press, 1988).

16. A good review of the literature on this topic is Margaret D. Chapman, "Women's Fishing in Oceania," *Human Ecology* 15, no. 3 (1987): 267–88. Two articles worth reading are Raymond Firth, "Roles of Women and Men in a Sea Fishing Economy: Tikopia Compared with Kelantan," in *The Fishing Culture of the World—Studies in Ethnology, Culture and Folklore,* 2 vols., ed. Béla Gunda (Budapest: Akadémiai Kiadó, 1984), vol. 2, 1145–70; and Kim Des Rochers, "Women's Fishing on Kosrae: A Description of Past and Present Methods," *Micronesica* 25, no. 1 (1992): 1–22.

17. Good reviews on these topics are Oliver, *Oceania,* vol. 1, 248–67; E. H. Bryan Jr., "Native Fishing in the Pacific: An Annotated Bibliography," in *The Fishing Culture of the World: Studies in Ethnology, Culture and Folklore,* 2 vols., ed. Béla Gunda (Budapest: Akadémiai Kiadó, 1984), vol. 2, 1025–1100; and Reinman.

18. Johannes, *Words of the Lagoon,* and Lieber have already been cited. Other impressive works include Lewthwaite, "Early Tahiti," and Gillett.

19. See Gillett, 31–43, for example, on inaccuracies in traditional knowledge.

20. For example, Firth, "Sea Creatures," and Andrew Pawley, "On the Classification of Marine Animals in Wayan," in *Science of the Pacific Island Peoples,* vol. 3: *Flora, Fauna, Food and Medicine,* ed. J. P. Morrison, P. Geraghty, and L. Crowl (Suva: Institute of Pacific Studies, 1994), 87–107. For the Linnaean classification system, see Daniel J. Boorstin, *The Discoverers: A History of Man's Search to Know His World and Himself* (New York: Vintage Books, 1985), 436–46.

21. See, for example, T. P. Bayliss-Smith, "Energy Use and Economic Development in Pacific Communities," in *Subsistence and Survival: Rural Ecology in the Pacific,* ed. T. P. Bayliss-Smith and Richard G. Feachem (London: Academic Press, 1977), 317–59.

22. Kenneth Ruddle and Tomoya Akimichi, "Introduction," in *Maritime Institutions in the Western Pacific,* ed. Kenneth Ruddle and Tomoya Akimichi (Osaka: National Museum of Ethnology, 1984), 1–9, especially 7–8.

23. Margie V. Cushing Falanruw, "Traditional Fishing on Yap," in *Science of Pacific Island Peoples,* vol. 1: *Ocean and Coastal Studies,* ed. John Morrison, Paul Geraghty, and Linda Crowl (Suva: Institute of Pacific Studies, 1994), 41–58; and McCutcheon.

24. Lessa, *Ulithi;* Ushijima; and Alkire, *Lamotrek.*

25. Don Rubinstein, "Native Place-Names and Geographical Systems of Fais, Caroline Islands," *Micronesica* 14, no. 1 (1978): 69–82.

26. Sudo. For a more general discussion of Micronesian tenure, see Mason, "Suprafamilial Authority."

27. The best study of indigenous tenure in Remote Oceania is Hommon. Hommon makes use of the wealth of nineteenth-century Hawaiian sources, most notably Kahaulelio. See also Mackenzie.

28. See particularly, Waitangi Tribunal, 77–119.

29. Oliver, *Tahitian Society,* 400–408; Ferdon, *Early Tahiti,* 257–69; and Gunson, "Pomare II."

30. The most recent study of this war is Sahlins, "The Return of the Event." Earlier studies were: Derrick, *History of Fiji,* and Tippett, "Fijian War." A more thematic treatment of Fijian warfare is found in Clunie, *Fijian Warfare.*

31. The most recent addition to this body of studies is I. C. Campbell, *"Gone Native" in Polynesia: Captivity Narratives and Experiences from the South Pacific* (Westport, Conn.: Greenwood Press, 1998).

32. Chappell, *Double Ghosts;* Judith Binney, "Tuki's Universe," in *Tasman Relations: New Zealand and Australia, 1788–1988,* ed. Keith Sinclair (Auckland: Auckland University Press, 1988), 15–33; and Howard.

33. Driessen, "Outriggerless Canoes" and "Outriggerless Canoes and Glorious Beings Revisited: A Reply to Robert Langdon," *Journal of Pacific History* 19, no. 4 (1984): 248–57. The opposing viewpoint is contained in Langdon, "Tupaia's Chart."

34. Sahlins, "Stranger-King."

35. Goodenough, "Sky World"; and William H. Alkire, "Land, Sea, Gender, and Ghosts on Woleai-Lamotrek," in *Culture, Kin and Cognition: Essays in Honor of Ward H. Goodenough,* ed. Mac Marshall and John L. Caughey (Washington, D.C.: American Anthropological Association Special Publication no. 25, 1989), 79–97.

36. Hviding, 31.

37. See, for example, Goodenough and Thomas, "Traditional Navigation," and Saul H. Riesenberg, "The Organisation of Navigational Knowledge on Puluwat," *Journal of the Polynesian Society* 81, no. 1 (1972): 19–56.

38. Minerbi, 88–89, based on Malo, 25–27.

39. Alkire, "Woleai–Lamotrek."

40. Gunson, "Tongan Historiography," and Geraghty, "Pulotu."

41. For example, see Alkire, "Porpoises," and Luomala, "Porpoises and Taro."

42. Luomala, "Sharks."

BIBLIOGRAPHY

Aitken, A. *Ethnology of Tubuai*. Honolulu: BPBM, 1930.

AJHR. "Report of the Select Committee on the Thames Sea Beach Bill." Wellington: Appendices to the Journals of the House of Representatives 1869. II, F–7 (1869), 1–18.

Akimichi, Tomoya. "Conservation of the Sea: Satawal, Micronesia." In *Traditional Fishing in the Pacific*, edited by Athol Anderson, 15–33. Honolulu: Pacific Anthropological Records 37, BPBM, 1986.

Alexander, W. D. *A Brief History of the Hawaiian People*. New York: American Book Co., 1891.

Alkire, William H. "Cultural Adaptation in the Caroline Islands." *Journal of the Polynesian Society* 69 (1960): 123–50.

Alkire, William H. *Lamotrek Atoll and Inter-Island Socioeconomic Ties*. Urbana: University of Illinois Press, 1965.

Alkire, William H. "Porpoises and Taro." *Ethnology* 7, no. 3 (1968): 280–89.

Alkire, William H. "Systems of Measurement on Woleai Atoll, Caroline Islands." *Anthropos* 65 (1970): 1–73.

Alkire, William H. *An Introduction to the Peoples and Cultures of Micronesia*. 2nd ed. Menlo Park, Calif.: Cummings Publishing Company, 1977.

Alkire, William H. *Coral Islanders*. Arlington Heights, Ill.: AHM Publishing Corporation, 1978.

Alkire, William H. "Technical Knowledge and the Evolution of Political Systems in the Central and Western Caroline Islands of Micronesia." *Canadian Journal of Anthropology* 1, no. 2 (1980): 229–37.

Alkire, William H. "Central Carolinian Oral Narratives: Indigenous Migration Theories and Principles of Order and Rank." *Pacific Studies* 7, no. 2 (1984): 1–14.

Alkire, William H. "Land, Sea, Gender, and Ghosts on Woleai-Lamotrek." In *Culture, Kin and Cognition: Essays in Honor of Ward H. Goodenough*, edited by Mac Marshall and John L. Caughey, 79–94. Washington, D.C.: American Anthropological Association Special Publication no. 25, 1989.

Allen, Rev. William. "Rotuma." *Australian and New Zealand Association for the Advancement of Science* 8 (1895): 556–79.

Amesbury, Steven S., and Michelle Babin. "Ocean Temperature Structure and the Seasonality of Pelagic Fish Species Near Guam, Mariana Islands." *Micronesica* 23, no. 2 (1990): 131–38.

Anderson, Athol, ed. *Traditional Fishing in the Pacific.* Honolulu: Pacific Anthropological Records 37, BPBM, 1986.

Anderson, Athol. "Slow Boats from China: Issues in the Prehistory of Indo-Pacific Seafaring." In *East of Wallace's Line: Studies of Past and Present Maritime Cultures of the Indo-Pacific Region,* edited by Sue O'Connor and Peter Veth, 1–34. Rotterdam: Modern Quaternary Research of Southeast Asia, vol. 16, Balkema, 2000.

Andia y Varela, Don Joseph. "Narrative 1774–5." In *The Quest and Occupation of Tahiti by Emissaries of Spain during the Years 1772–1776* (3 vols.), edited by Bolton Glanvill Corney, vol. 2, 224–318. London: The Hakluyt Society, 1915.

Anikouchine, William A., and Richard W. Sternberg. *The World Ocean: An Introduction to Oceanography.* Englewood Cliffs, N.J.: Prentice Hall, 1973.

Aoyagi, Machiko. "The Geographical Recognition of Palauan People." In *Islanders and their Outside World: A Report of the Cultural Anthropological Research in the Caroline Islands of Micronesia in 1980–1981,* edited by Machiko Aoyagi, 3–33. St. Paul's (Rikkyo) University, Tokyo: Committee for Micronesian Research, March 1982.

Arago, J. *Narrative of a Voyage Around the World.* Amsterdam: N. Israel and New York: Da Capo Press, 1971 (Bibliotheca Australiana reproduction of 1823 ed.).

Bahn, Paul, and John Flenley. *Easter Island Earth Island.* London: Thames and Hudson, 1992.

Bardach, John E., and Penelope J. Ridings. "Pacific Tuna: Biology, Economics, and Politics." In *Ocean Yearbook 5,* edited by Elisabeth Mann Borgese and Norton Ginsburg, 29–57. Chicago: University of Chicago Press, 1985.

Barratt, Glynn. *Carolinian Contacts with the Islands of the Marianas: The European Record.* Saipan: Micronesian Archaeological Survey Report no. 25, Division of Historic Preservation, Department of Community and Cultural Affairs, Commonwealth of the Northern Mariana Islands, August 1988.

Bàrrere, Dorothy B., ed. *Ka Poʻe Kahiko: The People of Old,* by Samuel Kamakau. Honolulu: BPBM, 1964.

Bàrrere, Dorothy B., ed. *The Works of the People of Old: Na Hana a ka Po'e Kahiko,* by Samuel Kamakau. Honolulu: BPBM, 1976.

Bàrrere, Dorothy B., ed. *Fragments of Hawaiian History,* by John Papa Ii (translated by Mary Kawena Pukui). Honolulu: BPBM, 1983.

Bayliss-Smith, T. P. "Energy Use and Economic Development in Pacific Communities." In *Subsistence and Survival: Rural Ecology in the Pacific,* edited by T. P. Bayliss-Smith and Richard G. Feachem, 317–59. London: Academic Press, 1977.

Bayliss-Smith, T. P. "Population Pressure, Resources and Welfare: Towards a More Realistic Measure of Carrying Capacity." In *Population-Environment Relations in Tropical Islands: The Case of Eastern Fiji,* edited by H. C. Brookfield, 61–94. Paris: Man and Biosphere Technical Notes 13, UNESCO, 1980.

Bayliss-Smith, T. P. *The Ecology of Agricultural Systems.* Cambridge: Cambridge University Press, 1982.

Beaglehole, J. C., ed. *The Journals of Captain James Cook on His Voyages of Discovery.* 4 vols. Cambridge: Cambridge University Press, 1955, 1961, 1967.

Beaglehole, J. C., ed. *The Endeavour Journal of Joseph Banks, 1768–1771.* 2 vols. Sydney: Angus and Robertson, 1962.

Beckwith, Martha Warren. "Hawaiian Shark Aumakua." *American Anthropologist* 19, no. 4 (1917): 503–17.

Beckwith, Martha. *Hawaiian Mythology.* Honolulu: University of Hawai'i Press, 1970.

Beechey, Frederick W. *Narrative of a Voyage to the Pacific and Beering's Strait, 1825–1828.* 2 vols. Amsterdam: N. Israel and New York: Da Capo Press, 1968 (Bibliotheca Australiana reproduction of 1831 ed.).

Beggerly, Patricia Price. "Hawaiian Initial Settlement: A Possible Model." In *Micronesian and Polynesian Voyaging: Three Readings,* 53–140. Honolulu: Pacific Islands Program Miscellaneous Work Papers, University of Hawai'i at Mānoa, 1976.

Belich, James. *Making Peoples: A History of the New Zealanders from Polynesian Settlement to the End of the Nineteenth Century.* Auckland: Penguin, 1996.

Bellwood, Peter. *Man's Conquest of the Pacific: The Prehistory of Southeast Asia and Oceania.* Auckland: Collins, 1978.

Bentzen, Conrad. *Land and Livelihood on Mokil, an Atoll in the Eastern Carolines.* Los Angeles: Coordinated Investigation of Micronesian Anthropology, 1947–49, 11, no. 2, June 1949.

Berg, M. L. "Yapese Politics, Yapese Money and the Sawei Tribute Network before World War 1." *Journal of Pacific History* 27, no. 2 (1992): 150–64.

Betzig, Laura, and Santus Wichimai. "A Not so Perfect Peace: A History of Conflict on Ifaluk." *Oceania* 61, no. 3 (1991): 240–56.

Binney, Judith. "Tuki's Universe." In *Tasman Relations: New Zealand and Australia, 1788–1988,* edited by Keith Sinclair, 15–33. Auckland: Auckland University Press, 1988.

Boddam-Whetham, J. W. *Pearls of the Pacific.* London: Hurst and Blackett, 1876.

Boorstin, Daniel J. *The Discoverers.* New York: Vintage Books, 1985.

Born, D.K.B. "Einigo Bemerkungen ubor Musik, Dichtkunst und Tanz der Yaploute." *Zeitschrift fur Ethnologie* 35 (1903): 134–42, 1903 (HRAF English translation no. 1186).

Boyden, S. *Biohistory: The Interplay between Human Society and the Biosphere Past and Present.* Paris: UNESCO and Park Ridge, N.J.: The Parthenon Publishing Group, 1992.

Branagan, David, ed. *Science in a Sea of Commerce: A day–by–day account of an 1820s south seas trading venture, based on the journal of Samuel Stutchbury, a scientific observer.* Northbridge, New South Wales: David Branagan Publisher, 1996.

Bridge, Admiral Sir Cyprian. *Some Recollections.* London: John Murray, 1918.

Broughton, William Robert. *A Voyage of Discovery to the North Pacific Ocean performed in His Majesty's Sloop Providence, and her tender, in the years 1795, 1796, 1797, 1998.* New York: Da Capo Press and Amsterdam: N. Israel, 1967 (Bibliotheca Australiana reproduction of the 1804 original).

Brower, Kenneth. *Micronesia: The Land, the People, and the Sea.* Singapore: Mobil Oil Micronesia Inc., 1981.

Bryan, E. H., Jr. "Native Fishing in the Pacific: An Annotated Bibliography." In *The Fishing Culture of the World: Studies in Ethnology, Culture and Folklore* (2 vols.), edited by Béla Gunda, vol. 2, 1025–1100. Budapest: Akadémiai Kiadó, 1984.

Buchanan, J., S. Kelso, and J. Wilkinson. "Journal, 1798–1799." SSJ, LMS, typescript in the possession of G. S. Parsonson, n.d.

Burley, David V. "Settlement Pattern and Tongan Prehistory: Reconsiderations from Ha'apai." *Journal of the Polynesian Society* 103, no. 4 (1994): 379–411.

Burrows, Edwin G., and Melford E. Spiro. *An Atoll Culture: Ethnography of Ifaluk in the Central Carolines.* 2nd ed. New Haven: HRAF, 1957.

Buzacott, Aaron. "Manners, Customs Language Religion etc of the Samoans." SSL Box 8, Folder 113—Cook Islands 1836–1837 May 30–March 10, Rarotonga to Navigator Islands, LMS, 1837. Hocken Library, Dunedin: Pacific Manuscript Bureau Microfilm copy.

Buzacott, Aaron. *Mission Life in the Islands of the Pacific.* Suva: Institute of Pacific Studies, 1985 (reproduction of 1866 ed.).

Cameron, I. *Lost Paradise: The Exploration of the Pacific.* Boston: Salem House, 1987.

Campbell, Archibald. *A Voyage Round the World from 1806 to 1812.* Honolulu: University of Hawai'i Press, 1967 (reproduction of the 3rd ed. of 1822).

Campbell, I. C. "Polynesian Perceptions of Europeans in the Eighteenth and Nineteenth Centuries." *Pacific Studies* 5, no. 2 (1982): 64–80.

Campbell, I. C. *A History of the Pacific Islands.* Christchurch: University of Canterbury Press, 1989.

Campbell, I. C. "European-Polynesian Encounters: A Critique of the Pearson Thesis." *Journal of Pacific History* 29, no. 2 (1994): 222–31.

Campbell, I. C. "The Lateen Sail in World History." *Journal of World History* 6, no. 1 (1995): 1–23.

Campbell, I. C. *"Gone Native" in Polynesia: Captivity Narratives and Experiences from the South Pacific.* Westport, Conn.: Greenwood Press, 1998.

Carrington, H., ed. *The Discovery of Tahiti: A journal of the second voyage of H.M.S. "Dolphin" round the World,* by G. Robertson. London: The Hakluyt Society, 1948.

Carroll, Vern, ed. *Pacific Atoll Populations.* Honolulu: University of Hawai'i Press, 1975.

Catherall, Sarah. "Waitangi Day Worries over Waka Safety—Training to Follow Tragedy." *Sunday Star Times,* Auckland, January 6, 2000, A6.

Chamisso, Adelbert von. *Werke, Bd.1: Reise um die Welt mit der Romanof-fischen Entdeckungs—Expedition in den Jahren 1815–18 . . . : tagebuch. Bd.11: Bemerkungen und Anisichten.* Leipzig: Weidmann'sche Buchhandlung, 1836.

Chamisso, Adelbert von. *A Voyage Around the World with the Romanov Exploring Expedition in the Years 1815–1818 in the Brig Rurik, Captain Otto von Kotzebue* (English translation by Henry Kratz). Honolulu: University of Hawai'i Press, 1986.

Chapman, Margaret D. "Women's Fishing in Oceania." *Human Ecology* 15, no. 3 (1987): 267–88.

Chappell, David A. "Beyond the Beach: Periplean Frontiers of Pacific

Islanders aboard Euroamerican Ships, 1768–1887." Ph.D. thesis, University of Hawai'i at Mānoa, 1991.

Chappell, David A. *Double Ghosts: Oceanic Voyagers on Euroamerican Ships.* Armonk, N.Y.: M. E. Sharpe, 1997.

Chatwin, Bruce. *The Songlines.* London: Picador, 1988.

Cheyne, Andrew. *Journal of a Voyage to the Islands of the Western Pacific in the Brigantine "Acis" A. Cheyne Commander* (log I 28/11/63–14/12/64 and 10/2/65–6/2/66). MS copy in possession of Dorothy Shineberg.

Chipen, Takashy, comp. *Uruon Chuk: A Resource of Oral Legends, Traditions and History of Truk.* 2 vols. Saipan: Omnibus Program for Social Studies—Cultural Heritage, Trust Territory of the Pacific Islands, July 1979 (copy in Micronesian Seminar Library, Kolonia, Pohnpei).

Christian, F. W. *The Caroline Islands: Travel in the Sea of the Little Lands.* London: Frank Cass and Co., Ltd, 1967 (new impression of 1st ed., 1899).

Claessen, Henri J. M., and Peter Skalnik. "The Early State: Models and Reality." In *The Early State,* edited by Henri J. M. Claessen and Peter Skalnik, 637–50. The Hague: Mouton Publishers, 1978.

Clunie, Fergus. *Fijian Weapons and Warfare.* Suva: Fiji Museum, 1977.

Clunie, Fergus. *Yalo i Viti—Shades of Viti: A Fiji Museum Catalogue.* Suva: Fiji Museum, 1986.

Cook, Captain James, and Lieutenant James King. *A Voyage to the Pacific Ocean undertaken by the command of his Majesty, for making discoveries in the Northern Hemisphere . . . in the Years 1776, 1777, 1778, 1779, and 17— in 3 volumes* (vols. 1–2 Cook, and vol. 3 King). London: G. Nicol, 1784.

Cordy, Ross. "The Effects of European Contact on Hawaiian Agricultural Systems—1778–1819." *Ethnohistory* 19, no. 4 (1972): 393–418.

Cordy, Ross. *Archaeological Settlement Pattern Studies on Yap.* Saipan: Office of Historic Preservation, Trust Territory of the Pacific Islands, August 1986.

Corney, Bolton Glanvill, ed. *The Quest and Occupation of Tahiti by Emissaries of Spain during the Years 1772–1776.* 3 vols. London: The Hakluyt Society, 1913, 1915, 1919.

Couper, A. D. "Indigenous Trading in Fiji and Tonga: A Study of Changing Patterns." *New Zealand Geographer* 24, no. 1 (1968): 50–60.

Craib, John L. "Settlement on Ulithi Atoll, Western Caroline Islands." *Asian Perspectives* 24, no. 1 (1981): 47–56.

Craig, Robert, ed. *The Palau Islands in the Pacific Ocean* by Karl Semper (English translation by Mark Berg). Mangilao, Guam: MARC, University of Guam, 1982.

Crawford, Peter. *Nomads of the Wind: A Natural History of Polynesia.* London: BBC Books, 1993.

Crosby, Alfred W. *Ecological Imperialism: The Biological Expansion of Europe, 900–1900.* Cambridge: Cambridge University Press, 1986.

Cruise, Richard A. *Journal of a Ten Months' Residence in New Zealand.* London: Longman, 1823.

Culliney, John L. *Islands in a Far Sea: Nature and Man in Hawai'i.* San Francisco: Sierra Club Books, 1988.

Cummins, H. G. "Tongan Society at the time of European Contact." In *Friendly Islands: A History of Tonga,* edited by Noel Rutherford, 63–89. Melbourne: Oxford University Press, 1977.

Damas, David. *Bountiful Island: A Study of Land Tenure on a Micronesian Atoll.* Waterloo, Ont.: Wilfred Laurier University Press, 1994.

Damm, H., P. Hambruch, and E. Sarfert. "Inseln um Truk (Polowat, Hok, Satowal)." In *Ergebnisse der Südsee-Expedition 1908–1910,* vol. II, B, VI, ii, edited by G. Thilenius, 1–288. Hamburg: Friederichsen, De Gruyter & Co., 1935 (HRAF English translation no. 1011).

D'Arcy, Paul. "Warfare and State Building in Hawai'i." M.A. thesis, University of Otago, 1992.

D'Arcy, Paul. "The People of the Sea." In *The Cambridge History of the Pacific,* edited by Donald Denoon, 74–77. Cambridge: Cambridge University Press, 1997.

D'Arcy, Paul. "No Empty Ocean: Trade and Interaction across the Pacific Ocean to the Middle of the 18th Century." In *Studies in the Economic History of the Pacific Rim,* edited by Sally M. Miller, A.J.H. Latham, and Dennis O. Flynn, 21–44. New York: Routledge, 1998.

D'Arcy, Paul. "Connected by the Sea: Towards a Regional History of the Western Caroline Islands." *Journal of Pacific History* 36, no. 2 (September 2001): 163–82.

D'Arcy, Paul. "Warfare and State Formation in Hawai'i: The Limits on Violence as a Means of Political Consolidation." *Journal of Pacific History* 38, no. 1 (May 2003): 29–52.

D'Arcy, Paul. "Island Environments and Cultural Divides since the Time of Dumont d'Urville." *Journal of Pacific History* 38, no. 2 (October 2003): 217–35.

Davenport, William H. "Marshallese Folklore Types." *Journal of American Folklore* 66 (1953): 219–37.

Davenport, William H. "Marshall Islands Navigational Charts." *Imago Mundi* 15 (1960): 19–26.

Davenport, William H. "Marshall Islands Cartography." *Exposition, the Bulletin of the University Museum of Pennsylvania* 6 (1964): 10–13.

David, Gilbert. "Dynamics of the Coastal Zone in the High Islands of Oceania: Management Implications and Options." In *The Margin Fades: Geographical Itineraries in a World of Islands,* edited by Eric Waddell and Patrick Nunn, 189–214. Suva: Institute of Pacific Studies, University of the South Pacific, 1993.

Davidson, J. W. "Problems of Pacific History." *Journal of Pacific History* 1 (1966): 5–21.

Davidson, J. W. *Samoa mo Samoa: The Emergence of the Independent State of Western Samoa.* Melbourne: Oxford University Press, 1967.

Davidson, J. W. "Lauaki Namalau'ulu Mamoe: A Traditionalist in Samoan Politics." In *Pacific Island Portraits,* edited by J. W. Davidson and Deryck Scarr, 267–99. Canberra: ANU Press, 1970.

Davidson, J. W. "Peter Dillon: The Voyages of the *Calder* and *St. Patrick.*" In *Pacific Island Portraits,* edited by J. W. Davidson and Deryck Scarr, 9–30. Canberra: ANU Press, 1970.

Davidson, Janet M. "Settlement Patterns in Samoa before 1840." *Journal of the Polynesian Society* 78 (1969): 44–82.

Davidson, Janet M. "Polynesian Outliers and the Problem of Cultural Replacement in Small Populations." In *Studies in Oceanic Culture History* (3 vols.), edited by R. C. Green and Marion Kelly, vol. 1, 61–72. Honolulu: Pacific Anthropological Record no. 11-13, BPBM, 1970.

Davidson, Janet M. "Preliminary Report on an Archaeological Survey of the Vava'u Group, Tonga." *Cook Bicentenary Expedition in the South-west Pacific,* Royal Society of New Zealand Bulletin 8 (1971): 29–40.

Davidson, Janet M. "Western Polynesia and Fiji: The Archaeological Evidence." *Mankind* 11, no. 3 (1978): 383–90.

Davidson, Janet M. "Auckland." In *The First Thousand Years: Regional Perspectives in New Zealand Archaeology,* edited by Nigel Pricket, 28–48. Palmerston North: The Dunmore Press, 1982.

Davies, John. "Public Journal, 21 August 1807–22 November 1808." SSJ 31, LMS Archives, London (AJCP mfm M2).

Davies, John. "Journal." SSJ, LMS, Held in School of Oriental and African Studies Library, University of London, n.d.

Daws, Gavan. *Shoal of Time: A History of the Hawaiian Islands.* Honolulu: University of Hawai'i Press, 1968.

Daws, Gavan. "The Death of Captain Cook." *Pacific Islands Monthly* (April 1984): 15–17, and (May 1984): 51–53.

De Beauclair, Inez. "The Stone Money of Yap Island." *Bulletin of the Institute of Ethnology, Academia Sinica* 16 (1963): 147–60.

De Beauclair, Inez. "On Religion and Mythology of Yap Island, Micronesia." *Bulletin of the Institute of Ethnology, Academia Sinica* 23 (1967): 23–36.

Debenham, Frank, ed. *The Voyage of Captain Bellinghausen to the Antarctic Seas 1819–1821.* 2 vols. London: The Hakluyt Society, 1945.

Dening, Greg. "The Geographical Knowledge of the Polynesians and the Nature of Inter-Island Contact." In *Polynesian Navigation* (3rd ed.), edited by Jack Golson, 102–31. Wellington: A. W. and A. H. Reed, 1972.

Dening, Greg, ed. *The Marquesan Journal of Edward Robarts, 1797–1824.* Honolulu: University of Hawai'i Press, 1974.

Dening, Greg. "Institutions of Violence in the Marquesas." In *The Changing Pacific: Essays in Honour of H. E. Maude,* edited by Niel Gunson, 134–41. Melbourne: Oxford University Press, 1978.

Dening, Greg. *Islands and Beaches: Discourse on a Silent Land, Marquesas 1774–1880.* Honolulu: University of Hawai'i Press, 1980.

Dening, Greg. *History's Anthropology: The Death of William Gooch.* Lanham, Md.: University Press of America, 1988.

Dening, Greg. *Performances.* Melbourne: Melbourne University Press, 1996.

Denoon, Donald, ed. *The Cambridge History of the Pacific Islanders.* Cambridge: Cambridge University Press, 1997.

Derrick, R. A. *The Fiji Islands: A Geographical Handbook.* Rev. ed. Suva: Government Press, 1957.

Derrick, R. A. *A History of Fiji.* Vol. 1. Suva: Government Press, 1968 (reprint of 1950 rev. ed.).

Des Rochers, Kim. "Women's Fishing on Kosrae: A Description of Past and Present Methods." *Micronesica* 25, no. 1 (1992): 1–22.

Diamond, Jared. "Twilight at Easter." *New York Review of Books,* March 25, 2004, 6–10.

Diapea, William. *Cannibal Jack: The True Autobiography of a White Man in the South Seas.* London: Faber & Gwyer Ltd, 1948.

Diaz, Henry F., and Vera Markgraf, eds. *El Niño: Historical and Paleoclimatic Aspects of the Southern Oscillation.* Cambridge: Cambridge University Press, 1992.

Diccionario Geografico Estadistico de las Filipinas—Historico 1851. Madrid: Pascual Madoz, 1851.

Dillon, Peter. *Narrative of La Pérouse's Expedition.* 2 vols. Amsterdam: N. Israel and New York: Da Capo Press, 1972 (Bibliotheca Australiana reproduction of 1829 ed.).

Dodd, Edward. *Polynesian Seafaring.* New York: Dodd, Mead and Co., 1972.

The Dominion. Wellington, February 25, 2000.

Douglas, Bronwen. "Rank, Power and Authority: A Reassessment of Traditional Leadership in South Pacific Societies." *Journal of Pacific History* 14, no. 1 (1979): 2–27.

Driessen, H.A.H. "Outriggerless Canoes and Glorious Beings: Pre-contact Prophecies in the Society Islands." *Journal of Pacific History* 17, no. 1 (1982): 3–28.

Driessen, H.A.H. "Outriggerless Canoes and Glorious Beings Revisited: A Reply to Robert Langdon." *Journal of Pacific History* 19, no. 4 (1984): 248–57.

Driver, Marjorie G., and Omaira Brunal-Perry, eds. *Carolinians in the Mariana Islands in the 1800s.* Guam: MARC and Division of Historic Preservation, Department of Community and Cultural Affairs, Commonwealth of the Northern Mariana Islands, 1996.

Ducker, Sophie C., ed. *The Contented Botanist: Letters of W. H. Harvey about Australia and the Pacific.* Carlton, Victoria: Melbourne University Press, 1988.

Dumont d'Urville, M. J. *Voyage au Pole Sud et dans l'Océanie sur les corvettes l'Astrolabe et la Zélée.* 5 vols. Paris: Gide, 1843 (HRAF English translation no. 1336).

Dunkin, E. "Far–off Vision." *The Leisure Hour* (1866): 512.

Dye, Tom. "Archeological Survey and Test Excavations on Arno Atoll, Marshall Islands." In *Marshall Islands Archeology,* edited by Tom Dye, 271–399. Honolulu: BPBM, December 1987.

Dye, Tom. "The Causes and Consequences of a Decline in the Prehistoric Marquesan Fishing Industry." In *Pacific Production Systems: Approaches to Economic Prehistory,* edited by D. E. Yen and J.M.J. Mummery, 70–84. Canberra: Occasional Papers in Prehistory no. 18, Department of Prehistory, RSPAS, ANU, 1990.

Dyson, Martin. *Journal.* Hocken Library, Dunedin: microfilm copy of journal and papers held in Mitchell Library, n.d.

Earle, Timothy. *How Chiefs Come to Power: The Political Economy in Prehistory.* Stanford: Stanford University Press, 1997.

Elder, J. R., ed. *The Letters and Journals of Samuel Marsden, 1765–1838.* Dunedin: A. H. Reed, 1932.

Ella, S. "The Samoan 'Taumua-lua.'" *Journal of the Polynesian Society* 7 (1898): 247.

Ellis, William. *Polynesian Researches: Hawai'i*. Rutland, Vt.: Charles E. Tuttle Co., Publishers, 1969 (reprint of new ed., 1831).

Ellis, William. *Polynesian Researches: Society Islands, Tubuai Islands, and New Zealand*. Rutland, Vt.: Charles E. Tuttle Co., Publishers, 1969 (reprint of new ed., 1831).

Elvin, Mark. "Three Thousand Years of Unstable Growth: China's environment from Archaic Times to the Present." *East Asian History* 6 (1993): 7–46.

Emerald. Ship's Log, March 5, 1834.

Emory, Kenneth P. *Kapingamarangi: Social and Religious Life of a Polynesian Atoll*. Honolulu: BPBM, 1965.

Enfield, David B. "Historical and Prehistorical Overview of El Niño/Southern Oscillation." In *El Niño: Historical and Paleoclimatic Aspects of the Southern Oscillation,* edited by Henry F. Diaz and Vera Markgraf, 95–117. Cambridge: Cambridge University Press, 1992.

Erskine, John Elphinstone. *Journal of A Cruise Among the Islands of the Western Pacific*. London: Dawsons of Pall Mall, 1967 (reprint of 1853 ed.).

Falanruw, Margie V. Cushing. "Traditional Fishing on Yap." In *Science of Pacific Island Peoples,* vol. 1: *Ocean and Coastal Studies,* edited by John Morrison, Paul Geraghty, and Linda Crowl, 41–58. Suva: Institute of Pacific Studies, 1994.

Farber, Thomas. *On Water*. Hopewell, N.J.: The Ecco Press, 1994.

Farrell, Don A. *History of the Northern Mariana Islands*. Saipan: Public School System, Commonwealth of the Northern Mariana Islands, 1991.

Feher, J. *Hawai'i: A Pictorial History*. Honolulu: BPBM, 1969.

Feinberg, Richard. *Polynesian Seafaring and Navigation: Ocean Travel in Anutan Culture and Society*. Kent, Ohio: Kent State University Press, 1988.

Feinberg, Richard, ed. *Seafaring in the Contemporary Pacific Islands: Studies in Continuity and Change*. DeKalb: Northern Illinois University Press, 1995.

Feinberg, Richard. "Introduction: Theme and Variation in Pacific Island Seafaring." In *Seafaring in the Contemporary Pacific Islands: Studies in Continuity and Change,* edited by Richard Feinberg, 3–15. DeKalb: Northern Illinois University Press, 1995.

Ferdon, Edwin N. *Early Tahiti as the Explorers Saw it 1767–1797*. Tucson: University of Arizona Press, 1981.

Ferdon, Edwin N. *Early Tonga as the Explorers Saw it, 1616–1810*. Tucson: University of Arizona Press, 1987.

Fijian Native Land Court. *Testimony of Bau*, VQ 284-88, Suva, n.d.

Finney, Ben R. "Voyaging." In *The Prehistory of Polynesia*, edited by Jesse D. Jennings, 324–51. Canberra: ANU Press, 1979.

Finney, Ben R. "The Ocean and the Quality of Life." In *The Emerging Marine Economy of the Pacific*, edited by Chennat Gopalakrishnan, 187–92. London: Butterworths, 1984.

Finney, Ben R. "Putting Voyaging Back into Polynesian Prehistory." In *Oceanic Culture History: Essays in Honour of Roger Green*, edited by Janet Davidson et al., 365–76. Dunedin: New Zealand Journal of Archaeology Special Publication, 1996.

Finney, Ben, Paul Frost, Richard Rhodes, and Nainoa Thompson. "Wait for the West Wind." *Journal of the Polynesian Society* 98, no. 3 (1989): 261–302.

Finney, Ben R., and James D. Houston. *Surfing: The Sport of Hawaiian Kings*. Rutland, Vt.: Charles E. Tuttle Co., 1966.

Firth, Raymond. *The History and Traditions of Tikopia*. Wellington: Polynesian Society Memoir no. 32, 1961.

Firth, Raymond. "Sea Creatures and Spirits in Tikopia Belief." In *Polynesian Culture History: Essays in Honor of Kenneth P. Emory*, edited by G. A. Highland et al., 539–64. Honolulu: BPBM, 1967.

Firth, Raymond. "Roles of Women and Men in a Sea Fishing Economy: Tikopia Compared with Kelantan." In *The Fishing Culture of the World: Studies in Ethnology, Culture and Folklore* (2 vols.), edited by Béla Gunda, vol. 2, 1145–70. Budapest: Akadémiai Kiadó, 1984.

Firth, Raymond, and Rosemary Firth. "Tikopia Songs of the Sea." In *Man and a Half: Essays in Pacific Anthropology and Ethnobiology in Honour of Ralph Bulmer*, edited by Andrew Pawley, 405–12. Auckland: Polynesian Society, 1991.

Fison, Lorimer. *Tales from Old Fiji*. London: The De La More Press, 1907.

Forbes, Litton. *Two Years in Fiji*. London: Longman, Green, and Co., 1875.

Fornander, Abraham. *An Account of the Polynesian Race*. 2 vols. Rutland, Vt.: Charles E. Tuttle Co., 1969 (reprint of the 1879 ed., vol. 2).

Forster, G. A. *Voyage round the World in His Britannic Majesty's Sloop, "Resolution"* . . . *1772–1775*. 2 vols. London: B. White, 1777.

Forster, J. R. *Observations made during a Voyage round the World*. London: printed for G. Robinson, 1778.

Fosberg, F. R., ed. *Man's Place in the Island Ecosystem: A Symposium*. Honolulu: BPBM, 1963.

Freycinet, Louis de. *Voyage autour du monde . . . éxecuté sur les corvettes de S. M. L'Uranie et la Physicienne, pendant les années 1817, 1818, 1819, et*

1820. 5 vols. Paris: Pillet Aîné, 1824–44 (HRAF English translation no. 1410).

Friedman, Jonathan. "Catastrophe and Continuity in Social Evolution." In *Theory and Explanation in Archaeology: The Southampton Conference,* edited by Colin Renfrew, Michael J. Rowlands, and Barbara Abbott Segraves, 175–96. New York: Academic Press, 1982.

Geraghty, Paul. "Pulotu, Polynesian Homeland." *Journal of the Polynesian Society* 102, no. 4 (1993): 343–84.

Gifford, E. W. *Tongan Society.* Honolulu: BPBM, 1929.

Gifford, E. W., and D. S. Gifford. *Archaeological Excavations in Yap.* Berkeley: Anthropological Records vol. 18, no. 2, University of California Press, 1957.

Gillett, Robert. *Traditional Tuna Fishing: A Study at Satawal, Central Caroline Islands.* Honolulu: Bishop Museum Bulletin in Anthropology no. 1, BPBM, 1987.

Gilson, R. P. *Samoa, 1830–1900: The Politics of a Multi-Cultural Community.* Melbourne: Oxford University Press, 1970.

Gladwin, Thomas. "Canoe Travel in the Truk Area: Technology and its Psychological Correlates." *American Anthropologist* 60, no. 5 (1958): 893–99.

Gladwin, Thomas. *East is a Big Bird: Navigation and Logic on Puluwat Atoll.* Cambridge, Mass.: Harvard University Press, 1970.

Golovin, V. M. *Around the World on the Kamchatka, 1817–1819* (English translation by Ella L. Wisnell). Honolulu: University of Hawai'i Press, 1979.

Golson, Jack, ed. *Polynesian Navigation.* 3rd ed. Wellington: A. W. and A. H. Reed, 1972.

Goodenough, Ward H. *Property, Kin and Community on Truk.* 2nd ed. Hamden, Conn.: Archon Books, 1978.

Goodenough, Ward H. "Sky World and This World: The Place of Kachaw in Micronesian Cosmology." *American Anthropologist* 88, no. 3 (1986): 551–68.

Goodenough, Ward H., and Richard Feinberg. "Epilogue: Seafaring in the Pacific, Past and Present." In *Seafaring in the Contemporary Pacific Islands: Studies in Continuity and Change,* edited by Richard Feinberg, 219–30. DeKalb: Northern Illinois University Press, 1995.

Goodenough, Ward H., and Stephen D. Thomas. "Traditional Navigation in the Western Pacific: A Search for Pattern." *Expedition* 29, no. 3 (1987): 3–14.

Gosden, Chris, and Christina Pavlides. "Are Islands Insular? Landscape vs. Seascape in the Case of the Arawe Islands, Papua New Guinea." In *Social Landscapes,* edited by Lesley Head, Chris Gosden, and J. Peter White, special issue of *Archaeology in Oceania* 29, no. 3 (1994): 162–71.

Green, R. C. "Near and Remote Oceania: Disestablishing Melanesia in Culture History." In *Man and a Half: Essays in Pacific Anthropology and Ethnobiology in Honour of Ralph Bulmer,* edited by Andrew Pawley, 491–502. Auckland: Polynesian Society, 1991.

Greer, Richard A. "Wandering Kamaainas: Notes on Hawaiian Emigration Before 1848." *Journal of the West* 6, no. 2 (1967): 221–25.

Grigg, Richard W., and Steven J. Dollar. "Natural and Anthropogenic Disturbance on Coral Reefs." In *Ecosystems of the World* 25—*Coral Reefs,* edited by Z. Dubinsky, 439–52. Amsterdam: Elsevier, 1990.

Grimble, Arthur. *A Pattern of Islands.* London: John Murray, 1952.

Guard, C. P., and M. A. Lander. *A Scale Relating Tropical Cyclone Wind Speed to Potential Damage for the Tropical Pacific Ocean Region: A Users Manual.* Mangilao, Guam: Water and Environmental Research Institute (WERI) Technical Report 86, University of Guam, 1999.

Gulick, Rev. L. H. "Micronesia—of the Pacific Ocean." *The Nautical Magazine and Naval Chronicle* 31 (1862): no. 4, pp. 168–82 (General Introduction and Ponape), no. 5, pp. 237–45 (Kusae), no. 6, pp. 298–308 (Marshalls), no. 6, pp. 358–63 (Island compass bearings), no. 8, pp. 408–17 (Gilberts).

Gunda, Béla. "Introduction." In *The Fishing Culture of the World: Studies in Ethnology, Culture and Folklore* (2 vols.), edited by Béla Gunda, vol. 1, 11–26. Budapest: Akadémiai Kiadó, 1984.

Gunson, Niel. "Pomare II of Tahiti and Polynesian Imperialism." *Journal of Pacific History* 4 (1969): 65–82.

Gunson, Niel. "John Williams and his Ship: The Bourgeois Aspirations of a Missionary Family." In *Questioning the Past: A Selection of Papers in History and Government,* edited by D. P. Crook, 73–95. St. Lucia: University of Queensland Press, 1972.

Gunson, Niel. "The Coming of Foreigners." In *Friendly Islands: A History of Tonga,* edited by Noel Rutherford, 90–113. Melbourne: Oxford University Press, 1977.

Gunson, Niel. "The Tonga-Samoa connection 1777–1845." *Journal of Pacific History* 25, no. 2 (1990): 176–87.

Gunson, Niel. "Tongan Historiography: Shamanic Views of Time and History." In *Tongan Culture and History: Papers from the 1st Tongan History*

Conference held in Canberra 14–17 January 1987, edited by Phyllis Herda, Jennifer Terrell, and Niel Gunson, 12–20. Canberra: RSPAS, ANU, 1990.

Gunson, Niel. "Understanding Polynesian Traditional History." *Journal of Pacific History* 28, no. 2 (1993): 139–58.

Gunson, Niel. "Great Families of Polynesia: Inter-island Links and Marriage Patterns." *Journal of Pacific History* 32, no. 2 (1997): 139–52.

Haddon, A. C., and James Hornell. *Canoes of Oceania*. 3 vols. Honolulu: BPBM, 1936, 1937, 1938.

Hae Hawai'i. Hawaiian-language newspaper, Honolulu.

Hambruch, Paul, and A. Eilers. "Ponape Part II." In *Ergebnisse der Südsee-Expedition 1908–1910*, vol. II, B, VII, II, edited by G. Thilenius, 1–388. Hamburg: Friederichsen, De Gruyter & Co., 1932, pp. 1–388 (HRAF English translation 1005).

Hamilton–Paterson, James. *Seven-Tenths: The Sea and Its Thresholds*. London: Vintage, 1993.

Handy, E.S.C., and E. G. Handy. *Native Planters of Old Hawai'i: Their Life, Lore, and Environments*. Honolulu, BPBM, 1972.

Hau'ofa, Epeli. "Our Sea of Islands." *The Contemporary Pacific* 6, no. 1 (1994): 148–61.

Hau'ofa, Epeli. "The Ocean in Us." *The Contemporary Pacific* 10, no. 2 (1998): 392–410.

Hawkins, Clifford W. "The Passage of Sail: European Sailing Ship Building in the South West Pacific." *The Great Circle* 5, no. 2 (1983): 87–97.

Helfrich, Philip, and Sidney J. Townsley. "The Influence of the Sea." In *Man's Place in the Island Ecosystem: A Symposium*, edited by F. R. Fosberg, 39–53. Honolulu: BPBM, 1963.

Helms, Mary W. *Ulysses' Sail: An Ethnographic Odyssey of Power, Knowledge and Geographical Distance*. Princeton: Princeton University Press, 1988.

Henry, Teuira. *Ancient Tahiti*. Honolulu: BPBM, 1928.

Hernsheim, Franz. *Südsee-Erinnerungen (1875–1880)*. Berlin: A. Hofmann, 1884 (HRAF English translation no. 1330).

Hezel, Francis X. "A Yankee Trader in Yap: Crayton Philo Holcomb." *Journal of Pacific History* 10, no. 1 (1975): 3–19.

Hezel, Francis X. *Foreign Ships in Micronesia: A Compendium of Ship Contacts with the Caroline and Marshall Islands 1521–1885*. Saipan: Historic Preservation Office, Trust Territory of the Pacific Islands, August 1979.

Hezel, Francis X. *The First Taint of Civilization: A History of the Caroline and Marshall Islands in Pre-Colonial Days, 1521–1885.* Honolulu: University of Hawai'i Press, 1983.

Hiroa, Te Rangi. "The Disappearance of Canoes in Polynesia." *Journal of the Polynesian Society* 51, no. 3 (1942): 191–99.

Hiroa, Te Rangi. *Arts and Crafts of Hawai'i.* Honolulu: BPBM, 1957.

Hocart, A. M. *The Life-Giving Myth and Other Essays* (Second Impression). London: Tavistock, 1973 (first published 1952).

Hockin, Rev. John Pearce. *A Supplement to the Account of the Pelew Islands.* London: G. & W. Nicol, 1803.

Hommon, Robert J. *Use and Control of Hawaiian Inter-island Channels— Polynesian Hawai'i: A.D. 1400–1794.* Honolulu: Office of the Governor of Hawai'i, 1975.

Horridge, Adrian. "The Evolution of Pacific Canoe Rigs." *Journal of Pacific History* 21, no. 1 (1986): 83–99.

Horridge, Adrian. "The Austronesians Conquest of the Sea—Upwind." In *The Austronesians: Historical and Comparative Perspectives,* edited by Peter Bellwood, James Fox, and Darrell Tryon, 135–51. Canberra: Department of Anthropology, RSPAS, ANU, 1995.

Houghton, Philip. *People of the Great Ocean: Aspects of Human Biology of the Early Pacific.* Cambridge: Cambridge University Press, 1996.

Howard, Alan. "Rotuman Seafaring in Historical Perspective." In *Seafaring in the Contemporary Pacific Islands: Studies in Continuity and Change,* edited by Richard Feinberg, 114–43. DeKalb: Northern Illinois University Press, 1995.

Howe, K. R. "Pacific Islands History in the 1980s: New Directions or Monograph Myopia?" *Pacific Studies* 3 (1979): 81–90.

Howe, K. R. *Where the Waves Fall: A New South Sea Islands History from First Settlement to Colonial Rule.* Sydney: Allen & Unwin, 1984.

Howe, K. R. *Nature, Culture, and History: The "Knowing" of Oceania.* Honolulu: University of Hawai'i Press, 2000.

Hughes, T. P., et al. "Climate Change, Human Impacts, and the Resilience of Coral Reefs." *Science* 301, no. 5635 (2003): 929–33.

Hunter, John R., et al. *The Dynamics of Tuna Movements: An Evaluation of Past and Future Research.* Rome: FAO Fisheries Technical Paper 277, 1986.

Hunter-Anderson, Rosalind L. *Yapese Settlement Patterns: An Ethnoarchaeological Approach.* Mangilao, Guam: Pacific Studies Institute, June 1983.

Hunter-Anderson, Rosalind L., and Yigal Go'ospan Zan. "Demystifying the Sawei, a Traditional Interisland Exchange System." *Isla* 4, no. 1 (1996): 1–45.

Hviding, Edvard. *Guardians of Marovo Lagoon: Practice, Place, and Politics in Maritime Melanesia*. Honolulu: University of Hawai'i Press, 1996.

Ibáñez del Carmen, Aniceto, Resano Francisco, et al. *Chronicle of the Mariana Islands* (English translation by Marjorie G. Driver). Mangilao, Guam: MARC, 1976.

Ibáñez y García, Luís de. *The History of the Marianas, with Navigational Data, and of the Caroline, and the Palau Islands From the Time of their Discovery by Magellan in 1521 to the Present* (English translation and annotation by Marjorie G. Driver). Mangilao, Guam: MARC, 1992.

Imthurn, E., and L. C. Wharton, eds. *The Journal of William Lockerby*. London: The Hakluyt Society, Cambridge University Press, 1925.

Intoh, Michiko. "Reconnaissance Archaeological Research on Ngulu Atoll in the Western Caroline Islands." *Asian Perspectives* 24, no. 1 (1981): 69–80.

Intoh, Michiko, and Foss Leach. *Archaeological Investigations in the Yap Islands, Micronesia—First Millennium B.C. to the Present Day*. Oxford: BAR International Series no. 277, 1985.

Irwin, Geoffrey. *The Prehistoric Exploration and Colonisation of the Pacific*. Cambridge: Cambridge University Press, 1992.

Irwin G. J. "The Colonisation of the Pacific Plate: Chronological, Navigational and Social Issues." *Journal of the Polynesian Society* 107, no. 2 (1998): 111–43.

Jackson, John. "Narrative by John Jackson of his residence in the Feejees." In *Journal of A Cruise Among the Islands of the Western Pacific* by John Elphinstone Erskine, 411–77. London: Dawsons of Pall Mall, 1967 (reprint of 1853 ed.).

Jarman, Robert. *Journal of a Voyage to the South Seas, in the Japan, Employed in the Sperm Whale Fishery, under the Command of Capt. John May*. London: Longman and Co. and Charles Tilt, 1838.

Johannes, R. E. "Traditional Law of the Sea in Micronesia." *Micronesica* 13, no. 2 (1977): 121–27.

Johannes, R. E. *Words of the Lagoon: Fishing and Marine Lore in the Palau District of Micronesia*. Berkeley: University of California Press, 1981.

Jonassen, Jon. "Diplomacy and Politics of Culture—the Case of Voyaging Canoes." Paper presented at Victoria University, Wellington, May 18, 1999.

Judd, Laura Fish. *Honolulu*. Chicago: R. R. Donnelly and Sons, 1966.

Kahananui, Dorothy, ed. *Ka Mooolelo Hawai'i*. Honolulu: University of Hawai'i Press, 1984.

Kahaulelio, A. D. "Fishing Lore from Ka Nupepa Kuokoa" (in 13 install-ments—February 28, March 7, 14, 21, 28, April 4, May 2, 16, 23, 30, June 20, 27, July 4, 1902), English translation by Mary Kawena Pukui, photocopy of typescript in Library of Hawai'i Institute of Marine Biology, University of Hawai'i, Honolulu, n.d.

Kamakau, S. M. *Ruling Chiefs of Hawai'i*. Honolulu: Kamehameha Schools Press, 1961.

Kane, Herb Kawainui. *Voyage*. Honolulu: Island Heritage Limited, 1976.

Kaplanoff, Mark D., ed. *Joseph Ingraham's Journal of the Brigantine Hope on a Voyage to the Northwest Coast of North America 1790–1792*. Barre, Mass.: Imprint Society, 1971.

Karlson, Ronald H., Howard V. Cornell, and Terence P. Hughes. "Coral Communities are Regionally Enriched along an Oceanic Biodiversity Gra-dient." *Nature* 429 (June 24, 2004): 867–70.

Kawaharada, Dennis, ed. *Hawaiian Fishing Traditions*. Honolulu: Kalamaku Press, 1993.

Kay, E. Alison, ed. *A Natural History of the Hawaiian Islands: Selected Readings*. Honolulu: University of Hawai'i Press, 1972.

Kay, E. Alison. *Little Worlds of the Pacific: An Essay on Pacific Basin Biogeography*. Honolulu: Harold L. Lyon Arboretum Lecture no. 9, May 9, 1979, Lyon Arboretum, 1980.

Kay, E. Alison, ed. *A Natural History of the Hawaiian Islands: Selected Readings II*. Honolulu: University of Hawai'i Press, 1994.

Keate, George. *An Account of the Pelew Islands, situated in the Western Part of the Pacific Ocean, composed from the journals and communications of Captain Henry Wilson, and some of his officers, who, in August 1783, were there shipwrecked, in the Antelope, A Pocket belonging to the Honorable East India Company*. 2nd ed. London: G. Nicol, 1788.

Keegan, John. *The Price of Admiralty: War at Sea from Man-of-War to Submarine*. London: Arrow Books, 1990.

Keesing-Styles, Esther, and William Keesing-Styles, eds. *The Journal of Thomas James Jaggar: Feejee 1838–1845*. Auckland: Solent Publishing, 1988.

Kelly, M., ed. *Hawai'i in 1819: A Narrative Account by Louis Claude de Saules de Freycinet*. Honolulu: BPBM, 1978.

Kimmerer, William J., and Ted W. Walsh. "Tarawa Atoll Lagoon: Circula-tion, Nutrient Fluxes, and the Impact of Human Waste." *Micronesica* 17, no. 1 (1981): 161–79.

King, Lester C. *Wandering Continents and Spreading Sea Floors on an Expanding Earth.* London: John Wiley and Sons, 1983.

Kirch, P. V. *The Evolution of the Polynesian Chiefdoms.* Cambridge: Cambridge University Press, 1984.

Kirch, P. V. *Feathered Gods and Fishhooks: An Introduction to Hawaiian Archaeology and Prehistory.* Honolulu: University of Hawai'i Press, 1985.

Kirch, P. V. "Exchange Systems and Inter-island Contact in the Transformation of an Island Society: The Tikopia Case." In *Island Societies: Archaeological Approaches to Evolution and Transformation,* edited by P. V. Kirch, 33–41. Cambridge: Cambridge University Press, 1986.

Kirch, P. V. "Prehistory." In *Developments in Polynesian Ethnology,* edited by Alan Howard and R. Borofsky, 13–46. Honolulu: University of Hawai'i Press, 1989.

Kirch, P. V., and Marshall Sahlins, eds. *Anahulu: The Anthropology of History in the Kingdom of Hawai'i.* 2 vols. Chicago: University of Chicago Press, 1992.

Kirch, Patrick Vinton, and Roger C. Green. *Hawaiki, Ancestral Polynesia: An Essay in Historical Anthropology.* Cambridge: Cambridge University Press, 2001.

Kittlitz, F. H. von. *Denkwurdigkeiten einer Reise nach dem Russischen Amerika, nach Mikronesien und durch Kamtschatka.* 2 vols. Gotha: J. Perthes, 1858.

Klee, Gary A. "Traditional Time Reckoning and Resource Utilization." *Micronesica* 12, no. 2 (1976): 211–46.

Kotzebue, Otto von. *A New Voyage Round the World in the Years 1823, 24, 25 and 26.* 2 vols. London: Colburn & Bentley, 1830.

Kotzebue, Otto von. *A Voyage of Discovery into the South Sea and Behring's Straits, in search of a North-east passage, Undertaken in the Years 1815, 16, 17, and 18 in the ship Rurick.* 3 vols. Amsterdam: N. Israel and New York: Da Capo Press, 1967 (Bibliotheca Australiana reproduction of 1821 ed.).

Krämer, A. "Truk." In *Ergebnisse der Südsee-Expedition 1908–1910,* vol. II, B, v, edited by G. Thilenius, 1–452. Hamburg: Friederichsen, De Gruyter & Co., 1932 (HRAF English translation no. 1009).

Krämer, A. "Inseln um Truk (Zentralkarolinen Ost, Lukunor, Namoluk, Losap, Nama, Lomarafat, Namonuito, Pollap-Tamatam)." In *Ergebnisse der Südsee-Expedition 1908–1910,* vol. II, B, vi, I, edited by G. Thilenius, 1–291. Hamburg: Friederichsen, De Gruyter & Co., 1935 (HRAF English translation no. 1010).

Krämer, A. "Zentralkarolinen, Part I (Lamotrek Gruppe, Oleai, Feis)." In

Ergebnisse der Südsee-Expedition 1908–1910, vol. II, B, x, I, edited by
G. Thilenius, 1–413. Hamburg: Friederichsen, De Gruyter & Co., 1937
(HRAF English translation no. 1013).

Krämer, A., and Hans Nevermann. "Ralik-Ratak (Marshall-Inseln)." In
Ergebnisse der Südsee-Expedition 1908–1910, vol. II, B, ii, edited by
G. Thilenius. Hamburg: Friederichsen De Gruyter & Co., 1932 (partial
English translation by Elizabeth Murphy), typescript held in Pacific
Collection, Hamilton Library, University of Hawai'i at Mānoa, Honolulu,
1985.

Krauskopf, Konrad B., and Arthur Beiser. *The Physical Universe.* 5th ed.
New York: McGraw Hill, 1985.

Kubary, J. S. *Ethnograpische Beiträge zur Kenntnis der Karolinischen Insel-
gruppe und Nachbarschaft, I: Die sozialen Einrichtungen der Pelauer.*
Berlin: A. Asher and Co., 1885 (HRAF English translation no. 1409).

Kubary, J. S. *Ethnograpische Beiträge zur Kenntnis des Karolinen—archipels.*
Leiden: P.W.M. Trap, 1895 (HRAF English translation no. 1179).

Labby, David. *The Demystification of Yap: Dialectics of Culture on a
Micronesian Island.* Chicago: University of Chicago Press, 1976.

Laevastu, Taivo, and Herbert A. Larkins. *Marine Fisheries Ecosystem: Its
Quantitative Evaluation and Management.* Farnham, Surrey: Fishing
News Books Ltd., 1981.

Lamb, W. Kaye, ed. *The Voyage of George Vancouver 1791–1795.* 4 vols.
London: The Hakluyt Society, 1984.

Lander, M. A. *Meteorological Factors Associated with Drought on Guam.*
Mangilao, Guam: Water and Energy Research Institute (WERI) Technical
Report 75, 1994.

Langdon, Robert. "What an Irish Algae-Hunter Told his Relations about the
South Seas." *PAMBU,* no. 8, March 1969, 1–4 (a commentary on Letters
on Fiji by Dr. William Henry Harvey, 1855, copies from the originals in
Trinity College, Dublin).

Langdon, Robert. *The Lost Caravel.* Sydney: Pacific Publications, 1975.

Langdon, Robert. "Of Time, Prophecy and the European Ships of Tupaia's
Chart." *Journal of Pacific History* 19, no. 4 (1984): 239–47.

Langdon, Robert. "The Impact of Castaways on Host Societies." *Journal of
the Polynesian Society* 98, no. 1 (1989): 91–93.

Langdon, Robert. "Castaways." In *The Cambridge History of the Pacific
Islanders,* edited by Donald Denoon, 69–74. Cambridge: Cambridge
University Press, 1997.

Latukefu, Sione. "King George Tupou I of Tonga." In *Pacific Island Portraits,* edited by J. W. Davidson and Deryck Scarr, 55–75. Canberra: Australian National University, 1970.

Laubenfels, Max W. de. "Ocean Currents in the Marshall Islands." *Geographical Review* 40, no. 2 (1950): 254–59.

Lay, William, and Cyrus M. Hussey. *A Narrative of the Mutiny on board the whaleship Globe.* New York: Corinth Books, 1963 (reprint of 1828 original).

Leach, Foss, and Graeme Ward. *Archaeology on Kapingamarangi Atoll.* Dunedin: Studies in Prehistoric Anthropology 16, Department of Anthropology, University of Otago, 1981.

Lessa, William A. "The Place of Ulithi in the Yap Empire." *Human Organization* 9 (1950): 16–18.

Lessa, William A. "Myth and Blackmail in the Western Carolines." *Journal of the Polynesian Society* 65 (1956): 67–74.

Lessa, William A. *Tales from Ulithi Atoll: A Comparative Study of Oceanic Folklore.* Berkeley: University of California Press, 1961.

Lessa, William A. "An Evaluation of Early Descriptions of Carolinian Culture." *Ethnohistory* 9, no. 4 (1962): 313–403.

Lessa, William A. *Ulithi: A Micronesian Design for Living.* New York: Holt, Rinehart and Wilson, 1966.

Lessa, William A. "The Social Effects of Typhoon Ophelia (1960) on Ulithi." In *Peoples and Cultures of the Pacific: An Anthropological Reader,* edited by A. P. Vayda, 330–79. Garden City, N.Y.: The Natural History Press, 1968.

Lessa, William A. "The Portuguese Discovery of the Isles of Sequeira." *Micronesica* 11, no. 1 (1975): 35–70.

Lessa, William A. *More Tales from Ulithi Atoll: A Content Analysis.* Berkeley: University of California Press, 1980.

Lessa, William A. "Comments on Settlement on Ulithi Atoll." *Asian Perspectives* 25, no. 2 (1987): 127–32.

Lessin, Alexander Philip, and Phyllis June Lessin. *Village of Conquerors, Sawana: A Tongan Village in Fiji.* Eugene: Department of Anthropology, University of Oregon, 1970.

Lesson, R. P. *Voyage Autour du Monde Entrepris par ordre du gouvernement sur la corvette "La Coquille."* 4 vols. Bruxelles: N.J.: Gregoir, V. Wouters & Co., 1839, (HRAF English translation no. 1324).

Lévesque, Rodrique, ed. *History of Micronesia: A Collection of Source Documents,* vol. 3, *First Real Contact 1596–1637.* Gatineau, Quebec: Lévesque Publications, 1993.

Levin, Michael J., and L. J. Gorenflo. "Demographic Controls and Shifting Adaptive Constraints on Eauripik Atoll." *Isla* 2, no. 1 (1994): 103–45.

Levison, M., R. G. Ward, and J. W. Webb. *The Settlement of Polynesia: A Computer Simulation.* Minneapolis: University of Minnesota Press, 1973.

Lewis, David. *We, the Navigators: The Ancient Art of Landfinding in the Pacific.* Canberra: ANU Press, 1972.

Lewis, David. *From Maui to Cook: The Discovery and Settlement of the Pacific.* Lane Cove, N.S.W.: Doubleday, 1977.

Lewis, David. *The Voyaging Stars: Secrets of the Pacific Island Navigators.* Sydney: Collins, 1978.

Lewis, David. "The Pacific Navigators' Debt to the Ancient Seafarers of Asia." In *The Changing Pacific: Essays in Honour of H. E. Maude,* edited by Niel Gunson, 46–66. Melbourne: Oxford University Press, 1979.

Lewthwaite, Gordon R. "Man and the Sea in Early Tahiti: Maritime Economy through European Eyes." *Pacific Viewpoint* 7, no. 1 (1966): 28–53.

Lewthwaite, Gordon R. "Geographical Knowledge of the Pacific Peoples." In *The Pacific Basin: A History of Its Geographical Exploration,* edited by H. R. Friis, 57–86. New York: American Geographical Society, 1967.

Lewthwaite, Gordon R. "The Puzzle of Tupaia's Map." *New Zealand Geographer* 26 (1970): 1–18.

Lieber, Michael D. *More than a Living: Fishing and the Social Order on a Polynesian Atoll.* Boulder, Colo.: Westview Press, 1994.

L Illustration. 11 Avril 1903, Paris, 1903.

Lingenfelter, Sherwin G. *Yap: Political Leadership and Culture Change in an Island Society.* Honolulu: University of Hawai'i Press, 1975.

Linnekin, Jocelyn. "Statistical Analysis of the Great Mahele: Some Preliminary Findings." *Journal of Pacific History* 22, no. 1 (1987): 15–33.

Linnekin, Jocelyn. "Contending Approaches." In *The Cambridge History of the Pacific Islanders,* edited by Donald Denoon, 3–36. Cambridge: Cambridge University Press, 1997.

Lloyd, P. C. "The Political Development of West African Kingdoms." Review article in *Journal of African History* 9, no. 2 (1968): 319–29.

Lobban, Christopher S., and Maria Schefter. *Tropical Pacific Island Environments.* Mangilao, Guam: University of Guam Press, second printing of 1997 first printing, 2001.

Lucatt, E. *Rovings in the Pacific from 1837 to 1849: by a merchant long resident at Tahiti.* 2 vols. London: Longmans, 1851.

Lukere, Vicki. "Mothers of the Taukei: Fijian Women and the 'Decrease of the Race.'" Ph.D. thesis, ANU, 1997.

Luomala, Katharine. *Voices on the Wind.* Honolulu: BPBM, 1955.

Luomala, Katharine. "Porpoises and Taro in Gilbert Islands' Myths and Customs." *Fabula* 18, no. 1 (1977): 201–11.

Luomala, Katharine. "Sharks and Shark Fishing in the Culture of Gilbert Islands, Micronesia." In *The Fishing Culture of the World: Studies in Ethnology, Culture and Folklore* (2 vols.), edited by Béla Gunda, vol. 2, 1202–52. Budapest: Akadémiai Kiadó, 1984.

Lutké, Frédéric. *Voyage Autour du Monde Exécuté par ordre de sa Majesté l'Empereur Nicholas Ier.* 3 vols. Paris: Firmin Didot, 1835 (vols. 1 and 2), 1836 (vol. 3) (HRAF English translation no. 1317 of vol. 1, no. 1318 of vol. 2, and no. 1319 of vol. 3).

Lutké, Frédéric. *Voyage Autour du Monde, 1826–1829.* 3 vols. Amsterdam: N. Israel and New York: Da Capo Press, 1971 (Bibliotheca Australiana reprint of 1835–36 ed.).

Lyons, Curtis. "Land Matters in Hawai'i." *The Islander* 1, nos. 18, 19, and 20 (1875): 103–19.

Mackenzie, Melody Kapilialoha. *Native Hawaiian Rights Handbook.* Honolulu: Native Hawaiian Legal Corporation, 1991.

Māhina, 'Okusitino. "The Poetics of Tongan Traditional History, Tala-ē-fonua: An Ecology-centred Concept of Culture and History." *Journal of Pacific History* 28, no. 1 (1993): 109–21.

Malo, David. *Hawaiian Antiquities: Moolelo Hawai'i.* 2nd ed. (English translation by Nathanial B. Emerson). Honolulu: BPBM, 1951.

Manu, Moke, et al. *Hawaiian Fishing Traditions.* Honolulu: Kalamaku Press, 1992.

Marck, Jeffrey C. "Micronesian Dialects and the Overnight Voyage." *Journal of the Polynesian Society* 95, no. 1 (1986): 253–58.

Martin, Captain Henry Byam. *The Polynesian Journal of Captain Henry Byam Martin . . . August 1846 to August 1847.* Canberra: ANU Press, 1981.

Martin, John. *Tonga Islands, William Mariner's Account.* 2 vols. 4th ed. Tonga: Vava'u Press, 1981.

Mason, Leonard, comp. *Select Writings on the Marshall Islands* (drawn from various HRAF English translations). Honolulu: Department of Anthropology, University of Hawai'i at Mānoa, 1947.

Mason, Leonard. *The Economic Organization of the Marshall Islanders.* Honolulu: U.S. Commercial Company Economic Survey, April 1947.

Mason, Leonard. "Arno: Story of an Atoll." Honolulu: Typescript draft held in Pacific Collection, Hamilton Library, University of Hawai'i at Mānoa, 1957.

Mason, Leonard. "Suprafamilial Authority and Economic Process in

Micronesian Atolls." In *Peoples and Cultures of the Pacific: An Anthropological Reader,* edited by A. P. Vayda, 299–329. Garden City, N.Y.: The Natural History Press, 1968.

Mason, Leonard. *Land Rights and Title Succession in the Ralik Chain, Marshall Islands.* Kolonia, Pohnpei: Final report on research for Iroij Lablab Kabua Kabua, Typescript manuscript held in Micronesian Seminar Library, n.d.

Massal, Emile, and Jacques Barrau. *Food Plants of the South Sea Islands.* Noumea: South Pacific Commission Technical Paper no. 42, 1956.

Masse, W. Bruce, David Snyder, and George J. Gummerman. "Prehistoric and Historic Settlement in the Palau Islands, Micronesia." *New Zealand Journal of Archaeology* 6 (1984): 107–27.

Masse, W. Bruce. "A Millennium of Fishing in the Palau Islands, Micronesia." In *Traditional Fishing in the Pacific,* edited by Athol Anderson, 85–117. Honolulu: Pacific Anthropological Records 37, BPBM, 1986.

Masse, W. Bruce. "Radiocarbon Dating, Sea-level Change and the Peopling of Belau." In *Recent Advances in Micronesian Archaeology, Micronesica: Supplement no. 2,* edited by Rosalind L. Hunter-Anderson, October (1990): 213–30.

Maude, H. E. "Pacific History—Past, Present and Future." *Journal of Pacific History* 6 (1971): 3–24.

McArthur, Norma. *Island Populations of the Pacific.* Canberra, ANU Press, 1967.

McCall, Grant C. "Little Ice Age: Some Proposals for Polynesia and Rapanui (Easter Island)." *Journal de la Société des Océanistes* 98, no. 1 (1994): 99–104.

McCluer, John. *Journal of a Voyage to the Pelew Islands 1790–1792.* Honolulu: Hamilton Library, University of Hawai'i at Mānoa, Microfilm UH 1202–2 (copy of British Museum MS ADD 19301 P50/5266), n.d.

McCoster, John E. "Fish." In *The Encyclopedia of the Earth: Oceans and Islands,* edited by Frank H. Talbot, 36–39. London: Merehurst, 1991.

McCoy, Michael. "A Renaissance in Carolinian-Marianas Voyaging." In *Pacific Navigation and Voyaging,* edited by Ben Finney, 129–38. Wellington: Polynesian Society Memoir 39, 1976.

McCutcheon, Mary Shaw. "Resource Exploitation and the Tenure of Land and Sea in Palau." Ph.D. thesis, University of Arizona, 1981.

McEvoy, Arthur F. *The Fisherman's Problem: Ecology and Law in the California Fisheries, 1850–1980.* Cambridge: Cambridge University Press, 1986.

McGowan, John A. "The Nature of Oceanic Ecosystems." In *The Biology of the Oceanic Pacific: Proceedings of the Thirty-Third Annual Biology Colloquium 1972*, edited by Charles B. Miller, 9–28. Corvallis: Oregon State University Press, 1974.

McLean, R. F. "Spatial and Temporal Variability of External Physical Controls on Small Island Ecosystems." In *Population-Environment Relations in Tropical Islands: The Case of Eastern Fiji*, edited by H. C. Brookfield, 149–76. Paris: Man and Biosphere Technical Notes 13, UNESCO, 1980.

McNeill, J. R. "Of Rats and Men: A Synoptic Environmental History of the Island Pacific." *Journal of World History* 5, no. 2 (1994): 299–349.

Meleisea, Malama, and Penelope Schoeffel. "Discovering Outsiders." In *The Cambridge History of the Pacific Islanders*, edited by Donald Denoon, 119–51. Cambridge: Cambridge University Press, 1997.

Menzies, Archibald. *Hawai'i Nei 128 Years Ago*. Honolulu: T. H. Press, 1920.

Merlin, M. D. "A History of Ethnobotany in Remote Oceania." *Pacific Science* 54, no. 3 (2000): 275–87.

Milet-Mureau, L. A. *A Voyage Round the World, performed in the years 1785, 1786, 1787, and 1788 by J.F.G. de La Pérouse*. 3-vol. English ed. London: J. Johnson Printer, 1798.

Minerbi, Luciano, Davianna McGregor, and Jon Matsuoka, eds. *Native Hawaiian and Local Cultural Assessment Project: Phase 1 Problems/Assets Identification*. Honolulu: University of Hawai'i Press, June 1993.

Mollat du Jourdin, Michel. *Europe and the Sea* (English translation by Teresa Lavender). Oxford: Blackwell, 1993.

Moon, Paul. "The Creation of the 'Sealord Deal.'" *Journal of the Polynesian Society* 107, no. 2 (1998): 145–74.

Moorehead, Alan. *The Fatal Impact: An Account of the Invasion of the South Pacific 1767–1840*. London: Harmondsworth, 1968.

Morey, C. J. "Wrecked on the Voyage to Lau." *Journal of the Polynesian Society* 41, no. 164 (1932): 310–11.

Morgan, Amanda A. "Mystery in the Eye of the Beholder: Cross-Cultural Encounters in the Western Caroline Islands with a Special Focus on Yap, 1525–1886." M.A. thesis in history, University of Hawai'i at Mānoa, 1994.

Morgan, Amanda. "Mystery in the Eye of the Beholder: Cross-Cultural Encounters on 19th Century Yap." *Journal of Pacific History* 31, no. 1 (1996): 27–41.

Morrison, J. P., P. Geraghty, and L. Crowl, eds. *Science of the Pacific Island Peoples*. 4 vols. Suva: Institute of Pacific Studies, 1994.

Morrison, James. *Journal*. London: Golden Cockerel Press, 1935.

Morton, Harry A. *The Wind Commands: Sailors and Sailing Ships in the Pacific*. Vancouver: University of British Columbia Press, 1975.

Moyle, Richard, ed. *The Samoan Journals of John Williams, 1830 and 1832*. Canberra: ANU Press, 1984.

Muller, Robert A., and Theodore M. Oberlander. *Physical Geography Today: A Portrait of a Planet*. 2nd ed. New York: Random House, 1978.

Müller, Wilhelm. "Yap." In *Ergebnisse der Südsee Expedition, 1908–1910, II: Ethnographie:B: Mikronesien*, 2, ii, edited by G. Thilenius. Hamburg: Friederichsen, De Gruyter & Co., 1917.

Munford, James Kenneth, ed. *John Ledyard's Journal of Captain Cook's Last Voyage*. Corvallis: Oregon State University Press, 1963.

Murakami, Alan. "*Konohiki* Fishing Rights and Marine Resources." In *Native Hawaiian Rights Handbook*, edited by Melody Kapilialoha MacKenzie, 173–95. Honolulu: Native Hawaiian Legal Corporation, 1991.

Nakayama, Masao, and Frederick L. Ramp. *Micronesian Navigation and Island Empires and Traditional Concepts of Ownership of the Sea*. Saipan: Study for the Joint Committee on The Law of the Sea Conference, 5th Congress of Micronesia, January 14, 1974 (copy held in MARC Library, Guam).

Nason, James D. "The Strength of the Land: Community Perception of Population on Etal Atoll." In *Pacific Atoll Populations*, edited by Vern Carroll, 117–59. Honolulu: University of Hawai'i Press, 1975.

Neich, Roger. "Samoan Figurative Carvings on Samoan Canoes." *Journal of the Polynesian Society* 93, no. 2 (1984): 191–97.

Neich, Roger. "Samoan Figurative Carvings and Taumualua Canoes: A Further Note." *Journal of the Polynesian Society* 100, no. 3 (1991): 317–27.

Nero, Karen. "The Material World Remade." In *The Cambridge History of the Pacific Islanders*, edited by Donald Denoon, 359–96. Cambridge: Cambridge University Press, 1997.

Nero, Karen. "The End of Insularity." In *The Cambridge History of the Pacific Islanders*, edited by Donald Denoon, 439–67. Cambridge: Cambridge University Press, 1997.

Nero, Karen. "Linkages between Yap and Palau: Towards Regional Histories." Kolonia, Pohnpei: unpublished paper held in Micronesian Seminar Library, n.d.

Nero, Karen Louise. "A cherechar a lokelii: Beads of History of Koror, Palau, 1783–1983." Ph.D. thesis, University of California, Berkeley, 1987.

Newbury, Colin. "Te Hau Pahu Rahi: Pomare II and the Concept of Inter-island Government in Eastern Polynesia." *Journal of the Polynesian Society* 76, no. 4 (1967): 477–514.

Newbury, Colin. *Tahiti Nui: Change and Survival in French Polynesia 1767–1945.* Honolulu: University of Hawai'i Press, 1980.

Newman, T. Stell. "Man in the Prehistoric Hawaiian Ecosystem." In *A Natural History of the Hawaiian Islands: Select Readings,* edited by E. Alison Kay, 599–603. Honolulu: University of Hawai'i Press, 1972.

Nicholls, Neville. "Historical El Niño/Southern Oscillation Variability in the Australasian Region." In *El Niño: Historical and Paleoclimatic Aspects of the Southern Oscillation,* edited by Henry F. Diaz and Vera Markgraf, 151–73. Cambridge: Cambridge University Press, 1992.

Nishimura, Asahitaro. "Fishing in Indonesia from the Marine Ethnological Viewpoint with Respect to Wallace's Line." In *The Fishing Culture of the World: Studies in Ethnology, Culture and Folklore* (2 vols.), edited by Béla Gunda, vol. 2, 677–703. Budapest: Akadémiai Kiadó, 1984.

Nordhoff, Charles. "Notes on the Off-shore Fishing of the Society Islands." *Journal of the Polynesian Society* 39 (1930): 137–73, 221–62.

Nunn, Patrick D. "Beyond the Naïve Lands: Human History and Environmental Change in the Pacific Basin." In *The Margin Fades: Geographical Itineraries in a World of Islands,* edited by Eric Waddell and Patrick D. Nunn, 5–28. Suva: Institute of Pacific Studies, 1993.

Nunn, Patrick D. *Oceanic Islands.* Oxford: Blackwell, 1994.

Oliver, Douglas L. *Ancient Tahitian Society.* 3 vols. Honolulu: University of Hawai'i Press, 1974.

Oliver, Douglas L. *Oceania: The Native Cultures of Australia and the Pacific Islands.* 2 vols. Honolulu: University of Hawai'i Press, 1989.

Orbell, Margaret. *The Illustrated Encyclopedia of Maori Myth and Legend.* Christchurch: Canterbury University Press, 1995.

Orbell, Margaret. *The Natural World of the Maori.* Auckland: David Bateman Ltd, 1996.

Pacific Commercial Advertiser. Honolulu, June 2, August 3, 1856.

Page, Harlan. *A Memoir of Thomas H. Patoo of the Marquesas Islands.* Andover, Mass.: American Tract Society, 1825.

Parkinson, S. *A Journal of a Voyage to the South Seas in His Majesty's Ship, the "Endeavour."* London: C. Dilly and J. Phillips, 1784.

Parmentier, Richard J. "Mythological Metaphors and Historical Realities:

Models of Transformation of Belauan Polity." *Journal of the Polynesian Society* 95, no. 2 (1986): 167–93.

Parmentier, Richard J. *The Sacred Remains: Myth, History, and Polity in Belau.* Chicago: University of Chicago Press, 1987.

Parry, John T. *The Sigatoka Valley—Pathway into Prehistory.* Suva: Bulletin of the Fiji Museum no. 9, 1987.

Parsonson, G. S. "The Settlement of Oceania: An Examination of the Accidental Voyage Theory." In *Polynesian Navigation* (3rd ed.), edited by Jack Golson, 11–63. Wellington: A. W. & A. H. Reed, 1972.

Parsonson, G. S. "The Nautical Revolution in Polynesia." Dunedin: Typescript copy held in the Hocken Library, 1975.

Pawley, Andrew. "On the Classification of Marine Animals in Wayan." In *Science of the Pacific Island Peoples.* Vol. 3: *Flora, Fauna, Food and Medicine,* edited by J. P. Morrison, P. Geraghty, and L. Crowl, 87–107. Suva: Institute of Pacific Studies, 1994.

Pearson, W. H. "The Reception of European Voyagers on Polynesian Islands, 1568–1797." *Journal de la Société des Océanistes* 26 (June 1970): 121–52.

Perminow, Arne Aleksej. "Between the Forest and the Big Lagoon: The Microeconomy of Kotu Island in the Kingdom of Tonga." *Pacific Viewpoint* 34, no. 2 (1993): 179–92.

Petit-Skinner, Solange. "Traditional Ownership of the Sea in Oceania." In *Ocean Yearbook 4,* edited by Elisabeth Mann Borgese and Norton Ginsburg, 308–18. Chicago: University of Chicago Press, 1983.

Pickering, Michael. "The Physical Landscape as a Social Landscape: A Garawa Example." In *Social Landscapes,* edited by Lesley Head, Chris Gosden, and J. Peter White, 149–61 (Special issue of *Archaeology in Oceania* 29, no. 3, 1994).

Porter, Captain David. *Journal of a Cruise made to the Pacific Ocean.* 2 vols. Upper Saddle River, N.J.: The Gregg Press, 1970 (reprint of 1822 ed.).

Pritchard, W. T. *Polynesian Reminiscences.* London: Chapman Hall, 1866.

Pukui, Mary Kawena, and Samuel H. Elbert. *Hawaiian Dictionary: Hawaiian–English English–Hawaiian* Revised and enlarged ed. Honolulu: University of Hawai'i Press, 1986.

Pukui, Mary Kawena, E. W. Haertig, and Catherine Lee. *Nana I Ke Kumu: Look to the Source.* Vol. 1. Honolulu: Hui Hanai, 1972.

Purseglove, J. W. *Tropical Crops: Volume One—Monocotyledons 1.* London: Longmans, 1972.

Quinn, William H. "A Study of Southern Oscillation-related Climatic Activity for A.D. 622–1990 Incorporating Nile River Flood Data." In *El Niño:*

Historical and Paleoclimatic Aspects of the Southern Oscillation, edited by
Henry F. Diaz and Vera Markgraf, 119–49. Cambridge: Cambridge University Press, 1992.

Ralston, Caroline. "Hawai'i 1778–1854: Some Aspects of Maka'ainana
Response to Rapid Cultural Change." *Journal of Pacific History* 19, no. 1
(1984): 21–40.

Rasmusson, Eugene M. "El Niño and Variations in Climate." *American Scientist* 73, no. 2 (1985): 168–77.

Reid, A. C. "The Fruit of Rewa: Oral Traditions and the Growth of the Pre-
Christian Lakeba State." *Journal of Pacific History* 12, no. 1 (1977): 2–24.

Reinman, F. M. *Fishing: An Aspect of Oceanic Economy: An Archaeological
Approach.* Chicago: Fieldiana Anthropology 56(2), Field Museum of
Natural History, March 1967.

Ridgell, Reilly, Manny Ikea, and Isaoshy Uruo. "The Persistence of Central
Carolinian Navigation." *Isla* 2, no. 2 (1994): 181–206.

Riesenberg, Saul H. "Tables of Voyages Affecting Micronesian Islands." In
R. T. Simmons, J. J. Graydon, D. C. Gajdusek, and Paul Brown, "Blood
Group Genetic Variations in Natives of the Caroline Islands and in Other
Parts of Micronesia." *Oceania* 36, no. 2 (1965): 132–70 (Riesenberg,
155–68).

Riesenberg, Saul H. "The Organisation of Navigational Knowledge on
Puluwat." *Journal of the Polynesian Society* 81, no. 1 (1972): 19–56.

Riesenberg, Saul H. "The Ghost Islands of the Carolines." *Micronesica* 11,
no. 1 (1975): 7–33.

Robertson, Russell. "The Caroline Islands." *Transactions of the Asiatic
Society of Japan* 5 (1877): 41–63.

Roe, Michael, ed. *The Journal and Letters of Captain Charles Bishop on the
North-west coast of America in the Pacific and in New South Wales
1794–1799.* London: Cambridge University Press for the Hakluyt Society,
1967.

Rogers, Robert F. *Destiny's Landfall: A History of Guam.* Honolulu: University of Hawai'i Press, 1995.

Rubinstein, Don. "Native Place-Names and Geographical Systems of Fais,
Caroline Islands." *Micronesica* 14, no. 1 (1978): 69–82.

Ruddle, Kenneth, and Tomoya Akimichi. "Introduction." In *Maritime Institutions in the Western Pacific,* edited by Kenneth Ruddle and Tomoya
Akimichi, 1–9. Osaka: National Museum of Ethnology, 1984.

Russell, Scott. *From Arabwal to Ashes: A Brief History of Garapan Village:
1818 to 1945.* Saipan: Micronesian Archaeological Survey Report no. 19,

Office of Historic Preservation, Commonwealth of the Northern Marianas, June 1984.

Russell, Scott, ed. *The Chamorro: A History and Ethnography of the Marianas* by Georg Fritz (English translation by Elfriede Craddock). Saipan: Division of Historic Preservation, 1984.

Russell, Scott. "Roots of the Falawasch." Mangilao, Guam: unpublished MS paper, MARC Library, n.d.

Russell, W. E. "Rotuma: Its History, Traditions and Customs." *Journal of the Polynesian Society* 51, no. 4 (1942): 229–55.

Rutherford, Noel, ed. *Friendly Islands: A History of Tonga.* Melbourne: Oxford University Press, 1977.

Sabatier, Father Ernest. *Astride the Equator: An Account of the Gilbert Islands* (English translation by Ursula Nixon). Melbourne: Oxford University Press, 1977.

Sack, Robert David. *Human Territoriality: Its Theory and History.* Cambridge: Cambridge University Press, 1986.

Sahlins, Marshall. *Moala: Culture and Nature on a Fijian Island.* Ann Arbor: University of Michigan Press, 1962.

Sahlins, Marshall. "The Stranger-King, or Dumezil among the Fijians." *Journal of Pacific History* 16, no. 3 (1981): 107–32.

Sahlins, Marshall. *Historical Metaphors and Mythical Realities: Structure in the Early History of the Sandwich Islands Kingdom.* Ann Arbor: University of Michigan Press, 1981.

Sahlins, Marshall. "Other Times, Other Customs: The Anthropology of History." *American Anthropologist* 85, no. 3 (1983): 517–43.

Sahlins, Marshall. *Islands of History.* Chicago: University of Chicago Press, 1985.

Sahlins, Marshall. "The Return of the Event, Again; With Reflections on the Beginnings of the Great Fijian War of 1843 to 1855 between the Kingdoms of Bau and Rewa." In *Clio in Oceania: Towards a Historical Anthropology,* edited by Aletta Biersack, 37–99. Washington, D.C.: Smithsonian Institute Press, 1991.

Sahlins, Marshall. "The Remembered Landscape of Oʻahu." In *Pacific History Papers from the 8th Pacific History Association Conference,* edited by Donald H. Rubinstein, 419–28. Mangilao, Guam: University of Guam Press and MARC, 1992.

Sahlins, Marshall. "The Discovery of the True Savage." In *Dangerous Liaisons: Essays in Honour of Greg Dening,* edited by Donna Marwick, 41–96. Melbourne: History Department, University of Melbourne, 1994.

Salesius, P. *Die Karolinen–Insel Jap.* Berlin: MS, c. 1907 (HRAF English translation no. 1027).

Salvat, B. "The Living Marine Resources of the South Pacific: Past, Present and Future." In *Population-Environment Relations in Tropical Islands: The Case of Eastern Fiji,* edited by H. C. Brookfield. 131–48. Paris: Man and Biosphere Programme, UNESCO, 1980.

Sánchez y Zayas, Don Eugenio. "The Mariana Islands: The Caroline Islanders." *The Nautical Magazine and Naval Chronicle* 35, no. 4, 205–13 (Rota, Agrigan, Tinian), no. 5, 253–66 (Saypan), 1866.

Sapper, K., et al. *Jap. Deutsches Kolonial–Lexikon II.* Leipzig: Quelle and Meyer, 1920 (HRAF English translation no. 1181).

Sarfert, E. "Kusae." In *Ergebnisse der Südsee-Expedition 1908–1910,* edited by G. Thilenius, II, B, IV. Hamburg: Friederichsen, De Gruyter & Co., 1932 (HRAF English translation no. 1007).

Sayes, Shelley Ann. "Cakaudrove: Ideology and Reality in a Fijian Confederation." Ph.D. thesis, ANU, 1982.

Scarr, Deryck. "Cakobau and Ma'afu: Contenders for Pre-eminence in Fiji." In *Pacific Island Portraits,* edited by J. W. Davidson and Deryck Scarr, 95–126. Canberra: ANU Press, 1970.

Scheltma, Rudolf S. "Long-distance Dispersal by Planktonic Larvae of Shoal-water Benthic Invertebrates among Central Pacific Islands." In *A Natural History of the Hawaiian Islands: Selected Readings II,* edited by E. Alison Kay, 171–86. Honolulu: University of Hawai'i Press, 1994.

Schmitt, R. C. "New Estimates for the Pre-censal Population of Hawai'i." *Journal of the Polynesian Society* 80, no. 2 (1971): 237–43.

Schneider, David M. "Typhoons on Yap." *Human Organization* 16, no. 2 (1957): 10–15.

Shannon, Sequoia, and Joseph R. Morgan. "Management of Insular Pacific Marine Ecosystems." In *Ocean Yearbook 10,* edited by Elisabeth Mann Borgese, Norton Ginsburg, and Joseph R. Morgan, 196–213. Chicago: University of Chicago Press, 1993.

Sharp, Andrew. *Ancient Voyagers in the Pacific.* London: Penguin, 1957.

Sharp, Andrew. *Ancient Voyagers in Polynesia.* Auckland: Paul's Book Arcade, 1963.

Sharp, G. D. "Fish Populations and Fisheries: Their Perturbations, Natural and Man-Induced." In *Ecosystems of the World 27: Continental Shelves,* edited by H. Postma and J. J. Zijlstra, 155–202. Amsterdam: Elsevier, 1988.

Shineberg, Dorothy, ed. *The Trading Voyages of Andrew Cheyne 1841–1844.* Canberra: ANU Press, 1971.

Sinoto, Yoshiko H., ed. *Caroline Islands Archaeology: Investigations on Fefan, Faraulep, Woleai, and Lamotrek*. Honolulu: BPBM, November 1984.

Sopher, David. *The Sea Nomads: A Study of the Maritime Boat People of Southeast Asia*. Singapore: National Museum of Singapore, 1977.

Spate, O.H.K. "The Pacific as an Artefact." In *The Changing Pacific: Essays in Honour of H. E. Maude*, edited by Niel Gunson, 32–45. Melbourne: Oxford University Press, 1978.

Spate, O.H.K. *The Pacific Since Magellan*, vol. 1, *The Spanish Lake*. Canberra: ANU Press, 1979.

Spate, Oskar H. K. "Islands and Men." In *Man's Place in the Island Ecosystem: A Symposium*, edited by F. R. Fosberg, 253–64. Honolulu: BPBM, 1963.

Spencer, Tom. "Changes in the Global Environment: Uncertain Prospects for the Pacific." In *Environment and Development in the Pacific Islands*, edited by Ben Burt and Christian Clerk, 243–63. Canberra: National Centre for Development Studies, ANU, 1997.

Spennemann, Dirk H. R. *Population Control Measures in Traditional Marshallese Culture: A Review of 19th Century European Observations*. Majuro: Report presented to the Population Co-ordination Committee, Alele Museum, 1990 (MS copy held in Micronesian Seminar Library, Kolonia, Pohnpei).

Spoehr, Alexander. *Saipan: The Ethnology of a War-Devastated Island*. Chicago: Fieldiana: Anthropology 41, Chicago Natural History Museum, February 11, 1954.

Stair, Rev. John B. *Old Samoa or Flotsam and Jetsam from the Pacific Ocean*. London: The Religious Tract Society, 1897.

Stannard, David. *Before the Horror: The Population of Hawai'i on the Eve of Western Contact*. Honolulu: Social Science Research Institute, University of Hawai'i, 1989.

Stimson, J. Frank. "Songs of the Polynesian Voyagers." *Journal of the Polynesian Society* 41, no. 163 (1932): 181–201.

Stimson, J. F., and D. S. Marshall. *A Dictionary of Some Tuamotuan Dialects of the Polynesian Language*. The Hague: Martinus Nijhoff, 1964.

Sudo, Ken-Ichi. "Social Organisation and Types of Sea Tenure in Micronesia." In *Maritime Institutions in the Western Pacific*, edited by Kenneth Ruddle and Tomoya Akimichi, 203–30. Osaka: National Museum of Ethnology, 1984.

Sunderland, J. P. "Letter of 23 July 1847." SSL 20, LMS, Pacific Manuscript Bureau Microfilm Series (copy held in Hocken Library, Dunedin).

Suter, Keith. *The History of the Development of the Law of the Sea.* Sydney: Humane Society International Inc. Australia, and World Wildlife Fund Australia, 1994.

Tamasese, Tui Atua Tupua. "Tamafaigā—Shaman, King or Maniac? The Emergence of Manono." *Journal of Pacific History* 30, no. 1 (1995): 317–27.

Teaiwa, Teresia. Review of *A New Oceania: Rediscovering Our Sea of Islands,* Eric Waddell et al. (eds.), Suva: University of the South Pacific School of Social and Economic Development, 1993, in *The Contemporary Pacific* 8, no. 1 (1996): 214–17.

Teiwaki, Roniti. *Management of Marine Resources in Kiribati.* Suva: University of the South Pacific, 1988.

Terrell, J. E., T. L. Hunt, and C. Gosden. "The Dimensions of Social Life in the Pacific: Human Diversity and the Myth of the Primitive Isolate." *Current Anthropology* 38 (1997): 155–96.

Tetens, Alfred. *Among the Savages of the South Seas: Memoirs of Micronesia, 1862–1868* (English translation by Florence Mann Spoehr). Stanford: Stanford University Press, 1958.

The Polynesian. Honolulu, 1846, 1852.

Thomas, John. "History of Tonga." Typescript copy of manuscript held in Mitchell Library, Hocken Library, Dunedin, n.d.

Thomas, Mifflin. *Schooner from Windward: Two Centuries of Hawaiian Interisland Shipping.* Honolulu: University of Hawai'i Press, 1983.

Thomas, Nicholas. "The Force of Ethnology: Origins and Significance of the Melanesia/Polynesia Division." *Current Anthropology* 30, no. 1 (1989): 27–41.

Thomas, Nicholas. "On the Melanesia/Polynesia Division: Reply to Comments." *Current Anthropology* 30, no. 2 (1989): 211–13.

Thomas, Stephen D. *The Last Navigator.* London: Hutchinson, 1987.

Thomas, William L., Jr. "The Pacific Basin: An Introduction." In *Peoples and Cultures of the Pacific: An Anthropological Reader,* edited by A. P. Vayda, 3–26. Garden City, N.Y.: The Natural History Press, 1968.

Thomson, Basil. *The Fijians: A Study of the Decay of Custom.* London: Dawsons of Pall Mall, 1968.

Thomson, Robert. "History of Tahiti." 3 vols. Typescript of unpublished manuscript in LMS Archives, London, in the possession of G. S. Parsonson, Dunedin, n.d.

Thrum, Thomas G., ed. *Collection of Hawaiian Antiquities and Folklore.* 6 vols. by Abraham Fornander. Honolulu: BPBM, 1916–19.

Thurman, Harold V. *Essentials of Oceanography.* Columbus, Ohio: Charles E. Merrill Publishing Co., 1983.

Tippett, Rev. A. R. "The Nature and Social Function of Fijian War." *Transactions and Proceedings of the Fijian Society for the Years 1951 to 1954* 5, no. 4 (1955): 137–55.

Tippett, Rev. A. R. "The Survival of an Ancient Custom relative to the Pig's Head, Bau, Fiji." *Transactions and Proceedings of the Fijian Society for the Years 1955 to 1957* 6, no. 1 (1958): 30–39.

Tippett, Rev. A. R. *Fijian Material Culture: A Study of Cultural Context, Function, and Change.* Honolulu: BPBM, 1968.

Titcomb, Margaret. *Native Use of Fish in Hawai'i.* 2nd ed. Honolulu: University of Hawai'i Press, 1972.

Toaru. *Talk of the Sea. Oral navigation Lore on Puluwat by Toaru as told to Peter Ochs* (English translation by Celestine Emwalu and William Bislent). MS copy in Micronesian Seminar Library, Pohnpei, MS 365 T9, 1971.

Tobin, A. *Land Tenure in the Marshall Islands.* Rev. ed. Washington, D.C.: Atoll Research Bulletin no. 11, The Pacific Science Board, June 1956.

Tolova'a, A. "Past and Present Practices in Agriculture and Fisheries in Samoa." In *Science of Pacific Island Peoples,* vol. 2: *Land Use and Agriculture,* edited by John Morrison, Paul Geraghty, and Linda Crowl, 223–30. Suva: Institute of Pacific Studies, 1994.

Tomczak, Matthias, and J. Stuart Godfrey. *Regional Oceanography: An Introduction.* Oxford: Pergamon, 1994.

Tonganivalu, Deve. "Ratu Cakobau." *Transactions of the Fiji Society for the Year 1912 and 1913* (1914): 1–12.

Trood, Thomas. "Far-off Vision." *The Leisure Hour* (1866): 485–86.

Tuggle, H. D. "Hawai'i." In *The Prehistory of Polynesia,* edited by Jesse D. Jennings, 167–99. Canberra: ANU Press, 1979.

Turnbull, John. *A Voyage Round the World in the Years 1800–1804.* Philadelphia: Benjamin and Thomas Kite, 1810.

Turner, G. *Nineteen Years in Polynesia.* London: John Snow, 1861.

Turner, G. *Samoa: A Hundred Years Ago and Long Before.* London: Macmillan, 1884.

Tute, Warren. "War at Sea." In *The Commanding Sea: Six Voyages of Discovery,* edited by Claire Francis and Warren Tute, 175–85. London: Book Club Associates, 1981.

Ushijima, Iwao. "The Control of Reefs and Lagoons: Some Aspects of the Political Structure of Ulithi Atoll." In *Islanders and their Outside World: A Report of the Cultural Anthropological Research in the Caroline Islands of Micronesia in 1980–1981,* edited by Machiko Aoyagi, 35–75. Tokyo: Committee for Micronesian Research, St. Paul's (Rikkyo) University, March 1982.

Vason, G. *An Authentic Narrative of Four Year's Residence at Tongataboo.* London: Longman, Hurst, Rees, Orme, 1810.

Vayda, A. P., ed. *Peoples and Cultures of the Pacific: An Anthropological Reader.* Garden City, N.Y.: The Natural History Press, 1968.

Vayda, Andrew P., and Roy A. Rappaport. "Island Cultures." In *Cultures of the Pacific: Select Readings,* edited by Thomas G. Harding and Ben J. Wallace, 5–12. New York: The Free Press, 1970.

Waddell, Eric, et al., eds. *A New Oceania: Rediscovering Our Sea of Islands.* Suva: School of Social and Economic Development, University of the South Pacific, 1993.

Waitangi Tribunal, Department of Justice. *Report of the Waitangi Tribunal on the Muriwhenua Fishing Claim, Wai-22.* Wellington: Department of Justice, 1985.

Wall, Coleman. *Catalogue of the Fiji Museum.* Suva: Fiji Museum, 1916.

Wall, Coleman. "Dakuwaqa." *Transactions of the Fiji Society for the Year 1917* (1918): 39–46.

Wallace, J. M., and S. Vogel. *El Niño and Climate Prediction.* Boulder, Colo.: UCAR Office for Interdisciplinary Earth Studies, Reports to the Nation, Spring 1994.

Waterhouse, Rev. J. *The King and People of Fiji.* London: Wesleyan Conference Office, 1864.

Weckler, J. E. "Land and Livelihood on Mokil, an Atoll in the Eastern Carolines." In *Coordinated Investigation of Micronesian Anthropology 1947–1949* 11, no. 1, University of Southern California, Los Angeles, 1949.

West, Rev. Thomas. *Ten Years in South-Central Polynesia.* London: James Nisbet & Co., 1865.

Wiens, Harold J. *Atoll Environment and Ecology.* New Haven: Yale University Press, 1962.

Wild, Alex, and John Hampton. "A Review of the Biology and Fisheries for Skipjack Tuna, *Katsuwonus pelamis,* in the Pacific Ocean." In *Interactions of Pacific Tuna Fisheries* (2 vols.), edited by Richard S. Shomura, Jacek Majkowski, and Sarah Langi, vol. 2, 1–51. Rome: FAO Fisheries Technical Paper 336/1 and 2 (1994).

Williams, John. *A Narrative of Missionary Enterprises in the South Sea Islands*. London: John Snow, 1838.

Williams, Thomas. *The Islands and their Inhabitants*, vol. 1 of George Stringer Rowe, ed., *Fiji and the Fijians* (2 vols.). Suva: Fiji Museum, 1982 (reprint of 1858 ed.).

Wilson, D. Parker. *Log of the Gypsy, kept by D. Parker Wilson, ship's surgeon, 23 Oct. 1839–19 mar. 1843*. M198, Records Room, Department of Pacific and Asian History, ANU, Canberra, 1839–42.

Wilson, James. *A Missionary Voyage to the Southern Pacific Ocean 1796–1798*. London: Praeger, 1968 (reproduction of 1799 original ed.).

Winkler, Captain. "On Sea Charts Formerly Used in the Marshall Islands." *Smithsonian Institute, Annual Report for 1899* (1901): 487–508.

Wood, C. F. *A Yachting Cruise in the South Seas*. London: Henry S. King and Co., 1875.

Woodin, Edward. *Log of the Schooner "Lady Leigh."* c2409, State Library, Hobart, 1861–65.

Worster, Donald. *The Ends of the Earth: Perspectives on Modern Environmental History*. Cambridge: Cambridge University Press, 1988.

Yamaguchi, M. "Sea Level Fluctuations and Mass Mortalities of Reef Animals in Guam, Mariana Islands." *Micronesica* 11 (1975): 227–43.

Youl, John. "A Journal of the Missionaries proceedings on Tahaete commencing March 8th 1806 and ending August 11th 1806—kept by John Youl." SSJ 2, LMS Archives, London (AJCP mfm M2).

Young, John. "Sailing to Levuka: The Cultural Significance of the Island Schooners in the Late 19th Century." *Journal of Pacific History* 28, no. 1 (1993): 36–52.

INDEX

About the Author

Paul D'Arcy lectures in Pacific and environmental history at the Australian National University. Born in New Zealand, he studied at Otago University and the University of Hawai'i at Mānoa before completing his doctorate at the Australian National University. He is a member of the editorial board of the *Journal of Pacific History* and has published a number of articles on Pacific indigenous and environmental history. This is his first book.

Production Notes for D'ARCY / THE PEOPLE OF THE SEA

Cover and interior designed by Leslie Fitch
with text in Sabon and display in Trajan

Composition by Josie Herr

Printing and binding by The Maple-Vail Book
Manufacturing Group

Printed on 60# Sebago Eggshell, 420 ppi